# CLAUDE VIVIER

BOB GILMORE

# CLAUDE VIVIER

A COMPOSER'S LIFE

UNIVERSITY OF ROCHESTER PRESS

The publisher and author gratefully acknowledge financial support from Société Gavigniès in the Netherlands and from Thérèse Smalt-Béland.

First published 2014

University of Rochester Press
668 Mt. Hope Avenue, Rochester, NY 14620, USA
www.urpress.com
and Boydell & Brewer Limited
PO Box 9, Woodbridge, Suffolk IP12 3DF, UK
www.boydellandbrewer.com

ISBN-13: 978-1-58046-485-7

ISSN: 1071-9989

**Library of Congress Cataloging-in-Publication Data**

Gilmore, Bob, 1961– author.
    Claude Vivier : a composer's life / Bob Gilmore.
        pages cm — (Eastman studies in music, ISSN 1071-9989 ; v. 109)
    Includes bibliographical references, discography, and index.
    ISBN 978-1-58046-485-7 (hardcover : alkaline paper) 1. Vivier, Claude,
1948–1983. 2. Composers—Canada—Biography. I. Title. II. Series: Eastman
studies in music ; v. 109.
    ML410.V8273G55 2014
    780.92—dc23
    [B]
                                                                    2013049531

A catalogue record for this title is available from the British Library.

This publication is printed on acid-free paper.
Printed in the United States of America.

*To Elisabeth, with love*
*and to Thérèse Desjardins, with gratitude and affection*

# CONTENTS

Appendixes

Illustrations follow page 146.

# PREFACE

One February evening in Amsterdam, some ten years ago, my partner, Elisabeth, dug out a videotape of Cherry Duyns's 1997 documentary film on Claude Vivier and we sat down to watch it together. Elisabeth, the daughter of a Quebecoise mother, appears briefly in the film as a viola player (or, more accurately, her right arm does, vigorously bowing a passage from *Zipangu*). I had heard some of Vivier's music as a student and liked it very much, but had paid it little attention in the years since. Still then in the early months of our relationship, we were pleased to discover this shared enthusiasm. The documentary, with its dark lamplit scenes of the Paris metro in the rain, the terrible story of Vivier's murder and its uncanny prediction in his last, unfinished composition *Glaubst du an die Unsterblichkeit der Seele* (Do you believe in the immortality of the soul), left me disturbed and spellbound.[1] After the film Elisabeth said that a biography of Vivier would make a wonderful story and that I should write it. Still reeling from the video and from the heart-stopping last moments of Vivier's final work, I told her it would be beyond me, my French was (then) not good enough—and it would be impossible to trace all the events surrounding his death.

The fact of Vivier's murder has, you might say, haunted the posthumous reputation of his music. It seems impossible to discuss his work without mentioning the cruel and sordid circumstances of his death. That death occurred not in the Paris metro, as people tend to assume—conflating the narrative of his last composition with the actual truth of the matter—but in his rented apartment on the rue du Général-Guilhem, at the hands of a young man he had invited home for the night. For some, Vivier's murder is the key to an understanding of his life and—more controversially—of his art.

That night I slept very little. I was deeply touched by the story of this death-obsessed creative artist. The biographer in me wanted to understand Vivier's apparent thirst for oblivion, for eternity, or—if such turned out to be a misinterpretation—to lay the myth to rest, to tell the true story, to hear the music without the webs of accumulated cod-psychoanalysis that clung to it. Deep in my insomnia, I reasoned: my French is not that bad; I can get help understanding the Quebec accent and language; I have researched equally bizarre and obscure things in the past. By morning, the reasoning had stopped, I had made up my mind, and this biography had begun.

Claude Vivier's music inhabits a shadowy realm between reality and the imagination. His is a world where human beings express themselves in invented languages more often than real ones; they are seduced by the allure of distant cities and embark on journeys, often symbolic ones, in search of love or companionship; and they are haunted by the omnipresence of death, which in Vivier's output holds dominion over everything else. All these themes characterize his largest works, the operas *Kopernikus* and the unfinished *Marco Polo*. Yet in the deepest sense the most frequently recurring subject in Vivier's compositions is himself: his works are unashamed revelations of his dreams, his fantasies, and his longings. The expressive intensity of his music, together with its compositional skill and innovation, makes his oeuvre among the most compelling of the late twentieth century.

This book is both a biography of Vivier and a critical study of his music. I have mixed these approaches in the pages that follow for two reasons. First, because it is my belief that practically everything Vivier composed was motivated by artistic impulses that are essentially autobiographical; this is as true of his first mature work, *Chants*, as it is of *Lettura di Dante*, *Liebesgedichte*, *Siddhartha*, *Journal*, *Pulau Dewata*, *Kopernikus*, *Lonely Child*, *Prologue pour un Marco Polo*, *Wo bist du Licht!*, *Bouchara*, and his last work, *Glaubst du an die Unsterblichkeit der Seele*. Vivier composed, in large part, in order to access an inner world: as a means of confronting pain, darkness, terror; as a means of negotiating a relationship with God; as a means of voicing his insatiable longing for acceptance and for love. Although his music is self-revelatory it is very much of its era: even in moments of unbearable emotional intensity, carefully crafted structural controls, usually mathematically based, are operating on various musical levels. Second, I believe that while it in no sense "explains" the music, biography can enrich our understanding of an artist's total oeuvre by unraveling the complex interaction of internal needs and external pressures that guided its unfolding. And if it is true, as I believe, that one does not really need to know anything of a composer's life in order to understand a particular work—which, if it is any good, will speak eloquently for itself—the reverse is not true: one cannot claim to understand Vivier's life without at least some understanding of his music. His devotion to his artistic vision made him the person he was.

As a biographical subject Vivier presents a range of difficulties, from the purely practical to the ethical. He lived in the age of the telephone, a period which, from the point of view of the biographer, is the black hole in twentieth century history between the era of the letter and the advent of e-mail and the hard disk. The long hours Vivier spent talking on the telephone to friends have left no trace other than in memory. Even more tantalizingly, the no less long hours he spent with the telephone receiver sitting on the top of his piano as he played through a new work in progress for the benefit of a sympathetic (or, sometimes, distracted and bored) ear on the other end of the line has left absolutely no trace either: several of his friends heard many of his finest compositions come into being, day by day, in this manner. For this reason, in my research I found it essential to supplement the written sources we possess with a great deal of oral testimony from close friends and colleagues. Furthermore, Vivier's was a short life, one spent with very little money and never with a truly stable home. He did not live long enough to write memoirs or to reevaluate his life. His days were lived in the full frenzy of youth, at top speed. The version of his own life that emerges in his written texts and letters is, so to speak, a first draft, raw and unedited, not a carefully polished rewrite; what we lose in terms of retrospection we gain in terms of honesty and immediacy.

Beyond the practical problems, there is the level of difficulty presented by the inner life. As with most composers, the relationship of Vivier's life and work is a complex one. "What was really going on," his friend Michel-Georges Brégent wrote, "in the soul of this abandoned child? Why this fear of the night ('Don't leave me in the dark'), this over-exuberance which covered the silence all around him, this laugh, this handshake, his great cries of joy, his multicolored wardrobe, his odors? Why too be so obviously extroverted when in private he was, on the contrary, so sensitive, generous, timid, open?"[2]

There is a chilling symmetry in Vivier's life: we do not know the exact time or circumstances of his birth, and we do not know the exact time or circumstances of his death. These two facts, troubling as they are, bring us up brutally against the limits of biography as a medium. Until now the facts and the contradictory explanations of both these events have never been thoroughly explored. In this book I have gathered together for the first time what we reliably know about Vivier's life and have studied the picture that emerges. While I take a view on the circumstances of his coming into this world and his leaving it, which the reader may not share, my hope is to have provided solid material on which to base other interpretations.

Not long after his death the idea of a biography of Vivier was hatched. In 1990 the Canada Council even pledged money for the project. But nothing came of the idea, and the project lay dormant for many years. Knowledge of Vivier's mind and work was helped considerably by the publication in 1991 of his writings, in the form of a double issue of the Montreal-based journal *Circuit*, with forty-nine texts edited and annotated by Véronique Robert. However, the publication, in French only, had limited circulation in Europe. Since then, as performances and recordings of Vivier's music have proliferated, serious scholarly work on the composer, whether musicological or biographical, has remained limited.

Shortly before leaving Montreal for the last time in June 1982, and giving notice on his apartment on the Chemin de la Côte-Sainte-Catherine, Vivier left various of his belongings (including his book collection and a great many miscellaneous things, including some music manuscripts) with his close friend Thérèse Desjardins. After his death, with these materials and with the effects shipped back from Paris as a basis, and having been granted authority by the Vivier family, Desjardins formed an organization at first named "Les Amis de Claude Vivier" and later the "Fondation Vivier." She began collecting clippings and reviews of performances of Vivier's music and copies of documents from his life, gradually assembling an extensive archive. With this material at my disposal I began work on this biography in the summer of 2002. I found it desirable to retrace many of the same steps, and to supplement these materials with extensive research of my own, including interviews and e-mail exchanges with Vivier's family, teachers, friends, and colleagues. Throughout, Madame Desjardins has been of inestimable help and support in my work. I should emphasize, however, that the portrait of Vivier that follows, and the interpretation of his music, represent solely my own viewpoint.

Amsterdam, October 2012

# ACKNOWLEDGMENTS

In the research for this book the most extensive debt I have incurred is to Madame Thérèse Desjardins, president of the Fondation Vivier in Montreal. From the time of our first meeting in Cologne in March 2002 she has encouraged me every step of the way, allowing me unrestricted access to the materials on Vivier she has assembled over the years, accommodating me for many weeks on my several trips to Montreal, driving me around the city, and helping me understand the broad Quebecois of some of Vivier's friends and family. Our many hours of conversation, at her home in Contrecoeur and on her several visits to Europe, were of inestimable help to my understanding of Vivier the man.

My work was supported in part by a grant from the British Academy in London, which made it possible to spend the autumn of 2003 in Montreal carrying out primary research.

Two sections of this book have appeared in slightly different forms as articles. My thanks to Calum MacDonald, then editor of *Tempo*, who published my analysis of *Lonely Child* as "On Claude Vivier's *Lonely Child*," *Tempo* 61, no. 239 (January 2007): 2–17; and to Jonathan Goldman, editor of *Circuit*, for publishing "Claude Vivier and Karlheinz Stockhausen: Moments from a Double Portrait," *Circuit* 19, no. 2 (2009): 35–49, which makes up part of chapter 4. I am also grateful to the staff of Boosey and Hawkes in New York, Vivier's publishers, for commissioning me to write the introduction to their 2012 brochure of his works and to write program notes for their published editions of some of his compositions, passages from which appear in this book.

Of the many friends, colleagues, teachers, and family of Claude Vivier I have spoken to or interviewed, either in person or by e-mail or telephone, I thank, in alphabetical order: Clarence Barlow, Machleen Batelaan, the late Gilles Beauregard, Frère Urbain Beauvais, Bernard Blanchard, Walter

Boudreau, Denys Bouliane, Paul Chamberland, Luc Courchesne, James Dashow, Daniel Dion, Peter Eötvös, José Evangelista, Lambert Ferrand, Martin Foster, Michel Gonneville, Denis Gougeon, Peter Hamlin, Bruno Hébert, Sophie Hébert, the late Hans Ulrich Humpert, Christopher Jackson, Gottfried Michael Koenig, Gisèle Vivier Labrècque, Serge Laflamme, Bertrand Lamoureux, Michael Laucke, Jean Laurendeau, Robert Leroux, Jos Leusink, Frère Jean Loiselle, John McAlpine, Tristan Murail, Marie-Danielle Parent, Louis-Philippe Pelletier, Christina Petrowska Quilico, Guy Plamondon, Philippe Poloni, Rober Racine, the late Horatiu Radulescu, John Rea, Véronique Robert, André Roy, Annemarie Ponse Smalt, Knut Sönstevold, the late Stan Tempelaars, Richard Toop, Barry Truax, Gilles Tremblay, Lorraine Vaillancourt, Pauline Vaillancourt, the late Jeanne Vivier, Kevin Volans, Frits Weiland, Walter Zimmermann. Only Karlheinz Stockhausen and Harry Halbreich failed to respond to my repeated requests for an interview. And while it is invidious to pick out individuals for special thanks—as every one of the above-mentioned made a valuable contribution—I gained considerable information and insight into Vivier from my meetings in Amsterdam with Clarence Barlow and in Montreal with Walter Boudreau, John Rea, and Gilles Tremblay.

My thanks to the staff in various institutions—at the Conservatoire de Musique in Montreal, the Institute of Sonology in The Hague, the Hochschule für Musik in Cologne, the Vivier Archives at the University of Montreal, and the Centre de Musique Canadienne in Montreal (especially its then director Mireille Gagné) for various forms of help and access to materials.

All translations from the French in this book are my own unless otherwise noted, although I would like to thank Marie Guilleray for her invaluable help; also, my thanks to Harald Muenz for his help with sources in German. Lucia Mense accompanied me to several of the places where Vivier lived in Cologne, as Thérèse Desjardins did in Montreal. Others with whom I had valuable discussions that encouraged my work on Vivier include Pierre Audi, Marc Couroux, Donnacha Dennehy, Taras Grescoe, Rozalie Hirs, Jean-Jacques Nattiez, Marc Sabat, and Rachid Safir. I would like to thank all at the University of Rochester Press, in particular Julia Cook, Tracey Engel, Sonia Kane, Ralph Locke, and Ryan Peterson. And special thanks to Christopher Fox for giving me peace of mind in the final stages of my work on this book.

The original suggestion that I write a biography of Claude Vivier came from my partner, Elisabeth Smalt. Throughout the long years of work on the project her love and support have sustained me and helped keep the idea of the book alive. Words cannot express my gratitude.

# CHAPTER ONE

# " THE FACT OF KNOWING I HAD NO FATHER OR MOTHER "

## 1 9 4 8 – 6 7

Together with the Kamchatka Peninsula in Siberia and the coastal mountains of British Columbia, Canada's Saint Lawrence Valley is among the snowiest places on earth. Winter in southern Quebec can last five long months, during which time as much as four meters of snow may fall on the streets of Montreal. The thermometer will drop to thirty below zero and stay there for days on end; evenings of raging wind and blowing snow can turn a walk to the corner *dépanneur* into a full-scale expedition. If winter defines much of our vision of the Quebec landscape and culture, there are compensations: Montreal, which is on the same latitude as Venice, is among the sunniest of winter cities, with an average of 350 hours of sunshine in the three months between winter solstice and spring equinox, transfiguring the blanket of snow with revivifying brilliance.

During the winter of 1947–48, a young woman endured a pregnancy through weather that was unusually harsh, even by Quebec standards.[1] She gave birth in the spring, in Quebec a short-lived season of ever-changing skies, a prelude to the heat of summer. In Montreal on April 14, 1948, her son was born, taken from her, and placed in an orphanage, where he would remain for the next two and a half years. It is the first and perhaps most poignant fact of Claude Vivier's biography that we do not know who this young woman was, not her name, her age, her ethnic origin, or her destiny. She is to us what she was to her son: a phantom who has left no trace on the historical record.

The young Claude was an abandoned child, one of roughly 3,000 born to "unknown parents" in Quebec in the year 1948 (3,000 is the official statistic; the actual number is almost certainly higher).[2] Following his birth he was placed in La crèche Saint-Michel run by the Soeurs Grises (Grey Nuns), a religious community that had been founded in Montreal in 1737 by a young widow named Marguerite d'Youville, the aim of which was to take care of the elderly, the infirm, and orphans, and to provide education.[3] According to one early document in the Vivier family, the young boy was known as "Claude Roger."[4] He was baptized in the church Saint-Enfant Jésus du Milen, on rue Saint-Dominique.

In the 1940s in Quebec the birth of an illegitimate child, with its implication of extramarital (usually premarital) sex, was almost universally regarded as a sin, a blasphemous violation of the basis of decent Catholic society. It was an act of shame, the traces of which had to be obliterated or at least concealed. More than a third of recorded illegitimate births took place in one particular institution, the Hôpital de la Miséricorde, which had a building in Montreal and another in Quebec City. Some more fortunate women gave birth in private maternity clinics, usually far from home, or at the home of distant relatives or, occasionally, in the family home, where their condition would typically be hidden for as long as possible. Of women admitted to an institution such as the Hôpital de la Miséricorde certain patterns can be discerned: they were usually French-Canadian and Catholic (Anglophone women were generally directed to other agencies such as the Salvation Army); the majority (approximately 60 percent) were between eighteen and twenty-two years old; roughly half were domestic servants; and roughly a third still lived with their families. For more than 80 percent, this was their first pregnancy. At that time, only about 12 to 14 percent of single mothers left the hospitals with their child.[5]

We have no idea where Claude's mother gave birth, but the likelihood is that she suffered terrible indignities during the term of her pregnancy and beyond. Quebec society regarded the pregnant, unmarried woman either as strong-minded and wicked, or as weak, ignorant, and perhaps mentally deficient. And whereas a considerable number of such women came to be pregnant from an act of sexual abuse, sometimes on the part of a relative, it was they who were generally seen as in need of repentance—having fallen, they must atone for their sin. (This judgment was sometimes applied even to women who encountered otherwise humane treatment in places like the Hôpital de la Miséricorde.) But the indignities did not end there. The mother not infrequently had little say in the name given to her child and little choice about whether or not to keep him—the pressures were immense from church, family, and society.[6] Perhaps most cruel of all, a woman would often be forced into the position of giving up her child "voluntarily" to protect him from the malicious prejudices surrounding bastard children in society at large.

Abandonment, in a sensitive mind, can be the most cruel of punishments—what Andrée Lévesque in her study of women in Quebec in the interwar years, *La Norme et les Déviantes*, calls "The Rejection of Motherhood."[7] We cannot draw a tidy line under the matter. For Vivier, the fact of abandonment—or, as he usually expressed it, the fact of knowing he had no father or mother—kept resurfacing in his work, in his imagination, and as something he experienced as a daily reality, casting a long shadow over his life. If none of his surviving written documents express particular anguish about this condition, treating it instead with an almost magical awe, it could be said that his music tells a different story. The text Vivier wrote for *Lonely Child*, his "long song of solitude," dares, with heartbreaking poignancy, to say the words that the young Claude himself never heard from his birth mother—"O beautiful child of the light / sleep sleep sleep on / sleep / dreams will come / sweet fairies will come to dance with you, marvelous one / the fairies and the elves will celebrate you / the joyful farandole will intoxicate you / Friend / sleep my child." These words are to be sung by a soprano; but there is the sense of Vivier identifying with his birth mother, speaking—as though through her lips—to his own infant self, with a song of immense tenderness and consolation.

Claude's birth mother, so painfully absent from his life, exerted a hold over his imagination that was possibly even stronger than it would have been had she been physically present. Another of the several compositions that deal directly with the subject is *Journal*, again to a text by Vivier himself. The work, he wrote, "is mainly inspired by the very fact that during the greatest part of my childhood I was always looking for my own mother, who I thought was somehow Polish, [by] mystical concepts which I also hold from my childhood where Christmas was a big event and where reality was not the one I was, in fact, living but the one I was taken from in a very strange fashion."[8] Neither here nor anywhere else in the surviving documentation does Vivier suggest why he believed his mother was anything other than French-Canadian. In most of his projections she is

usually eastern European and—not infrequently—Jewish, thereby implying (by Jewish law) that he himself was a Jew. Her being Polish is certainly
possible: tens of thousands of Poles came to Quebec following World War
II, a mixed group of intellectuals, concentration camp survivors, refugees,
and soldiers.[9] But there is no evidence of any sort that this was actually the
case. Vivier's friend Philippe Poloni recalls Vivier telling him a different
version in which his mother was Jewish German and father Italian: "he
thought that his father was a conductor, or his mother was a musician, and
they met in Montreal. Or something like that, something very romantic.
He always said he spoke good German and good Italian because he had a
natural connection with those two languages as he had some Italian and
some Jewish German blood in his veins."[10]

The program note to *Journal*, quoted above, contains several other
phrases that seem significant. Vivier writes that in his childhood he felt
that "reality was not the one I was, in fact, living but the one I was taken
from in a very strange fashion." What does he mean? Is the suggestion
that "reality" is the life with his birth mother that was denied him, and
that his actual life, with his adopted family, is somehow unreal? And, if
so, why does he then say he was taken from that reality "in a very strange
fashion?" Given that he was probably taken from it by the prevalent social norm—that is, by the contemporary mores of church and society
and their negative attitude to single parenthood—he seems to be suggesting that he finds these mores "very strange," implying a strong condemnation of the treatment to which his birth mother may well have
been subjected.

Vivier returned to the theme of his abandonment in another piece
of writing from the same year as the "Notes on *Journal*." This is perhaps the most revealingly autobiographical of his writings, a piece titled
"Introspection d'un compositeur," written in 1978 for the Montreal journal *Sortir*. There he writes:

The fact of knowing from the age of six that I had no father or mother
gave me a marvelous dream universe; I fabricated my origins as I wanted, pretended to speak strange languages. The reality that I encountered
every day was alas of a very hard kind, muscular. I wasn't left alone
to dream of these marvelous lands and these charming princesses; the
reality I encountered was only violence and pettiness. So I entered the
great mystic period of my life; I discovered that my suffering finally had
a meaning, that my real mother resembled the Virgin Mary, my whole
sensibility became refined and increasingly I drew a veil around myself:
finally I was protected![11]

This text offers a wonderful snapshot of Vivier's inner world. He professes a distaste for the brutal, muscular nature of everyday reality where violence and pettiness go hand in hand and keep intruding upon his dreaming. At the same time, he takes comfort from a Catholicism that finds meaning in suffering, believes that his "real" mother resembles the Virgin Mary, and adopts a mystical outlook on life, protecting himself by a veil, one that keeps reality at a distance. The mystical outlook of which he is speaking in these young years is fueled largely by daydreaming and by a vague sense of God's benevolent protection. The adolescent self he is describing has not yet discovered that other veil through which he would soon start to view the world: the veil of art.

The circumstances of Vivier's birth pose, for his biographer, complex ethical questions. When the laws changed in Quebec at the beginning of the 1980s and it became easier to begin the search for one's birth parents, Vivier decided he wanted to try to trace his mother and asked his close friend Thérèse Desjardins to help him.[12] The search, barely begun, was terminated at his death only a few years later, with her identity still unknown. The biographer's dilemma, then, is: should one continue the search begun by Vivier himself?

It is entirely possible that Vivier's birth mother is alive as I write these words, and will be alive to see the first publication of this biography of her son. If we go with what is statistically a 37 percent possibility that she was a *fille-mère*, an underage mother of, say, seventeen or eighteen when her son was born, she herself would then have been born as recently as 1930 or 1931. If we imagine her in her early twenties when Claude was born, but unmarried, she would, as I write, be in her early eighties. The likelihood of one or the other of these scenarios being true is quite high—most abandonments were a consequence of underage pregnancies out of wedlock. What is virtually certain is that the woman in question had, or has, no idea that her son grew up to be a composer, one of the most notable figures in late twentieth-century music.

My decision has been to leave Vivier's birth mother alone, largely out of respect for the humiliations I imagine her to have suffered at the time of her son's birth. The fact is that it was the mythic, indeed mystical, aspects of the matter that were so important to Vivier's inner world. It is the state of unknowing—the gateway to the "marvelous dream universe"—that is finally the most salient fact of Vivier's relationship with his birth parents. A similar image of the benevolent, protecting nature of the older woman comes across also in this brief vignette Vivier provided of his adoptive grandmother: "My grandmother, whom I only knew very fleetingly, had been a little island of affection and security for me. I remember that after her death, I always tried to find the same in other old women. They always awoke in me feelings of farewell, of eternity."[13]

We know nothing about the first two and a half years of Claude's life, the period he spent in the orphanage. One family legend that Vivier himself came to believe, which is possibly apocryphal, is that he was an unusually late developer with speech. His friend Michel-Georges Brégent noted, after Vivier's death, that "until the age of six Claude was thought to be deaf and dumb," a claim he no doubt picked up from Vivier himself.[14] While this seems rather implausible if taken literally, it may nonetheless have some basis in fact.

At Christmas 1950, Armand and Jeanne Vivier came to the orphanage with their eighteen-year-old son Marcel and their seventeen-year-old daughter Gisèle. They didn't quite find what they wanted. Gisèle Vivier recalls: "We all went, the whole family to the crèche. My mother wanted a girl (I had lost a baby sister). But there were only boys, so the choice of a boy was made for us."[15] While this claim that the orphanage had no girls might at first seem surprising it is most probably true. Chantale Quesney, author of a doctoral dissertation on the Montreal Société d'adoption et de protection de l'enfance, comments:

> It is a fact that adoptive parents preferred little girls to little boys. To the point that in the 1950s, the orphanages in Quebec had practically only boys to offer up for adoption. But we don't know why. Some say that the parents wanted to preserve the line by avoiding introducing a new masculine element. Because a girl did not ensure the continuation of the name, she seemed therefore more "neutral." It's possible. My sources however point to a more concrete reason. It seems that the parents, not knowing the exact origin of the child, would have preferred a little girl whose character was likely to be calmer than that of a little boy. In summary, it was thought that a little girl was "less trouble" than a little boy. It seems that this issue was particular to Quebec, because I am not aware that elsewhere, in the United States for example, the adoption agencies would have been confronted with this type of problem.[16]

The Vivier family took Claude home with them. He was one of the lucky ones: many children never came out of the orphanages, or only after many years and immense psychological damage. Bruno Roy's harrowing *Mémoire d'asile: la tragédie des enfants de Duplessis* (1994) portrays the anguish, humiliation, and moral guilt of those children, like himself, who grew up in the orphanages of Montreal at that time. Some five years older than Vivier, Roy was placed in an orphanage at birth and transferred at the age of seven to a "medico-pedagogical institute," Mont Providence, which accepted those orphans believed to be responsive to attempts at education. The institute was rebranded as a psychiatric hospital four years later, and all the orphans who happened to be there, irrespective of their individual conditions or histories, were declared mentally ill and denied education. (It emerged years later that the religious communities received greater financial support from Duplessis's government for a mentally ill "patient" than for an orphan.)[17]

The Vivier family was a poor, working-class, in most respects typically French-Canadian family. Armand Vivier (1905–88) had served for four and a half years in the army during and just after the war, and had been stationed in England and in Holland. "He said it was very beautiful in Holland," his daughter Gisèle recalls, "he said it was a very welcoming and beautiful country."[18] When he came back from the war he was offered a job in the Canadian Post Office (many army men, on their return, were offered jobs in the civil service) but did not like it, and opened a repair shop on rue Duluth servicing the hydraulic systems on trucks. He was helped there later by his son, Marcel. His wife was Jeanne Vivier, née Masseau (1910–2009).

The question arises why the Viviers should wish to adopt a child so many years after the births of their two children, Marcel in January 1932 and Gisèle in February 1933. (The baby girl that the Viviers had lost was born, according to Gisèle, even earlier, in 1930, and died at the age of three months.) Gisèle explains: "At the time my parents adopted Claude, my mother didn't go out much, so the doctor advised her to take a child." According to her daughter, Jeanne suffered from sinusitis, which made her dizzy, and she had frequent falls; as a result she stayed housebound much of the time. But related to their decision, whether as cause or effect, may have been some form of protracted grieving for the lost child: "My mother lost a baby girl, she wanted to have another girl."[19] And yet the adoption took place fully twenty years after the loss of the baby, and long after the birth of Gisèle herself. Another family legend is that Armand Vivier promised his wife they could have another child when, or if, he came back from the war. Perhaps adoption was a way of fulfilling his promise.

However, after a few weeks they took the young Claude back to the orphanage. A surviving letter to the Vivier family dated February 28, 1951, from Paul Contant, director of La Société d'adoption et de protection de l'enfance on rue Sherbrooke in Montreal, reads: "Dear friends, Given the return of the child, please find enclosed your marriage certificate which we no longer need."[20] The return of the young boy to the orphanage has three possible explanations. One is that the family took him to their house for the Christmas period only, always with the intention of returning him once the festivities were over: this was a quite common custom at that time. The second possibility is that Jeanne Vivier took a dislike to him. Thérèse Desjardins remembers Madame Vivier complaining (in her presence and that of Vivier himself, on a visit in the early 1980s) that he threw a piece of wood at her in a fit of temper. A third possibility is that the forty-year-old Jeanne simply found him too much to handle. Gisèle Vivier remembers that "my mother was sick and she said 'I cannot keep the boy,' and my father and my brother didn't talk to my mother." Because they were angry she returned him? "My father said: 'when we take somebody we keep him, it's impossible to throw him away,' and now she took him back."[21] According to the recollections of Gisèle Vivier the legal adoption of the three-year-old Claude took place in August 1951, at the cours Juvénile, rue Saint-Denis and boulevard Saint-Joseph, in Montreal. "After she adopted him everything was OK, everything was under control."[22]

The family lived at 5042 rue Lejeune, a small street between avenue Laurier and boulevard Saint-Joseph, and only a few blocks east of the apartments on avenue du Parc and Côte-Sainte-Catherine where Vivier would spent most of his adult life. Today the street has considerable charm: it is tree-lined, rather small-scale with mostly small red-brick houses with wooden window frames and balconies, set between busy, prosperous thoroughfares. In 1951 it was still a poor backstreet, almost a slum. These postwar years were, however, times of marked growth in Quebec. Montreal proper, in the 1951 census, had over a million inhabitants; the island had a further 300,000, bringing the total in the greater metropolitan area to 1,358,075. Quebec itself then had a population of over 4 million, compared to 18,250,000 in Canada as a whole; ten years later, Quebec would have grown to account for 28.8 percent of the population of Canada.[23]

As a young boy Claude seems to have been quite a charmer. He smiled easily and often, and enjoyed the usual round of games and slapstick comedy that make children laugh. Gisèle, fifteen years older, adored him, perhaps thinking of him almost as her own child. "He was a brother that I was happy to have," she remarks, "because he came to my family in the Christmas time. I think he liked me."[24] She recalls further:

We'd often go out together. He loved to play in the snow, to go for sleigh rides, tobogganing. He loved to rock back and forth. One day he fell and his nose was bleeding, the poor boy. Once my father and mother were out shopping. I was washing the floor. When my parents returned, Claude put my mother's hat in the bucket of water, took it in and out, it was so funny I nearly died laughing. I took him two or three times on the "golden tramway." In the parc Lafontaine we watched films, he asked questions the whole time, people laughed when they heard him. He was very clever. Always humming, always in a good mood, a lovely smile. He hated it when people raised their voices, he was very gentle. In the evenings he liked me to show him the Mont-Royal cross. . . . He had his little friends, Hamel, Latreille. Claude was a ray of sunshine; he was what I wanted as a brother. . . . My father said he was his lucky charm. For me Claude was more than a brother, if I had stayed at home instead of getting married, I would have loved him like a mother loves her own child.[25]

Signs of the adult Vivier would occasionally show themselves. "One day at church, it was quite full on Sunday, and Claude let out this enormous yawn, he was bored. . . . I wanted to die I was so embarrassed. He liked to make noise."[26] This attention-seeking yawning would also characterize the somewhat older Claude's behavior when he was bored at new music concerts. Yet beyond the good-natured affection between Gisèle and Claude, there were shadows over the house on rue Lejeune. Jeanne Vivier was often sullen and uncommunicative, and there were tensions between Armand and his eldest son Marcel. Gisèle Vivier says simply, "We weren't a united family . . . we were a strange family." How did this affect the young Claude? "Claude was in his own world, he wasn't in our world."[27]

Gisèle married François Labrecque on August 27, 1955, when Claude was seven; he was brought to the wedding. She left the family home at that point, living with her husband in Ville Saint-Michel, a city that would be annexed to Montreal in the late 1960s. Marcel Vivier had also already married and left home. Gisèle still saw quite a bit of Claude, and remembers especially their ritualistic trips to the "sugar parties" in the spring, a fixture of the Canadian social calendar, involving visits to a *cabane à sucre*, the "sugar shack," to make maple syrup. In late March, after a sufficient number of cold nights and sunny days, the sap in the maple trees starts its rise. The watery liquid seeps through notches cut into the bark, and thence into tubes that take it through the maple groves into the *cabane à sucre*. A surviving snapshot from the spring of 1958 captures the nine-year-old Claude and his big sister on one such trip.

✳ ✳ ✳

It is heartbreaking to realize that the happy, innocent young boy who looks out at us from the Polaroid photographs of that time may already have experienced a further traumatic event that would have an influence on the course of his life in the years immediately ahead. According to Vivier, his first sexual experience was around the age of eight, when he was raped by an uncle.[28] Oncle Joe and Tante Aline, Claude's godparents, lived on the ground floor of the same house on rue Lejeune: Aline was the sister of Armand Vivier. According to Gisèle Vivier, "that's where he did the job": it was there that Oncle Joe sexually abused the young Claude.[29] The event took place one Sunday when the rest of the family was out attending Mass. Vivier told a priest in confession, who insisted he inform his parents, because, according to Thérèse Desjardins's recollections of Vivier's story, "otherwise I will not give you forgiveness." Claude told his mother (we do not know how long after: days? weeks? months?), which caused a scandal: "she was furious [with Claude]," recalls Gisèle.[30] This, according to Desjardins's recollections, set in motion a chain of events: the family left rue Lejeune not long thereafter, and eventually Claude was sent away from home altogether to boarding school, and would only live with his adoptive family for short periods during school holidays.

The story of his rape relies, then, not exclusively on the testimony of Vivier himself, but is confirmed by his sister. He told the story to a great many of his adult friends, and it clearly continued to play on his mind. But almost everything about the incident and its aftermath cries out for interpretation.

To begin with, both Thérèse Desjardins and her son Bruno Hébert, who heard the story independently of each other, remember that when Vivier told it there was no sense that he necessarily disliked what happened or was even particularly traumatized by it. On the contrary, at least in his later tellings, it was made to sound like a positive experience.[31] (This may, of course, have involved Vivier's giving the story a lighthearted or matter-of-fact cast to hide deeply buried memories of painful humiliation.) And his mother's anger, a classic example of blaming the victim: was it out of a spirit of "I told you so," that the child who had thrown a piece of wood at her at the age of two was still causing trouble in the family and should have been left to rot in the orphanage after all? Or because she herself was fearful of her brother-in-law, maybe even aware of his misdemeanors? Another possible consequence of the rape, although here the causality is not at all clear, lies in Vivier's statement that, because of the chain of events that followed, his uncle "saved my life"; when an opportunity arose to have the boy educated away from the family home, it met with his parents' consent and, it seems, his mother's great relief.[32] At any rate, Oncle Joe's sexual adventures with young boys seem not to have ended with Claude, and continued for some years. Gisèle Vivier, when asked about this, replies simply: "well, that's life I suppose . . . there's nothing to be done . . . this sort of thing happens in families, no?"[33]

The young Claude attended two primary schools: first, the École Saint-Louis, on rue Saint-Dominique, a short walk away from the family home on rue Lejeune; then, after the move of the Vivier family north of the city, the École Saint-Jean in Pont-Viau.[34] Armand and Jeanne Vivier moved north when Claude was nine or ten. Pont-Viau is a neighborhood in the southern part of Laval, at that time a town, and today the largest suburb of Montreal. Whatever the part played in the decision by the presence of Oncle Joe, moving to Laval was a common enough occurrence in those years. The family was moving from an old property in a downbeat part of Montreal to a newer and larger house with a garden, a proper bath, and other modern conveniences they had lacked on rue Lejeune. Gisèle Vivier explains that her father would buy a house in rundown condition, renovate it, and then sell it, and that he made money doing it.[35] This perhaps accounts for their frequent moves during Claude's early adolescent years around Pont-Viau, where we have addresses for them at 9 rue Cousineau, 134 rue Cousineau, and 398 Saint-André, before they settled at 60 rue Proulx by 1964; the family still lived at this last address at the time of Vivier's departure for Europe in 1971. The house on rue Proulx was an important one for Claude because it was where he had his first piano. Claude himself did not enjoy these moves as much as his father did: "I remember when I was a child and we moved house—I went around the streets looking for friends, but came back to the house with my head down, still with no friends."[36]

The direction his schooling subsequently took came about through a chance encounter. Either through the École Saint-Jean, or perhaps through contacts at church, he met a member of the Frères Maristes (the Marist Brothers), a religious order that had come to Canada in 1885, establishing a community at Iberville, some thirty miles from central Montreal. The order stemmed from the work of a French priest, Marcellin Champagnat (1789–1840), who created some forty-five schools in France, with a view to providing a religious education for poor and sometimes homeless young people. In Quebec the Frères Maristes founded first the Collège d'Iberville, then the Juvénat Notre-Dame (in 1892) and the Juvénat Saint-Joseph (in 1945): Vivier would attend the latter two of these schools.

Vivier's mother recalls that although they had to pay some money for the schooling there, the education provided by the Frères Maristes cost very little.[37] Thus the young Claude received a very good education of a kind that was unlikely to have been available to him otherwise. More important, these were boarding schools: from the age of thirteen the adopted son would spend most of his time outside the family unit. Vivier attended three such schools in succession, namely, the Juvénat Inférieur Notre-Dame, in Iberville (today École secondaire Marcellin-Champagnat, Saint-Jean-sur-Richelieu), September 1961–June 1963; the Juvénat Supérieur Saint-Joseph, in Saint-Vincent-de-Paul (in what is now Laval), September 1963–June 1965; and the Noviciat des Frères Maristes, in Saint-Hyacinthe, September 1965–late 1966 or early 1967.

A Juvénat is a Catholic secondary school, directed by priests, that offers a foundation for pupils who want to become Christian brothers (frères). Claude's fellow pupil Bertrand Lamoureux describes it more circumspectly as "a place of development where we encourage young people towards the religious life, more or less in the hope that they will proceed in this direction."[38]

Frère Jean Loiselle, then in his early forties, a softspoken man who taught Vivier at the Juvénat for several years, does not recall specifically how the young Claude came to the schools of the Frères Maristes. The most usual way was that the frères recruited from among the local community—Claude may have met one of them at church or elsewhere. Frère Loiselle emphasizes that when the children entered such schools, generally at thirteen, it was for educational purposes, not because they had already decided on a religious vocation. "However, the young people needed to have given a sign of good will."[39] He remembers the cost of the education at that time to be around thirteen dollars a month, which covered both education and lodging. This was an average figure: less well-off parents may have paid even less. Bertrand Lamoureux recalls: "Families paid for lodging a monthly sum of about thirty dollars. Families who couldn't manage that amount paid twenty dollars, or ten dollars, or even nothing, in that case. At the noviciat [the most advanced stage, from the age of seventeen], families no longer paid at all."[40]

The days were "well filled," says Loiselle, with a considerable though not exclusive emphasis on religion. The boys had a Mass every morning, and prayers in the evening. There were times off: 4:00 p.m. every afternoon was a recreation hour when the boys could do as they liked, Thursday afternoons were free, and there were several free periods on Sundays. It was most likely in those free periods that Claude began to pursue his burgeoning interest in music and poetry. Although the school library did not have many specialist books on modern music, it had quite a few general works and encyclopedias.[41]

There is every indication that Claude took fairly easily to his new environment. A photograph dated September 1961 shows him standing proudly in his school uniform by a statue of Marcellin Champagnat outside the main school building. The two years he spent at the Juvénat Inférieur Notre-Dame were essentially preparatory, although, even here, the academic standard would have been higher than he was used to. Later, at the Juvénat Supérieur Saint-Joseph he studied Latin as part of his *méthode* (first year); to this was added Greek during his *versification* (second year). By the end of this latter year the class had shrunk from thirty-four to twenty-four pupils; some, realizing the religious vocation was not for them, withdrew; and the strictness of the school's standards is shown in the fact that no new students were admitted into the *versification* without having completed their *méthode*. Claude's results at the Juvénat Supérieur Saint-Joseph, however, were extremely impressive. In the first year, he was first in his class of thirty-four pupils, with an end-of-year average exam mark of 79 percent; and in his second year he was second out of twenty-four pupils with an average of 81 percent.

It is during his studies at the Juvénat Supérieur Saint-Joseph in Saint-Vincent-de-Paul that we first encounter Vivier in his own words. Several little texts of his were published in *L'Écho*, the magazine of the Juvénat: "Musique" and "En musicant" [*sic*] (during 1964–65); a humorous pseudo-biographical note on his fellow pupil Serge Bélisle, alongside a retaliatory piece by the friend in question (June 1965); and poems titled "L'Amour," "La Passion," and "Postulat" (all 1965). Of these six pieces, the first two, on music, are naturally of most interest. The little article titled "Musique" (written at the age of sixteen) begins with the revelation that modern music not only means "the *yé-yé*, the twist and all the rest": modern music is "dodecaphony, polytonality, polyrhythm, atonality." Clearly, he is already an enthusiast for modern music, and displays a knowledge of various big names including Schoenberg, Stravinsky (*Petrushka*), Milhaud, Auric, Honegger (*Jeanne d'Arc au Bûcher*), and Bartók.[42] The second text from the same year, "En musicant," is a brief description of Beethoven's Ninth Symphony. His poems of the time are also not without interest. Véronique Robert, editor of the posthumously published collection of

Vivier's writings, comments about "L'Amour": "apart from the frankly painful style, it is striking to note that many of the themes that will return in the works of Vivier the composer were already obsessing him at the age of 17: the unhappy child looking for love and happiness with an allusion, at the end, to the consolation brought by music."[43]

It is thanks to his short description of fellow pupil Serge Bélisle that we have the earliest character sketch of Vivier himself, from June 1965 (when he had recently turned seventeen). Bélisle's sketch reads:

> "O sole mio!" How many times have you heard someone humming this melody? He's a good guy: dark eyes and hair, his glasses sometimes on the end of his nose and his trousers rarely straight. Yes, Claude can be irritating. This song suits you well. You are the sun of the juvénat. We never saw your face darken from any of our arguments. Sometimes, if things were difficult, you had your piano to console you. In class, if the situation became difficult, you were the one who saved us by a sudden change of attitude. In the area of verbal expression also we appreciate you, and when everyone and even Molière were neglecting you, you passed even this hurdle with the help of music. Yes, Claude, despite our sometimes nasty teasing, we respect you and wish you every happiness.

In his reply, Vivier wrote: "I must already leave this little island of pure and healthy happiness where my impulsiveness has caused some silly things, but . . . I am ready, my knapsack of hopes and dreams on my back. I thank my teachers and my fellow pupils. They helped me to cast my rod and attach it to a shining star: my vocation. You have taught me to stay attached to it despite everything. Finally I see, in the mist, after the storms, my dream becoming concrete. The way is in sight. Thank you."[44] Although it is not completely clear here which "vocation" he is referring to, presumably at this stage—being about to enter the seminary at Saint-Hyacinthe—he means a religious one rather than the life of a musician.

His mother claimed that Claude began piano lessons at the age of fourteen, therefore during his time at the Juvénat Inférieur Notre-Dame.[45] His parents subsequently bought him a piano, which was installed in their home on rue Proulx. In his later school years Claude even made some extra pocket money from his music: according to his sister, he gave some music lessons, and he played the piano for the ballet school in nearby Ahuntsic. He also became fond of the organ, and went anywhere he could to practice, becoming familiar with many of the churches in the area. Vivier recalled to Thérèse Desjardins that at school the piano was kept locked and only he had the key. This is confirmed by Frère

Loiselle; "yes, it was his responsibility." On the other hand, Loiselle is sure that at the school "there was no piano teacher at that time."[46] In short, the Frères Maristes willingly tolerated, but could not do much actively to help, his burgeoning musical talents.

For all his enjoyment of playing, the young Claude's most important musical epiphany came about in quite different circumstances. Referring in the autobiographical text "Introspection d'un compositeur" to the "long period" he spent "au juvénat et au postulat," in other words between the ages of thirteen and eighteen, he remarks: "My encounter with music dates from this time, at a Midnight Mass. It was to change my whole life. Unwittingly, I had found the ideal instrument to express my search for purity and also the very reason for my future existence."[47] Some years later, he elaborated: "it was the first time that I felt in contact with sound, with a certain kind of purity . . . and that's why my music is always looking for purity, like the purity of a child, a candor and a happiness."[48] He seems to be referring to Mass at the Juvénat Supérieur Saint-Joseph. "I got to know music when I was at the juvénat. . . . I recognized music in a Midnight Mass we sang. I was extremely pious, I had faith, I wanted to be a pure human being, to give myself totally, and for me music . . . is a way of achieving my own redemption. In that sense I am very Catholic."[49] His friend Philippe Poloni recalls: "He heard the organ and the choir singing, and I remember he told me he turned his head very very slowly because he thought he was going to see God or a great light or something, it was so magnificent. He knew that he had found something that would change his life."[50]

In September 1965, at the age of seventeen, Claude began his studies at the Noviciat des Frères Maristes in Saint-Hyacinthe, a city east of Montreal on the Yamaska River. This was a natural progression, but now emphasis was placed even more strongly on a religious orientation. In his first year there, he took his Belles-Lettres (his "postulat"), "a mixture of secular sciences and religious sciences." The first part, from September until the middle of February, consisted only of *matières profanes* (Latin, mathematics, French, English). Beginning six months before the investiture, religious sciences were added. Claude's investiture took place on August 15, 1966, at the end of his first year in Saint-Hyacinthe, a crucial moment in the life of one possibly contemplating life as a religious brother. The second year was his "noviciat," the preparatory year for those contemplating a religious vocation (normally a five-year process). But, says Urbain Beauvais, his director of studies and "maître des novices," "he only did a few months."[51] Interrupting his studies, Claude left at some point midway through the academic year, either late in 1966 or early in 1967. The explanation we accept for this is crucial to an understanding of the life Vivier then followed.

Despite the intensity of the studies the pupils were obliged to pursue, the place acquired the nickname *La Villa du Bonheur*, the Villa of Happiness. During his time there, contact with his family was even more restricted than it had been at the Juvénat Saint-Joseph. (The composer Denis Gougeon has suggested that Vivier's accent, with its rolling "r," was developed at the seminary, and may even have represented a desire to fit into his new "home" environment.[52]) Holidays at the Juvénat had been short, even at Christmas, where he was obliged to stay in school until after the messe de minuit, but at least the summer—from the last week of June to the beginning of September—was free. At the seminary at Saint-Hyacinthe, he hardly saw his parents at all: pupils did not go home except for very special events such as funerals. Claude's fellow pupil Gilles Beauregard remarks that "at that time the idea of the noviciat was that it was a time of retreat from the world, a break; it was a sort of enclosure."[53] It was a year essentially devoted to religious studies, of the Bible, the Church, Christology, Theology. However, "in the musical domain there was Gregorian chant, which Claude liked, choral singing; he made many arrangements." Saint-Hyacinthe had roughly forty students spread over the two years, and "we were together the whole time. It was a very large property, so there was a lot of work": each student had to help maintain the place, being assigned various responsibilities.[54] As regards sport, "Claude wasn't very adept": but he liked swimming, and most evenings would do several laps in the school's indoor pool.

Claude made, albeit briefly, one musical acquaintance during his time there: a fellow pupil named Bertrand Lamoureux, who was already quite an accomplished pianist. Unlike Claude himself, Lamoureux had not already spent some years in the juvénat but entered directly into the noviciat, with a view to a religious vocation. "I therefore came in to the noviciat with a certain musical reputation, because I had won the Jeunesses Musicales de Granby competition, a few years earlier, playing Khatchaturian's Toccata for piano. I was therefore a pianist in the making. Claude was expecting to have the chance of living with a fellow student who knew and loved music, which was the case with me. . . . But, the year I went in to the Noviciat, Claude left."[55]

His school friend Gilles Beauregard describes the different sides of the adolescent Claude's character:

Claude was very original; already you could see that he had a rather exceptional character. On the other hand there was a sad aspect to Claude because we knew he was an adopted child. He didn't hide any of these things; he was very open, so we knew that his family wasn't very warm, that he wasn't very well accepted there. At school Claude was very popular, he had no enemies. Claude wasn't someone who was bullied at school: we liked to joke about him, we liked to make him react (because his reactions were always very strong), we liked to tease him; but we weren't mean to him. I think he was happy.

According to Beauregard it was poetry, perhaps even more than music, that was Claude's favorite subject: he loved Rimbaud, and the Quebec poet Émile Nelligan; he would often recite poems for his friends. The first of his musical compositions that his school friends remember was a song, *Océano Nox*, setting a poem by Victor Hugo. (Unfortunately, the manuscript of the song is lost.) Already at the Juvénat, as we have seen, his musical interests were strongly in evidence: Beauregard, however, perceptively remarks that Claude "hadn't received a good musical education when he was young. He learned things himself, it was a personal interest." He therefore lacked the training from a young age to be a real performer, but recognized this, while regretting it. Beauregard recalls Claude playing the Rondo alla Turca by Mozart. "At that time he played quite simple pieces, especially Tchaikovsky, that was his favorite. . . . In terms of modern music he was already interested in Bartók. We teased him by calling him Belua, the Latin word meaning 'the beast.' *Belua* Bartók." And further: "He talked to us about Schoenberg. We had no idea who that was, but he had already found Schoenberg." Beauregard notes also that Vivier's inclinations toward modern music matched his tastes in poetry.[56]

There is no doubt that Vivier himself felt his religious leanings were equally strong at this time. "When I was very young—well, 17 or 18," he told an interviewer, "I studied intensively all the psalms on the love of God. And perhaps that's the faith I have. The faith in the love of God. That's the faith I have deep inside me."[57] His faith is expressed in various of the writings he published in *La Villa du Bonheur*, the magazine of the seminary at Saint-Hyacinthe; but so, too, is an increasing sense of loneliness, a need to express a longing for company close to anguish, feelings that seem to run counter to his profession of religious faith. Véronique Robert has suggested that there may be an autobiographical aspect to Vivier's poem "Le clown," published during his first year at Saint-Hyacinthe, in which the clown "laughs without laughing . . . When he laughed, / He laughed in tears / Because he cried, / No-one knew . . . .!"[58] Another text, "Conte de Noël," published at Christmas 1965, expresses the emotional difficulty of being alone during this season, without family: "alone like that at Christmas you cry even more!"[59] Gilles Beauregard says of Vivier during this period: "He had a great need for communication, perhaps a need for acceptance; precisely because of his rather unhappy childhood, he always had this need for affection and recognition." On the other hand, "he wasn't deprived of it because Claude was without doubt the most popular of anyone there."[60]

If he was so popular, why then did he leave? For here begins one of the main strands of the mythology Vivier developed for himself—the ex-Catholic *frère* turned bohemian artist and flamboyant homosexual—and, as might be expected, several different types of explanation are on offer. To begin with, one of his teachers, Urbain Beauvais, the "maître des novices" at Saint-Hyacinthe, says:

> Claude was very sensitive, very nervous . . . he was someone who lived life from the inside. He lived so much inside of himself that from time to time he perhaps forgot what was happening around him . . . one day he came to see me. He told me how he did his meditation. He took a text, and inwardly he was so transported by music and poetry that during his meditation, without intending to, he began to compose poetry or music inwardly. That was his meditation! Claude was very interesting. He was cheerful, he was lively, but excessively sensitive and excessively inward-looking. He was so absorbed by what was going on inside him, so much thinking inside himself, that he sometimes forgot about the reality surrounding him. I think his career depended a bit on that. He left the community not because he didn't pray but because for me his orientation—music, poetry, all that—perhaps it would not have suited him to stay in the community . . . Perhaps it was too structured; he wasn't the type to be structured, Claude . . . I think his orientation wouldn't have fitted with the orientation of the community.[61]

In other words, Beauvais felt the eighteen-year-old Claude simply did not have the sort of discipline needed for the religious vocation, that he was too closely attuned to an inner imagination that valued music and poetry above all else. Claude's friend Gilles Beauregard tends to agree: "it was painful but I think ultimately he would have had difficulties later on. . . . Claude wasn't made for the religious life."[62] (To clarify, the Frères Maristes were a religious community of brothers, not priests; Vivier was not assuming he would become a priest with the power to celebrate Mass or administer sacraments, and was more likely aiming at becoming a teacher, possibly even a music teacher.)[63]

Vivier himself gave rather different interpretations from the sensible and, as such, quite plausible explanation given by Beauvais and Beauregard. Véronique Robert, editor of the posthumous collection of Vivier's writings, notes that his leaving the Noviciat was due to "lack of maturity," without however giving any source for this explanation.[64] But it is particularly its timing, midway through the school year, that seems to require explanation, with its vague suggestion of an incident or event of some sort that triggered his departure. At least two of Vivier's friends independently picked up the idea from the composer himself that the cause was some sort of sexual impropriety. Thérèse Desjardins remembers Vivier telling her that he had to leave because he was having sexual relations with other boys; and Clarence Barlow, himself an ex-Catholic, talking to Claude about his seminary days, remembered Claude telling him "he'd tried to seduce a *frère* or two, and they found out about it and threw him out."[65] If either of these somewhat conflicting memories are accurate, we may of course wonder whether either is truly the case, or—as with Vivier's account of his rape—a show of bravado to cover the pain of his being asked to leave. Urbain Beauvais, on being asked why Vivier left the seminary, did not mention any such thing, nor any "lack of maturity," merely that the "excessively sensitive" nature of the eighteen-year-old Claude was unsuited to the vocation of a religious brother. His school friends Bertrand Lamoureux and Gaston Robert, talking of this together, were clear that "there was no 'scandalous' or spectacular element (of a sexual nature for example) that brought about this expulsion. It was simply a question of understanding."[66] This may well be the case: of course, it could also be that certain things were simply not spoken about, and that the more scandalous truth of the matter was simply not known to Vivier's school friends.

There is another important element to the eighteen-year-old Claude's character that may or may not be relevant to his abandonment of a religious vocation: his emerging homosexuality. In his "Introspection d'un compositeur," Vivier remarks that, during his years with the Frères Maristes, "I discovered brotherly love [*l'amour-amitié*] and my sensibility could express itself more freely"—already an advance, emotionally, on the lack of warmth of his family, his adoptive mother in particular. He goes on:

> End of religious studies: I decide to enter the conservatoire and am successful. But there remains one element not yet expressed: my sexuality. Still a Catholic, it is difficult for me to believe I am a homosexual. But more and more another certainty grows in me: I am a composer! and the communicator that I am cannot bother with such a minor problem. For now, it is music that needs me. And I have to accept being a representative

of my society all the way. Later I learned that it was more than music that
needed me but Life in the most creative and universal sense of the term!
The decision was made.[67]

In other words, however potentially troubling, and although still unex-
pressed, his homosexuality was less urgent a matter than the realization
that his real calling was to be a composer and that he must surrender not
only to music but to "Life." Asked whether Vivier's homosexuality was obvious during his time at Saint-Hyacinthe, Gilles Beauregard replied: "It was
evident; perhaps we weren't perceptive enough to understand it that way at
the time . . . what we took as a need for affection." Beauregard recalls that
Vivier's nickname at the school was "Cherami," because he would often
begin a remark to a friend by saying "Cher ami, look at this," or "Cher ami,
come here," and so on. "Sometimes, I remember, he'd try to befriend someone, wanted to talk to him, to work with him, and the boy didn't connect
with him at all, wouldn't answer or would say 'Claude, you're annoying
me.' I know Claude suffered because of this. It was what was called at that
time 'amitiés particulières': Claude had the novel *Les amitiés particulières*
by Roger Peyrefitte; that was perhaps a sign." (The novel treats of the relationship between an older boy and a younger boy at a strict Catholic
boys' school in France, and ends in disaster after the priests keep voicing
their disapproval with heavy-handed tactics: despite their condemnation
of these "special friendships," some of the priests harbor sexual feelings for
the boys.) "But of course given the religious nature of the noviciat it was
not a place where he could easily express these sentiments or even make
what today would be called a 'coming out.' It was not possible, and perhaps
he himself had to live in an ambiguous way. I don't know. . . . He didn't find
anybody, I can say, who was really a friend of the heart, who loved to read
his poems, to talk with him. . . . Physically Claude was not really beautiful.
He had a large nose, big ears . . . he had very intelligent eyes, very penetrat-
ing, but physically he wasn't very attractive." He believes Claude suffered
because of this: "We didn't tease him in these areas because we knew that
would have hurt him."[68]

The Conseil de sélection advised Claude to withdraw from the seminary at Saint-Hyacinthe during the school year 1966–67, after only some
months of his noviciat. The decision was made, according to Frère Beauvais,
on the basis of "the evaluation of the fellow students who were living with
him at that time. . . . I think that his orientation would not have agreed
with the orientation of the community. . . . Community life with rules: he
wasn't cut out for that."[69] Bertrand Lamoureux adds: "Urban [Beauvais]

tells me that the decision to leave came from the postulant or the novice, but that in fact there was a discussion. We know that if a *maître de novices* found that someone was not made for the religious life, he would manage to convince the postulant or the novice of his point of view."[70] Vivier told his friend Michel-Georges Brégent that he suffered greatly because of this rejection from Saint-Hyacinthe, and that he would certainly have become a *frère* were it not for this expulsion.[71] His mother also remembered his crying after being asked to leave the seminary.[72] Beauregard adds: "Perhaps he experienced it as a third rejection. His mother rejected him at birth, he had been in an adopted family that rejected him, and he had found a milieu where he had been relatively happy: perhaps he saw that as yet a further rejection."

Claude left Saint-Hyacinthe and returned to his parents' house in Pont-Viau. Quite apart from his broken heart, there was now the problem of money. According to the recollections of his mother, he found at job at Goineau & Bousquet, a large hardware store that had a branch in Pont-Viau, in their lumber department; but the work was too hard on his hands so he stopped. He also worked at Eaton's department store in Montreal, and in a restaurant, but for some reason "ça pas marché" (that didn't work out).[73]

At the age of eighteen Claude was even more of an oddity in Pont-Viau than he was when the family had first arrived there. A Pont-Viau acquaintance, a year younger than Claude himself, recalls:

> We lived two streets away from him. I remember we heard him singing very loudly when he passed by on the pavement in front of our house. I was in service at Mass with him. Young people made fun of him because he was so out of the ordinary. He already had effeminate manners, laughed loudly and behaved strangely. But he was unreachable. Nothing seemed to affect him. Even when people were making fun of him he just started over again the following day. You would notice him. He wasn't the type to pass by unnoticed.[74]

Another vignette of the young Vivier at this time comes from Bertrand Lamoureux, his former school friend, who has a memory of the nineteen-year-old Claude in the summer of 1967, shortly before he began at the Conservatoire:

> One year later, at the time of my investiture, August 15, 1967, Claude came to visit my friends and offered me a piece for organ, which I couldn't manage even to read (it was handwritten). He took it straight back, saying he wanted to make some improvements. It was then he told me he was

going to study composition at the conservatoire. I remember saying to him: You see, it's a good thing you're not still in the Marist community: by staying in the community there is no way you could develop yourself in an area like composition. Maybe you could do some teaching but not composition. I also felt that composition was a domain that suited the eccentric and hypersensitive being that he seemed to be, even more so because he never had the chance to follow regular piano lessons (fortunately, some would say).[75]

Claude continued to make good use of the piano in his home on rue Proulx, as well as the organs in the various churches: his sister recalls that "he ran round all the churches in Pont-Viau to play the organ."[76]

The earliest two compositions of Vivier that are still extant are both organ pieces: one or perhaps both date from the year 1967, the year he entered the Conservatoire, although we do not know if it was either of those, or yet another, that he showed to Lamoureux.[77] The first is an extended piece titled *L'homme*, eight pages of manuscript (not dated, but below Vivier's name at the top of the first page is his parents' phone number in Pont-Viau). The second, which bears the date 1967, is called *Invention sur un thème pentatonique*: it is only eighteen measures long, and does not seem really finished in musical terms, although a double-bar is drawn before the last chord. Both pieces speak a modern language, although far from fluently. The *Invention* takes its main theme (a simple descending pentatonic scale starting on A) through several brief adventures and transpositions, but runs into rhythmic problems. Keen as the young Vivier was to experiment with quintuplets and sudden splashes of rhythmic energy, the piece seems to resist a settled tempo; if the busy figuration is to be intelligible to the ear, the fastest conceivable tempo would already make the statements of the main theme seem turgid.

We may wonder if the pomp and circumstance surrounding Expo '67, the noisy celebration of Canada's one hundreth birthday that ran from April to October that year, made much of an effect on the nineteen-year-old Claude. The expulsion from Saint-Hyacinthe was perhaps too recent and the new excitement of his life at the Conservatoire had not yet begun. In the summer of 1967, he still had much to learn, and much to sort out.

# CHAPTER TWO

# " I  W A N T  A R T  T O
# B E  A  S A C R E D  A C T ,
# T H E  R E V E L A T I O N
# O F  F O R C E S "

## 1 9 6 7 – 7 1

The Conservatoire de musique in Montreal has a nomadic history, having been obliged to relocate several times in its relatively short existence for reasons of expansion, renovation, or economy. During the period of Vivier's studies there, 1967–70, it was located in the premises of the former Palais du commerce at 1700 rue Berri, in what was felt by general student consensus to be "a horrible building" with poor soundproofing: the present state-of-the-art facilities on avenue Henri-Julien were still several decades in the future.[1] The place had a long prehistory, with the pianist Léo-Pol Morin and the composer Claude Champagne proposing as early as 1927 to the Quebec government to open a state-funded conservatoire that would be free to students, one in which talent and a willingness to develop would be the only admission criteria. That year, Morin had visited conservatoires in Brussels and Paris and proposed them as models in the columns of the Montreal newspaper *La Patrie*. The Montreal Conservatoire finally opened its doors in March 1943, proudly claiming to be the first institution of higher musical learning in North America operating entirely under state subvention. Its first director, Wilfrid Pelletier, steered the place for eighteen years, and was succeeded in

1961 by the cellist and conductor Roland Leduc. The director during Vivier's studies there was the composer Clermont Pépin (1926–2006), who took up his duties in the year of Vivier's arrival.[2]

Enrolling at the Conservatoire in the autumn of 1967 brought Vivier into steady contact, for the first time, with a professional musical environment. Although he continued to live with his parents in Pont-Viau, not only was he now in the company of other young students whose tastes and aspirations resembled his own, but he had access to the teaching of a range of professionals of broad experience, many of whom had studied in Europe with distinguished practitioners. During his years at the Conservatoire, Vivier studied piano with the American-born pianist Irving Heller; "écriture" (harmony and counterpoint) with the composer and pianist Isabelle Delorme; fugue with the organist Françoise Aubut-Pratte; and, most important of all, analysis and composition with the composer Gilles Tremblay. The teaching he received reflected the strongly French orientation of the Conservatoire. The director, Pépin, had spent several years in Paris studying with Honegger and Jolivet, and attended Messiaen's analysis class (at the same time as the young Stockhausen). Both Heller and Delorme had studied composition in Paris with Nadia Boulanger; Aubut-Pratte had been a student in Paris of both Messiaen and Marcel Dupré, and was one of the first to play their organ works widely in Canada; and Gilles Tremblay acknowledged frankly in an interview published in 1962 that "my true master is Messiaen."[3] But despite the French roots of its teaching, by the late 1960s the Conservatoire, and the Montreal new music scene as whole were opening their eyes to the world more widely than ever before: the many gifted young musicians who passed through the Conservatoire's doors on rue Berri during Vivier's studies are indicative of larger social and political changes taking hold in Quebec during this period.

While the Montreal of Claude Vivier's youth was very different from the cosmopolitan Montreal of today, the city even then was in the throes of transformation. In the 1960s, Quebec, like the rest of the industrialized world, was profiting from unprecedented economic growth and low unemployment, which brought great waves of social reform and strengthened the idea of the province's uniqueness within Canada. "The idea of being Québécois, as opposed to French-Canadian, became fashionable," notes Montreal writer Taras Grescoe, "as did the notion of forming a distinct nation, one defined by language and culture rather than religion."[4]

That a western society should still feel itself to be "defined" by religion as late as the 1960s is worthy of note. We can gain some sense of the background to the Quebec cultural landscape of the 1960s by looking at an incident some years earlier, a celebrated page of Quebec's cultural history but one practically unknown outside its borders. In August 1948, a few months after Vivier's birth, Paul-Émile Borduas, a professor of drawing and decorative arts at Montreal's École du Meuble, deposited four hundred copies of a mimeographed pamphlet at the Henri Tranquille bookstore on rue Sainte-Catherine in downtown Montreal. Titled *Refus global* (Total refusal), the manifesto was signed by sixteen individuals, nine men and seven women—a group that the Montreal press named "les automatistes," consisting of painters, photographers, dancers, poets, a psychiatrist, and a window decorator at a well-known jewelry store. Ignored by the majority of the population, *Refus global* provoked a scandal, albeit a short-lived one, among certain elites. Essentially an attack on the domination of the Catholic Church in Quebec society, the manifesto—barely three thousand words long—was written, somewhat in the style of André Breton's stream-of-consciousness prose, for maximum shock value. It opens by describing the people of Quebec as "a small people huddling under the shelter of the clergy, who are the only remaining repository of faith, knowledge, truth, and national wealth." The document is not only antichurch ("To hell with holy water and the French-Canadian tuque") but also antipolitical: it denounces much but offers relatively little of a genuinely constructive nature, and many of its proposed reforms are irrational in the extreme. "Make way for magic!" it declares at one point, "Make way for objective mysteries! Make way for love!" At its climax, in a flourish of impressive but rather hollow rhetoric, it proclaims:

> We must abandon the ways of society once and for all and free ourselves from its utilitarian spirit. We must not willingly neglect our spiritual side. We must refuse to turn a blind eye to vice, to scams masquerading as knowledge, as services rendered, as payment due. We must refuse to live out our lives in the only plastic village, a fortified place but easy enough to escape from. We must insist on having our say—do what you will with us, but hear us you must—and refuse fame and privilege (except that of being heard), which are the stigma of evil, indifference and servility. We must refuse to serve, or to be used for, such ends.[5]

*Refus global* is an idealistic manifesto written by artists dreaming of a less stifling society, one more attuned to their anarchic aspirations and desires. It requires a leap of the imagination today to appreciate just how shocking its passionate but ultimately innocuous spoutings must have seemed in the political climate of the late 1940s. But these were the dark days of rule by the conservative government of Maurice Duplessis and the Union Nationale, which dominated Quebec politics from 1944 to 1959 with the full support of the Catholic Church. The backlash against the manifesto brought consequences for some of those who had put their name to it: Borduas himself, fired from his teaching post, first produced a milder sequel (*Projections libérantes*) in the attempt to defend himself, then left Quebec altogether, settling initially in New York and later in Paris, where he died in 1960 at age fifty-four. Nonetheless, *Refus global* has maintained a mythic importance in Quebec culture. The Mouvement laïque québécois in 1998 awarded its Prix Condorcet, an annual prize given "for the defense of secularity and freedom of thought," to all signatories of the manifesto; and several commentators regard it as one of the crucial steps toward *La Révolution tranquille* (the Quiet Revolution), "an episode that transformed Quebec into one of the more liberal and culturally vibrant societies on the continent."[6]

The term "Quiet Revolution" is generally taken to have been coined in an unsigned article by a journalist from Toronto's *Globe and Mail* who, observing the many changes happening in Quebec, declared that what he was witnessing was nothing short of a revolution, albeit a quiet one. Although there are discrepancies in its usage and meaning from within Quebec, the Quiet Revolution has broadly come to mean "the period of political, institutional and social reforms brought about between 1960 and 1966 by the liberal government of Jean Lesage," which came to power following the death of Maurice Duplessis in September 1959.[7] This latter event is generally heralded as the end of Quebec's *Grande Noirceur*, the Great Darkness; the opening word of the speech given by Premier Paul Sauvé following Duplessis's death, "Désormais . . ." (From now on . . .), predicted that nothing in Quebec would ever be quite the same.[8] The years of the Quiet Revolution saw a great number of reforms: the creation of new universities, the revamping of the health system, the nationalization of hydroelectric dams, and the setting up of a complex system of social services (with all its attendant bureaucracy). Ex-priests married ex-nuns, joined the government, and participated in the transformation of the institutions that until then had been agents of clerical control. Future prime minister Pierre Trudeau, one of the key players in the revolution, commented that "the Holy Church" was being replaced by "the Holy Nation."[9]

Indeed, these apparently liberal reforms—some more successful than others—went hand in hand with new expressions of national identity. August 1968 saw the premiere at Montreal's Théâtre du Rideau Vert of the play *Les Belles-Soeurs* by Michel Tremblay (no relation to Vivier's future teacher Gilles Tremblay: Tremblay is a common surname in Quebec). This was an affectionate portrayal of working class society in a poor area of a great metropolis, written entirely in *joual*, the Montreal street French with which Tremblay had grown up, in which "je suis" becomes "chus" and "pas du tout" is "pantoute." While intended by its author simply as a realistic portrait of a slice of the life of his native city, the play became the subject of heated debate, with the accusation that it encouraged the debasement of Quebecois French. (Unrelated to Tremblay's work, but in the very same year, then federal justice minister Pierre Trudeau said his compatriots should stop demanding more rights and work on improving their "lousy French.")[10]

But a cultural flare-up such as *Les Belles-Soeurs* sent, at best, a few sparks into the prevailing cultural shadow. The conventional rhetoric surrounding the Quiet Revolution—that a retarded province suddenly, in the space of a few years, emerged from a century-long dark age into the brilliant light of liberalism, social progress, and joie de vivre—is too easy, too journalistic an interpretation to be credible. While much that was good indeed followed from Lesage's reforms—only in 1964, for example, was the Civil Code amended to give married women rights they had enjoyed in the rest of Canada for decades—old attitudes die hard, and the "collective mind" of much of Quebec society was slower to lay the old ghosts to rest. The composer John Rea, who came to Montreal from Ontario in the early 1970s to teach at McGill University, felt himself in the midst of "a nineteenth-century value system, which was quite suffocating. This was a complicated society, a hidden religious structure. A Catholic model of the world and human values was still resonant. Quebec then was a society under very strange pressures."[11]

Musical modernism came much later to Montreal than to New York or Boston, and made itself heard at first in an atmosphere of incomprehension and indifference. The musicologist Odette Vincent has identified three crucial dates that "mark the official entrance of Quebec musical life into Modernity: the organization of the first concert of contemporary music in 1954, the formation of the group Musique de notre temps in 1956 and, in 1961, the holding in Montreal of the first International Week of Contemporary Music organized by Pierre Mercure."[12] The first of these, in May 1954, was a concert given by three young composers who were also talented pianists, Serge Garant, François Morel, and Gilles Tremblay. The program consisted of works by Webern (the Variations Op. 27), Messiaen (three of the *Vingt Regards sur l'enfant Jésus*, *Neumes rythmiques* and *Île de feu* no. 1), Boulez (the *Première Sonate*, first movement), and new pieces by all three young Montreal-based composers. Whatever its significance historically as the first outing in Quebec for the trailblazing works of recent Modernist piano music, the concert did not in itself herald the emergence of a "Montreal school": Tremblay thereafter disappeared to study in France for a long period (until 1961), while Garant, just back from his stay in Paris, became the main *animateur* of the whole new music scene. The following year, Garant organized a concert commemorating the tenth anniversary of the death of Webern, a composer crucial to the new music of the era.

The apparatus of modernism entered the Montreal scene gradually. Garant was already writing atonally in his first major work, the *Musique pour saxophone alto et fanfare* of 1948; his progressive immersion in the music of the Second Viennese School and enthusiasm over the first available recordings of Varèse led him to compose works like *Nucléogame* (1955), arguably the first Canadian work involving tape. Serialism was increasingly in evidence throughout the fifties: Clermont Pépin produced his first serial work, the String Quartet no. 2, in 1955. And Quebec was then blessed with another quite individual modernist talent, sadly neglected today: Pierre Mercure, a composer of energy and originality who was killed in a traffic accident in 1966 at the age of thirty-eight. Electronic music, despite the interest shown in it by Garant, was slow to emerge: in 1961 Gilles Tremblay, just back from Europe, presented Quebec's first full program of electroacoustic works at Orford. In August that same year Pierre Mercure directed la Semaine Internationale de Musique actuelle, inviting twenty-nine composers including Cage, Kagel, Stockhausen, Xenakis, and Wolff. (Only two of the twenty-nine featured composers, Garant and Mercure himself, were from Quebec.)[13]

Before he began at the Conservatoire it is doubtful that Vivier knew very much of this repertory. It is also unlikely that he had composed much more than a handful of songs, organ and piano pieces, almost none of which have survived; Vivier's friend Michel-Georges Brégent recalled an early *Prélude pour piano* written near the beginning of his studies but later apparently destroyed.[14] In applying to the Conservatoire the prospective students would submit whatever compositions they had, and would take an aural exam and be interviewed. Gilles Tremblay's earliest memories of Vivier are of someone with "a very good ear," a "curiosity" and a "desire" for music.[15] "At the very beginning," Tremblay admits, "I had no idea that he was so tremendously gifted. I did feel that something was there but I couldn't guess, and I say this in all simplicity, I could not have predicted the music that he was going to write."[16]

In 1969, while Vivier was studying with him, the journal *Musicanada* published a feature on Tremblay, in which he was asked to describe his most profound musical experiences and his favorite composers. His response is interesting, if only because these enthusiasms could scarcely have failed to influence the twenty-year-old Vivier in some way: "Bach, almost the entire oeuvre," Tremblay begins, then "Mozart, mainly the piano concertos"; Monteverdi's *Vespers*; madrigals; Varèse's *Intégrales*; the Masses of Machaut; Stravinsky's *Le Sacre du printemps*; Messiaen's *Le Livre d'orgue*, *Chronochromie*, *Le merle de roche* (Book 6 of the *Catalogue d'Oiseaux*); Boulez's *Pli selon pli*; Stockhausen's *Zeitmasse*; and recordings of Indian and Balinese music. Asked "What interests you the most in the current streams of composition?" he replies in terms of his emphatic belief in innovation, the hallmark of Modernism: "the generous spirit of research, embracing risk without being paralyzed by fear. I mean research in the largest and most poetic sense—moving forward."[17] To this statement of belief he added another, in a television interview in 1974: "My profession as a composer is a way of saying Hallelujah."[18]

When Vivier began at the Conservatoire, Gilles Tremblay was thirty-five and had been teaching there for five years. He had already acquired a reputation as an inspiring and punctilious teacher. His influence, then still nascent, would continue to grow: the composer John Rea, assessing his contribution, calls Tremblay an "unprecedented catalyst" for a whole generation of Quebec composers, a teacher without parallel in the Canadian music world. "Religion had a lot to do with it," Rea says; Tremblay, himself a devout believer, was in some respects "like a priest." He had imbibed the "ecstatic tradition" from his own teacher, Messiaen, so there was a "religious metaphor still at work there."[19]

Tremblay's were "great classes," says Walter Boudreau, who began studying at the Conservatoire toward the end of Vivier's time. The analysis class was at 9:30 on Wednesday, and the composition class at 9:30 on Thursday. It was "un cours magistral," modeled on Messiaen's classes, with the piano in the middle of the room; Tremblay sat there, with the students gathered around him, and would analyze a score. He was "a sweet man," says Boudreau, "fatherly"; the class was "much more than the sum of its components" because "we became a family." Often the classes would continue until 1:30 p.m., when they would all take lunch together, sometimes walking along to rue Ontario to a vegetarian restaurant called Les Petits Oiseaux where they could eat a plate of salad and beans for a dollar and carry on discussions about music, politics, or anything else. Tremblay, says Boudreau, was "a teacher with disciples." The discussions were "frank, sometimes heavy": all the students were "passionate about what they were doing, rejecting a lot."[20]

How did Vivier seem to his teacher? "He had a fantastic gift of curiosity," recalls Tremblay, "he was eager to know. He was so eager to know that he was sometimes very tiring, because he would follow me in the corridors after the lessons and ask me questions." This lack of social sensitivity was displayed not only toward his teacher. "Claude was sometimes unbearable with the other students," Tremblay admits. "I had a class that ended at 1, and at 12 precisely Claude began very slowly to unwrap his lunch and to eat it, the others telling him to shut up." (A legacy, perhaps, from the highly structured routine he had experienced with the Frères Maristes.) And yet, "everybody loved him."[21]

Tremblay's teaching consisted of analysis, which took the form of a weekly group lesson, and composition, which was equally divided between group teaching and one-to-one tuition. He refused to teach only contemporary music, believing that "music was a whole," so he would range around various historical periods and epochs, declining to follow neat chronological lines. He analyzed Gregorian chant, classical music, Bach, a lot of Mozart, and contemporary music; in Vivier's "second or third year of study I made a big analysis of Berg's *Wozzeck*. I did it specially for him." Even though Tremblay at that time knew almost nothing of his young student's background, he felt "this work was very important for him"; he speculates that Vivier saw at the end of *Wozzeck* "a reflection of his own destiny"; the impoverished, mentally unbalanced soldier becomes progressively more of an outcast from society.

Vivier "was the most serious student I ever had," Tremblay concludes, "extremely serious." And with his other teachers? "He did not do much piano," Tremblay thinks, "he was not a very good pianist. With me he worked a lot. This guy was always laughing, making jokes, but at the end he was the one who went the most deep, especially in analysis." Did his role in the young Vivier's life extend beyond the purely pedagogical? "I was not conscious of replacing a father," Tremblay says.

> One day at the Conservatoire we had a reading with the orchestra of some student things. I conducted and afterwards I invited Claude and a few others to a Chinese restaurant. I'd known him for a while but I noticed I never saw his parents at concerts. . . . I asked if he had brothers and sisters, and he said "Yes, I have, but . . ." and then he said, very loudly, "I am a bastard!" And he told me a delicious story: that his parents went to the orphanage, and "my sister Gisèle thought I was so beautiful that they took me!"[22]

Vivier's admiration for Tremblay knew no bounds, and extended even to the occasional attempt to poach a student from another institution and bring him to the feet of the master. During his second year at the Conservatoire he met Michel Gonneville, two years his junior, who was studying piano and composition at the École de musique Vincent d'Indy in Outremont, a borough north of downtown Montreal.[23] The two got into conversation there one day in the café; Vivier was extremely friendly, enthusing so loudly about his studies with Tremblay that Gonneville became curious and, upon finishing at the École de musique, enrolled in Tremblay's class at the Conservatoire. Gonneville remembers the young Vivier as "very expansive," "exuberant," somebody who radiated a sense of joy but yet exhibited a "moral concern" for the world. They had long conversations, mostly with Vivier talking; already it was clear, Gonneville says, that he had ambitions to be a composer. Much of the talk centered around the vicissitudes of the new music scene, with constant analyses and counteranalyses of the music and the aesthetic standpoint of the composers then being played at concerts such as those of the SMCQ, the recently founded Société de musique contemporaine du Québec, led by Serge Garant. At that time a more conservative wave was also prominent on the Montreal scene, represented by composers like Jacques Hétu and André Prévost who, although a few years younger than Tremblay or Garant, seemed less progressive in outlook. Prévost was a fan of the music of Berg, with which his own music shared a certain Expressionist intensity. Garant, then teaching at the University of Montreal, talked incessantly about Webern and Boulez: his compositions of that period show an unmistakable debt to a Boulezian aesthetic, which the musicologist Richard Toop has characterized as "an aura of elegant abstraction [with] lots of xylorimbas and vibraphones."[24] But "Tremblay's scope," says Gonneville, "was wider."

The fact of Vivier encountering students at institutions other than his own is entirely characteristic. During his years at the Conservatoire he would go from time to time to the Faculty of Music at the University of Montreal to attend Garant's composition workshops and classes in analysis. The percussionist Robert Leroux, who saw Vivier "sporadically from the time he was still a student at the Conservatoire," remarks that at this time "Claude 'haunted' all the schools and was certainly very curious to hear and see the new works that were being played there."[25] One day, by chance, he ran into his old school friend Bertrand Lamoureux. "I saw Claude again," Lamoureux remembers, "at the University of Montreal, in the Faculty of Music which was at that time on the rue Chemin de la Côte-Sainte-Catherine. I was then studying clarinet. Claude came to the faculty on occasion, I think among other reasons to see Serge Garant. I remember, one day, his showing Garant a composition he had just done. With great gestures and an exuberance that was characteristic of him, he was explaining what happens in the piece. Garant seemed to be listening with a sceptical ear."[26]

At the Conservatoire itself Vivier formed several lasting friendships with fellow composition students. The earliest was with Michel-Georges Brégent, who began in the same year as Vivier himself. Brégent recalled their first meeting: "Conservatoire de musique, 1967, I am at the piano in the middle of working on my *Grande Toccate-Sonate Barbare*. Someone knocks at my door. It was Claude. He wanted to know who this crazy guy was. After two hours of unforgettable conversation which led to an embrace, we were One. We discovered everything together."[27] Toward the end of his studies a new student appeared at the Conservatoire who would remain one of Vivier's closest friends: Walter Boudreau. A few months older than Vivier himself, Boudreau had beaten an unorthodox path to contemporary music, studying classical piano, jazz saxophone, and playing in various rock and jazz bands while still in his teens; he already had something of a name as a jazz musician on the Montreal circuit. But in 1968 his musical horizons had widened on hearing a concert in Montreal of music by Garant, Tremblay, Bruce Mather, and Karlheinz Stockhausen. Boudreau had heard of the young Vivier before encountering him in Tremblay's class. A pop-singer friend, Louise Forrestier, had been taking music lessons from someone who, she told Boudreau, looked like a "strange young priest": it was Vivier. Once Boudreau began regularly attending Tremblay's classes, he started to see quite a bit of the strange young priest, both there and privately: Vivier, he, and Michel Gonneville would often spend time in the apartment of their fellow student Michel-Georges Brégent and talk about "music, religion, politics, sex." They quickly became firm friends, although Boudreau immediately realized that Vivier's relatively low level of performance skills would limit the amount of practical music making they could do together. On one occasion, looking for a pianist to play an arrangement he had made of the first movement of Bach's D-minor Concerto for a concert at the Place des Arts, Boudreau showed the score to Vivier who took it into a practice room at the Conservatoire saying, "I'll do it, I'll do it!" He came back half an hour later, Boudreau remembers, "drippily" admitting he could not really manage it. (Although Boudreau himself and Michel-Georges Brégent were already very involved in the world of pop music, Boudreau recalls that Vivier was "interested, sort of," but showed no desire to join that world.)[28]

In class, Boudreau recalls, Vivier was "very loud and very obnoxious." Asked to explain this, Boudreau suggests that this aspect of his friend's character might have been the result of two things: his physical appearance and his "sexual stand." He thinks Vivier was "very unhappy" about his physical appearance. He had glandular problems, so his feet would smell, and he had bad breath. Moreover, in Quebec at that time homosexuality was "one heavy thing, so you'd either hide it, or if you came out you'd have to be *un fol*, and very extravagant." Boudreau believes it was a lifelong problem for Vivier—that his love life both then and subsequently was "never gratifying." He agrees with the apparent paradox noted by Tremblay, that Vivier could be "unbearable" and yet was "loved" by everyone in the class. Vivier, Boudreau says, could be "like a clown, . . . often the saddest people. I think this is one of the reasons why Claude was so obnoxious, because he was very deeply unhappy." For all that, they had many good times together, Vivier enjoying "but never totally fitting in with" the gang of friends that surrounded the charismatic Boudreau: besides Gonneville and Brégent this included fellow Conservatoire composition students Raynald Arseneault, Richard Boucher, and Yves Daoust.[29]

Boudreau believes the unhappiness he detected in his friend had its origins in his early history.

> Claude was an abandoned child. All that fucked-up turmoil! He managed for a short while. His genius managed to use this as a kind of catharsis to give us those wonderful pieces of music, because otherwise . . . There's so much pain in his music, it's terrible. Yet Claude was a clown, in life, with people. How could he disguise this terrible insecurity? By being an asshole. And by being so loud. He'd come up anywhere, at a party for example, and French-kiss any girl . . . his behavior was a way of getting attention that he wouldn't have got purely on the basis of his looks. Claude would sit at a concert, and if the piece was boring he'd let out this incredibly loud yawn; you'd know that Claude was there.[30]

Vivier's clown-like nature and his tendency toward exhibitionism are seen in an incident from March 1969, around the middle of his second year of study at the Conservatoire. Each year several composition departments from various schools both in the northeastern United States and Canada (the Eastman School of Music, Bennington College, Columbia and Princeton Universities, the University of Toronto, McGill University, the Conservatoire in Montreal, and others) would organize a symposium for student composers, with one of the schools acting as host. That year the host institution was McGill University. The Canadian composer Harry

Somers, then forty-three, fresh from the success of his opera *Louis Riel* commissioned for the Canadian centennial the previous year, was asked to speak about his use of the voice in his compositions. "I decided to 'sing' my lecture," Somers recalled. "I sketched an outline starting simply with 'breathed' sounds. . . . I moved naturally to 'voiced' sounds, to fully sung, and finally expired on a breath."[31] "Somers was in fact performing an early version of what would become his *Voiceplay*, a wordless but sound-full (of new vocal techniques) lecture-demonstration for actor/singer," recalls the composer John Rea, who was in the audience. Then,

> at the end point in the proceedings, Claude, who was sitting near the moveable low-rising stage, and who may have thought like others in the hall that either Harry was pulling everyone's leg, or that he was simply unprepared, or that a new form of music was being foisted upon the unsuspecting, or all of these put together, jumped up from his seat, mounted the stage, and like the agit-prop street theatre of the day did a mocking, mirror-like copy of Somers's performance. The hapless Somers was startled, to be sure (today we'd say it was a kind of artistic terrorist attack), but the monkey-business did not last too long, Harry recovered his composure, went on with his things, and Claude left the stage shortly thereafter. Needless to say, everyone talked about the event that night, and for the days following.[32]

Rea adds: "In looking back, and reflecting upon all of the vocal music that Vivier would write over the next number of years, it would be foolish to underestimate the value of this 'traumatic' event in the genesis of his nonsense-word languages."

Vivier's studies at the Conservatoire in Montreal not only encouraged him to compose but also gave him a grounding in "écriture," the study of traditional harmony, counterpoint, fugue, and orchestration, skills in which he was relatively deficient at the time he entered. There is no indication that this kind of study, considered drudgery by many students at the time (as well as before and since), particularly bothered him. Indeed, he retained the manuscripts of some of the exercises he produced at the Conservatoire, indicating a certain fondness for them. Among them are orchestrations of Bach's Fugue in C-sharp Minor (from Book I of *Das Wohltemperierte Klavier*), Debussy's *La fille aux cheveux de lin* and *Ondine* (from the *Preludes*); Vivier's manuscript for the latter has conducting symbols at the bottom of the staves, suggesting it may have been tried out by the Conservatoire orchestra, perhaps even with Vivier himself wielding the baton. Besides these, he retained a sheaf of sketches and neat copies for the many fugues he produced under the tutelage of Françoise Aubut-Pratte. There are various loose pages showing multiple attempts to write presentable fugue subjects and countersubjects in two voices; abandoned beginnings of what were presumably intended to be more extended pieces; and a number of complete four-voice fugues in various keys, all written out in the old clefs (soprano, alto and tenor C-clefs, and bass clef). They show him grappling earnestly with fugal form: countersubjects, false entries, or passages of stretto are often indicated as such, clearly showing the didactic intent of these pieces. Aubut-Pratte seems to have given him fugal subjects to work with, so we find two fugues on subjects by her own teacher, Marcel Dupré, and a lively one in F minor on a subject by Aubut-Pratte herself. Only one of the surviving fugues is on an original theme (the manuscript proudly states "sujet: Vivier"), an intense piece that plows on relentlessly in a highly chromatic D minor for seventy-nine measures before ending on an enigmatic cadence in D major with a final tonic triad with added second and sixth.

Vivier meanwhile made further attempts at original composition. From the end of his first year at the Conservatoire, we have the piece that he would regard as his Opus 1, the first item to be retained in his catalog of works: the *Quatuor à cordes* (1968), titled *Quatuor à cordes* no. 1 on the manuscript, but it remained his only work in the medium. Two movements only are extant; the second movement was originally marked "3° mouvement," but this has been crossed out and "2° pièce" written above it. It is therefore not clear whether the piece had at some point another movement, now lost or destroyed. It is also not clear whether the second of the surviving movements, which ends extremely abruptly at the end of a page without a concluding double bar line, is actually complete.

The quartet, under the name *Quatuor en deux mouvements*, was the first work of Vivier's to be played in a public concert. The performance, the only one the piece would receive during his lifetime, was given on August 10, 1968, as part of a concert titled "Musique d'Aujourd'hui" at the Festival Orford near Magog, some 120 kilometers east of Montreal. The performers were participants in the JMC (Jeunesses Musicales du Canada) music summer camp: Hansheinz Schneeberger and Anka Moravek, Norbert Blume and Eric Wilson.[33] The performance was conducted by the Romanian-born French composer Marius Constant, presumably a practical expedient in putting together a performance by relatively inexperienced young

performers of a difficult—and, in some places, rather badly notated—new
work with limited rehearsal time. The concert began with Vivier's quartet
and continued with the Webern Concerto, Op. 24, Niccolo Castigliani's
*Tropi*, André Jolivet's *Douze inventions pour douze instruments*, Ravel's
Sonata for violin and cello, Marius Constant's *Pièce pour trois*, and Edgard
Varèse's *Octandre*. Vivier, who had received a bursary that summer from
the JMC to study piano with Karl Engel, was able to attend the performance. Constant took it upon himself to make numerous markings on the
manuscript with a thick ink pen, showing that he regarded the piece as a
student work and its composer as being in need of some assistance. These
markings include: conducting symbols, added more or less throughout,
intended to help him beat through the frequent changes of time signature in the music; the superscription of time signatures above the systems,
which occasionally contradict Vivier's own;[34] and various verbal tempo indications (e.g., "Lent," "Assez vif," "Animé," etc), whereas Vivier tended to
use simply metronome marks to indicate tempo changes. Moreover, some
additional metronome marks have been added by Constant where Vivier
has none.[35] In all of these cases it is impossible to know which of these inscriptions represent the wishes of Vivier, as expressed verbally during rehearsals of the piece, and which are simply Constant's own interpolations.
Moreover, we should not assume that the 1968 performance of the quartet,
even with Vivier present, represented anything like a "definitive" interpretation. The young and inexperienced composer was, and would remain for
some years, shy about stating his own interpretative preferences too boldly
in the presence of performers. The resulting manuscript looks in places
like a battlefield, and in a few places it is unclear exactly whose handwriting one is seeing. (At the age of twenty Vivier's handwriting was still in
flux and he was experimenting with at least two distinct styles, both of
which, and more, are in evidence in the manuscript of the quartet.)

Vivier and his teacher Gilles Tremblay differed in their evaluation of
the piece. Tremblay remembers it as "not very well sounding," but on the
other hand it was clear that Vivier "believed in it very much."[36] Listening
to it now—the first professional performance was not until 2005—there
is little to distinguish the quartet from the prevailing modernist idiom
of the time. It is atonal, full of characteristically Webernian "expressive"
sevenths and ninths; the meter changes almost every measure, as though
to eliminate any possibility of metric regularity; and the music expresses
itself in short bursts, with rapid changes of texture, tempo, dynamic, and
mood. It is intensely serious throughout, even solemn. The music is closer
to Viennese atonality than to Messiaen, but this seems to result less from a

clear aesthetic decision than from the fact that a quasi-Expressionist idiom simply came more easily to the twenty-year-old composer, still trying to learn the language of modern music.

Vivier's compositional explorations took quite a different turn a few months later, in *Ojikawa*, for soprano, clarinet, and percussion (four timpani and vibraphone). This is the earliest of his extant vocal works, and in it we find the first use of the "invented language" that would come to characterize the majority of his subsequent vocal compositions. The invented language—a subject to which we shall return as its importance in Vivier's output grows—is essentially a succession of nonsense syllables that are generally combined into "words" in his scores by the use of hyphens. The syllables are empty of semantic significance, but individual syllables or their combinations may certainly suggest or invoke images and associations in the listener's mind. (No scholar has yet undertaken a systematic exploration of Vivier's "nonsense" texts.) The opening of the text, for example, "O-ji-ka-wa," means nothing in particular (although "Ojikawa" is a relatively common Japanese surname); its constituent syllables are subsequently combined into constructions like "Ni-ê-do-ka-wa o-ji-ka-wa Na-a-a-ou-vi-na Ou-vi," none of which mean anything either, but seem to express a childlike delight in making up words and, in the process, repeating syllables almost as though they were notes in a melody. In *Ojikawa* this invented language is combined—again, from the standpoint of Vivier's later work, prophetically—with passages in French, in this case a version of Psalm 131, from the group of fifteen psalms known collectively as the Song of Ascents. The text begins, in Vivier's version, "Seigneur mon coeur ne s'enfle pas d'orgueil, mon regard ne se fait pas arrogant" (in the King James version: "Lord, my heart is not haughty, nor mine eyes lofty: neither do I exercise myself in great matters, or in things too high for me. / Surely I have behaved and quieted myself, as a child that is weaned of his mother: my soul is even as a weaned child").[37] The text is thus one of humility and simple faith, though as Véronique Robert has observed, "we find in it the theme of childhood and the image of the child resting in its mother's arms, an image to which Vivier was never insensitive."[38]

It is tempting to speculate on the meaning of the text of *Ojikawa* overall, with its eccentric combination of nonsense with an Old Testament psalm. Certainly, nothing in the music suggests that the Biblical text is being ridiculed by the nonsense surrounding it; on the contrary, the psalm setting is perhaps the most beautiful part of the work. (It was this very section that was later sung at Vivier's funeral.) Perhaps more indicative of the intent of the piece is the wish expressed in the psalm text to return to the state of being a child, to behave purely and humbly in the face of human striving; the "nonsense" may, in its own way, bear this out. Once the psalm has been sung, the closing section of the work sets the text "Porphyre Éden, enfant Éden, enfant porphyre enfant." The child finds himself in a Garden of Eden made of porphyry, the beautiful purple-red rock much valued as building material in the monuments of the ancient world. How should we interpret this curious line, if not as the earliest of the numerous visions of paradise that infuse Vivier's work? The text of *Ojikawa* contains two things that recur in the composer's later work: the psalm text itself is used again in *Liebesgedichte*, and porphyry, the magical substance, recurs in the text of *Journal* ("Our hands will touch marvelous colors / [Is it true that] Carabosse the fairy has here her castle of porphyry?"), and in *Kopernikus*.

Ojikawa had a curious debut. Vivier showed the score to Tremblay, who was encouraging, and mentioned the piece to the Conservatoire's director, Clermont Pépin.[39] Pépin helped have the piece selected for performance at the same Symposium of Student Composers at McGill University in March 1969 that saw Vivier's curious interaction with Harry Somers. The problem was that no soprano could be found who was equal to the demands of the vocal part, so Pépin asked Jean Laurendeau, who had just begun teaching both clarinet and ondes Martenot at the Conservatoire, if he would agree to play the soprano part on the ondes. Laurendeau was enthusiastic, so he met Vivier and showed him how the instrument worked. Certain changes were made in the interests of making the music sound idiomatic in its new instrumentation: Laurendeau remembers, for example, suggesting that some of the octave sweeps in the soprano part be changed into two-octave sweeps on the ondes, to give an equivalent impression of brilliance and movement. He also remembers an incident at the premiere that he took as a sign of the easygoing temperament of the young Vivier. In rehearsal, generally the three musicians would skip the soprano solo (ondes solo, in their case) in the middle of the work, the setting of the psalm text, so by the time of the performance the clarinetist and percussionist had forgotten it was there. Laurendeau began his ondes solo only to have the other two players simultaneously begin the final section of the work, a set of mobiles. Because of the generally atonal nature of the music it sounded reasonably convincing, and probably few among the audience realized anything had gone wrong; but Laurendeau remembers a loud laugh from Vivier at the back of the hall. "We were very grateful!"[40]

The experience of *Ojikawa* led to a new work, the earliest of Vivier's commissioned pieces. Jean Laurendeau asked him to write a piece that would be suitable for the tours he undertook at the time for the Jeunesses

Musicales du Canada. (The JMC, which had hosted the premiere of Vivier's *Quatuor*, was a nonprofit organization created to encourage the pursuit of music among Canada's young people and to help talented performers and composers develop their careers in Canada and abroad.) This was not a paid commission, Laurendeau explains, "as Claude was still a student," but he remembers Vivier's being delighted at the invitation. In the end the work he produced, *Prolifération*, for ondes Martenot, piano, and percussion, was largely unsuited to the audience of young people for which it was intended: it was, Laurendeau says, "too avant-garde," but nonetheless had "lots of light, lots of life"; it was "quite revolutionary in a way."

In fact Laurendeau found the piece both disturbing and inspiring. "May '68 was still fresh in our memories. . . . In this atmosphere, *Prolifération*—an explosive, spring-like piece—seemed to me a sort of joyous and agreeable Molotov cocktail."[41] "In this spirit I made two red covers for my copy of the score, red like the Little Red Book of Chairman Mao!" *Prolifération* is the most advanced work Vivier had produced to that time, and the score is filled with contemporary techniques that he had encountered thanks to Tremblay's classes. Chief among them is the use of aleatoric, or chance, procedures, which are combined with theatrical elements. At the beginning, "the three musicians come onstage as though they don't know each other"; they begin to play a mobile, a musical form pioneered by Earle Brown (and later utilized by Boulez among others) in which the musicians' material is fully notated, but its synchronization is left open—rather like a Calder mobile, where individual pieces take on a spatial relationship to each other that is determined largely by circumstantial factors such as air currents in the room or direct physical contact. *Prolifération* also contains three sections titled "jeu," involving improvisation and various degrees of nonsynchronicity of the players' material. In the work's final section, the musicians progressively replace their instrumental sounds with spoken words; at the end they leave the stage still talking. The work invites the active participation of the players in a way that is worlds apart from the completely determined *Quatuor* (although the last section of *Ojikawa* is a step in an aleatoric direction). Laurendeau remembers Vivier talking too much in the first rehearsals and having to ask him to be quiet. He also remembers sitting down in the breaks, still thinking about the piece, discussing with Vivier and the other players what it was, what they could do with it. "We had the feeling we had to bring it to life." For Laurendeau himself, now beginning a settled life as a recitalist and a professor at the Conservatoire, "Claude was a representation of some aspect of freedom."[42]

*Prolifération* received its premiere at the New England Conservatory of Music in Boston in April 1970, in a concert as part of that year's symposium of works by young composers from various North American colleges. The concert consisted of works by four students of Tremblay: Vivier's work began the program, and then came new works by Yves Daoust, Raynald Arsenault, and Michel-Georges Brégent. There was even a brief review in the Canadian periodical *La Scène musicale* in June, calling the concert "the most fascinating of the whole conference."[43] Laurendeau evidently believed in Vivier's piece, as he programmed it several times subsequently: he even had a dispute with Gilles Lefebvre, the director at that time of the Jeunesses Musicales du Canada who, for all his respect for Vivier, told Laurendeau that his idea to program *Prolifération* in the SMCQ series (in October 1971) was crazy; "he said Claude was 'far too young,' 'you'll kill him in the egg.'"[44] But the performance was a success, and *Prolifération* became the first piece to make Vivier's name known in Montreal. The work's European premiere followed in March 1972 at the ninth Festival d'Art Contemporain at Royan, France. A review in the Montreal paper *Le Devoir* noted that "*Prolifération* by Claude Vivier had at least the merit of being an authentic creation by the young Quebec generation."[45]

The original manuscript of *Prolifération* from 1969 is apparently no longer extant. We have only the revised version made by Vivier in 1975–76, though the differences were probably not that substantial. Laurendeau played it with Louis-Phillippe Pelletier and Serge Laflamme, whose recording of the piece was released on an LP by RCI (Radio Canada International) in 1973, and later with Lorraine Vaillancourt and Robert Leroux.[46] By the time of this second version in 1976, Laurendeau noticed a profound change in Vivier compared to the student he had first met some eight years earlier. Vivier, he says, had become "le musicien," and was much more active in working with and advising the players. The new version attempted to "de-contemporary-music–ize the piece," says Laurendeau: "especially in the improvisatory passages, Claude would object that 'oh, that's too Contemporary Music.'" At that time Laurendeau had struck up a friendship with the composer José Evangelista, and they would listen together, occasionally with Vivier also, to recordings of nonwestern music such as Gagaku. Laurendeau was "steeped in" such experiences when they did the second *Prolifération*, and it filtered into his improvisations. Vivier accepted this: it was, says Laurendeau, "a work that includes diverse approaches."[47] Vivier continued to make changes to the piece in rehearsal. At the time of the later performances, the percussionist Robert Leroux recalls, "Claude then didn't hesitate to modify the tempi, make cuts, etc. I found it quite courageous on the part of a composer of serious music to not hesitate to 'correct' one of his works with the passage of some years."[48] The various changes Vivier brought to *Prolifération* show, as much as anything else, his continuing belief in the piece. They are less a criticism of the first version than an acknowledgment that the new music world had moved on in the interim, and that there was no need for the piece to remain stuck with the clichés of the late 1960s avant-garde.

The other substantial work from Vivier's years as a student in Montreal is his most ambitious undertaking to that time, *Musique pour une liberté à bâtir*, written probably in 1968 or 1969, and scored for women's voices and orchestra. The work has never been performed, which fact is not so surprising given the untidy state of the manuscript. Indeed, the piece would be difficult to perform today without consulting the composer. The manuscript is in several parts: a first part of twenty-three pages, then a short aleatoric second part of two pages (at the start of which Vivier has written "the three events of this part are played in a random order, following one another without interruption"); then a long section, twenty-four pages, with the title "Musique pour une liberté à bâtir II." The piece begins with "extremely violent" music for four trumpets and piano, as though a call to arms, followed by a brief "joyous" passage for two ondes Martenot. This gives way to orchestral passages that alternate between fully notated material and moments when the conductor cues entries of material in free rhythm from players scattered around the orchestra. The manuscript shows Vivier fascinated by the look, as well as the sound, of modern music, making use of recent developments in notation, but in the process creating pages that are sometimes difficult to make sense of, especially rhythmically. There are quite a few passages of controlled improvisation and mobiles, and one moment, in part 2, when the three trumpets separate themselves from the orchestra and walk into the hall. The aggressive brass music returns toward the end, before the final "song of the light," with the singers singing a calm, chant-like melody to a Latin text. The piece is ambitious and imaginative, but is the product of a young composer still exploring the language of contemporary music and making discoveries, some of them too recent to be fully assimilated, and some of them perhaps uncomfortably close to the work of his teacher. Gilles Tremblay remarks that "at the beginning he was imitating too much—especially with these aleatoric parts, which I did use very much at that time."[49]

Perhaps the most curious aspect of *Musique pour une liberté à bâtir* is its title, which seems to be a response—unique in Vivier's output—to the political climate of the times. (The title can be translated as "Music

for Freedom," or, literally, "Music to Build Freedom.") Vivier's friend
Martin Foster, who was another member of Tremblay's class, recalls that
"although I grew up in Quebec, like most anglos of my generation I was
only partly aware of the French fact of my home province. My time at
the Conservatoire changed all that. Claude was a fervent separatist in
those days and he took pleasure in introducing me to the serious nature
of Quebec's desire for self-determination."[50] Not only were the protests of
May 1968 in Paris still fresh in the public consciousness, but Quebec was
going through its own period of upheaval, at the end of a decade when
the Quiet Revolution was giving way to new initiatives. The Liberal Pierre
Trudeau became prime minister of Canada in June 1968, which seemed
in many people's eyes to herald a new era in Canadian politics. But there
were dissenting voices. The Parti Québécois, formed that October, partly
as an outgrowth of the expansion of the francophone bourgeoisie in the
province, had the aim of fighting for political, economic, and social independence for Quebec; in their eyes Trudeau's policies were not nearly radical enough.[51] Quebec also had its own spate of political activism in these
years, such as the huge demonstration on the campus of McGill University
on March 28, 1969, in support of the "français movement," with protesters
urging the primarily anglophone university to respond more fully to the
linguistic reality of Quebec. We do not really know what sort of "liberté"
Vivier's title invokes, whether a specifically Quebecois one or a less politically focused kind. The fragmentary text does not help: on the final page,
titled "Chant de la lumière," the choir sings "il n'y a pas de plus grand
amour que de donner sa vie pour ceux qu'on aime" (there is no greater
love than to give one's life for those one loves). But in any case this work,
like most of the other ambitious works Vivier would produce in the years
immediately ahead, proved impossible to hear in performance. Its declaration of support for "liberté," however genuine, was still confined to his
own imagination.

Vivier's years at the Conservatoire culminated in 1970 with his being awarded first prize in analysis and first prize in composition. His final analysis
paper was on Varèse's orchestral work *Arcana* (1925–27), the enthusiasm
for which he had acquired from his teacher. "My specialty was Varèse," says
Tremblay. "I think very few people at the time did this. I met Varèse, I went
to meet him in New York when I was the age Vivier was then, nineteen,
twenty years old. I had heard his music. When I discovered that this giant

was living in New York . . . when you are very young, you know, you are not so self-conscious, so I went to see him; and he was very nice with me, with this young provincial from Quebec."[52] Vivier's analysis of *Arcana*, 127 typewritten pages plus more than a dozen pages of handwritten music examples and errata, is dated Montreal, April 28, 1970. Tremblay himself had not really analyzed the piece. "I thought it was a little dangerous," Tremblay recalls. "I wasn't sure he knew enough, but he did it . . . for him it was very useful to do it, an excellent thing for his own development."

At that time two commercial LPs of *Arcana* existed—Robert Craft's with the Columbia Symphony Orchestra and Jean Martinon's with the Chicago Symphony Orchestra—but Vivier's analysis is more concerned with the notes on the page than with the sound of the music in performance, about which he makes hardly any comment at all. He views the piece as dividing into six unequal parts.[53] After brief discussions of the "principal moments" of the work, its rhythmic material, and its "treatment of intervals," he plunges into an immensely detailed description of the piece, carefully scrutinizing every rhythmic figure and every vertical pitch collection. With regard to present-day analytical thinking on Varèse, it is perhaps surprising that Vivier says so little about timbre and the choices of instrumental sonority;[54] but this thesis is pioneering work, one of the first detailed analyses of a work of Varèse ever submitted to a North American institute of higher learning.

Overall, Vivier's studies at the Conservatoire were an overwhelmingly positive experience. He was nineteen when he enrolled and twenty-two when he graduated, although he continued to hang around the Conservatoire (and other music schools in the city) for another year. Those years saw the usual late-adolescent emotional ups and downs in his spirits. Jean Laurendeau recalls one evening seeing a surly Vivier sitting on the desk of the caretaker of the Conservatoire, leaning over to him and saying, "Don't you think, M. Charrette, this conservatoire is a graveyard?"[55] (But what composer has never entertained such thoughts about their place of study?) And socially he was known for being, at times, hard work: Bertrand Lamoureux recalls one of his teachers remarking, "Claude Vivier? He's at the limits of the bearable."[56]

In his final year at the Conservatoire there is one sign that the religious life in which he had for so long been immersed had not entirely left his mind. In the middle of February 1970, he went on a five-day retreat to L'Abbaye cistercienne d'Oka, a large gray-stone monastery in the village of Oka, on the northern bank of the Ottawa River (the Rivière des Outaouais), about an hour and a half by public transport southwest of Pont-Viau. L'Abbaye cistercienne, known in English as the Abbey of Notre-Dame du Lac, was a Roman Catholic order of contemplative monks, originated by a small group of Trappist monks who had escaped the French Third Republic and immigrated to Quebec in the 1880s. By the time Vivier encountered it, the settlement in Oka consisted of a group of some 150 monks, settled in a sizable property that included a large church, a library, and a refectory. It was famous throughout Quebec because of an exquisite semisoft cheese made there, *le fromage d'Oka*.[57] Vivier found the abbey to be a place of rest and spiritual refreshment, and he would make occasional visits there for the rest of his life. Following this February visit he returned for another five days in early June.[58]

✶ ✶ ✶

If the Conservatoire had given the young Vivier a strong foundation on which to build, the summer of his graduation saw him take one determined step further toward his vocation as a composer. In July 1970, he went for the first time to Europe to attend the summer courses in new music in Darmstadt, a city in central Germany just south of Frankfurt, famous for its Jugendstil architecture. Darmstadt had been for more than a decade a byword for the newest developments in contemporary music. The summer courses had been in existence since 1946. The musicologist Richard Toop explains that they "had been designed as a way of reconstituting new German music in the wake of the Nazi years of prohibition":[59] they were cosmopolitan in outlook, and attracted students from all over Europe and, increasingly, the whole world. The image of Darmstadt as the epicenter of musical Modernism—an image that persists to the present day—was well in focus by the end of the 1950s. Throughout the 1960s the presence of a generation of composers that had came to prominence in the previous decade—Boulez, Nono, Stockhausen, Ligeti, Kagel, Pousseur—ensured that the courses were a platform, a mouthpiece, and a breeding ground for the radical young generation.

Darmstadt presented Vivier with a larger range of new music than had been accessible in Montreal, and introduced him to many composers whose names were new to him. There were concerts every evening during the two weeks of the course: that summer he could have heard large-scale orchestral works such as Pousseur's *Couleurs croisées*, Morton Feldman's *First Principles*, Bruno Maderna's Violin Concerto, orchestral works by Hans-Joachim Hespos, York Höller, and Hans Zender, and smaller works by Rolf Gehlhaar, Vinko Globokar, Kagel (*Atem*), Ligeti (Ten Pieces for Wind Quintet), Edison Denisov, and Bernd Alois

Zimmermann. The composition teachers that year were Ligeti, Pousseur, and Stockhausen; all gave lectures on new music, their own included, and attended performances of their recent works. Ligeti analyzed his Second String Quartet and *Kammerkonzert* and gave his "Subjective reflections on New Music 1957 to 1970." Pousseur spoke on *"Engagierte Musik* today." Stockhausen's lectures, according to the *Darmstädter Beiträge zur Neuen Musik,* the Ferienkurse's official organ, centered on "Micro- and Macrocontinuum," "Meta-collage and Integration," "Expansion of the Tempo Scale," "Feedback," "Spectral Harmonics and Expansion of Dynamics," and "Spatial Music."[60] While Gilles Tremblay's classes had introduced him to Stockhausen's music, hearing the forty-one-year-old composer in person could hardly fail to intensify Vivier's interest.

Far from being overawed and made to feel humble by the celebrated and talented company around him, Vivier evidently wanted to make his mark on the summer courses. If he could not yet manage it as a composer, not having a piece of his own played that summer, he would do it through another show of exhibitionist behavior. Clarence Barlow, then a student of Bernd Alois Zimmermann, recalls:

> There was a piece by Günther Becker [*Disposition X*] being done, I believe in the Sporthalle, involving a lady rolling around in a fishnet suspended above the audience. She had very little on. When she came down they tried to cover her up with cloth so nobody would see her. Suddenly you noticed this young man who had begun to wriggle around and do a kind of funny dance during the piece. In those days, of course, the society was much more liberal, so he was allowed to continue—nobody came to say "Stop this!"—and we were all watching him rather than the lady. He was getting into all kinds of lascivious positions, with very tight trousers if I remember right; maybe his green satin trousers. That's when I first saw Claude. I got terribly embarrassed and thought, this person would certainly not be somebody I'd like to meet, I just wouldn't know how to deal with him. He made quite a scene of himself in public.[61]

Vivier may well have planned to attend Darmstadt again the following summer, but in January a press release announced that from that point forward the courses would happen only every other year: there would be none in 1971.

The piece he was working on during his weeks in Darmstadt was *Hiérophanie,* for soprano and ensemble (two flutes, clarinet in B♭, horn, three trumpets, tenor trombone, bass trombone, and two percussionists). The first version of the score is signed "Heidelberg, août 1970"; it is a big, ambitious, rather chaotic score, eighty-nine pages, with a clear indication at the end that "this is not the definitive version; it's a first version!" (A second version, much neater and now requiring only fifty-six pages, is signed "Montréal le 8/1/71.") The scoring for wind and percussion perhaps invokes the Varèse of *Hyperprism* and *Intégrales*, but the addition of the soprano voice and the use of aleatoric and semi-improvised elements, and the movement of players around the stage, make the piece firmly of its era. Work on *Hiérophanie* occupied Vivier over a period of six months or more, from the summer of 1970 to the completion of the neat copy of the score in January 1971. It is clear that the twenty-two-year-old composer wanted to produce a substantial work, one surpassing in ambition even what he had attempted in *Musique pour une liberté à bâtir*, and the extensive folio of sketches he produced, with its grids of dynamics, numbers, and pitch charts, is a testimony to his determination to make the work embody much solid compositional effort.

The introductory notes to the manuscript show that the piece embodies a scenario of sorts. The eleven instrumentalists are conceived in three groups: Vivier suggests that stage lighting might help to differentiate them. The percussion symbolizes "the transcendental" (early in the piece the second percussionist sings and plays an "Alléluia"). The first group of the other instrumentalists (initially the three woodwinds, first trumpet, and two trombones, though its constitution changes as the piece progresses) symbolizes "the loving human"; and the second group (initially the other two trumpets and horn) represents "egotism." These two groups are, respectively, the "good" and "bad" sides of humanity. The symbolism of the soprano is not explicitly stated. When she finally enters midway through the piece she first has to cry out "in a horrible way" for seven seconds; then, more calmly, she sings the first of the two Delphic Hymns from ancient Greece, believed to date from around 138 BC, and probably the world's oldest surviving music notation.[62] Then she quietly intones the words "vie," "mort," "silence," "parole," followed by five Greek names. At the work's culmination, she sings, in Latin, a Salve Regina, a traditional Catholic prayer to the Virgin Mary for mercy; Vivier uses its traditional chant melody.[63] In its final moments, *Hiérophanie* also contains the first appearance of a literary source that would return periodically through Vivier's output: Lewis Carroll's *Alice's Adventures in Wonderland*. Toward the end of the piece the horn player reads unspecified passages from the novel while walking around the hall. At some point he or she stops reading, and the work ends with the soprano, unaccompanied, singing the last phrases of the Salve Regina in total darkness.

*Hiérophanie*, then, seems to be a complex enactment of the human predicament. The musicians go through the range of motions and interactions Vivier has devised for them, all apparently to no end: they move around, they improvise, they play and hum music that reminds them of their childhoods, they call out the names of gods, they play "musique de club 'commercial,'" and at one point they swap instruments with each other, all amid the occasional spiritual exhortations of the percussionists. The soprano seems like a being from another time, or rather other times, her main contributions being a Greek hymn to Apollo and a Christian prayer to the Virgin Mary. It is all quite difficult to make sense of, until we realize that much is revealed by the work's title: *hierophany*, from the Greek roots "hieros," meaning sacred or holy, and "phainein," meaning to reveal or to bring to light, signifies the *manifestation of the sacred*. Vivier almost certainly came across the word in the writings of the Romanian-born historian of religion Mircea Eliade, several of whose books he owned, who used the term as an alternative to the more specific but restrictive term "theophany," meaning the appearance of a god.[64] Eliade argued that the idea of the sacred gave the world value, direction, and purpose, and that in traditional societies, myths described "breakthroughs of the sacred (or the 'supernatural') into the World": to these moments of manifestation he gave the term *hierophany*.[65]

It may be that we can read Vivier's *Hiérophanie* more autobiographically, as a sort of rite of passage in his own personal quest for manifestations of the sacred. Among the sketches for the piece he retained two pages of (verbal) notes, in which he outlines a sevenfold division of the piece. The seven stages progress through, successively: "communication" (represented by the physical contact between the players at the start, who take turns to sound a note on the tam-tam); "meditation" ("the birth of the individual," represented by silence and then by children's music); "contact with primordial and primitive time" (the passage from darkness to light, and the birth of sound); "the first time of man (childhood)" (attraction, dreams, spontaneity); "the primitive" (instinct, memory, death, anguish); "passage" (formalism, "ritual of the sonorous world," "symmetrical alternation"); and "childhood," leading at the end to a sense of the "great sacred." This reads almost as an allegory of a child's own passage to religious or spiritual awakening or, on a larger scale, that of humanity as a whole. As though in confirmation of this sort of reading of the piece, Vivier writes at the end of the notes, "Salve Regina; manifestation; path of the pure young man." More than three years after his expulsion from the Noviciat des Frères Maristes, Vivier shows himself still concerned with making sense of what he had learned there, and asking, now through the medium of his music, questions about the true way of the young man, pure of heart. But like its freedom-proclaiming predecessor, this musical rite of passage remained unheard: *Hiérophanie* was to wait forty years for its premiere.

✳ ✳ ✳

The experience of Darmstadt in the summer of 1970 had clearly whetted Vivier's appetite to absorb European culture more deeply. That autumn he applied to the Canada Council for a "Bourse de Perfectionnement Pour Artiste," a postgraduate grant, for the academic year 1971–72: his application is date-stamped October 14, 1970. His original plan was to go to Paris. Under "Short description of your project," he lists:

 a. Studies at the ORTF research centre in Paris with Pierre Schaeffer.
 b. Studies with Olivier Messiaen and Gilbert Amy at the Conservatoire National de Paris in analysis and composition.
 c. Work with Maurice Béjart in Brussels. I already have his agreement on this.
 d. To compose and meet artists living in Paris.

In the light of subsequent events it is interesting to see how much his ideas at this time were still clearly influenced by Gilles Tremblay, not least the very choice of Paris itself, and the intention to study with Messiaen. The wish to work with Pierre Schaeffer, then the leading exponent of *musique concrète* and other forms of electronic music, is no surprise either (Tremblay had worked with him in Paris some ten years earlier); but it is unclear quite what he proposed to do with the famous choreographer Maurice Béjart who, despite championing the music of several avant-garde musicians, would surely have been unlikely to want to work with so inexperienced a young composer. As referees for his application, he listed Tremblay, Serge Garant, and Maryvonne Kendergi, the tireless radio broadcaster, teacher, propagandist for Canadian music, and founding member of the SMCQ, in which latter connection Vivier had gotten to know her. He asked the council for $4,000 (the maximum applicable), for twelve months beginning June 1, 1971.[66] In the event, none of the plans he listed, apart from the rather vague one under (d), actually came to fruition.

  Shortly after submitting the application he received the tragic news that his actor and playwright friend Yves Hébert, known under the pen name Yves Sauvageau, had committed suicide at the age of twenty-four.

Despite his youth, Sauvageau had already won prizes in a Radio Canada competition for young authors, and was now working as an actor and writing plays. He performed widely with the Jeunes comédiens of the Théâtre du Nouveau Monde based at that time in Montreal's Place des Arts, and the year before his death joined the Enfants de Chénier at the Théâtre du Même Nom.[67] Vivier mentions Sauvageau at the end of the introductory note—in essence, a short essay on the subject of death—that prefaces the score of his vocal work *Musik für das Ende*, composed some months later, and again, after a passage of some years, in his text "Introspection d'un compositeur": "Some years ago I met Yves Sauvageau; shortly before his death, he told me that I should establish a monastery for artists where they could finally express themselves openly, where their creative activity could finally find favorable ground. Some time later, the poor man died."[68] Some eight years after Sauvageau's suicide, the idea of a monastery for artists, where the spiritual journey embodied in a work like *Hiérophanie* might be understood, was still resonating.

He expressed a similar religious aspiration even more strongly in an article titled "Truth and Revolution: A Quebec Composer Facing the Musical Act," published in the newspaper *Le Devoir* on Friday December 4, 1970, only some weeks after hearing the news about Sauvageau. The article begins:

> I want art to be a sacred act, the revelation of forces, the communication with these forces. The musician must organize no longer just music, but sessions of revelation, sessions of the incantation of forces of nature, forces that existed, exist and will exist, forces that are truth. . . . To become a priest, to organize ceremonies dedicated to these forces, to find the soul of humanity . . . To organize revelations of which priests are the interpreters and of which the composer is the medium.[69]

The article argues forcefully for "pure creative work," free from commercial constraints and, interestingly in the light of Sauvageau's remark, for new places for art, both "defined" and "not defined." The text is passionate and idealistic, if rather vague on specifics, and is underscored with a note of impatience and even anger at the state of things. The same tone is found in a companion piece written around the same time, "Notes of the evening," which begins even more truculently with an epigraph that is a quotation from Artaud's *Le Théâtre et son double*: "To be like victims burnt at the stake, signaling through the flames."[70] This text also deals with the place of artistic endeavor in today's world, and shares the tone of indignation and anger he had found in Artaud. Here, the path of the creative artist is likened to that of the monk, and art itself is felt to be eschatological or apocalyptical:

> If you want to be a flare of freedom, you have to walk alone, without speaking, in silence. . . . There is only one language, that of the end; and when you talk, you will only use this language, forgetting about the language of your companions. For when you talk, you talk to all the beings past, present and future, from here and from there. . . . We share the same path, to the same end, and the only language is that of the end, of true universality.[71]

Without being stated explicitly, the grand theme hanging over these two texts is death, or, as he prefers to say here, "the end." The making of art is seen as a religious intention aimed, as is everything else in life, at death, which is viewed quite clearly in religious, even Catholic, terms as the ultimate resolution of life's suffering. Only through death, the text says, do we find "true universality." It is interesting to see Vivier confronting this theme in his writing just as it was emerging as one of the main subjects—arguably *the* main subject—of his music.

Both "The Musical Act" and "Notes of the Evening" were included in a book titled *Musiques du Kébèk*, edited by Raôul Duguay, published by Montreal's Éditions du Jour in 1971. Vivier had met Duguay through Walter Boudreau, with whom in 1967 Duguay had formed the colorful and bizarre collective L'Infonie, with musicians from various backgrounds playing in a range of styles including free jazz, classical, contemporary, and rock, and involving visual artists and poets. The band already had an enthusiastic cult following in Quebec. About the book, the autodidactic Duguay—singer, songwriter, poet, trumpet player—recalls: "My school, my only real school, has always been in listening precisely and carefully to the works of others. So much so that I wrote a book called *Musiques du Kébèk* in 1971, which consisted of a synthesis of all the musics that could be heard in Quebec at that time."[72] While not sharing Duguay's populist outlook on the role of music in Quebec society, Vivier nonetheless found him enjoyable company. Duguay even claims that it was Vivier who notated his main hit song: "If you had come in to the little student café at the CEGEP in Limoilou [in Quebec City], ten or twelve years ago [around 1971], you would have caught Claude Vivier in the middle of finishing, in public, the first arrangement for piano of the 'Bitttàtibi,' my first song. You would also have heard a rather special version of *Poppy Nogood* by Terry Riley for piano and trumpet."[73]

For the early part of 1971, Vivier is only sketchily present in the historical record. The single surviving document we have of him from this time is a photograph, taken in Montreal in March 1971 on the occasion of a visit by Stockhausen to the city for two concerts of his music by the SMCQ. The photograph, by Bruno Massenet, captures Vivier in an uncharacteristically reticent moment: with rakishly long hair, but smartly dressed, he stands behind Serge Garant and István Anhalt as they listen to the words of the ponytailed Stockhausen, comfortably seated on a couch.[74] We would love to know what transpired between the recently graduated student and the famous composer-guru at that meeting, or others during Stockhausen's stay. By the time of our next documented trace, the plans to study in France that Vivier had confidently proposed to the Canada Council in the autumn have vanished, and instead he has set his sights on Germany. (Had his original intentions come to fruition, he would have been in Messiaen's class at the same time as Gérard Grisey and Tristan Murail.) The Canadian periodical *La Scène musicale* dated June 5, 1971, reported: "Claude Vivier will leave for Germany in May and travel across Europe to compose and finish his studies. Before leaving Canada, he finished *Hiérophonie* and is intending to present this work in Europe." In the event no such presentation ever took place: in Europe, though, he found plenty of other projects to keep him busy.

Before leaving Canada Vivier worked "for two months" on a project at the National Arts Centre in Ottawa.[75] He was asked to do the music for a play for which little documentation has survived; Vivier himself, in a grant application to the Canada Council in October 1972, mentions among his performed works "Musique du Spectacle Femmes" in Ottawa. There he met the poet André Roy, working as a stage manager at the National Arts Centre, who recalls it as a "play about feminism." Vivier "didn't believe in the play," says Roy; "it was low pay but at least it was paid!"[76] The music Roy recalls, "vaguely," as "rock music" for a trio of musicians including electric guitar. Vivier stayed with him in Ottawa for three or four days while he was finishing the music, working all night long until the morning, and leaving behind an incredible mess in the bedroom, including some three or four sheets of music, presumably sketches or drafts of music for the play. (A few years later the two met in Montreal: Roy told him he still had those pages, to which Vivier replied, "Oh, put them in the garbage!") Vivier himself, uncharacteristically, did not keep such notation as he had for the music, and by the time of a grant application in 1974 was no longer listing the event among his "main achievements on the professional level," showing his lack of enthusiasm for the music. Another useful aspect of his time in Ottawa was that he worked "with tapes machine [*sic*] and I have done a lot of montage and recording during this time," possibly in connection with sound effects for the play.[77] (Electronic music had not been among his studies at the Conservatoire.)

André Roy recalls that Vivier was learning German at the time of his visits to Ottawa, doubtless in preparation for his forthcoming departure for Europe, and that he would speak to various people in German to practice. Vivier left Montreal for Europe in May 1971. He would be gone for more than three years.

# CHAPTER THREE

# " T O   P U S H   M Y
# L A N G U A G E   F U R T H E R "

## 1 9 7 1 – 7 2

For a young Canadian composer at the beginning of the 1970s, the decision to study in Europe was not uncommon. In Vivier's case, had encouragement been needed, it would have come amply from Gilles Tremblay, who had himself as a younger man studied in Europe for a period of seven years. Study in Europe was more than simply a "finishing school": in the eyes of an important minority in Quebec it was a passport toward an international career and a crucial step away from parochialism. Relatively few of Vivier's fellow students at the Conservatoire followed suit—Michel-Georges Brégent and Walter Boudreau, for example, were too committed to their bands and their various other musical activities to think of leaving Quebec at this point—but quite a few of them came to Europe in the summers, and occasionally for longer periods. During the three years he would spend in Europe, Vivier would see various Montreal friends from time to time and even make the acquaintance of people who would remain friends back home, such as the Spanish-born José Evangelista.

For Quebec composers, however, the destination of choice had overwhelmingly been France. The two most prominent figures of the Montreal-based musical avant-garde, Tremblay and Garant, had both spent important years in Paris; Vivier's decision to study in Germany was unusual. The first address we have for him in Europe, on a document dated June 20, 1971, is on Stürzelberger Weg in Köln-Worringen, the most northern

part of Cologne.[1] The fact that the document in question is his registration
form for study at the Institute of Sonology in the Netherlands, however,
is significant. He had come to Cologne in May in hopes of studying with
Stockhausen, then newly appointed as a professor at the Hochschule there,
but was, at first, refused. Clarence Barlow, who also applied that summer,
tells the story:

> Stockhausen I know took offense at his looks and his smell—Claude had
> this sheepskin coat which exuded a certain sheep odor—and maybe his
> way of talking, which had a certain namby-pamby quality. Stockhausen
> gave us a job to do—we were supposed to write something based on the
> formula from his *Mantra*; each one of us got a photocopy of the formula.
> So we all sat around this table—we had two or maybe three hours to write
> a piece. Anyway, Stockhausen loved my handwriting and said, "Oh, you
> English are so excellent in writing"—I think he thought I was going to be
> one of his copyists. At the end of the exam he showed me Claude's score.
> He said, "Just look at this! look at this writing! would you accept some-
> body like this as a student? This man will never be a good composer, with
> writing like that!" And Claude was refused. His piece was called *Übung
> sur "Mantra."* And that's when we became friends, because he hung out
> in Cologne then.[2]

A change of plan was thus called for, and in late June Vivier applied to
the Institute of Sonology, then located at Utrecht State University, to study
with Stockhausen's former colleague Gottfried Michael Koenig. Whether
this was Stockhausen's suggestion or someone else's we do not know; it is
interesting nonetheless that Vivier's second choice of place of study still
emphasizes work in electronic music. He was accepted in Utrecht for the
beginning of the academic year in October.

In Cologne in July 1971, he completed *Musik für das Ende*, for twenty
voices (in three unequal groups, two groups of five and one of ten), the
singers also playing percussion. Vivier also sometimes referred to the piece
by its French title, *Musique de la fin*. This work, like the two articles he had
written back in Canada a few months previously, was a response to the
suicide of his playwright friend: in an interview published in a Montreal
newspaper three years later he described it as "a grand funeral ceremony
written in memory of Yves Sauvageau."[3] The title page bears a dedication
to two friends he had made in Germany, Peter Eötvos and Joachim Krist,
both composers who had studied in Cologne and regular members of the
Stockhausen Ensemble. But the piece is dedicated also to "die Leute [*sic*]
die heute sterben werden" (to the people who will die today). "Living in

the midst of beings destined for death I have often reflected upon this. Instinctively I see these beings no longer in life but in death. In my dreams I was living more and more the strange ceremony of beings who vanish for ever, who become an 'infinite moment' in the eternal silence."[4] The piece, never performed in Vivier's lifetime, again calls for movement of the musicians on stage, something that had been so important a part of *Hiérophanie*. Here Vivier specifies more sober activities, and ends up with a semitheatrical work that is quite distinct from the music theater of Kagel and that seems almost to look forward prophetically to the late plays of Beckett, sharing something of the strange, quasi-ritualistic nature of *Quad* or *Nacht und Träume*. The work is concerned not only with death but with personal identity and human communication. Almost as though he were directing a play, Vivier specifies three types of "fundamental relationship" between the singers: the first, shown in the score by the use of a plus sign (+), means that "two beings reach so deep a mutual understanding that they exchange their music and finally become one music"; the second, notated with a minus sign (−), is the opposite ("from this one music the beings return gradually to their own music"); and the third, indicated by a slash (/), is that "certain beings remain solitary and have no contact with the others." Toward the end of the work comes a moment that is almost too raw in its autobiographical significance: "a being comes into the hall . . . he walks in and asks the following questions: Where do I come from? Who am I? Where am I going? He talks louder and louder, walks faster and faster, gets annoyed!"[5] This "being" seems the very incarnation of the composer himself; it is perhaps the first but certainly not the last time we find a "Vivier character" in his work. The scenario of *Musik für das Ende* as a whole shows Vivier using music to ask questions about human interaction, solitude, and existential despair. Musically, the piece uses the same kind of controlled aleatoric textures as his previous pieces and also incorporates moments of quite different kinds of music, although here they are newly composed rather than "found" (as was the case in *Hiérophanie*): a fragmentary "kirie eleison" [*sic*] in B minor, for example, or two solos that are chant-like but rhythmically irregular and chromatic. But once again, despite mentioning in a letter to a Montreal friend a possible performance in Munich in December, he was never to hear the work, or have the opportunity to learn from seeing it performed.[6]

With *Musik für das Ende* finished and his acceptance to the Institute of Sonology in the Netherlands confirmed for October, he ended up spending the rest of the summer in France, studying privately with someone who would become an important mentor, one who has received too

little attention in the existing literature on Vivier: the composer and conductor Paul Méfano. It is interesting that Vivier should have gravitated
not to one of the "inner circle" of French musical life but to Méfano; here
again the point of contact was probably Gilles Tremblay. Born in Iraq in
1937, Méfano had grown up in France where he had studied at the conservatoire. His teachers had included Milhaud and Messiaen, and he had
followed classes by Boulez, Stockhausen, and Pousseur. Several of his
early works were conducted by Maderna and championed by Boulez's
Domaine Musical. He had recently come back to France after two years
in America and one in Berlin, and settled in Chilly-Mazarin in the southern suburbs of Paris. Thanks to a contract with Salabert publishers, he
was able to make a living as a composer, conductor, and concert orga-
nizer. In the years ahead, Méfano was to become known as founder and
principal conductor of the Ensemble 2e2m, which in the summer of 1971
had not yet gotten started.

In France in the early 1970s, the new music landscape was still very
much dominated by Pierre Boulez, who had established an aesthetic stran-
glehold on the whole scene. The fact that Boulez was present in almost every aspect of French musical activity, and would remain so at ever higher
levels throughout his career, cast a long shadow over the generation that
followed. The Boulezian aesthetic, powerfully seductive for some composers, entailed a highly calculated approach to rhythm and harmony, an
aura of intellectual abstraction, a love of novel colors, a brusqueness and
even violence of expression, and an avoidance of sentiment or warmth.
Méfano, as well as several other young composers like Gilbert Amy and
Jean-Claude Éloy, were initially seen as Boulezian in musical outlook: but
as one commentator has remarked, Méfano "had too slight a respect for
orthodoxy to become the member of any cenacle, no matter how attentive he was to the fashions of his contemporaries, and was ill cut out to
be a continuator of Boulez"; his music had "the elegance found in Boulez
but neither the remoteness nor the austerity."[7] He was considered a young
composer to watch.

A letter written from Paris to his Montreal friend Pierre Rochon gives
us a glimpse of Vivier's attitudes and activities in the summer of 1971.
Ensconced in the Hotel de Blois, an *hôtel de passe*—possibly also a brothel—on rue Vavin in the heart of Montparnasse, Vivier describes France
as "a terrible country," adding that "I love Germany as much as I hate
France." The letter also shows that, whatever Vivier's later reverence for
his teacher-to-be Stockhausen, the idolatry was not there from the start:
perhaps he was still hurt by Stockhausen's rejection.

I'll stay in Paris until October and in October I'll leave for Utrecht for the Studio of Koenig. So I need to learn Dutch!

At the moment I'm analyzing with Paul Méfano the "Soleil des eaux" by Boulez; extraordinary but all the same the complete opposite of my music. And I'm composing; you know this music I started with Luc, well it's come quite far, I messed everything up and found myself with three choirs! found myself with people who sing for brief moments about their past or talk about it, found myself with voices | sound | word | rhythm for each and which develop according to fundamental principles of human relations, found myself with a psalm, a procession and finally the whole thing will be performed in December in Munich; isn't that marvelous. In the meantime I've begun a work for string quintet, two wind quintets and one brass quintet. Strange music which finishes with the voice of the author saying: "I have nothing anymore, nothing to say." Towards the end I'll probably add a vocal quartet!

So in short I've been pretty busy. But what's happening in Montreal, anything new? is Serge OK, how did the concerts with the SM go? I've only had very little news from Montreal so send me some!

Stockhausen's musicians are very good, I like them a lot, they've given me a lot, perhaps more than Stock. who is always a bit distant and doesn't understand my warm manner which means I'm always shaking hands with people! I heard Sternklang a new work; it's five times Stimmung but much less good. He's preparing "Trans" for Donaueschingen I hope that will be better. I must say that the vision he gives to the group in "Aus den Sieben Tagen" and what really comes from the group bothers me a lot. They're all "professional musicians."[8]

The piece referred to in the letter, for string quintet, two wind quintets, and brass quintet, would occupy him through his move to Utrecht and beyond, emerging in January 1972 as *Deva et Asura*—though without the "voice of the author" at the end, unlike the autobiographical presence in *Musik für das Ende*.

It may well be that Vivier heard the premiere at Donaueschingen, on October 16, 1971, of Stockhausen's *Trans*, mentioned in the letter. Clarence Barlow recalls going there with Vivier either that year or the following, and learning a good deal more about his friend as a result. They had no place to stay, Barlow recalls,

but Claude said, "I'll fix it up." So he wrote a little sign saying, "Anybody got a bed for the night for the two of us?" and he stood at the entrance of the concert hall displaying it. I thought, oh God, you can't go anywhere with him! But a young chap coming out said, "Come!" The two of us followed. And we were put up in his living room, I was at one end and

Claude was at the other—fortunately, because during the night Claude
began to make noises in his sleep. I'll never forget the sound he made—it
was as if somebody had attacked him or something.[9]

✶ ✶ ✶

The Institute of Sonology was located at Plompetorengracht 14-16, a big,
imposing, three-level red brick building in the center of Utrecht. (It moved
to the Royal Conservatory in The Hague only in the following decade, long
after Vivier's time.) If you came out of the Sonology building, turned right,
and walked along the canal, you would soon come to the Voorstraat and
the lively part of town. If you turned left on Voorstraat, kept straight on for
a couple of minutes, then crossed over another canal, the broad, tree-lined
Buitengracht, the street becomes the Biltstraat, today a busy, noisy shopping street. A little way along on the left-hand side is no. 32, an ugly, modern, flat-roofed building that for years provided cheap accommodation for
generations of students. Vivier lived at Biltstraat 32a during the months he
spent in Holland.

Unusually, given that teaching in the Institute was in English, and
that he probably had no intention of spending more than a year in
Utrecht, he began to learn Dutch. He acquired the nickname Meneer
Mooi (sometimes Monsieur Mooi); "mooi," meaning "beautiful," was
the most frequently used word in his Dutch vocabulary. Given the smat-
tering of German he had also acquired by now, his conversations with
Dutch friends would use a mixture of English, Dutch, and German,
sometimes in the same sentence. The most abiding memory among his
Dutch friends, however, is not so much a linguistic one as the omnipresence of the malodorous sheepskin jacket that would be a regular fixture
in the Vivier wardrobe in the months ahead.

Although this was his first experience of Holland—the country
his father had loved during the war—Vivier was not completely isolated there. During the 1971–72 year his friend Clarence Barlow, together
with two other students he had met in Cologne—the young composer
Walter Zimmermann and the English trumpeter and composer Alan
Cartwright—would commute once a week to Utrecht. They would arrive
on Monday evening and stay where they could, crashing on floors and
couches (although neither Barlow nor Zimmermann recalls ever sleeping in Vivier's room). They would attend all the classes happening on
Tuesdays at the Institute for Sonology—Gottfried Michael Koenig on algorithmic composition, Stan Tempelaars on perception, psychoacoustics,

and computer applications—then work in the studios all afternoon into the evening (students had, in practice, twenty-four-hour access to the facilities), and would set off again for Cologne on Wednesday morning. Occasionally Vivier would come with them. Barlow, more sophisticated than the others in handling computers, recognized that his friend's grasp of some of the teaching there was limited: "I don't think Claude really learned very much about sonology, but he knew his way around in a studio, and was able to put things together."[10]

The institute had begun life in 1960 as a Studio for Electronic Music, when equipment from the acoustics department of Philips Research Laboratories in Eindhoven (where Varèse had made his *Poème Électronique*) was moved to Utrecht State University. It became known as the Institute for Sonology only in 1967; the name was chosen to make the place sound more like a university department than a commercial recording studio (by analogy with words like "phonology" as used in linguistics).[11] The teaching was intended as a single-year curriculum, with no degree or diploma at the end; students were free to choose the subjects they were interested in. Stan Tempelaars, who taught there, recalls Vivier's era as a "special time," and Vivier himself as an "interesting figure."[12]

Since its inception the institute's facilities had been purely analog, based on tape manipulation. However, in 1970, at great expense, the institute had acquired its first computer, the enormous PDP-15, which was phased into the teaching curriculum the year Vivier arrived, although he himself did not use it. Indeed he complained that the Institute was in the grip of "a fierce computer sickness . . . people . . . want to put together everything on computer without understanding its essence . . . finally man tries to find gods almost everywhere."[13] A highly international mix of students came, attracted by the new possibilities, Tempelaars says, "as by a magnet." During 1971–72 the institute was home to work by somewhat older composers (including Berend Giltay and Simeon ten Holt from Holland, Wolf Rosenberg and Erhard Grosskopf from Germany, and Nicole Lachartre from France, all of whom had come there to learn the new electronic techniques—in their cases, tape-based ones) and by students around Vivier's age, including the Norwegian-born Knut Sönstevold and Olav Anton Thommessen, the American Peter Hamlin, and the Canadian Barry Truax.[14]

The institute's director was Gottfried Michael Koenig, a German composer then in his mid-forties, who had previously worked for several years at the electronic studio of West German Radio (WDR) in Cologne, assisting many of the young composers there—including Kagel, Ligeti, and Stockhausen—in the realization of tape pieces. Frustrated with his situation in Cologne, he had accepted an offer to take charge of the Utrecht studio in 1964, "to help develop it, and to give it an international profile."[15] Koenig's new obsession was computer music, and in Utrecht in the 1960s, he developed his computer composition programs Project 1 and Project 2, which gave an important impetus to the further development of algorithmic composition systems. In 1971 he introduced a sound synthesis program, SSP. His own background had been in music, so he was sympathetic to the composers attracted to the institute as well as those students with a more scientific orientation. Tempelaars describes him as a "very liberal man."

Koenig was to be Vivier's main teacher during his year in Utrecht. He remembers Vivier as a determined young composer with "something to say."[16] (Fellow student Peter Hamlin recalls him as "an exuberantly friendly guy gushing with creative energy.")[17] The other teacher to whom Vivier gravitated was the Swiss-born Luctor Ponse, a genial man of mixed Dutch-French parentage, who had been living since the mid-1930s in Holland, where he made a name for himself as a brilliant pianist and composer. Their friendship developed in no small part because Ponse was a native French speaker. He took the young Vivier under his wing to some extent, inviting him occasionally in the evenings to dine with his family on their houseboat in the village of Loenersloot, a longish bus ride from Utrecht. Ponse's widow, Annemarie Ponse Smalt, remembers the two speaking animatedly together in French; she found Vivier "a very warm, lively, spirited person" with a "lost child" quality.[18] Her husband told her that he found Vivier "not well formed" musically—by which he probably meant that his instrumental skills were quite low level (certainly by Ponse's own standards) and that he had not had the sort of rigorous training that Ponse himself had had in France and Switzerland in his teens. Nonetheless, Ponse helped Vivier realize the two main tape compositions he produced at the Institute of Sonology.

Vivier attended various other classes, including those of Tempelaars (who remembers him as "not a regular in my class—it was probably too mathematical for him"), the Swiss composer Werner Kaegi, and Frits Weiland, who lectured on the history of electronic music. And while his attitude to the institute seems to have been generally positive, he was not exempt from the usual ups and downs of the young creative artist trapped within the walls of academia. Frits Weiland recalls Vivier coming to one of his lectures one morning, slumping his elbows down on the desk, head in hands, and staring blankly for most of the lecture with a look of boredom and disdain on his face.[19]

"I think this was a very happy time in his life, as it probably was for most of us who were studying at the institute at that time," says Vivier's fellow student Knut Sönstevold.

> It had not always been like that for Claude. "You know they did terrible things to me," he once said to me, referring to what had happened to him when he was a child. When Claude had something to say, everyone had to listen carefully. I remember specially one late night when I was about to go home from the studio. There was a grand piano in the classroom, and Claude was sitting there improvising on it. The special thing was the way he was using his voice at the same time. It sounded like a mixture of singing and crying. It did really touch you. To expose his feelings in this way! One of his favorite expressions was "We got to do that!" talking about some concert project where special things were to happen.[20]

Barry Truax also remembers the lack of emotional inhibition of the twenty-three-year-old Vivier.

> He was very "bohemian," usually wearing boots and a big fleece-lined coat (always quite smelly) and sometimes with a boyfriend in tow as well. We were good friends but the more emotional and mystical he became as a Francophone, the more Anglo I seemed to become. He was of course very exuberant and voluble, and I remember that his occasional outbursts with a word like "Scheisse!" in class would offend Koenig. But overall, he was "molto simpatico" as they say in Italian, though hardly the saint he has become in some later portrayals . . . he was always excited and passionate about his discoveries, particularly when Stockhausen was inspiring him. I think he was already listening to Indonesian music at that stage too (which could readily be heard in Holland at that time though I don't know if Claude ever went to any concerts of that type as I did).[21]

Truax's mention of Vivier's "boyfriends" is the earliest clear recollection we have of the young composer publicly displaying his homosexuality. While he surely had experiences in this area during his years of study at the Montreal Conservatoire, we have no reliable information on this aspect of his life at that time.

And yet, another friendship that began in his year in Utrecht makes it clear that Vivier's sexuality was, at the time, anything but a settled matter. Some of the condemned houses in the area around the train station, several of them already abandoned, became the center of a squatters' scene that would house quite a few students. Among them was Machleen Batelaan, then studying at Utrecht's Akademie voor Expressie door Woord en Gebaar, which taught aspiring teachers of drama. In 1971 she was living in one such house on the Riemstraat, close to the station and now long since demolished. Among the visitors she remembers showing up there are Claude Vivier, Clarence Barlow, and Walter Zimmermann. She immediately liked the young Canadian, whose lost quality—which she describes with the Dutch word *zwerver*, a homeless person—"really touched me." They had "very intimate and long talks" together on the Riemstraat, and she was charmed by his attempts to speak Dutch and by the fact that he claimed to be able to read palms (even though "his predictions didn't come true!"). Their talks were "all to do with identity— where are you coming from, where are you going?" She describes him as "a universal believer"; they would talk about religion, and she remembers his conviction that "we are in a body for a short time, but there is something before and something after."[22] He would sometimes eat at her place, and they would go out together in Utrecht, usually in company, sometimes to dance at the newly opened student disco Woolloomooloo on the Janskerkhof—"for Claude every day was like a party." Later they became lovers, although in the sexually adventurous climate of the early seventies theirs was not an exclusive relationship, and they never considered themselves a couple, nor were they so considered by anyone else. "Those were hippie times," she says. "We had good physical relations . . . Claude was a soft, warm man. We had a very good time together, and many nice nights. He was very touched by the fact he could have a good relationship with a woman." The sexual contact between the two became stronger when she saw him again the following year in Cologne: there, she says, "we really found each other." But it was only something "for that moment," "like ships passing"; they each had "a busy life, other friends." "With Claude," she says, "I was aware of his deep fear of not being in life . . . there was always a drive to smash through any glass barrier."[23]

Vivier and Batelaan also hatched plans to develop work together. She introduced him to her friend Jos van Dijk, and remembers the three of them talking in van Dijk's attic room about making a performance in the Janskerk in Utrecht, with sounds and movements, making use of the huge space of the church. But the plan came to nothing.

For all this, Vivier was well attuned to the gay scene in Holland. Early in 1972 he wrote to Pierre Rochon:

The Dutch penis seems to be similar to the Quebec one. Here the boys are wonderfully handsome and the gays make a lot of noise by unifying their sexual revolution and the political one. The open-mindedness of people here is very wide and I love that. Indeed the Dutch are colder and less impulsive than the Québécois; they think and reflect a lot which sometimes causes me problems with the lovers I find. Well, that's life I suppose.

Politically Holland is <u>very</u> capitalist but the people themselves much less so, they have a very high sense of the social and a quite rare sense of community, they're a bit like the Chinese of America.[24]

No sooner had Vivier arrived in Utrecht in the autumn than he was obliged to think about plans for the following academic year. In an application date-stamped October 20, 1971, he applied again for a "Bourse de Perfectionnement pour Artiste" from the Canada Council for the year beginning June 1, 1972. He wrote: "My project, which I've already begun this year, is as follows: Main studies in Utrecht at the Institute of Sonology. Studies in Cologne with Stockhausen at the Musik Hochschule. Studies in Paris with Paul Méfano who is helping me to clarify my thoughts about Utrecht and Cologne and who brings the French point of view. . . . So the place where I will live is Utrecht, and work also in Paris and Cologne."[25] The grant application was successful and the council awarded him the customary $4,000 for the year. His plans changed somewhat when he applied at the end of January 1972 for the summer course at the Institute of Sonology: a handwritten inscription at the top of his registration form says "afgewezen mondeling" (turned down, verbally) March 22, 1972, and it also says "Vivier niet" (Vivier: no). We do not know whether this was actually a rejection on academic grounds or the institute simply had no available space that summer.

Vivier was one of the more productive students at the Institute of Sonology in 1971–72, so if he was indeed ejected from the place it can hardly be as a result of idleness. Ironically, the first composition he completed in Utrecht, on January 8, 1972, was the large instrumental piece he had begun in Paris in the summer, scored for four quintets (two wind quintets, one string quintet with double bass, and one brass quintet of three trumpets and two trombones), and titled *Deva et Asura*. It is tempting to listen for the influence of his work in the electronic studio in the instrumental writing, but such a connection is speculative at best and no more true of this work than

many others of the period that exploit recently developed extended playing techniques, transforming the conventional sounds of the instruments.

In Hinduism, Deva and Asura—more commonly given in the plural,
the Devas and the Asuras—are half brothers, the children of Kashyap, the
ancient Hindu sage, himself a second-generation descendant of the creator Brahma. ("Deva" is the Sanskrit word for god or deity that, in modern
Hinduism, means any benevolent supernatural being.) The Asuras are the
half brothers of the Devas, but are power-seeking deities, sinful and ma-
terialistic. A simple reading of the work's title, therefore, seems to imply
the unity within an apparent dualism or dichotomy. A Deva and an Asura
may represent opposing values, benevolent and malevolent, respectively,
but because of their blood bond they are more like two sides of one coin
rather than polar opposites. Besides, it is possible to change from one to
the other: the Vedic god Varuna is an Asura who later became a Deva.

Vivier's piece, lasting about eight minutes, is indeed an alternation between two types of texture, one sustained, serene, rather otherworldly, and
the other highly disjointed, abrupt, and aggressive. At the beginning of
the piece the sustained texture takes the form of chromatically ascending
and descending lines, beautiful but apparently directionless. After some
two and a half minutes this is briefly disturbed by a wild outburst from the
two wind quintets in turn. Serenity is restored, but serenity of a fractured
kind, and it is not long before noisy brasses shatter the mood. Calm again
returns, but now with many woodwind multiphonics and trills and with
flutter-tonguing on the trumpets creating a constant nervous motion inside the sustained textures. The disjointed music reappears suddenly and
begins for the first time truly to dominate the aural surface, quite covering
the sustained material continuing underneath. The last page of the score
is an enigmatic coda, with nothing but multiphonics on bassoons, oboes,
and clarinets, and a final "pure" tone on flutes, horns, and trombone with
a hazy aura of string harmonics.

*Deva et Asura* is quite straightforward to read programmatically. The
basic contrast is between calm and agitated material, and between long
tones and short ones, the contrast offset by unifying features: an overrid-
ing aura of chromaticism; a general rhythmic irregularity and complexity;
and a constant textural evolution, in which the sustained notes, by means
of multiphonics, harmonics, and flutter-tonguing, begin to acquire even
more "grain" than the wild, virtuosic, note-filled outbursts, such that one
sort of material almost becomes indistinguishable from the other. Here
again Varèse casts a passing shadow in terms of general sonority as well as
in the concision of the musical argument; but, more than ever before, we

see Vivier conceiving a large ensemble (twenty players) as a conjunct of clearly defined and separable consorts of instruments, not so very differently from what he would do in the great works of the following decade.

Having completed the thirty-one-page manuscript score Vivier felt quite exhausted, as he told Rochon.

> I have lots of work but I have to tell you that my two last pieces [*Musik für das Ende* and *Deva et Asura*] particularly exhausted me, especially following "Musik für das Ende" and the logical consequences it had in itself. These are two pieces where I tried to see music from two angles that I haven't approached yet, that's to say structure and a free play with sound. I needed to do this in order to push my language further, you might call my pieces in my output "transitional works or studies or sketches," however these pieces are now "works" which is to say someone (whether me or someone else) in the course of his life has to formulate precise gestures in order to go further.[26]

Given that *Deva et Asura* was the fourth large-scale work in a row not to receive a performance, working in the medium of tape must have been a considerable relief: now he could work with the sonic material directly, and all of his compositional decisions would be immediately audible in the studios on the Plompetorengracht. The first piece he made there was *Variation I*: the box containing the stereo master tape has the date February 22, 1972, and records that the piece was "réalisé par Claude Vivier et Luctor Ponse." In the published listings of works composed there, the Institute of Sonology was insistent on distinguishing between a piece that was merely a "study," that is, one with primarily didactic intent, and a "concert" piece. Vivier was adamant that *Variation I* was the latter: "I . . . finished an electronic piece for four channels (10 mn 26 sec), they asked me if it was a concert piece or a study, it's absolutely a piece to be heard, so a concert piece."[27]

As the title suggests, *Variation I* is highly abstract (as opposed to concrete) in nature. It is a good-natured, undemonstrative piece, highly idiomatic and effective in its modest way. Its basic materials are sequences of very short clicks and chirps, which sometimes sound like birds, or the buzzing of insects, or of tongue clicking or tut-tutting. These sequences are continually subjected to vari-speed treatment, with sudden manic shifts in tempo from fast to hyperfast yielding extremely high-pitched chirruping sounds. Vivier also exploits the spatial potential of his four-track medium, with lines traveling between speakers around the space. In the latter part of the piece he uses filtering effects to create more sustained, pitched sounds.

Vivier's next tape work was of a crazier kind and, uniquely for him, was a collaboration with another composer: Peter Hamlin, a fellow student a couple of years younger, who was spending a year in Utrecht in the midst of his studies at Middlebury College, Vermont. Like Vivier himself, Hamlin had had little studio experience before coming to the institute, and felt "a little overwhelmed there—maybe a little bit out of place as a liberal arts undergraduate with a fierce interest in electronic music but not yet a lot of training."[28] Together they made thirty-five minutes of tape music for a multimedia event on the theme of chance to be held at the University of Utrecht. The label on the original tape bears the date March 10, 1972, and the tape box says: "Peter Hamlin Hall-music (right track) / Claude Vivier Stair-music (left track) / Random Music (Stadium [correctly, Studium] Generale: Toeval [chance]), 1972." Vivier himself described the work as an "environment for an exhibition."[29]

Hamlin recalls of his Utrecht experience:

> Vivier was outgoing and exuberant, and would pull us into the studio to show us something he was working on. He didn't have any false modesty, which I found refreshing—he loved what he did and always seemed very excited about it.
>
> The studios at the Institute were modular—various pieces of analog gear and effects that you would patch together for the sounds you wanted. (Much of the gear was designed and built right there—one of the amazing features of that place was that they had their own lab where circuits could be designed and built right on premises.) There were a few manufactured synths, but mostly the studios were just huge collections of various sound generators, effects, and recording equipment. There was a wonderful kind of purity to it—just electronic sounds engaged on their own terms, without the overlay of traditional musical performing devices, scales and metrical rhythms.
>
> They had "pancake" tape reels—10½" reels with the tape wound on a hub but without the metal flanges to protect it. (It seemed that each of us, at least once, held the pancake in the wrong way so that the hub fell through the middle and the tape all spooled out onto the floor.) We had stands with small guides and rollers so that you could make long tape loops—loops that wound around the room, or even out into the hall and into the neighboring studio. If I'm remembering correctly, the Chance piece I did with Claude made use of that sort of technique—you could literally have sounds that reappeared only after a minute or more and loops so long and unsynchronized that you didn't get any sense of a pattern. You could get several unsynchronized loops to create unpredictable interactions between them.

Early in the academic year I recall feeling frustrated with my own work. I was really not sure how to approach these freeform studios, how to get interesting musical sounds out of them and mold them into pieces. At about this time, Claude gathered a group of us into one of the studios, the same one I had been struggling with, and played the most remarkable, jangling, screeching, rich, gorgeous sound I had ever heard. "Le cri de la bête!" he exclaimed. He then showed us how a sound had gone through a reverb spring at too high a level, rattling the spring to create such an otherworldly utterance.[30]

Perhaps the most engaging music Vivier produced in Utrecht is the final tape piece he made there, *Hommage: Musique pour un vieux Corse triste*, the tape box dated May 8, 1972. This is a substantial and complex work, twenty-seven and a half minutes in duration, music that suggests levels of feeling deeper than his level of technical accomplishment can really convey. Vivier later explained to an interviewer in Montreal the circumstances that triggered the piece:

In a train taking me from Rotterdam to Antwerp, I met an old Corsican, completely drunk, whom everybody was afraid of. For my part I decided to get him into conversation and the idea came to me to record him discreetly with the little machine I had on me. I wanted to eternalize him, transcend him, take him out of the context of the train, to transform this meeting into an ecstatic vision, through the medium of electroacoustic music.[31]

The work begins in the "real world" with a recording made in Utrecht's train station, with platform announcements in Dutch, footsteps, whistles, slamming doors, even the sound of Vivier clearing his throat. But soon we are taken to a stranger place, with long, sustained, "dirty," constantly fluctuating tones, as though the swishing sounds and rhythms of the train journey had taken on a bizarre, hallucinatory quality. The old drunkard appears disruptively nine minutes into the piece, his voice becoming gradually more aggressive and incoherent. By twelve minutes he has gone. Fifteen minutes in, and the "dirty" texture has cleared somewhat; we are left mostly with the long steady tones, howling like wind blowing through the cracks in an old house. But the Corsican returns, briefly but audibly, at twenty-two minutes; the menace has not entirely gone away. In the closing minutes the howling tones are overlaid with purer sounds of definite pitch, sounding like voices in the reverberant spaces of a large church.

But this programmatic description fails to convey the emotional impact of *Musique pour un vieux Corse triste*, as the quality of the sounds—crude

though they are, some of them derived from manipulation of the recording of the old man's voice—manifest the musicality of Vivier's ear, so that
the work overall adds up to more than the sum of its parts. The piece is
striking, too, in being the first of Vivier's works to explore one of the characteristic themes of his output: violence. In this case the old Corsican is
aggressive and out of control rather than actively violent, but he is nonetheless a disturbing and repugnant aural presence. Vivier's act of engaging him in conversation, which is not really apparent in the work, is an
act—if not of love, then at least of acceptance, embracing a dissolute, ab-
ject creature and looking in him for qualities of transcendence and eternity. Something of the "universal believer" side of Vivier that Machleen
Batelaan noticed comes across in this piece, or perhaps a hippie-style belief
in love and peace, an acceptance of one's fellow man. But surely we also
hear in this piece Vivier flirting with danger, like the moth to the flame,
smashing recklessly through another "glass barrier."

Vivier himself evidently retained a fondness for *Hommage: Musique
pour un vieux Corse triste*, as he used an extract from it a decade later in
the soundtrack for his semiautobiographical film *L'Homme de Pékin*. It
is in fact the only one of his tape works to have a real afterlife. The music
for the exhibition on chance was an occasional piece, produced for that
particular event and never revived; and we have no record indicating that
Vivier returned to *Variation I*. Indeed, after his year in Utrecht he did very
little work in electronic studios. The following year, in Cologne, he worked
on another substantial tape piece that was never finished. Aside from that,
the only other tape music in his career is the brief incidental music for a
production of Büchner's *Woyzeck* in Ottawa in 1976. Interestingly, however, prerecorded sounds of various kinds find their way into several of
his instrumental and vocal works: the playful, anarchic (and optional) bits
of classical music in *Désintégration*; the ritualistic sound of a large door
opening and closing at the beginning and ending of *Learning*; the sound
of foghorns near the beginning and at the end of *Bouchara*; the conversation between composer and poet originally part of *Prologue pour un Marco
Polo* (before Radio Canada inadvertently erased the tape); and, most notably, the prerecorded speaking voices in *Wo bist du Licht!* It may well be
that Vivier, in company with a great many of his contemporaries, was finally not convinced by tape music as a medium. His tape pieces, rather like
those of Ligeti, form an intriguing if modest body of work early in a career
that would ultimately play itself out along quite different musical lines.

Apart from his work at the institute, we have little idea about such
involvement as Vivier may have had with Dutch musical life specifically,

as opposed to his ongoing interest in European musical developments in a more general sense. He would escape occasionally to Cologne and sometimes to France (*Prolifération* was performed on March 31, 1972, at the Festival d'Art Contemporain in Royan, but it is not known whether he attended). He told Pierre Rochon:

> As to interesting music that's going on in Europe there's not a lot, the French have had the Boulez malady or the G.R.M. [the *Groupe de Recherches Musicales*, founded by Pierre Schaeffer] malady, the Germans that of Adorno (except for Kagel who does extraordinary things) Stock. who remains Stock. with his bizarre contradictions but very much a genius; as for everybody else it doesn't seem to me there's a whole lot going on. I think the great musical streams will come from America, that's the only place where the face of music has really, deeply changed (from the need to ignore the past and from lack of tradition) I don't believe the country that carries on its back such a long and heavy tradition can really carry the revolution that has hardly begun, that we have hardly begun.[32]

We would love to know, for example, if he was aware of the new musical directions then erupting in nearby Amsterdam. In May 1972, a few days after Vivier finished *Hommage: Musique pour un vieux Corse triste*, the young composer Louis Andriessen presented for the first time his composition *De Volharding*, together with the eponymous ensemble he had formed to play it, before a noisy, raucous public in Amsterdam's Carré Theatre—a work building on exactly those new kinds of American music (chiefly minimalism) that Vivier seemed to sense held the seeds of renewal for European music. It is ironic that Vivier and Andriessen seem never to have met; nearly four decades later, as a much-venerated, aging enfant terrible, Andriessen would declare that "the only composer to influence me in the past ten years is Vivier."[33]

During the spring in Utrecht, concurrently with his work in the electronic studios, Vivier was laboring on another large-scale instrumental piece that he began not long after completing *Deva et Asura*: a work for two pianos titled *Désintégration*. It is perhaps the work of his that most defiantly proclaims allegiance to a late-modernist aesthetic, specifically a postserial one. Given the choice of the two-piano medium (although the piece seems to have been conceived with no particular performers in mind), the ghost of a work like Boulez's two books of *Structures* for two pianos seems discernible in the hinterland. Indeed the jagged, even aggressive quality of much of the then-contemporary Parisian new music seems imprinted on this piece, and the desire to make a large statement in the two-piano medium would seem to owe more to the "cold," intellectual example of Boulez than to the exotic colors and textures of Stockhausen's *Mantra* (1970), which Vivier had probably not actually heard at the time he began the work. *Désintégration* was still unfinished when he left Utrecht in the summer, and he brought it with him in July to Darmstadt, where he had enrolled for a second taste of the summer courses.

✳ ✳ ✳

The Darmstadt summer courses in 1972 ran over eighteen days, from July 20 to August 6. The resident composers that summer were Kagel, Ligeti, Stockhausen, Xenakis, and Wolff. (Vivier wrote in his October 1972 grant application to the Canada Council that he had attended lectures by four of these at Darmstadt that summer: curiously there is no mention of Xenakis.) The *Arbeitsgruppen* (working groups) that the directors formed that year discussed subjects that, collectively, give a snapshot of some of the pressing concerns in new music in 1972: "Notation and sound result"; "Political music"; "Collective composition"; "New music—not for children?"; "Tonality in new music"; "Electronic Studio techniques"; "Computer techniques"; "Contact with the VCS 3"; and "New instrumental techniques and notation." The timetable of the summer courses gives an indication of the fare on offer. The intrepid student could attend an interpretation masterclass with the organist Gerd Zacher at 10:00 a.m., enjoy a leisurely (if tasteless) lunch before a 2:30 p.m. lecture by Xenakis followed by a 4:30 p.m. lecture by Ligeti, and then attend an 8:00 p.m. concert of new music from Bucharest. Ligeti was unusual in presenting his lectures three times over, in English, French, and German (on consecutive days).[34] Naturally, Stockhausen's lectures were of interest to Vivier, as were the works of Stockhausen performed that summer: *Stimmung* (on August 3), *Kontakte* (on August 5), and *Mantra* (on August 6). Among younger composers, Clarence Barlow caused a minor scandal with his minimalist *Textmusik* for piano, played by Herbert Henck (Vivier translated the verbal score of the work into French for its later publication by Feedback Studios); the performance caused a storm of protest with booing and sarcastically exaggerated applause from many in the audience, but Vivier was among the genuinely enthusiastic, and Stockhausen himself, according to Barlow, was "not antagonistic."[35] Vivier made one of his rare ventures into public performance by playing tam-tam in the performance, on August 5, of *Flood for the Eternal's Origins*, by the young Romanian composer Horatiu Radulescu, having been "very impressed" by Radulescu's seminars, "Theorie meiner 'Plasmatischen Musik,'" in the Kompositionsstudio on July 21 and 22.[36]

Some 200 students were in attendance that summer, most of them staying at the Georg-Büchner-Schule (which the Ferienkurse had begun to use only that year). Just over a quarter of them were from Germany; there were quite a few Hungarians, Americans, Romanians, Yugoslavians, and smatterings from other countries including Canada, among whom were Vivier's old friends Walter Boudreau and Raoul Duguay. The young American composer James Dashow recalls Vivier as "one of the very vivacious French-Canadians that enlivened stodgy old Darmstadt with their quasi-anarchic presence . . . those folks were not all that interested in the 'official' or semi-official activities as much as they were interested in making waves, musical and political." Another student at Darmstadt that summer was the French composer Gérard Grisey, then twenty-six; he, Vivier, and Boudreau became "beer buddies" and would hang out together. Boudreau recalls that "a lot of the stuff that was being forwarded to us in Darmstadt, both the food and the music, made us puke"; indeed, James Dashow recalls Boudreau "standing up on one of the tables in the lunch hall and shouting, THIS SALAD SUCKS!"[37] Meanwhile, the performance of *Stimmung* and the attendant workshop on the new vocal techniques of the piece had unleashed waves of satire: Boudreau remembers himself, Vivier, and Grisey amusing themselves by incessantly imitating the vocal overtone sonorities of *Stimmung* as they walked around the town or on trams, much to the annoyance of one particular driver who threatened to throw them off if they didn't stop.[38]

With the benefit of hindsight, the 1972 Darmstadt courses seem to have signaled a turning point in the intellectual dominance of the postwar avant-garde over the new music scene. James Dashow feels that "1972 was a time when the old structuralists seemed to have become automated versions of themselves."[39] Following lectures by musicologists Carl Dahlhaus and Reinhold Brinkman there was an animated discussion in which the middle-aged avant-garde was accused of conspiring to exclude the young.[40] This sentiment, expressed in various ways, had been in the air for a few years. Stockhausen was the main focus of many of the attacks, with the accusation that both by the number of his pieces performed at the summer courses and by his guru-like presence as teacher, he and his ideology were overly domineering and blocked other approaches. From another perspective, the quasi-religious aspects of his work were found bothersome by many of the participants. Beginnings of revolt against what was perceived as Stockhausen's domination of the Ferienkurse had already begun in 1969, when his "seminar series" turned out to be performances of text pieces from his *Aus den Sieben Tagen*, with the result that he was accused of obscurantism, elitism, imperialism, and exploitation of the students. In the 1972 discussion, Ligeti protested that he would be delighted to hear stimulating new work by the younger generation, work that was not simply an imitation of what had gone before, but that little was forthcoming.[41] Some of the young composers themselves did not disagree: James Dashow feels that "the desperate attempts to find something new, rather than let things evolve gradually, made many of the musical 'trends' into slightly ridiculous exercises in self-indulgence. 'Letting it all hang out' was thought by many to be the solution to the excesses of the structuralists."[42] We do not know if Vivier was present at this discussion, nor his attitude to these sentiments; in any case the years that followed would see the period of his deepest immersion in Stockhausen's thought.

With the course finished, and the performance of *Mantra* by the brothers Kontarsky on the final Sunday evening still ringing in their ears, Vivier, Boudreau, and various others took a train to Paris. "I nearly kissed the sidewalk of the Gare de l'Est," says Boudreau, "and took Claude right there and then to eat a good salad and drink some wine." Vivier, he believes, was "coming back to Paris to hang around Méfano."[43] In Paris some three weeks later, on August 26, 1972, Vivier completed the thirty-eight-page manuscript of *Désintégration*. "The idea of the piece," writes Richard Toop, "is that a basic rhythmic grid, initially populated by fistfuls of notes, is gradually 'eaten away'; at first the pianists alternate, but as the process of erosion gets under way, they increasingly overlap and interlock."[44] "This work," Vivier noted, "was entirely predetermined, not a single note at any moment was left to chance."[45] Clearly for him, unlike some of his fellow participants at Darmstadt, the intellectual dominance of the postwar generation of musical "structuralists" was far from over.

# " A  N E E D  T O  C O M M U N I C A T E  W I T H  T H E  R E S T  O F  T H E  C O S M O S "

## 1 9 7 2 – 7 4

"In his works Stockhausen wants to expand the field of human consciousness, to show us new planets," wrote Vivier in December 1978 of the music of his former teacher. "But who is Stockhausen the man? In *Momente*, at the moment 'KK' (K: Klang/sound and K: Karlheinz) he gives us his self-portrait: a great call, solitary and sad; his need to speak comes from a great solitude, from a need to communicate with the rest of the cosmos."[1] It is striking that these last words seem to apply equally well to teacher and student: for what better characterization could there be of Vivier's own music than "a great call, solitary and sad," its particular blend of expressive intensity and disciplined calculation issuing from "a need to communicate with the rest of the cosmos?" Reading Vivier's text, a brief program note written for a performance of Stockhausen's *Mantra* by the SMCQ in Montreal, it is clear that the reverence he feels toward his former teacher's work is tinged with empathy for its expressive aims—even with a degree of identification with the person of its creator.

That Stockhausen played a crucial role in Vivier's musical development is beyond question. In the autobiographical note Vivier supplied for a performance of his *Lettura di Dante* in Toronto in 1975, he noted: "Born in Montreal in 1948. Born to music with Gilles Tremblay in 1968. Born to composition with Stockhausen in 1972." Indeed, the widespread view is that, during the years he studied formally with Stockhausen at the Hochschule für Musik in Cologne (1972–74), Vivier hero-worshipped the German composer. Gilles Tremblay feels that Vivier was *ébloui* (dazzled) by Stockhausen;[2] while Vivier's fellow student Kevin Volans recalls that, at that time, "the general perception of Claude was that he was THE Stockhausen student. He idolized him, and idolized his way of working. It was intriguing how Claude managed to reconcile that with his own sort of mystic Catholicism"[3]—almost as though, Volans seems to imply, Vivier viewed his teacher as a sort of god. The English musicologist Richard Toop, Stockhausen's teaching assistant for the academic year 1973–74, recalls that "Claude was by far Stockhausen's most loyal adherent in the class (in fact, I think of loyalty as one of Claude's key characteristics), and the only one to share Stockhausen's spiritual outlook to any significant degree."[4] Clarence Barlow, another student in the Stockhausen class, had at that time begun to react against much of his teacher's music and its overall aesthetic, and found Vivier's reverence toward Stockhausen regrettable, even problematic: "I didn't like the way Claude just worshipped Stockhausen."[5]

In all probability Vivier had finally been accepted formally as Stockhausen's student by the time of the 1972 Darmstadt courses. His handwriting having not noticeably improved in the year since his rejection, the received version of the story—whether apocryphal or not—is that he secured his place at the Hochschule through flattery. As Gilles Tremblay tells it, Stockhausen asked him why he wanted to study with him. "Vivier said: Because you are the greatest composer in the world. That was enough: the only entrance test!"[6] Besides his composition studies with Stockhausen from 1972 to 1974 he studied electronic music with Hans Ulrich Humpert and, in his second year, analysis with Richard Toop.

Stockhausen gained his professorship in Cologne in the autumn of 1971 when the suicide of Bernd Alois Zimmermann, the previous year, created a vacancy.[7] During the two years Vivier studied with him, Stockhausen's class contained a wealth of extraordinary creative talent, including Clarence Barlow, László Dubrovay, Robert HP Platz, Wolfgang Rihm, and Kevin Volans. A detailed picture of Stockhausen's thought at the time Vivier first got to know him emerges from two books, *Stockhausen: Conversations with the Composer* by the American journalist Jonathan Cott, based on conversations recorded in February and September 1971, and *Stockhausen on Music*, a collection of lectures and interviews compiled by Robin Maconie, part 1 of which collects lecture transcripts from 1971. (Vivier's copy of Cott's book, presently in the Archives of the Fondation Vivier, is inscribed: "einen wunderschönen Monat Mai 1974/ lieber Vivier/ wünscht Ihnen herzlich/ Ihr Stockhausen.")[8] Both books show clearly the breadth of Stockhausen's interests in music as well as outside it. He speaks extensively of the consciousness-widening effect of his travels, of his belief in intuitive music, of his love of electronic technology, of his interest in the tastes and behavior of the younger generation and, at length, of his own musical ideas. The mesmerizing nature of Stockhausen's conversation is readily apparent from viewing the extant film recordings from these years of lectures he gave in England, some of which form the basis of *Stockhausen on Music*.[9] They make it clear that he was no ordinary teacher. His ideas roll forth in slow but practically perfect English, his eyes seeking contact with every person in the room as he speaks. They are mesmerizing performances, especially to one as thirsty for knowledge and guidance as the twenty-four-year-old Vivier. Beyond his immediate charisma, however, there were more complex sides to Stockhausen the man. Clarence Barlow comments that, overall, Stockhausen was "a mixture of charm and arrogance. I can very easily put it down to self-defense in terms of his arrogance; his charm was provoked by a compliment. So if I asked him a question about one of his pieces he'd be all charm and say, 'Oh, you must come and visit me.' But if you had one slight word of criticism his hackles would go up and he'd become totally arrogant."[10]

The affinity the young Vivier felt for his teacher was compounded by the similarities between them, peculiarities shared by few others in their immediate surroundings. Both Stockhausen and Vivier were Catholics, or rather ex-Catholics who had evolved a free-thinking attitude within a basic paradigm of belief. Vivier had retained an essentially spiritual outlook, still believing in God while having no specific doctrinal allegiance. Stockhausen, for his part, remarked: "Until 1960 I was a man who related to the cosmos and God through Catholicism, a very particular religion that I chose for myself almost as a way of opposing the post-war Sartrean nihilistic attitudes of the established intellectuals. . . . And then I began to float because I got in touch with many other religions."[11] If the basis of Vivier's belief was less intellectual, less studied than Stockhausen's, the two men's views nonetheless intersect at a certain point. We recall Vivier's comment regarding his time at the juvénat that "I was extremely pious, I had faith, I wanted to be a pure human being, to give myself totally, and for me music . . . is a way of achieving my own redemption. In that sense I am very Catholic."[12] Music as a means of achieving personal redemption: Stockhausen might well have concurred.

Beyond their respective backgrounds in Catholicism, Vivier shared— and perhaps was consciously steered by his teacher toward—Stockhausen's more idiosyncratic interests in mysticism and the occult. Thus Gilles Tremblay and others believe that it was Stockhausen who introduced Vivier to—or at least encouraged his interests in—occult texts such as *Les Clavicules de Salomon*, a text on magic first published in Paris in 1825 from which Vivier drew in compiling the text for *Chants* in 1972–73, and *The Urantia Book*, a collection of unorthodox texts on spirituality first published in Chicago in 1955 that would later become important to the conception of aspects of Stockhausen's own *Licht* cycle, and to which parts of *Donnerstag* (1978–80) make explicit reference.[13] (Overall, though, Vivier's later work could be said to move away from the mystical content that infuses early pieces like *O Kosmos!* and parts of *Chants*, as well as "middle-period" works like *Journal* and *Kopernikus*, toward the broadly humanist content of the works of the *Marco Polo* opera.)

On a more personal level, both Stockhausen and Vivier shared a sense of uncertainty about their origins—genuine uncertainty in Vivier's case, and willful uncertainty in Stockhausen's. As we have noted, Vivier was obsessed by the identity of his birth mother in particular and, toward the end of his life, expressed a wish to trace her.[14] Around the time he started to teach Vivier, Stockhausen began to indulge a curious fantasy about his own origins. While in his case we have the certainty that he was born in the village of Mödrath, not far from Cologne, on August 22, 1928, to Simon Stockhausen and his wife Gertrud, in a sketchbook from 1975 he wrote: "In connection with the composition *Sternklang* [1971] I closely watched the star constellations in Kürten. From my study as well as from the kitchen my attention focused time and again on the constellation Canis Major and the star Sirius. Without knowing the reason why, I had fantastic visions of being a descendant of Sirius. . . . Since then my curiosity about Sirius has slowly and steadily grown."[15] It is not known how much of this revisionist personal mythology, if any, he shared with Vivier, who may at this time have been wholly unaware of this curious parallel between them; but nonetheless for both men the question of their origins became a fantasy world, a place for sometimes irrational flights of the creative imagination.

On a personal level, despite the evident loyalty shown by Vivier to his teacher, Richard Toop has observed that "paradoxically, Stockhausen never seemed to take Claude as seriously as he took most of the other students."[16] The reason for this is not clear, but the attitude was not exclusive to Stockhausen. Walter Zimmermann, who was not officially a Stockhausen student but who knew the group well, recalls that several of the students used to tease Vivier a good deal, however good-naturedly, and would often make fun of him.[17] We may perhaps put this down to some sort of personal incompatibility between Vivier's "warm manner" (as he had expressed it to Pierre Rochon) and the more reserved manner of Stockhausen; whether or not Vivier himself perceived things this way we do not know.

The first address we have for Vivier in Cologne in the autumn of 1972 is Vogelsanger Weg 26, a pleasant, respectable suburban street in Lindenthal in the far west of the city.[18] Cologne was, musically, a less vibrant city than Paris, but Vivier still retained his dislike of France and showed every sign of being quite content to be once again in Germany. The year's studies at the Hochschule, on the other hand, got off to what for some students was an inauspicious start. Stockhausen, having just had the premiere of *Alphabet für Liège* in September, was now busy supervising the rehearsals of *Momente* for the forthcoming first complete performance (the "Europa Version") of the work, to be given in Bonn on December 8, and insisted his students attend the rehearsals rather than offering them formal lectures. For some this was incredibly boring and frustrating, but it seems not to have been so for Vivier. Indeed, he would continue to follow various of Stockhausen's rehearsals during the remainder of his studies in Europe: in an undated letter to Serge Garant, probably from February 1973, he writes: "I'm getting ready to go to London in March, to attend rehearsals of works by Stockhausen." This devotion may not have been entirely devoid of self-interest: in the same letter to Garant, Vivier adds that in Paris "my piece for three women's voices has every chance of being played, and as well the Stockhausen Group has agreed to play a 'Live electronic' piece." The latter work, sadly, never materialized.

It was during the weeks observing the rehearsals for *Momente*, Vivier later wrote, that he experienced a sort of vision, a revelation of "the very essence of musical composition," which brought about "a sort of laying bare of my soul." He had written nothing in the three months since he had arrived in Cologne, but now this vision gave rise, in December, to the beginnings of a new work, *Chants*, which represented for him "the first moment of my existence as a composer":

My whole life spread out before me, letting me glimpse the outline of
the face of a sad child who wanted to express something imposing but
was not yet capable of it. These memories became mixed into a strange
dream: in a great cathedral were three tombs, one of which had fallen
over. I ran to tell the priest. This good old man talked about the death
which had just befallen them, strangly the death transformed itself into
a white eagle which grabbed me with its big claws and flew me above the
earth. At the end of this night, I had the sense of having attended my own
rebirth, and the being I was until then seemed mixed with the transhis-
torical breath of Life.[19]

The original title was to be *Reinigung* (purification). He described the work
a few years later as "a song of death both human and celestial": a requiem,
"three women in the presence of death and their three shadows, the seventh voice being my own in the middle of this ritual of death, the voice
that has forgotten what it wanted to say but feels it is important and that
finally goes its own way." The work was scored for seven female voices,
"three principal women's voices and four secondary women's voices": the
singers, mostly the three principals, also play percussion at various points,
as had been the case in *Musik für das Ende*. The texts are partly by Vivier
himself and partly extracted from Christian liturgy (chiefly the Requiem
Mass) and *Les Clavicules de Salomon*. Again we note an autobiographical presence—the seventh voice, "my voice in the middle of this ritual of
death" which, midway through the work, repeats insistently in German,
punctuated by strokes on a bass drum, "ich wollte was sagen / ich weiß aber
nicht mehr / was ich sagen wollte" (I wanted to say something / but I don't
know anymore / what I wanted to say).

In fact *Chants* as a whole says a great deal, although what exactly it
"says" is not easy to put into words. It was not Vivier's first work to be
inspired by the subject of death, and would not be his last. The subject is
here confronted energetically, and in a great variety of tones of voice—
from the serious and solemn through the hysterical (perhaps at times
mock-hysterical) to the dryly humorous and grotesque ("no I don't want
to die I'm afraid the servants in the house will give my flesh to be eaten
by the Earth"). Ghosts of his French-Canadian Catholic past flit by, as in
the sequence where the principal mezzo recalls: "When I was a child an
old woman died I had to pass through three cathedrals to see her in her
tomb she smiled at me like she was calling me." The music is complex, although once again with a clear eye to melodic line (after the more textural-
gestural orientation of *Deva et Asura* and the pointillistic orientation of
*Désintégration*). It is described well by Christine Menneson:

In *Chants*, simple systems unify a discourse structured by highly dif-
ferentiated characters. The musical characters—such as plainchant style
(tenuti with or without percussion), recurrent timbre-chords, very close
counterpoint from which "vocal peaks" and rhythmic modes emerge—
[alternate] with the poetic characters—phrases making sense or not, and
symbolic forenames—which emerge from textures of spoken words, the
right way round/backwards, and phonemes. The choice of articulations,
the prosodic speeds, the voiced/unvoiced timbres, the choice of resonators, the dynamics, throw into relief various sound planes in a perspective of innumerable vanishing lines.[20]

The work, lasting some twenty minutes, is highly intense and dramatic,
and Vivier continued to imagine various possibilities for how it might be
staged, some of them rather bizarre. "Some of his ideas seemed a bit crazy
at the time," recalls Kevin Volans: "seven sopranos in seven coffins, for example; the Cologne establishment couldn't take that seriously."[21]
During the months he worked on *Chants*, the rest of his studies were
proceeding apace. He had begun electronic music studies with Hans
Ulrich Humpert, who had just taken over from Herbert Eimert as director
of the studios at the Hochschule. But, as Clarence Barlow recalls, "studying
with Humpert meant you had access to the studio and then after one lesson, the very first time, you were pretty much left on your own."[22] Unlike
the studios in Utrecht, students were not allowed to do the hands-on work
themselves and continually had to ask the studio technicians to execute
tasks for them, even simple things like splicing tape. Perhaps this explains
why Vivier ultimately spent relatively little time there and did not produce any finished tape pieces. Two letters written from Germany mention
a tape work in progress: one to a Montreal friend early in 1973, and one
to a producer at Radio-Canada sometime during the second year of his
studies in Cologne, referring to a piece called *Signes* as one of three works
he would like to include in a broadcast about his own music.[23] More interesting for him than pure tape music was the prospect of writing a "live
electronic" work for the Stockhausen Group, which in the early months of
1973 remained a possibility.[24] And he was working on something else at
the time that was never finished: in the letter to the Montreal friend just
cited, he writes, "I'm trying to finish a piece for 9 instruments," a work of
which we otherwise have no knowledge.[25]
He interrupted work on *Chants* to produce a short choral piece on a
text of his own, *O! Kosmos*, the manuscript dated "Köln 13/2/73."[26] This
music, written for soprano, alto, tenor, bass (SATB) chorus and largely
homophonic, is much simpler than the more complex interweaving of

voices in *Chants*. *O! Kosmos* would be a relatively conventional exercise in contemporary choral writing were it not for a few idiosyncratic touches. Midway through, a solo soprano voice begins to speak the last two lines of the text—"[May the heat of the seven suns / and the music of the supra-dimensional temple /] at last unite the beings / of all dimensions"—in a loop, over and over, as though she has fallen into a trance: we are whisked out of the world of choral music toward the experimental speech-music of Robert Ashley or Alvin Lucier. Then, at the end, the same soprano repeats, accelerating, a teasing little cadential figure ("ta ta-ra ta ta") that seems to have no relation whatsoever to the music around it. The solo soprano stands out from the rest, the joker in the pack: first she seems like a stoned hippie and then a clown. Both seem like self-projections of Vivier himself, as though he were standing outside and commenting on his own creation.

The same year, 1973, Vivier produced a companion piece, *Jesus erbarme dich*, also for SATB chorus. Shorter and simpler again than *O! Kosmos*, this is a beautiful setting of the single German phrase of the title ("Jesus have mercy"), almost entirely without eccentric touches (the "almost" being one wordless outburst by the sopranos after the first full choral passage). The music makes much expressive use of the interval of the semitone, especially melodically: Vivier uses it, rather as Bach did, in phrases with a lamenting or supplicatory quality. This piece is perhaps the most satisfying music he had produced to that time, modest, elegantly shaped and heartfelt. It opens a door that Vivier chose not to go through, opting instead to follow more ambitious conceptions, and less neatly containable ones, in the years ahead.

Meanwhile, he was about to have the premiere of *Désintégration*—amazingly, the first public performance of any new work of his since *Prolifération* three years earlier. He was in London briefly in early March to attend Stockhausen's rehearsals with the London Sinfonietta (preparing performances and recordings of various works, including the premiere of *Ylem*, the superb results subsequently released on Deutsche Grammophon). From there he headed to Paris, where Paul Méfano had arranged a performance of *Désintégration* with his new Ensemble 2e2m, based in Champigny-sur-Marne. (The ensemble's name was shorthand for "*études et expressions des modes musicaux*.") Despite his increasing devotion to Stockhausen, Vivier still had a very high regard for Méfano's teaching, and their irregular periods of contact led to work of a high degree of intensity. Méfano's daughter Nathalie recalls: "Claude . . . lived in our house. Claude's fantastical character and freedom of imagination provoked my father to submit him to a very fierce and unified kind of discipline as regards his creative conceptions."[27] One of Méfano's suggestions was to add string parts to *Désintégration*, perhaps as a way of counteracting the increasing sparseness of the texture as the rhythmic grid is progressively eaten away throughout the piece. Vivier duly obliged by adding sustained lines throughout, for four violins and two violas. However, when it came to the premiere in March 1973, Vivier had a further idea of how to liven up the latter part of the piece. Méfano recalls:

> He came to Paris, and we worked together. He lived with me for several months [August–September 1972] to write *Désintégration* for two pianos and six strings. And it was my first quarrel with him, at the concert with this piece, because he said to me: "I'm going to give you a surprise. But of course I'm not going to tell you what it is, because it's a surprise." And the surprise was: I was conducting *Désintégration*, and I saw that there were tape recorders beside the pianists. And then at the moment when the chords completely thin out and there are only the last spasms of the work with the sustained strings, the pianist pushed the button on the tape recorder; and what you heard was their favorite pieces of classical music, or symbolist music, or . . . in other words Claire de Lune by Debussy, the Appassionata Sonata, things like that. I was very angry. I said to him, "listen Claude, you're making fun of me because we worked for months on this piece and we thought it was the disintegration of contemporary music." . . . I said to him, "you must be of your time." Back then it was a necessary step for him during that year. "And here you're presenting that as though it's a liberation to hear Debussy, or Beethoven. But you're going against our time!" . . . I was so annoyed with him.[28]

Indications for when the tapes begin are clearly shown in the final manuscript copy of the piece, on page 82; and the final page has the instruction "Band ausblenden!" (Fade out the tape!). Richard Toop remarks of this moment in the piece:

> As an act of sheer eccentricity, undermining the accumulated rigor of the preceding twenty minutes, this seems entirely typical of Vivier. Yet as I recollect, when asked about this, Claude was slightly evasive. Was it meant to underline the discrepancy between his music and the tastes of conservatoire prodigies (he assumed the recording would be of Schumann, Chopin or something similar)? Or to highlight the "aliveness" of the present, as opposed to the mechanical repetition of the past (the recordings were to be wilfully "low-fi")? Or was it that he wanted the element of "love" to be present at least somewhere in the performance? It was never quite clear.[29]

The premiere of *Désintégration* seems to have brought about a slight, albeit temporary, cooling of Vivier's relationship with Méfano, and it is noteworthy that Méfano's name for the first time disappears from the list of referees Vivier had to provide for the Canada Council in his grant application that October.[30] The two remained in sporadic contact, however, and it was not the last time Méfano would program his works. Perhaps the intensity of Vivier's devotion to Stockhausen replaced the need for other mentors. Méfano's anger apart, Vivier did not much enjoy the overall experience:

> This concert I have to say was really foul and badly organized, full of mistakes, finally not good at all I must say; my piece for 2 pianos went well except that the silly Méfano didn't notice that it was written for 4 violins and 2 violas and not for 3 violins 3 violas; so a viola had to play a violin part. France is backward, bourgeois and badly organized which meant that everything I had to go through before this concert was simply atrocious and disgusting.[31]

The Paris experience did not, however, shake his confidence in the piece. In May he had some correspondence with the SMCQ in Montreal about Gilles Tremblay's suggestion that they perform it in the first concert of the new season, in October 1973; he sent off the two-piano score at the end of June but did not have the string parts, and suggested that they have them copied in Montreal.[32] Somewhere along the line plans stalled, and the projected Montreal performance never took place. But he still wanted very much to have the piece heard in Germany.

On May 1, he took a room in a large house, Im Stavenhof 18, where his friend Walter Zimmermann lived. This location was much more central than Vogelsanger Weg, and could hardly be more different in character: as Richard Toop describes it, "the alley where Walter lived was a flagrant brothel street on the edge of the Turkish quarter."[33] Vivier's room was "very small," Zimmermann says, and there was not much privacy: "the toilet was by the staircase, and Claude had to leave his room and walk over to my room to brush his teeth in the washing place under my 'Hochbett.'"[34] Vivier befriended some of his new Turkish neighbors, and learned some Turkish and some Arabic. Clarence Barlow recalls his

> announcing one evening that we had all been invited over for dinner at the home of some Turkish people he had met who lived around the

corner on the Weidengasse. When the day came we were at a concert and forgot all about it. Claude said suddenly, "oh, these people must have been waiting for hours!" and we went there, and they had candles all over the place, and were politely waiting. That was typical of Claude—he'd make friends with people at the drop of a hat.[35]

Im Stavenhof 18 became the scene of many happy memories, with many long discussions about music and many exuberant parties. Barlow says:

They were grand times. We were all sexually liberated. One night I was flirting heavily with a young lady I'd met, and we were both lying on Walter Zimmermann's bed, a loft bed. Wolfgang Rihm was also sitting on the same bed with a glass of wine in his hand. We looked over the edge of the bed at some point, and saw Claude on top of a lady. This lady was someone I'd had something with, and her husband was in the other room with a friend of mine. All we could see was Claude's back, completely naked, his buttocks moving at a regular pace, and two female thighs jutting out on both sides. Wolfgang looked over the balustrade and said, in his inimitable accent, "It looks like a poster!" The next day Claude appeared in the Hochschule, in the canteen, and he'd hardly entered the room when he yelled out "I'm bisexual!" Everybody looked at him.[36]

Indeed sexual contact with women was by now a regular thing in his life, rather to his own concern. He wrote to his friend Pierre Rochon:

My private life is going very well except that I make love more and more with girls, something that in itself is very pleasant. I must say that many parties end up in an orgy, the Germans also seem to do orgies not badly in a way that everything is not badly mixed together but anyway you still end up in a girl's vagina! On the other hand German gay guys are not very amusing in general and the most beautiful boys always end up asking you for money which is not very interesting. In this way I miss Montreal, its life is much more healthy! Given that I have neither time nor money to waste on all that, at some point I'm going to retire from the gay life of Cologne.[37]

A couple of recollections from the Cologne years by Vivier's fellow student John McAlpine, a young pianist recently arrived from New Zealand, perhaps put the matter of Vivier's sexual frankness in context. In the Hochschule the men's toilets were located one floor higher than the women's toilets; McAlpine recalls that Vivier could never see any good reason why he should have to climb one extra flight of stairs simply to use the bathroom, so would unapologetically make use of the women's toilets on a regular basis. "I don't recall any of the female students particularly object-ing," McAlpine adds. This perhaps shows Vivier's unembarrassed attitude to bodily functions generally, whether sexual or otherwise.

McAlpine also recalls Vivier's tendency in Cologne to cross the road whenever he felt the need rather than walking to a corner crossing; some-times he would hold up his hand to stop cars so he could do so. This behav-ior is, of course, dangerous as well as highly exhibitionist; but McAlpine's sense is that Vivier did not see it in these terms, the fulfillment of his own immediate need being more compelling than how his behavior was per-ceived or judged by others.[38]

The group of friends who gathered around Im Stavenhof was aug-mented in the summer of 1973 by the arrival of Kevin Volans from South Africa. As a teenager Volans was already an accomplished pianist, and gave his first broadcast recitals (Liszt, Chopin, Messiaen) at the age of twenty-one. He had been in Darmstadt in 1972 and had now come to Germany to study with Stockhausen; he would make his home there for some years, eventually becoming Stockhausen's teaching assistant. In becoming ac-quainted with the Cologne circle, Volans felt that Vivier "wasn't that highly regarded by the New Music establishment. And certainly Claude was not practical—in the two-piano piece, for example, there's a lot of systems composition, and it was very difficult to play. . . . He was a bit like a street dog, a shaggy dog, sniffing about, running around here and there, sort of uncontrollable. He was not bourgeois in any shape or form—and it was odd that we were friends, because I was seen as very bourgeois." He seemed, Volans says, "a little unfinished, rather rough, a bit of a loner; he seemed never to invite people back to his place."[39] As a newcomer to Cologne Volans was welcomed by people like Vivier and Barlow. Richard Toop observes, "I think they appreciated each other's 'otherness' within the general Cologne context."[40]

By the end of his first year's studies with Stockhausen, Vivier had com-posed not only *Chants* but, as he mentions in a letter to Serge Garant in mid-June, had begun planning what would eventually become *Lettura di Dante*, which was originally to have been premiered in Cologne and in Budapest and gone on tour; in the end, the premiere did not happen until the autumn of 1974 when he was back in Canada. In the same letter he mentions two projects that he had in mind: one for four voices (one of which would be his own), and one for six percussionists, piano and three voices, for which he asked Garant if it would be possible to have an SMCQ commission.[41]

In July, Vivier headed south for a holiday, visiting Venice and the Côte d'Azur with a couple of German friends. On July 18, he sent a postcard from Hyères to Walter Zimmermann: "Nice vacation, pissed drunk and puked—! (in my tent!) Was in Venice—great city, didn't find any friends but a lot of girls." His two German friends, not used to his ways, added a postscript, asking Zimmermann: "Does Claude get up to this nonsense with you the whole day as well? My God!"[42] "The holidays went very well," Vivier told Pierre Rochon, despite the fact that his passport was stolen at some point on his travels, "but I don't like to talk about holidays because they're not part of my most pressing interests."[43]

By the time studies began again in the autumn of 1973, things had changed: Barlow left for India in September, his period of study at an end, and Kevin Volans took over his flat. Vivier himself, bothered by the cramped living conditions in the Im Stavenhof house, had by now moved on, to Neuhöfferstrasse 32, a pleasant apartment house just across the Rhine and opposite the Köln Messe/Deutz train station. He would live there for most of his second year of study at the Hochschule, finally moving back across the river and north to Weissenburgerstrasse 46A the following summer.

Stockhausen's teaching usually took the form of extended sessions at his home in Kürten, a small community about thirty kilometers east of Cologne in the rural Bergisches Land. Despite the doubts entertained by a few members of the class, this teaching was clearly of enormous interest to Vivier, even if the direct influence on his work is not always immediately evident. Richard Toop recalls: "Stockhausen analysed *Mantra* in detail during the 1972–73 classes. I don't remember Claude saying anything about this, and I don't find any trace of it in, say, *Lettura di Dante*, much of which was composed at the piano anyway. Stockhausen also analysed the Europa version of *Momente*, which undoubtedly impressed Claude."[44]

In his second year in Cologne, Vivier took analysis classes from Toop himself, who had now become Stockhausen's teaching assistant. "The deal was that I would give two 2-hour analyses classes a week," Toop recalls, "one on Stockhausen's work, and the other on whatever I liked, but with the understanding that it would usually be 20th century, and probably post-war. In addition, I and the students would go to Stockhausen's house in Kürten about once a month for a long (4-hour +) session." As to what specifically Toop himself taught that year:

Of Stockhausen I remember spending quite a lot of time on the Nr. 4 *Klavierstücke*, and *TRANS*. From other composers, I know I looked at various pieces of Webern, Cage's *Sonatas and Interludes*, the Barraqué Sonata, and Boulez's Third Sonata (I remember we spent an afternoon coming to the conclusion that despite all the hieroglyphics, there were basically only two—or was it three?—routes through "Constellation-Miroir," plus some minor variants). In addition, I think I looked at some of the pieces arising from Gottfried Michael Koenig's Project 2 programmes. We made a collective realisation of Dieter Schnebel's *Glossolalie*, to which Claude contributed a wonderfully bizarre episode that involved eating money, or something like that (bear in mind that this was also the Joseph Beuys era in neighboring Düsseldorf!). But we also spent a lot of time discussing general issues. A significant factor here was that the classes were not held at the Musikhochschule, but in my flat, which was just a few minutes walk away.[45]

Toop elaborates that Im Stavenhof, where Walter Zimmermann still lived, "was barely 500 meters away, but even this short distance encapsulated some basic social divisions. Where I lived, in Kleverstrasse, there was a modestly endowed Polish Consulate to the left of my flat, and above it, according to the house owner, was a very discreetly run brothel.... So my flat's location was comparatively 'conformist,' whereas Walter's was emphatically not."[46] Toop's apartment had a front room big enough to accommodate a good many people. "So while the classes formally ran from 2–4, at 4 my then wife Carol would bring in cakes, tea, and cheap red wine, and things would continue more informally (sometimes till about 10 p.m.). And in addition to the Stockhausen students, other people like John McGuire, Walter Zimmermann, Georg Wolff and the organist Daniel Chorzempa would sometimes sit in." And Vivier?

To be honest, our main problem with Claude was his total disinclination to wash—some of the more nasally squeamish class members found this very hard to cope with. No, Claude was always enthusiastic, and threw himself into whatever matter was on hand. This of itself may have seemed a little naive to some of us, but that's because Claude was, above all, spontaneous. We couldn't resist teasing him at times, but it was done in an entirely friendly spirit, not a malicious one. And compositionally, pieces like *Désintegration* put Claude rather ahead of most of the students in terms of concrete achievements. ... When Stockhausen urged all the course participants to write choral pieces on (preferably non-Christian) sacred texts in response to a request from a German choral director—his own contribution being the opening section of what became *Atmen gibt das Leben*—only Claude responded with any enthusiasm, though I think Robert Platz also came up with something eventually.[47]

Vivier liked and admired Richard Toop, writing to Pierre Rochon: "Passionate work with Stock's assistant, he really knows the repertoire of contemporary music, with someone like him you can see a bit more clearly what's going on in today's music."[48] Toop extended him some special favors as well. "He would come and compose at my old Broadwood grand, where I naturally left him to get on with things. . . . I had a little daughter, Samantha, already very blonde and cute at the age of 1–2 years, and once the classes were over and refreshments were brought in, Samantha too was let loose. Claude adored her, but she found him a little scary (he was probably too intense), and tended to head for John McGuire, a sweet, archetypally laid-back Californian."[49]

The presence of Kevin Volans on the Cologne scene seems to have inspired Vivier toward a new project, mentioned in the grant application he submitted in October to the Canada Council. He outlined his plans for the coming year: "To finish the summer semester with Stockhausen then go to Darmstadt. To go to South Africa to study African musics in Johannesburg. This project therefore includes a voyage to south Africa." The Canada Council seems to have asked for more information, as he wrote them a further letter in an attempt to explain and justify his request: "Already in October at the same time as my course with Stockhausen I will have to learn 2 African languages. Probably around January I will go to South Africa to study African music. This project is terribly important for me because for me to spend one year at the sources of music and to understand the fundamental reasons for music is terribly important, essential to the formation of a composer."[50] Now, for the first time, the council turned down his request, and he had to face the fact that when his grant expired in summer he would have to find some new means of support in Germany or, more likely, return to Canada.

His contacts back home received a jolt early in 1974 in the form of a curious misunderstanding between him and Serge Garant. In the early summer, Vivier had written to Garant, reporting on his compositional work and inquiring about the possibilities of a performance in Montreal through Garant's SMCQ, and even of a commission. He explained that, having failed to enthuse the Collegium Vocale in Cologne in taking on *Chants*, he hoped the piece might be done in Montreal, offering by way of justification a perhaps not very clearly expressed argument: "My music has to use Canadians in order that Canada can develop a musical life that is strong and very professional and also internationally exportable. When I say internationally exportable, that means it has to rank at the level of current research in contemporary music."[51] Garant latched on to this last phrase, that Canadian music life has to "rank at the level of current research," hearing in it an unintended criticism and surely reading more into the phrase than Vivier intended. Garant wrote a lengthy response that was published under the title "Une letter de Rome" in the *Cahiers canadiens de la musique* later in the year. He claims to be shocked by Vivier's cold-blooded tone, and takes issue with his "badly formed" and vague argument, reading into it the far-fetched implication that Vivier was suggesting the SMCQ should play only truly contemporary music and not music of figures such as Varèse, Webern, and others, and that Garant's championing of contemporary music was not sufficiently up to date. Garant's biographer Marie-Thérèse Lefebvre writes that his response perhaps shows "a sort of justification for his own confusion regarding 'current research.'"[52] Vivier replied on March 8, apologizing for the misunderstanding, assuring him that no criticism was intended and that he was arguing only for more performances, broadcasts, and recordings of new Canadian work in general, not only his own. Having sufficiently smoothed Garant's ruffled feathers, the two remained on good terms. Lefebvre even feels the misunderstanding may have been "an important stimulus to Garant's new orientation" in the years ahead.

In the same letter, Vivier reported on the premiere of *Chants*, which had just taken place in Cologne in the context of a concert of works by Stockhausen's students. "The concert was very successful, but the performance was dreadful: 60% of the notes were wrong; but despite everything, you could still get an idea of the piece!"[53] Vivier later claimed the work took nearly 200 hours of rehearsal for its first performance, the atmosphere rather fraught. He conducted the performance himself.[54] The concert was reviewed in the *Frankfurter Allgemeine Zeitung*. The reviewer wrote that this "nervöses Mezzofortestück" was one of the less derivative pieces of the concert, while roughly out of the same stable as Stockhausen's *Momente*.[55] Naturally Vivier hoped for further performances of the work. In a letter to Garant a few weeks later he reported that Paul Méfano wanted to program *Chants* for May 10, but that it would not be possible "because my soprano doesn't want to sing anymore (she says it's dangerous for her voice)."[56]

The spring of 1974 was a productive period ("I'm working like a madman"); by April he had finished a new large-scale work, *Lettura di Dante* for soprano and seven players, and had made a revised score of *Désintégration* ("97 pages of music, hideous work"); he was also planning "a new electronic piece which I hope to finish in July," bragging to Garant that "this piece is going to be incredible." He enthused that "the serial school . . . which has led us to the atom" had also shown how other parameters—duration, tempo, color, density, dynamics—could be explored in greater depth and their musical potential realized. The letter ends: "I've always been passionate, crazy about music, and believe me it's wonderful."[57]

However, there was the more down-to-earth problem that he was running out of money. Much to his relief, in mid-May he received a letter from Maryvonne Kendergi, then recently appointed president of the SMCQ, saying that Gilles Tremblay had told her of his money problems and of his request for an advance on the commission the SMCQ had offered him for 1975–76; although this was not possible, she herself gave him an advance of DM 1,239.16 (equal to $500 Canadian, equivalent to one-eighth of his annual grant from the Canada Council). Madame Kendergi went further than her word, writing again a few days later with the news that the SMCQ commission for 1975–76 was now all arranged. He wrote back gratefully to thank her, saying that the money would enable him to finish things in Cologne, but also that he was looking into the possibility of staying longer in Germany, telling her of plans to have *Désintégration* performed at the end of July and to have *Chants* performed that same summer at Darmstadt. He optimistically assured her that his new work, *Lettura di Dante*, the neat copy of which he completed in mid-July, "could be put on without difficulty" by the SMCQ, and of how delighted he would be to have the piece done there before the planned performance in Budapest the following year.[58] They offered him $1,200 for a new work, half of which he would get on acceptance of the commission and half on receipt of the finished score. He was already able to announce the proposed title: *Liebesgedichte*.

Thanks to a Hessichesland bursary, Vivier was able to attend the Darmstadt Ferienkürse again this summer, the twenty-seventh session. In 1974 the courses ran from July 22 to August 8. Kagel, Stockhausen, Xenakis, and Wolff were there, but not Ligeti. Also much in evidence were two young composers from Stockhausen's circle, Peter Eötvös and Johannes Fritsch. Of Stockhausen himself there was a revival of *Mikrophonie I* (from 1964); one of the "intuitive pieces" from the set *Für kommende Zeiten* (1968–70); and of new works, the *Indianerlieder* and *Herbstmusik*, neither of which met with particularly favorable response, though some students were intrigued with the melodic qualities of the *Indianerlieder*.[59]

For Vivier himself the main excitement was the performance of *Désintegration*, which was given twice, first in the Aula of the Musikhochschule in Köln at the end of July, then on Friday, August 2 in the Georg-Büchner-Schule in Darmstadt. It was performed by pianists Herbert Henck and Christoph Delz, with string players Saschko Gawriloff and members of his class (Kalevi Aho, Vjera Katalinic, Andreas Pflüger, Jacqueline Ross, and Claes Pearce). The Cologne concert consisted of Cage's *Concert* for piano and orchestra of 1958 (played by Richard Toop and four wind players), Franco Donatoni's *Black and White no. 2* for two pianos from 1968, Cornelius Cardew's *Autumn 60* and *Material*, also from 1960, and finally *Désintegration*, with Vivier conducting. A reviewer from the *Kölner Stadt-Anzeiger* wrote that the strings, with their strained voices in high positions, sounded at best like the Prelude to *Lohengrin* played by an amateur orchestra.

> In this thin Klangsuppe the massive piano entries splash and plop with calculated irregularity. The longer the piece lasted, the more the listeners gradually moved from an unwilling nervousness into a sort of valium-effect in which one couldn't care less about the music. But even that didn't last forever. Vivier must have noticed, because after about half an hour he played a tape of The Old Castle from Mussorgsky's *Pictures at an Exhibition*. Of course he merely demonstrated what is usually the case in this old Hochschule building, namely that at concerts you always hear pieces from neighboring rooms that are absolutely not on the program.[60]

The reviews for the Darmstadt performance were no more positive: the critic of the *Darmstadter Tagblatt* felt that the length (at his estimate of "a good half hour") was "in a grotesque and brutal relationship with the content, an old problem with new music in the second half of our century."[61]

The 1974 courses marked Stockhausen's last teaching at Darmstadt until 1996, and a mood of unease was sometimes evident among the students in his lectures. Wilhelm Schlüter, responsible for most of the administrative aspects of the summer courses, reported that on August 9, the day after the close of the courses, the panel in charge had already stated that for 1976 they required a "total change."[62] The main reason for this appears to have been a walkout from one of Stockhausen's seminars, which Schlüter stated was orchestrated by three participants with Marxist leanings.

In his exhaustive study of Darmstadt in the years 1968–84, the English composer and musicologist Martin Iddon notes:

The minutes of the meeting of 27 December 1974 state that Stockhausen *could* be reinvited, but only in the case that a new composition of sufficient quality was available. Even in this case, Stockhausen was to be restricted to a single seminar and a single concert. Aloys Kontarsky acerbically stated: "For all that, if Karlheinz writes his *Wohltemperiertes Klavier* tomorrow, he obviously comes back." This criticism of the decreasing standard of Stockhausen's work is particularly damning, given that Kontarsky had been for many years one of Stockhausen's staunchest collaborators.[63]

It seems clear that Stockhausen wanted very much to be reinvited, and was not happy about this rejection. When Ernst Thomas, the director, mentioned the cost of Stockhausen's concerts as one reason for not inviting him for 1976, Stockhausen replied that he did not insist on having concerts and might be prepared to accept a lower rate of remuneration for his teaching.[64]

Many of the criticisms of Stockhausen centred on the quasi-religious aspects of his work. At the 1974 courses the young composer Gerhard Stäbler, together with colleagues Johannes Vetter and Jürgen Lösche, published yet another political pamphlet for distribution among the participants, supposedly under the auspices of "The Initiative for the Foundation of a Union of Socialist Producers of Art." The pamphlet mercilessly satirizes the spiritual aspects of Stockhausen's recent work:

> The blessing has befallen the participants of the International Ferienkurse for New Music in Darmstadt to receive in quiet devotions the holy consecration of higher truths from the mouth of St. Stockhausen. In order to ensure the unchecked flow of his divine spirit, St. Stockhausen demands absolute subordination to the single condition dictated by him: to absorb without contradiction the master's brilliant wisdom in "PEACE and QUIET." "PEACE and QUIET" for Saint Stockhausen therefore means not optimal working conditions for all participants, but complete stillness for Saint Stockhausen himself. All who make the slightest movements will be penalized via disciplinary measures.[65]

How should we understand this assault on Stockhausen's position, and his removal from the Darmstadt courses? Musicologist Paul Griffiths has written of the "failure of faith" in the idea of a common language of new music—the serial language, with all the universalist claims made for it by Stockhausen in his teaching and writings—which rendered much of the content of the Darmstadt courses irrelevant to the younger generation.[66] Martin Iddon has moreover suggested that "the continuing presence of Stockhausen [at Darmstadt] was of primary significance in creating the impression of a dearth of talented younger composers. Stockhausen overshadowed the younger prospects, in a way that might not have been the case had Boulez and Nono remained to provide a counterbalance."[67]

As to Vivier's attitude to this perceived debasement of his teacher's standing in the German new music world, we can only speculate. However, a snippet of information gleaned by Iddon from Wilhelm Schlüter, who was for many years librarian at the Internationales Musikinstitut Darmstadt, gives a fairly clear indication.

> On the day the Stäbler, Vetter et al. pamphlet was printed, Schlüter met Vivier late in the evening in a restaraunt in Darmstadt. Vivier had apparently had enough of the traditional lamentable standards of Darmstadt catering. He was, however, evidently in an extremely bad mood. Schlüter asked what the problem was and Vivier said he was afraid he'd only be able to explain properly how angry he was in French! He then showed his copy of the pamphlet to Schlüter. This, it seems, was the first knowledge that the Darmstadt administration had of the protest that was to come in one of Stockhausen's later lectures.[68]

Vivier was in any case not present to witness firsthand the fallout from the Darmstadt debacle, as he returned to Montreal that summer, his Canada Council grant used up, and would not return to Europe for another two and a half years. What we can say with certainty is that he retained his belief in Stockhausen's work and continued to regard him as a mentor, someone with whom he hoped to retain contact and to consult whenever possible for moral support and guidance. In the report that Vivier submitted to the Canada Council in the early months of 1977, following the premature ending of what was intended to be a yearlong trip to Asia, he noted: "I therefore decided to bring my journey to an end, to spend some time in Paris to get back into composition and afterwards to go to Cologne to review everything again with Stockhausen and my composer friends. It was very important to me to take some time with Stockhausen to look at everything and to clarify my ideas on the situation."[69] To "clarify my ideas": that was always Vivier's wish, and in that quest Stockhausen had helped him enormously. Nearly three years after the end of their period of formal contact, Vivier still regarded the German composer in much the same light as he always had.

Asked by the Montreal music critic Claude Gingras in September 1974 what he had learned from Stockhausen, Vivier replied:

Above all, to be able to be strong enough in front of Stockhausen so that my own ideas would stand up. Then, especially, to think of music before everything else. To be able to make the link between the whole abstract side of a piece (its structure) and the music that results. That's to say to be able to translate the visions one has. That's to say, to be a composer . . . to be able to structure a thing and at the same time to hear the result. To be extremely critical of myself and the music I write and the other musicians I hear. . . . What I learned from Stockhausen: the craft of writing . . . how to organize general proportions, to expand my vision of durations. He is the greatest living musician because he's the greatest composer. He leads music into the future and at the same time he changes your way of hearing music from the past. With him, you understand Mahler better, you understand Ockeghem better.[70]

Walter Boudreau, who attended Stockhausen's classes at Darmstadt in 1972, has perceptively noted that studying with Stockhausen was "like spending forty days in the desert," a sort of purification. He feels the results for Vivier were highly beneficial because *Chants* marks a real turning point in his oeuvre. Boudreau had stayed briefly with Vivier after the Darmstadt courses in 1972 when Vivier was working on *Désintégration*. He feels the Stockhausen experience "cornered Claude into facing what was his music and what wasn't"; the outcome was that Stockhausen set Vivier on a path that led ultimately to the development of the personal voice of his later works.[71]

Are there any examples of actual borrowings in the work of the two men? The musicologist Jean-Noël von der Weid finds in *Chants* "numerous pigments derived from Stockhausen's *Momente*," without however specifying exactly what these pigments are.[72] Richard Toop, on the other hand, has suggested that Stockhausen "may have made a minor appropriation from Claude's work: the Indian bells to which the mime in *INORI* exits are distinctly reminiscent of the end of Claude's *Chants*, whose premiere Stockhausen attended."[73] Paul Griffiths has noted that Vivier's orchestral work *Siddhartha* (1976) is close to then-recent Stockhausen,[74] and the influence of Stockhausen on this particular work has been exhaustively explored in an article by the composer Jean Lesage, who has written: "The work illustrates in an exemplary way the influence of Karlheinz Stockhausen's compositional techniques on Vivier's thought as much as the latter's fascination with certain procedures characteristic of oriental musics, such as the Indian raga."[75] It is hard not to see a similarity between the concept and structure of Vivier's *Learning* (1976) for four violins and percussion, described by its composer as "learning melody," and Stockhausen's *Tierkreis* (1974–75), which consists of twelve melodies, each representing one of the signs of the zodiac. The idea of structuring a large-scale composition in the form of a succession of melodies, however elaborate and unconventional, was certainly a radical one at that time.

There are, of course, more fundamental techniques in Vivier's work that have close parallels in that of Stockhausen, but that nonetheless do not originate with him and are not unique to his work. For example, Vivier's commitment to precompositional calculation and the extensive preworking of material never faded, as can be seen by the substantial port-folios of sketches he left for works throughout his lifetime. Stockhausen was intensely committed to what Kevin Volans has described as "work-ing through all the possibilities of the material" and to preplanning, an attitude that Vivier shared. Interestingly, Stockhausen's abandonment of precompositional working in the "intuitive music" of the late 1960s and early 1970s has no real parallel in Vivier's work.[76]

It is clear, finally, that what Vivier learned from Stockhausen went beyond specific compositional techniques into what may be called more "cosmic" matters. Asked by Jonathan Cott about his relationship "as a German composer to the musical and spiritual awarenesses you arrived at in Japan and Bali," Stockhausen replied: "You see, once you've achieved a certain independence from the natural forces and your heritage, you can become someone who also discovers within himself the Balinese and the Japanese. That's why it's wrong to say, 'He's influenced by the Japanese.' What I've actually experienced is that I came to Japan and discovered the Japanese in me. I immediately wanted to become that 'Japanese,' because it was new to me that I could live like that."[77] Again, this could be Vivier talking. "Stockhausen wants to expand the field of human consciousness," Vivier had written: in this wish the German composer found a ready and loyal accomplice in his Canadian student.

✳ ✳ ✳

A final souvenir of Vivier in Europe from the summer of 1974 comes from Richard Toop.

> I think I was probably staying with my parents in England, a Kentish vil-
> lage somewhere near Shoreham. One day there was a phone call in the
> mid-afternoon. It was Claude. Out of the blue, he had arrived at Dover
> at daybreak, hitched various rides to somewhere in the vicinity, and was

now at the local rail station. I went to find him. Clearly he had hardly a penny in his pocket, but he presented me with a bottle of Johnny Walker Black Label whisky, as if that were the very least he could do. That was pure Claude.[78]

In August 1974 Vivier returned to Montreal after three years' absence. The performance of *Lettura di Dante* the following month was his immediate concern; after that, his professional future was a complete blank.

# CHAPTER FIVE

# " SOMETHING DIFFERENT IS COMING, SOMETHING MORE PRECISE, MORE CLEAR "

## 1974–76

Vivier's return to Montreal in August 1974 was the result of economic necessity and not of any conscious wish to reintegrate himself in the Canadian scene, no matter how positive a spin he tried to put on the matter in his recent correspondence with Serge Garant. Had his grant application for a further year's study (including the proposed trip to South Africa) been successful, he would certainly have remained in Europe, perhaps indefinitely. It is tantalizing to imagine how differently his music would have developed had he stayed. The years immediately following his departure saw the beginnings of what in retrospect may be seen as two of the most important European new music tendencies of the 1970s, *la musique spectrale* in Paris and *die neue Einfachheit* in Cologne, both of which—especially the former—would mark Vivier's own work profoundly when he encountered them a few years later. Now twenty-six, he had no option but to move back temporarily to his parents' house in Pont-Viau while looking for a place of his own in Montreal and some source of income.

The immediate anxieties connected with his homecoming were offset by the excitement of the premiere of *Lettura di Dante* by the SMCQ, the performance arranged for the Salle Claude-Champagne at the University of Montreal on September 26. The work, completed in Cologne in July, was equal in ambition to anything he had produced to that point. It is scored for solo soprano with a Varèse-like ensemble of oboe, clarinet, bassoon, trumpet, trombone, viola, and percussion. Garant had agreed to conduct, and the singer was the young soprano Pauline Vaillancourt, then making her debut with the SMCQ. She found the piece "very very hard, really at the limit of possibility"—not least because so much of the part is in the very highest register of the voice—but she was determined to sing what he had written rather than ask him to make changes. She worked with Vivier both on the music and on the theatrical conception of the work, and remembers finding him "quite sure of himself, and of the work, yet he was still nervous about the performance."[1]

In an interview at the time of the premiere, Vivier explained the origins of the piece. During his time in Cologne, he recalled,

> I studied the Italian language—its musicality had always fascinated me. At the beginning I intended to use texts in six languages and all my sonic material was ready. One day, sitting on the terrace of a café, I heard—in my head—an old Italian man reciting passages from the famous text of Dante [*The Divine Comedy*]; it was then that I opted to use Italian exclusively. During the performance, we don't see the singer, at least not at the start. The work, which leads us from hell to heaven, will be a beautiful trip. . . . Towards the end the curtain opens: we see the singer saying "I have seen God" in deaf-and-dumb language, very religiously, then she repeats it in Italian.[2]

The Dante text—mostly sung while the singer is still behind the curtain—is not intended to be the primary focus of attention. It was, Vivier remarked, "used less for its traditional meaning than for its affective meaning, the 'feeling' that you get hearing a text by Dante."[3] In keeping with this, the text "Ho visto dio" (I have seen God), which forms the most striking part of the piece—when, after more than fifteen minutes, the curtain opens and the singer finally becomes visible—is not in fact from Dante, but is Vivier's own invention. The singer, once she appears, begins by mouthing the three words silently while simultaneously forming them in sign language. Then she intones them audibly thirteen times against a slow, steady pulse on a muted nipple gong. It is a marvelous effect, almost as though God has intervened to grant her the power of speech.

In his program note for the premiere Vivier remarked that, compositionally, *Lettura di Dante* was built "on a melody consisting of six cells of one, two or three notes, which are constantly repeated and slightly modified by the soprano." But he insisted that the use of a single melody as basis for the work had nothing to do with the similar technique of Stockhausen's *Mantra*.[4] "It's very melodic, the form is clear, beautiful, pure, very balanced, but it's not at all nostalgic, I have the feeling that the music does not have the right to impose itself on the listeners. On the contrary, contemporary music should make them want to be free, to leave, to raise themselves to another planet."[5]

Some commentators have suggested that Vivier's wish to downplay the Stockhausen influence on *Lettura di Dante* is slightly disingenuous. In an article on Vivier's melodic writing, Janette Tilley argues that *Lettura di Dante* represents a "simplified application" of the *Mantra* technique:

> Like *Mantra*, the melody unfolds over a long period with the limbs of the melody separated by pauses of varying duration. The piece consists of seven repetitions of the melody, six of which are sung by the soprano with only a few minor changes to the order of limbs. The penultimate statement of the melody appears in the instrumental texture with the "limbs" superimposed and out of order. Furthermore, whereas the pitch of each limb remains fixed through the six vocal repetitions, they undergo operations of transposition and inversion in the instrumental statement. . . . [The] rigidity of pitch that *Lettura* displays reveals a fundamental difference between teacher and student and suggests either a misunderstanding of the *Mantra* principles or an intended over-simplification of the compositional process. . . . Vivier's *Lettura di Dante* submits to traditional procedures by presenting simple variations of the original melody. Each limb undergoes its own variation procedure but the pitches of the melody remain fixed throughout the work. Nowhere in *Lettura* does the original melody expand or contract, nor do the characteristic transformations of each limb extend to other limbs or statements of the melody.[6]

Such considerations would of course only be picked up by the most astute listener to the piece in performance. Stockhausen's presence can nonetheless be felt more directly in the solemn, ritualistic nature of the work and in the quasi-oriental use of percussion to punctuate melodic phrases (itself by this time something of a new music cliché). The placing of one of the most important performers behind a curtain has a precedent in Stockhausen's placing of a string orchestra behind a magenta-lit gauze in *Trans* a few years earlier.

More important, *Lettura di Dante* is another of Vivier's death-filled visions, a piece that views our world as merely a temporary stopping place before the next. In the program note he commented that the piece was marked by

> the beauty and the purity that old people and children inspire in me, or by the closeness to death that my father and mother always imposed on me. A vision of an inaccessible world in a life where money and power lead everything. A life full of solitude. I certainly think of the solitary beings that we all are when I write. I no longer think of the future or the past but of a sort of vanished present, a sort of immaterial joy mixed with the sadness of the child who has lost his mother.[7]

The concert, presented on September 26, 1974, in Montreal and repeated the following day at the National Arts Center in Ottawa, also contained pieces by Luis de Pablo, the Montreal composer Donald Steven, Paul Méfano's *Lignes*, and ended with Varèse's *Ecuatorial*. The reviews were mixed but on the whole not positive. Most encouraging was that by Gilles Potvin in *Le Devoir*, who felt that, "recently returned from a long stay in Europe," Vivier showed himself to be "a musician of talent . . . he has ripened . . . at first tortuous, not very promising, he manages to lead us, and his music then acquires an unexpected expressive richness, the singer . . . inviting us to ecstasy while the curtain opens on her, only to close again while the music goes its way."[8] The English-language *Montreal Star* described the staging: "The soprano is concealed behind a gauze curtain, centre stage, and spotlights bathe the ensemble in amber and green. The work is divided into six main sections, each of them featuring a solo and as many as six instruments . . . in the last section, the curtain is drawn slowly aside to reveal Vaillancourt in a green glow, making supplicatory gestures towards the ceiling, and repeating over and over, 'Ho visto Dio' (I have seen God)." The reviewer felt Vivier had learned much from his studies with Stockhausen about instrumentation and form, "though he still has a tendency to extend insubstantial ideas in a very self-indulgent manner. His own commentary on the work betrays a premature world-weariness; he talks of his new sensibility, 'a sensibility which I have always noticed in derelicts ("les robineux" in Montreal) since my childhood.'"[9] More damning was the review in *La Presse* by Claude Gingras, who had previewed the event some days earlier: "On paper it is very intelligently written, very complicated. To listen to, it is extremely long, by turns fascinating, monotonous and pretentious."[10] Vivier wrote an angry reply to Gingras's review which *La Presse* published on October 8 under the title "Est bien vu ici qui

veut être médiocre" (We can see here exactly who is mediocre); in it he
hotly, if unjustifiably, accuses Gingras of finding his work inferior to that of
Varèse only because it was Canadian. The exchange marked the beginning
of years of mutual hostility between Vivier and the unrepentant Gingras.[11]

As important to him as the critics were the reactions of his fellow composers, many of whom he had not seen during his years in Europe. Gilles
Tremblay was delighted: "for me, for Serge Garant, for other friends, I
think we discovered the real Claude Vivier with this work. This work is
fantastic, beautiful, very direct, very deep. It was marvelous to discover
that Claude had opened his being, *son être*. It reveals the mystic part of
the music of Vivier." Tremblay feels this work has the same "necessity"
as *Lonely Child*, and for him these two pieces are the "twin summits" of
Vivier's output.[12] Among the younger generation, Walter Boudreau was
also at the premiere, because at that time "I was following Serge Garant
around. I liked the end but not the beginning." (Boudreau recalls that in
the rehearsals Vivier sat in the auditorium not saying much "because he
was so pleased anyone would play his music; and maybe he was still a little
in awe of Garant.")[13] José Evangelista, whom Vivier had gotten to know
in Darmstadt that summer, was impressed by the "very haunting" ending.
So too was John Rea, a young Toronto-born composer who had recently
taken up residence in the city.[14]

Yet for all the approbation of his colleagues, *Lettura di Dante* has remained a little-known item in Vivier's catalog, having been revived only
infrequently since its initial performances. It sounds slightly dated today,
a work bound to, rather than transcending, its era. To the Montreal and
Ottawa audiences it must have sounded very European, although undeniably accomplished. But there can be no doubt of the importance of the
event for Vivier himself. *La Scène musicale* noted that "this concert 'cel-
ebrates,' in a way, the return and the official recognition of a 'young composer to watch!'"[15]

The preview article in *Le Devoir* allows us to trace a few other items of
concern to Vivier at the end of his European studies. One is, as he told the
interviewer Jacques Thériault, "Improvisation in contemporary music is
finished, at least for me. Something different is coming, something more
precise, more clear. . . . I'm talking about written, fixed scores. However,
improvisation is not excluded; but it's during the preparatory sessions for
the work that the musicians have the chance to take part in it."[16] This is a
response not only to an important strand of Stockhausen's recent work
but also to the tendency in some new music since the late 1960s to equate
improvisation with political and social freedom. Composers as different as

Franco Evangelisti and Vinko Globokar, both Darmstadt veterans, turned overwhelmingly (and polemically) to improvisation around this time as, for different reasons, did young American composers like Terry Riley or Frederic Rzewski. With his limited keyboard skills Vivier himself was no improviser, which may partly account for his determination to look elsewhere for a way forward: yet it is striking, even so, how accurately his words—"something more precise, more clear"—describe the nature of the major works he himself would produce in the following decade.

To the same interviewer Vivier remarked: "This last work, like that for seven female voices [*Chants*], marks the beginning of a new asceticism, or rather a new sensibility." This is in keeping with a curious remark in the program note, one that the reviewer from the *Montreal Star* had picked up on, where Vivier writes: "This music tends towards a new sensibility, a sensibility I always noticed amongst homeless people (in Montreal, 'les robineux') ever since my childhood."[17] Here, admittedly, it is hard to know what he really means, and harder still to relate the remark to *Lettura di Dante*. The Quebecois slang term *robineux* refers to homeless people, generally alcoholics, the word "robin" a derivation from the American "rubbing alcohol" (or, in British English, surgical spirit), something that could be drunk in desperation if no normal alcoholic drink was available. But quite why or how *Lettura di Dante* might be said to tend toward the sensibility of *les robineux* is not at all apparent. The ghost of the old drunkard of *Hommage: Musique pour un vieux corse triste* seems to pass by, although the connection seems mostly in Vivier's own imagination rather than in the music itself. Might it be that in some strange way he is here identifying, as a young homeless and penniless creative artist, with the dregs of humanity, the clochards and the *robineux* who, throughout his brief life, would always arouse his sympathy and compassion?

The months following the premiere were difficult for him, and readjusting to life in Montreal proved quite a struggle. He had found a room at 6325 rue de Gaspé, roughly equidistant from the metros Beaubien and Rosemont, described by a friend as "a fairly deathly room at minimum rent and totally impersonal. Of course, no piano and, as a substitute, an almost empty refrigerator in the corridor."[18] He took a part-time job teaching electronic organ in a Montreal music store, Galipeau Musique, which brought in forty dollars per week.[19] His friend Pierre Rochon interviewed him a few months later for the magazine *La Scène musicale*, and described how during the autumn Vivier "felt himself sinking dangerously into depression, sadness, creative impotence. His 'friends' kept a distance, the telephone rang rarely, and it was only because of the personal generosity of some anonymous members of the Montreal musical milieu that Claude could get back into composition seriously."[20] He had the SMCQ commission for *Liebesgedichte*, but although ideas for the work were already taking shape, the premiere would not be until the following season, so there was no immediate pressure to work on the score. It must have been with some relief when, on December 4, he was able to write a letter accepting a new commission to write a number of short "pièces imposées" for the Tremplin International Competition to be held in Montreal the following June, for which Les Concours de Musique du Canada Inc. would pay him $400 per month for six months.[21] His letter does not specify how many pieces were asked for: he would produce eight in the months ahead.

Despite his low spirits he would occasionally engage with the music scene of the city. In October he was interviewed by Nicole Bisaillon for the radio series Carnet Arts et Lettres in connection with the forthcoming SMCQ program presenting Mauricio Kagel and Le Théâtre musicale de Cologne. Less characteristically, he picked up some paid work making song arrangements for "boîtes à chansons" in Montreal and Quebec City, small, informal, smoky venues that often gave aspiring chansonniers their first public platform. Things had improved somewhat by the new year, by which time he had found some part-time teaching, both at the University of Montreal and at CEGEP Montmorency in Laval, the latter "at a level that interests and stimulates him," according to one interviewer.[22] (The CEGEPs—an acronym for *Collège d'enseignement général et professionnel*—had been established a few years previously by the Quebec provincial government with the aim of preparing pupils for university-level study.)

Rochon's interview for *La Scène musicale*, from February 1975, quotes Vivier further on the state of new music. The contemporary composer, he told Rochon, has a choice:

> By the simple fact that he's a creative artist . . . the composer has a rope around his neck. Society seems to give him a place, of course, but any extreme stance that he takes is received severely, especially by the critic who, instead of really trying to understand, disguises his ineptitude by treating the situation with contempt or indifference. In parallel with this situation . . . the idea of the "salon" or "the elite" is still very present. Or that of "me, I'm a *freak*, I don't belong to anything": two parallel attitudes which, deep down, follow the current fashion.[23]

Asked about his feelings about being back in Canada, he replied:

> I am a citizen of the world, even if Montreal remains my first port of call;
> and it's in being plainly, truly Quebecois that I become a citizen of the
> world. My Quebec nature is acquired and I don't feel any need to justify
> it, to constantly redefine it in relation to other nationalities . . . something
> is happening in Canada and in Quebec that has to be said and perhaps
> can only be said here. Unfortunately, we lack large-scale horizons; the
> musicians are good but the means are limited.

He complained about the lack of regular access to an electronic studio,
quite unlike the situation he had experienced in Utrecht and in Cologne;
and, with one brief exception in the summer of 1976, true electronic music makes no further appearance in his output. At the end of the article
he makes an intriguing prediction, true in the case of several composers
but not himself. Talking about the difficulty of funding orchestras to properly rehearse new work, he remarked: "In North America, I think now
that the only solution consists of attaching oneself to a group dedicated to
its own time, at risk of being badly paid, of not 'selling' the product . . . a
group determined to join itself assiduously with the creative effort of the
composer." Meanwhile, he had begun work on the pieces for the Tremplin
International Competition. They were intended for the ominously named
"Third Elimination" of the International Stepping Stone section; contes-
tants were given the pieces on June 4 for performance, from memory, on
Sunday June 22, 1975. Vivier produced a total of eight short pieces during the winter, spring, and summer, all of them similar in length (between
five and nine minutes), four of which—*Pièce pour flûte et piano*, *Pièce pour
violon et piano*, *Pianoforte*, and *Hymnen an die Nacht* (for soprano and
piano) were performed during the final of the competition. There were
twelve finalists, four sopranos, one flautist, six pianists, and one violinist,
so Vivier, had he been there—which it seems he was not, for reasons unknown—would have heard four different performances of *Hymnen an die
Nacht* and six of *Pianoforte*, including one by Louis Lortie, who won the
competition overall with a prize of $3,000. The prize of $350 for the best
performance of one of the Vivier pieces went to the then fifteen-year-old
Vancouver violinist Gwen Hoebig.[24]

Besides the four works performed that day, it is not clear whether
all of the remaining four short pieces from 1975 were intended for the
Tremplin competition. One that surely was is the *Pièce pour violoncelle et
piano*, which was not played only because no cellist reached the final. *Pour
Guitare* remained unperformed for some months until it was taken up by

the young Montreal guitarist Michael Laucke, to whom Vivier retrospectively dedicated it.[25] We are less sure about the *Improvisation pour basson et piano*, which, despite the existence of the manuscript, remains one of Vivier's least-known works; there is no record of a public performance of the piece in the composer's lifetime. Certainly not intended for the competition, or at least not successfully so because postdating it, is *Pour violon et clarinette*, the manuscript signed "Halifax le 5/8/75"; it may be that Vivier produced this piece after the event simply to fulfill the terms of the original commission. During these months he was working simultaneously on the score of *Liebesgedichte* for the SMCQ, the first draft completed on April 17 and the neat copy dated May 5. And at the beginning of April he spent a week at L'Abbaye cistercienne in Oka, the place of spiritual refreshment from which he had derived such solace prior to his years in Europe.

Taken collectively, the eight short pieces of 1975 form an impressive outpouring. Vivier responded well to the demands of having to produce a lot of music in a short space of time, something he had never had to do before. Our wish to trace his development through the eight pieces is thwarted by the fact that only three of them are dated precisely (*Pièce pour flûte et piano*, February 16; *Pièce pour violon et piano*, March 9; *Pour violon et clarinette*, August 5). But certain tendencies are clear nonetheless. Overall one might say that the pieces represent genuinely transitional work between the student Vivier of works like *Chants* or *Lettura di Dante* and the composer he was to become. *Pianoforte* combines common-practice elements of the time, such as retrograde and inversion of melodic lines, a quasi-serial use of dynamics, and sudden, short-lived changes of tempo and mood, with features more directly associated with Stockhausen, notably the use of single or multiple grace notes before the notes in a melody (indeed the opening two-voice texture of this piece and those for flute and for violin, with their reiterated notes and ornamentations, are not so far away from the opening of Stockhausen's *Mantra*). *Pianoforte* ends with an intriguing eleven-measure coda which is the first clear use of overtone-derived harmony in Vivier's output. Above a *fff* statement by the left hand in octaves of the melodic contour of the opening melody of the piece, the right hand, ***ppp***, plays chords made up of selected overtones of each of the bass notes in turn (or, more accurately, approximations of overtones; the seventh or eleventh, in particular, correspond only very approximately to the equal-tempered intonation of the piano).[26] From Stockhausen he would have learned to think of these chords as approximating particular formant regions of a complex tone. This passage, as we shall discuss later, is similar (but not identical) to Vivier's use of spectral "colors" in his later works.

It is interesting, moreover, that in a collection of pieces that might broadly be characterized as Expressionist in tone, Vivier makes use of an intervallic palette that is much more varied than the endlessly reiterated sevenths and ninths characteristic of much Webernian (and post-Webernian) Expressionism. In particular, the interval of the minor tenth (octave plus a minor third) emerges as a characteristic sonority of these pieces; the *Pièce pour flûte et piano* ends with a whole descending chain of them, and Vivier sometimes plays with alternating minor and major tenths in these works as he does later to such poignant effect in *Lonely Child, Bouchara,* and elsewhere. In *Pièce pour violon et piano* he has the violinist play whole chains of sixths, something often found in the piano music of Chopin or Liszt but unacceptable to the Darmstadt-based avant-garde. Perhaps the most memorable sonority in the whole collection is the widely spaced dyad A♭–C that begins *Hymnen an die Nacht*, a sonority that remains in the air for a long time before being replaced by a more modern-sounding minor seventh. There are moments also when melodic fragments are heard over a drone, as in one passage in *Pièce pour flûte et piano* (on B) or in the original version, with piano accompaniment, of *Pour Guitare* (on D and A). In these and other ways, Vivier breaks away from the restrictions of the postserial language present in parts of his earlier works and introduces both old and new kinds of tonal relations.

Vivier's use of a text by Novalis—pseudonym for the German early Romantic writer Georg Philipp Friedrich von Hardenberg (1772–1801)—in the only vocal piece of the set, *Hymnen an die Nacht*, is intriguing. Although candidates in the Tremplin competition came largely from English- and French-speaking Canada, the deliberate use of a foreign language for the singers is not in itself so unusual; in that sense German would be the obvious candidate. The passage in question, the opening lines of the fifth part of Novalis's *Hymns to the Night*, has a complex significance in the context of Vivier's output. It describes the ancient world, a world filled with gods and with the living light of the sun, which rises each morning from the sea. The passage that Vivier sets stops there, before Novalis goes on to describe the one "dreadful" thought that frightens all the souls of this world: Death, which brings "anguish, pain and tears" in its wake. Indeed, after setting Novalis's phrase "Unendlich war die Erde—der Götter Aufenthalt, und ihre Heimat" (boundless was the Earth—the abode of the gods and their home) Vivier has the temerity to inject a few phrases of his own: first "reich an Kleinodien und herrlichen Wundern" (rich in gems and great marvels), an elaboration, if a slightly unnecessary one, on the picture Novalis gives of the ancient world; and then a few snippets of child language ("Ti ta ti ti ta"), set to falling major and minor thirds, the same kind of teasing gesture he had used in *Chants. Hymnen an die Nacht*, therefore, is a vision of paradise, even—thanks to Vivier's textual intervention—a rather child-like vision, in which thoughts of Death are not permitted. And yet the complete text of Novalis's long poem-sequence ends with a section titled "Sehnsucht nach dem Tode" (Longing for Death), and his *Hymns to the Night* as a whole views night as the threshold between life and death, and death as an intermediary between this world and the next. As such, this short vocal piece shows Vivier immersed in his characteristic themes, offering here a kind of prelude to ideas he would explore in greater depth in later works.

The last of the short pieces written that year, the *Pièce pour violon et clarinette* composed in Halifax in early August, is an intriguing afterthought to the set.[27] Although sharing broad similarities of language with the earlier pieces, this one is even more stridently confident in its tonal anchors, the F♯ of the beginning, the C♯ of the second section. The piece is essentially a study in chromatic scale playing, and for the majority of the time, the two players do just that in a lively interplay, often either in rhythmic unison or antiphonally. And while the resulting figuration seems perhaps less varied than the rich coloring of harmony in the earlier pieces, we can see—with the benefit of retrospect—Vivier wiping the slate clean, purging his harmonic world of unwanted residues of earlier manners before embarking on the adventures of his next major works, *Siddhartha* and *Learning*.

The Tremplin competition in June brought Vivier's name before a certain cross section of the Canadian public, but in career terms he was making slow progress. At the beginning of that month he had signed a contract with Les Éditions musicales transatlantiques in Paris for the publication of *Chants*, which was a promising step, and a couple of months later he heard that the Secretariat d'État à la Culture in Paris had decided, thanks to the intervention of Paul Méfano, retrospectively to commission the piece with a view to a new performance at the Festival International de Champigny. He would receive 4,000 francs for the commission.[28]

Meanwhile he was still teaching at CEGEP Montmorency, but purely out of financial necessity. He later told an interviewer that he was "not liked" there, and Walter Boudreau says plainly that Vivier was "a catastrophe" as a teacher.[29] And while we have no details of his teaching experiences or the difficulties he may have encountered, it is not hard to imagine the twenty-seven-year-old Vivier restless to compose and to build a career, to push further as a creative artist, rather than to impart his knowledge to groups of Laval teenagers. It must therefore have been a relief to be able to end his involvement there that summer and to accept an apparently more promising part-time position at the University of Ottawa, in charge of the Atelier de musique contemporaine—which meant, essentially, running the contemporary music ensemble. The Ottawa Music Department had come into existence only some six years previously under the direction of Françoys Bernier, an energetic man and former artistic director of the Orchestre symphonique de Québec who was enthusiastic about contemporary music and had recently organized a Messiaen Festival (with Messiaen in attendance) and a Festival of French music in the department. Vivier's contract was for a fixed term of seven months, from the beginning of October 1975 to the end of April 1976. He would be paid at an hourly rate of twenty dollars, and was employed for one hundred hours of work in total.[30] He took lodgings at 21 rue Stewart, a short walk from the department, although at first he still maintained his Montreal apartment, now 6435 rue Saint Denis #102, and would make frequent commutes between Ottawa and Montreal by bus during the autumn and winter.

During the late summer he had been approached by the Youth Orchestra Association of Canada to compose an orchestral work for the following season. This, like the Ottawa job, was a welcome sign of recognition from within Canada, and yet he was as restless as ever. His thoughts seem never to have been far away from the prospect of how to disappear again, not necessarily back to Europe, but to experience more of the world. He spent a few days at L'Abbaye cistercienne in Oka in the middle of September, perhaps indicating the need for a brief respite from the struggles going on inside him.

He now had another important premiere approaching, the most substantial he had had since *Lettura di Dante* almost exactly a year earlier. This was *Liebesgedichte*, scored for four solo singers (SATB) and eight instrumentalists (two oboes, clarinet, bassoon, two horns, and two trumpets), the neat copy of which he had finished in early May.[31] The work and its title (Love poems) had been in his mind since the end of his time in Cologne, and was once again intended for the SMCQ, which had now moved their base from the Salle Claude Champagne at the University of Montreal to the Salle Pollack at McGill University; it was in the Salle Pollack that the premiere of *Liebesgedichte* took place on October 2, 1975, conducted by Serge Garant. It was preceded by Stravinsky's *Symphonies of Wind Instruments*, and after the intermission Garant conducted a work by Vivier's Toronto-based contemporary John Hawkins, and Messiaen's *Couleurs de la Cité Céleste*. Vivier dedicated the work "affectueusement" to Maryvonne Kendergi, president of the SMCQ, who had helped secure the commission, even advancing him money that rescued him during his last lean weeks in Cologne. "My connection with Claude took the form of affection," she recalled some years later. "A sort of mutual adoption, mother/son. Without having been part of his everyday life, I always felt Claude was a warm presence, needing attention and to exchange tenderness. A sort of perpetual childhood."[32]

The "love" explored in *Liebesgedichte*, Vivier wrote, was "partly the love of a child, a naïve, tender love. The love of God for human beings and also the love of human beings for God."[33] The text includes quotations from several sources, principally fragments in Latin from Virgil's *Eclogues* (Bucolics), the earliest of the Roman poet's great works, a heady mixture of reflections on contemporary politics, mythology, and love both specifically homosexual and not; it also includes a passage from Psalm 131, "Seigneur mon coeur ne s'enfle pas d'orgueil" (My heart is not proud, O Lord), which Vivier in his program note calls "the psalm of spiritual childhood." The majority of the time, however, the singers must negotiate Vivier's "invented language," the nonsense syllables that had been a recurrent feature of his vocal works ever since *Ojikawa*. *Liebesgedichte* includes a Vivier text titled "Chant d'amour," which begins:

> Rèste Bouyjdè Kalmiya
> O Vien distèrdo eusdè
> eusien dijteurdov kourdièsa
> Kourdièsa alderdo Diosa
> Térosia

Whatever the intention expressed by Vivier in his program note, quoted above, the concept of *Liebesgedichte* may also be seen in more broadly autobiographical terms as an expression of the complexities of love in all its myriad forms, erotic, spiritual, compassionate, sociopolitical, irrational. If Vivier's own nonsense text here may perhaps be taken as child-speak, its "content" expressive—at a stretch—of the child's need for love, then the use of Virgil broadens considerably the range of love referenced in the work. Vivier's program note goes on to discuss the music in highly technical terms, almost as though to forestall any misconception that a work on such a theme would imply any lessening of the rigor of his musical language. He also tells us that the music grew from his memory of a melody composed some years earlier, during his studies at the Montreal Conservatoire.

> In 1968 I composed an extraordinary melody and even today it has not left me. This melody was completely intuitive. One afternoon I harmonized it in four parts, still intuitively, and certainly with love. Finally I divided it into twelve groups, each one containing between one and twelve chords. Then I spread the music out in time, I gave each series of chords a duration following very precise proportions. Then I gave to each chord in my groups a duration forming a scale of harmonic proportions. Each part was then given a character, a tempo and a tendency (past, present or future).[34]

The scoring of the work he conceived as implying "three quartets: voices, wind, and brass," which partly explains the use of the number twelve in his compositional procedures (notwithstanding its plethora of symbolic associations, not least in serial music). Harder to understand is his reference to the "tendency" of each part: we would love to know what he means by "past, present or future" in this context.[35] *Liebesgedichte* marks a clear step beyond *Lettura di Dante* in terms of originality, at times looking forward to the Vivier of *Kopernikus*. But it can be a difficult experience for the audience, partly because of its length—twenty-eight minutes—and partly because its form and direction are extremely difficult to grasp at first listening. The reviewers at the premiere, which was part of a weeklong festival, were generally positive. The French critic Jacques Lonchampt, reviewing the event for *Le Monde*, wrote that *Liebesgedichte* was "full of passion, and also of confusion, but it gives evidence of a real joy in sound."[36] Gilles Potvin in *Le Devoir*, meanwhile, remarked rather didactically that "there is more and more confirmation of Vivier's talent but he still needs to learn to keep to the essentials. He needs to learn to separate the wheat from the chaff. But his last work marks clear progress on his 'Lettura di Dante' from last year. The treatment of voices, for example, is interesting but the continual repetition of the same procedures leads to monotony."[37] *Liebesgedichte* has remained one of Vivier's "sleeping" pieces, only rarely revived since its premiere: a deeper acquaintance with its complexities still awaits us.

Meanwhile he had begun his commuting existence to Ottawa, but was simultaneously planning a further prolonged absence from Canada. In early October he applied again for a Bourse de Perfectionnement Pour Artiste from the Canada Council for the year September 1976 to September 1977, his first such application since the unsuccessful one of two years earlier.

This grant will allow me primarily to finish my "Maritimes," a work that I will have begun around April 76. This work, which lasts about an hour, needs various recordings and also a staging. But the main use of my grant will be a personal study trip to India, Burma, Java and Bali. For me the result will be a deeper knowledge of these cultures that are so important for a composer and, finally, a work to be called "Journal d'un voyage en Orient" with all that it contains by way of recordings and probably the writing of a work of analysis.

At this stage his plans included India, Burma, Java, and Bali "and probably Japan." He asked for $7,000 plus $500 "production costs," and $1,000 travel costs. And we note the two new projected works that were in his mind, neither of which would come to fruition in the way he planned. Within a few months he heard that his application had been successful, and he was able to tell the Belgian musicologist Harry Halbreich that he was planning to be in Asia "for a year" beginning in October: "I'm planning lots of composition and certainly a lot of thinking about music and its fundamental forms of expression! I'll probably make a book!"[38]

The news must have cheered him through the winter months, as there were few performances of his music during this year to sustain him. *Chants* was revived at the New Music Concerts series in Toronto; and in the spring of 1976 the Festival Singers of Canada conducted by Elmer Iseler gave the Canadian premieres, in Toronto, of *Jesus Embarme Dich* and *O! Kosmos*, and took them on tour. (They made a good impression: Michael Schulman in the *Globe and Mail* remarked that Vivier's works "offered some rhythmic excitement and extremes of volume . . . plus inventive use of audible aspiration, hisses and speech," while in the same paper John Kraglund commented that *Jesus Erbarme Dich* was the "least familiar and otherwise most memorable of [the choir's] four selections.")[39]

Vivier's personal life during his months in Ottawa is a mystery. He was probably quite lonely, submerging himself in work on his orchestral piece. In March, with the score finished, he jumped at the chance to go see his Cologne friend Walter Zimmermann, who was briefly in Chicago working on his book *Desert Plants: Conversations with 23 American Musicians*, to be published later in the year. But the trip was a fiasco, as he reported to Zimmermann (here translated from his idiosyncratic German) when safely back at 21 rue Stewart.

I traveled from Ottawa to Detroit by bus! 10 hours that took! In Detroit, I've tried to reach you, the phone number was apparently wrong! I looked then for the name "Rosenbaum" in the phone book but there was none!

> I was really very tired and did not know any more what to do! A border guard even came to me and asked me what I was doing there! Showing passport, giving explanations, showing money, and so on! I was completely lost. So I went straight to the airport and flew to Montreal! I was really confused![40]

The reason he could not find "Rosenbaum" in the telephone book was that the friend Zimmermann was visiting in the States was in fact the composer David Rosenboom. As well as showing his enduring loyalty to his European friends, the incident also shows Vivier's spontaneous and disorganized nature, leaving home without a contact address or accurate phone number for his intended destination.

The musicologist Louise Duchesneau was a student at the University of Ottawa at the time. She remembers that Vivier

> would come in every day and practice piano in one of the practice cubicles. He would play the beginning of Chopin's Revolutionary Etude (Op. 10 no. 12) or Mozart's Alla Turca and then break off after a few bars and improvise. The thing we all remember is that we didn't *hear* Claude as much as we *smelled* him. The cubicles had a common ventilation system so that the odors would spread as fast as the sounds of the playing. He never took a bath or showered (maybe he didn't have anything in his room) and he smelled rather "strong." He would also go for lunch or dinner to a restaurant very close by (called El Paso, I think) and eat the fantastic rice pudding they had there. It was in that restaurant that Claude spoke his famous statement about me: "She's cute, that girl, she looks like a boy." I suppose he meant it as a compliment. Of course, we all recognized Claude's laugh at a great distance, very loud and a bit creepy.[41]

Vivier's laugh—a series of loud, rapid staccato bursts—was instantly identifiable. Gilles Tremblay recalls being at a concert in Paris and not knowing Vivier was in the auditorium until he heard the laugh; whatever its exuberance, it was, Tremblay says, a laugh that "was hiding something."[42] His friend Thérèse Desjardins remarks: "It was a fabricated sound . . . he invented that sound, it wasn't natural. But with him it became natural."[43] It is a laugh that expresses nervousness, a clear seeking for attention; but, judging by the surviving recordings, rarely, if ever, does it seem to express joy.

On February 28, 1976, he completed his commission for the National Youth Orchestra of Canada: *Siddhartha*, a twenty-eight minute work for large orchestra divided into eight instrumental groups. He dedicated the piece to his composer friend Michel-Georges Brégent. *Siddhartha* was inspired, in a way that Vivier never made explicit, by the 1922 novel of that name by Hermann Hesse, a novel widely read by the young people of Vivier's generation. (It was turned into an English-language film in 1972, directed by Conrad Rooks; Vivier may have seen the film during his studies in Germany.) Set in ancient India, Hesse's novel tells of the spiritual journey of a young man in search of enlightenment. He passes from asceticism to a more worldly existence, seeking fulfillment in business and love, and then returns to an ascetic life. The book became cult reading among the younger generation in the sixties and seventies, particularly among those questioning the values of capitalist lifestyles.

Vivier's *Siddhartha* embodies a highly unusual conception of the orchestra and was the most ambitious work he had realized to that time. It is therefore all the more tragic that he never heard the piece performed. An article in the Ottawa paper *Le Droit* in the summer of 1977 explained: "Once the work was finished, those responsible invoked the 'difficulty' of the score to justify excluding it from their program."[44] We do not know for sure whether the decision was made by the would-be conductor of the piece, Marius Constant (who had directed the premiere of Vivier's *Quatuor à cordes* in 1968), but it seems likely. In any case, the news must have been devastating (although the causality implied later in the same article—"So Vivier packed his bags and left for the Orient"—is not quite accurate: he had heard of the successful outcome of his grant application before news reached him of the cancellation of *Siddhartha*).

Despite the attention-grabbing opening, with a single pitch (F$\sharp$) bursting into the air like a brilliant firework exploding in the night sky, *Siddhartha* makes relatively little tutti use of its enormous orchestral body, the whole second half of the piece proceeding much of the time in chamber-music combinations with music of surprising intimacy and delicacy. Earlier parts of the piece show greater bravura, with a predilection for sonorous brass and bell outbursts of boldness and confidence. György Ligeti perceptively commented that "With Vivier, we see already the Asian influence in . . . *Siddhartha*, composed before his journey"; and indeed in parts of the piece Vivier configures a kind of western gamelan of metallic percussion (the score asks for eight percussionists), which makes its voice heard clearly amid the strident orchestral sonorities.[45] (By the mid-seventies such melodic, lyrical, quasi-Asian use of percussion was nothing new—it can be found variously from Messiaen's *Turangalîla-Symphonie* [1948] through West Coast American percussion music to Britten's ballet *The Prince of the Pagodas* [1957]).

In his analysis of *Siddhartha* the Canadian composer Jean Lesage has shown how the structural heart of the work is a long melody in seven parts, each part longer than its predecessor, and each introducing at least one new pitch until we reach the total chromatic gamut of twelve notes in the seventh part. The melody is stated at the opening of the work and develops into what Walter Boudreau, who conducted the belated premiere, has called "a fantastic galaxy of ideas and emotions." Technically, this puts us in mind of Stockhausen's formula technique as exemplified in *Mantra* and subsequent works, where a long melody becomes the basis of an extended composition. Indeed, Lesage argues that Stockhausen's influence can be felt at every level of *Siddhartha*, both as regards the large-scale plan of the work and the note-to-note details, such as a predilection for Fibonacci-series proportions, and the use of a "chromatic scale" of tempo relationships.[46] He also suggests that the use of this melody is the basis of the connection with Hesse's novel:

> In Hesse's novel, the hero evolves through various human encounters and existential experiences. In Vivier's score, a single monody is transformed during various cycles of expansion and contraction of its intervals. The work rests entirely on the projection in time and space of a single evolving melody and its interaction with the episodic satellite melodies, in the image of the principal character who is transformed, towards enlightenment, through a series of ephemeral encounters with the secondary characters of the novel.[47]

Lesage also speculates that Vivier may have wanted to draw attention, in a work inspired by a novel set in India, to an analogy between Stockhausen-inspired formula melody and the nature of the raga of Indian music. A raga is neither a simple scale or mode nor a melody, but somewhere in between, having a character or a flavor that differentiates it from a simple linear sequence of pitches, and yet being not as precisely elaborated or as fixed as a melody. Much the same can be said of the formula melody of *Siddhartha*. Moreover, a further Indian analogy can be drawn in the persistence of the single pitch F♯ of the opening, doubled at the octave and used as accompaniment to the melodic material, having a function not unlike that of the drone maintained by the tambura in a performance of an Indian raga. (Vivier had composed, and then withdrawn, an even more explicitly Indian-style drone in the original version of *Pour Guitare* written a few months earlier.) However closely these speculations may or may not coincide with Vivier's own thought processes, it is clear that *Siddhartha* as a whole represents a considerable widening of the expressive nature of his musical language, in several directions at once: toward a greater clarity and "simplicity" ("simplicity" of the kind being explored independently by several of his Cologne colleagues, with whose music Vivier was by now rather out of touch); toward digesting and assimilating Stockhausen's thought, and being able to move beyond it; and toward what we might describe as a broadening of his musical consciousness away from the stimulating but also claustrophobic world of Cologne-based new music. *Siddhartha* shows Vivier's music at a time of momentous change.

✳ ✳ ✳

His contract at the University of Ottawa at an end, Vivier returned to Montreal in the spring, with thoughts of his forthcoming Asian adventure never far from his mind. Between then and his departure in September he revised one old work and completed two new ones. He finished a new score of *Prolifération* in Montreal on April 24, probably in connection with the planned performance at the Centre Culturel Canadien in Paris that autumn (in a program of "Musique pour ondes Martenot" put together by Tristan Murail). The two new works were *Learning*, for four violins, a percussionist playing claves and Balinese gong, and tape, the manuscript dated August 11, 1976; and incidental music for a production of Büchner's play *Woyzeck* at the National Arts Center in Ottawa, set to open that October. While the latter is a merely a curiosity item in Vivier's catalog, *Learning* is one of his finest works, and shows him courageously delving deeper into the new terrain that *Siddhartha* had opened up.

Described by Vivier as "l'apprentissage de la mélodie" (learning melody), and originally subtitled "Ceremony of the Beginning," *Learning* is one of his most haunting and individual creations. It is dedicated to the Montreal-based violinist Martin Foster, whom Vivier had known from his time in Gilles Tremblay's class. We have no record of a public performance of the piece in Vivier's lifetime, though from a study of the manuscript it seems that the piece was at least tried through not long after it was written, as there are fingerings and various other performance indications (some in Vivier's hand) scribbled on the pages.[48] Vivier did not simply forget about *Learning*; five years after composing it he recycled parts of the work into *Et je reverrai cette ville étrange*, for the Toronto ensemble Array. This is the only instance of this type of reworking in his whole career, indicating his continuing faith in the music. *Learning* is a sequence of fifteen melodies, the beginnings of each of which are signaled by the percussionist by a tap on the claves; his gong strokes indicate the beginnings of the five unequal sections into which the fifteen melodies are grouped. These sections comprise one, five, two, four, and three melodies respectively. Also notated in the score are the occasional movements of the players onstage, and their desired facial expression ("neutral, even impassive"). The whole piece has the feeling of a strange ritual being enacted for an unknown purpose, in which the percussionist appears to be guiding the violinists in their study of melody.

The piece begins in darkness with the prerecorded sound of a door opening. The percussionist enters, wearing wooden shoes, and walks to the center of the stage where he sounds a Balinese gong, cueing a fade-up of lights ("blue dominant plus a bit of red," says the score); he then sounds the claves, indicating that the first melody may begin. The violinists, divided into pairs on either side of the hall, play while walking to the stage. This first, long melody is made entirely from five notes, C, D♭, E♭, F, G♭, and is the most tonal (or, more accurately, modal) music Vivier had so far written, functioning mostly as though in D-flat major. At the beginning the musicians play a phrase in parallel thirds, which returns, ritornello-like, throughout the melody; between its appearances they play melodic lines in unison, adding embellishments at times. This is strikingly original music, highly memorable, devoid of harmony or counterpoint in the usual sense, and monochrome (although richly so) as we hear only the timbre of the four violins with no special effects or extended techniques. As the piece proceeds and one melody follows another, the players are asked sometimes to depart from the notated line (which is not usually quite as straightforwardly tonal as the opening melody) and produce variations or embellishments on what they have just played. Occasionally, Vivier even asks particular players to improvise a transition passage that gradually transforms what they have been playing into a new figure heard later on in the melody. For the violinists, the whole thirty-minute piece is a demanding and exhausting "lesson." If the idea of structuring a whole work around a sequence of melodies perhaps owes something to the example of Stockhausen's *Tierkreis* (1975), a sequence of melodies for each of the twelve signs of the zodiac, *Learning* is a major work that could be by no other composer than Vivier.

Georg Büchner's play *Woyzeck* is one of the most frequently performed works of German theater. Begun in 1836 and left unfinished at the time of the author's early death the following year, it was not seen in public until 1913 in Munich and was almost immediately turned into an opera by Alban Berg, first performed in 1925. A letter to Vivier dated July 13, 1976, from Jean Herbiet, artistic director of the Théâtre Français of the National Arts Center in Ottawa, acknowledges his willingness to commission incidental music for the play for their 1976–77 season. The guarantee was of twenty-four evening performances and four matinées, opening on Monday October 4 and continuing to the end of the month.[49] They promised him a complete text of the play in English, French, and German by August 15. Vivier's income statement for that year shows $2,320 received from the National Arts Center, as well as expenses for "studio costs" of $610. The novelty of the production was that it was to be for marionnettes. It was directed by the German-born director and puppeteer Felix Mirbt, who made several such stagings of classic plays at the National Arts Center in those years: the presentation involved visible "readers" who spoke the voices for the characters, while clearly visible puppeteers ("manipulators") controlled puppets representing the characters.[50] Years later, Mirbt recalled that Vivier made the music for the production in the electronic studios at McGill University.[51]

The incidental music for *Woyzeck* is the last pure tape music in Vivier's catalog. The tape that survives in the Vivier Achives, however, is very odd, consisting as it does of a forty-second fragment of percussive music—a sound-world close to the Varèse of *Ionisation*, in which we hear a militaristic snare drum, bass drum, timpani, piano, a range of differently tuned tom-toms, gong, and cymbal, the music prefaced and concluded by a recording of a door opening and closing (the same gesture begins and ends *Learning*). On the tape this forty-second percussive fragment appears, identically, twenty-four times in succession, with the thirteenth appearance, uniquely, being an abbreviated version of only twenty seconds; then, near the end, we have another forty-second snatch, this time of Thomas Arne's *Rule, Britannia!* played by a military band, before a final return of the percussive fragment. Today we have, of course, no sure way of knowing how this tape was used in the performances. Did Vivier really compose only forty seconds of music for the production? He himself was not able to attend the October performances in Ottawa, as by then he had begun his new adventure: the trip to Asia.

# CHAPTER SIX

# " A  J O U R N E Y
# I N T O   T H E   D E P T H S
# O F   M Y S E L F "

## 1 9 7 6 – 7 7

In 1981 Vivier told an interviewer: "My whole relationship with Asian music was one in which I avoided all possible preconceptions. I didn't want to do anything about it before going there. I just wanted to put myself there, like a child, and learn it out of nothingness."[1] While this is probably a fair reflection of his state of mind as he began his journey in September 1976, preconceptions could not be entirely avoided. Writing to Harry Halbreich that March, he had commented that one of his intentions when there, besides composing, was "a lot of thinking about music and its fundamental forms of expression." This perhaps reflects his feeling—a common idea in the minds of western intellectuals—that Asian music had remained closer to these "fundamental forms of expression" than had contemporary European music, a sense that the musicologist Curt Sachs had captured in the title of his 1962 book *The Wellsprings of Music*. In that sense, right from the outset, Vivier's trip was a sort of pilgrimage, a wish for musical—and, we may safely assume, personal—refreshment and renewal.

In making a journey such as this he was following in the footsteps of several close friends and mentors. In the previous decade, Stockhausen had become something of a world traveler. He wrote and spoke extensively about his recent experiences, notably in Japan, where his music was featured prominently at the 1970 World Fair in Osaka. Gilles Tremblay had made a visit to Bali, Java, and Korea in 1972, where he had wanted to experience firsthand "the relation of the sacred and art"; and his Montreal composer colleagues John Rea and José Evangelista had recently returned from Bali, brimful of enthusiasm for its music and culture.[2] This is worth remembering given the myth that has arisen in some of the writing on Vivier: that his travels in Asia in the autumn of 1976 somehow mark him out as a great composer-traveler, a musical Marco Polo restlessly moving onward in search of new experience and inspiration—that, in short, as one recent article puts it, his was "a life dictated by travel."[3]

Even a casual examination of the facts dispels this myth. To begin with, he terminated what was supposed to have been a yearlong adventure after only about five months, explaining in his report to the Canada Council that by that point he was "nervously and physically" exhausted, and felt the need to digest his experiences from the perspective of a western environment. Second, he never attempted another such trip (in the six years that remained to him), neither in the form of a return visit to the places he had seen during those months nor in terms of striking out to new lands. If the phenomenon of mass tourism can be said to have already been in full swing by the 1970s, then Vivier was simply someone who showed no interest in it. Compared to the experiences that many young people of the next generation have accumulated by the age of twenty-eight, the idea of Vivier-as-traveler is a nonstarter. The truth of the matter is simple: by now he lived the life of a composer first and foremost, and every other pursuit was entirely secondary. The needs of his music dictated how he shaped his life. In this case, the lessons he learned and experiences he absorbed during his months in the east profoundly affected his musical outlook from that point onward.

In late July he had received a check from the Canada Council that gave him $2,800 as the first half of his grant, expenses of $500, and travel costs of $1,894. This was a quite healthy sum, and on this basis he managed to visit Japan, Singapore, Bali, Java, Thailand, Iran, and Egypt in the months between September 1976 and January 1977. While abroad he purchased two notebooks in which he wrote down things of importance during his travels. Neither notebook is remotely full, and many blank pages remain in both. The first is a small, hardback, Chinese-made notebook with a black cover and red binding, on the first pages of which Vivier has noted: "Journal d'un voyage en Asie. / already begun. / this journal contains musical problems which I will try to solve." The second notebook is slightly larger; Vivier has stuck a label onto its floral cover, saying simply "journal d'un voyage en Asie." (This description, Vivier acknowledged, was an allusion to Hermann Hesse's 1932 novel *Die Morgenlandfahrt*, especially in its French translation, *Le Voyage en Orient*.)[4] Leafing through the notebooks, which are still extant among the papers of his archive, we see that these are indeed notebooks rather than journals; there is little in the way of diary material or self-reflection in them, but instead many musical notations, attempts to learn the various languages he encountered (particularly Indonesian), addresses and phone numbers, brief descriptions of his musical and cultural experiences and, toward the end of the second notebook, a plan (in words) for a new composition inspired by his Asian journey. He seems to have kept the two notebooks concurrently; and while they contain far less material than the Vivier scholar might hope, they nonetheless offer some insight into his thoughts during these months.

His first port of call was Japan. In Tokyo on September 20 he wrote a text on his thoughts and experiences there, which was published in *Musicanada*.[5] It presents his impressions of Kabuki theater, its theatrical concepts, the roles of the performers and the nature of the music.[6] But rather quickly, after only a few paragraphs, it becomes philosophical:

> The basic problem that presents itself is the following: here I am with my culture and my language in a land where the culture and language are totally different! To understand the word-to-word, literal meaning of these musics and these ceremonies, I have to in a way become Japanese myself, but is this finally so interesting? It seems to me it's much more interesting to immerse myself in this culture, this art of living and only understand the spirit.

Already, after a matter of days in a new culture, Vivier was feeling the handicap imposed by not knowing the language, a situation that he had not previously experienced (in Utrecht he had quickly picked up some Dutch and in Cologne some Turkish, so he could speak a little to his Turkish neighbours). It is also amusing to see how his attempts at objective, ethnomusicological reporting (of Kabuki, or of Bunraku, the traditional Japanese puppet theater, a brief discussion of which concludes the text) quickly dissolves into meditations on his own work. In tandem with this little article, the very first page of his notebooks identifies five immediate areas of importance derived from his exposure to Japanese arts, which are scribbled down as though a note to himself on things to consider in his own work: "Express the essential"; "Different linguistic articulations"; "homophony of gesture-voice, heterophony of gesture-voice, counterpoint of gesture-voice"; "the ceremony"; "proportions." The notebook goes on to reflect on the matter of perception, of which he distinguishes five kinds: "A) direct perception (moments) / B) perception of my imagination / C) perception of what I believe it to be / (Prior experiences and an evolution in perception) / D) global perception / E) abstraction from all context (relations established by myself)." While these thoughts seem prompted by his encounter with different forms of Japanese theater, and are reflections on how he as an outsider experiences it, as distinct from how a Japanese observer might, Vivier again seems to reach for generalities based on his experience. Embedded in this passage is an attempt to separate out different forms of perception: direct, immediate, sensory impressions (A, and perhaps E); perception mediated by thought and the operation of the rational intellect (C, and perhaps D); and a kind of creative perception, the sort that immediately transforms what it sees into material for art (B).

From Japan he proceeded via Hong Kong to Singapore, where he noted that "As with all towns in Asia the west has had a big influence on this town!" The next page of his notebook has the simple inscription "Bells: joy. ecstasy." From there the next stop was Indonesia.

We do not know whether Vivier expected in advance that Bali would be the defining encounter of his Asian journey—"I was told a great deal, but you really have to live there to really see and understand," he noted— but it made by far the deepest impression.[7] "What I found in Asia I found in Bali," he told an interviewer, "a poetry of enormous sadness, the sadness that life and death can bring to someone."[8] From the time of his arrival he was plunged into an island filled with gods, demons, and sorcerers, with thatched tents, pavilions, temples, and palaces, with aromatic smells and colorful sarongs, and with the sound of rituals and ceremonies and music being played somewhere from morning to night.

He spent one week in Yogyakarta, where he began learning Indonesian; he later claimed that within a month he could speak the language quite well.[9] He would walk around with a dictionary, looking up the words for things as needed. He then proceeded to Bali, where he remained for the best part of three months. In Denpasar, the capital city in the south of the island, he found a cheap hotel not intended for tourists but rather for locals (or for Javanese), and stayed there for the remainder of his time. He immediately set about studying Balinese music in the traditional manner: by learning to play it. He had accumulated the names of a number of teachers, but once in Denpasar he quickly gravitated toward KOKAR (the Conservatory for Traditional Performing Arts), the main music school there, and inquired about lessons. Soon he found himself studying *gangsa*, a metallophone that is one of the main melody instruments in the Balinese gamelan, as well as playing *kempli*—a small kettle gong played with a cord-wrapped mallet that plays a steady beat, keeping the time—with one particular gamelan that accompanied "a ceremony of the consecration of a house" for a solid hour. Perhaps inspired by this experience, the second of his notebooks opens with "BALI. The concept of pulsation. Rhythm is a series of balances or imbalances around an axis."[10] As in Japan, Vivier was concerned to engage with Balinese culture as a whole rather than simply extrapolating the music from its larger context. He attended several trance ceremonies, fascinated by the power of the gamelan to mark stages in the long event, and the *arja*, the dance dramas that could run all night. On the other hand he disliked the *kecak* performances mounted for tourists, which were invariably shorter and more palatable than the true Balinese versions, and made a point of avoiding them. More so than in Japan, he was concerned to try to write down in musical notation, as well as to express in words, various Balinese musical techniques, especially rhythmic ones. He put together a short article that was published in *Musicanada* in February 1977, under the title "Letter from Bali: Island of Dreams for Composers?" There, after a short introductory section in which he proudly reports his acquisition of a Balinese name—"Nyoman Kenyung" (the third born laughing)—he goes on to offer "some technical remarks on Balinese music," under three headings: "The concept of pulsation" (the quotation about rhythm taken from his notebook, cited above); what he calls "Tridimensional concept (left-right-change)," itself not a concept that is familiar to a Balinese musician, but refers to the alternation of left and right hands in playing rhythmic patterns in the music; and "the concept of displaced 'time,'" his way of describing the interlocking rhythms of Balinese music (so that a musician who would seem, from a western perspective, to be playing on the offbeat all the time is, according to Vivier, playing "not a cross-rhythm but [a rhythm] with time displaced to the right"). His article ends with some thoughts on Western cultural dominance:

> Here in Den Pasar [*sic*] western pop music or Mantovani is gradually replacing Balinese music. They offer a sort of musical soup in hotel lobbies or in shows for tourists.
>
> Culturally, humanity is presently living through an extremely important transitional period. A process is in motion which slowly but surely is bringing together the different cultures of the world to find one terrestrial culture. It seems that this movement is headed more towards an impoverishment than an enrichment. More and more the non-western cultures are literally drowned by western culture without any exchange of culture which would have been desirable for human thought.

What we want is the conscious man, who carries within him all the
traditions that the earth has brought us. We want a human being who
by his/her uniqueness can truly reunify the rest of humanity. The future of music cannot be seen without the essential contribution of other
cultures. The human spirit can only be cosmic when implementing the
whole of its cultural heritage.[11]

These last are words with which Stockhausen may well have concurred, but
by now there is a change: Vivier is capable of speaking unapologetically for
himself, no longer as the starstruck student but as a great-composer-in-
the-making, drawing together the various ideas necessary to form his art.

Vivier also profited from a sense of reciprocation with the Indonesian
musicians he befriended. Telling them that when he composed he felt as
if he had entered a trance, they understood him completely and assured
him this was very similar to how they felt playing music. A sense of reci-
procity also showed in the fact that he was not asked to pay for his lessons,
but rather to give something in return. Among other things he played his
teacher a cassette of Mozart's Requiem, which the teacher did not much
like, and a cassette of the premiere of Liebesgedichte, which, to Vivier's
own surprise, he did—Vivier felt he grasped its changing moods very
sensitively.[12]

For all the excitement of the discoveries he was making in Bali, and
the many charms of the island and its people, he would occasionally miss
home. Gilles Tremblay recalls once receiving a phone call in the middle of
the night: "It was Claude calling from Denpasar: 'I heard there is a revolution!' (It was the time of the election, the first time the Parti Québécois
was elected to form the government of Quebec.) I said, Claude, it was very
democratic, there were elections, there's no fighting in the streets! He
seemed a little disappointed."[13]

On December 26 Vivier wrote a second, shorter letter from Bali, on
pink airmail paper, possibly also intending it for Musicanada, but if so it
was not published there. There may be good reason as the letter, written
toward the end of his stay (it begins "I will soon have to leave this island")
shows him openly expressing his uncertainty about what he intends to do
with the knowledge he has acquired—the feeling, expressed by many artists before him, of being temporarily overwhelmed by the immensity of
the culture around him.[14] The letter ends: "as in the story where the master
asks the pupil what he has learned and the pupil repeats shyly by heart
what the master said, upon which the master responds by giving him a slap
and asks the pupil to come back when he understands, I don't want to get
a slap and I certainly don't want to write Balinese music!"[15]

His departure from Bali was marked by two incidents that touched him deeply and brought him again a sense of the love he had felt there: "how can one not speak of love when a friend, by way of farewell, dances for me, when an old woman offers me a piece of fruit for my journey to Java because for her the furthest you can go from Bali is Java!"[16] In the last of his writings about Asia for *Musicanada*, written in January 1977 and published in shortened form in their May issue under the title "Return from Bali," he describes his time on the island as "a lesson in love, in tenderness, in poetry, and in respect for life."[17] His love for Bali and for the kindness and tenderness shown him by the Balinese people is apparent throughout his text. He deplores the exploitation of the Balinese by Western domination. He writes about the music, specifically the timbre, form ("what interested me most in Balinese music is its form"), the technique of *kotekan* (the fast rhythmic interlocking of parts), the vertical and horizontal aspects of the music, and the role of the individual instrumental voices in the whole. He is also impressed by the integration of art and music making with everyday life: "Ultimately, the most important thing is life, a life that is full and happy, the deep feeling that each instant is a marvelous discovery, the sense of dispassionate listening and seeing."

From Bali he proceeded, via Java, to Thailand. From this point onward his journey becomes more obscure and there are fewer traces of his activities. Of Thailand the notebooks record, enigmatically:

Thailand.
1 melody
2 octaves and intervals in octaves!
3 . . . (tremolo)! Important.

On a curriculum vitae submitted to Radio-Canada several years later, the section outlining his studies concludes with mention of "Studies in Bali and in Chiang Mai (Thailand)," so he seems to have made some serious attempt to study Thai music.[18] The notebooks record the name of the "Dramatic School of Arts, Chiang Mai," but in truth we have simply no idea where or what Vivier studied. In any case he was not there for long, probably at most a fortnight.

Thereafter, the feelings of nervous exhaustion he described to the Canada Council seem to have increased. He abandoned his plans to go to Burma and India "for the simple reason that it seemed to me impossible to learn yet another language and to mix with people as I did in Bali and to some extent in Thailand."[19] He went on instead to Iran, "where all I did was to follow blind singers in the market place in Shiraz"; some months later, these blind singers would become the codedicatees of his virtuoso piano piece *Shiraz*.

The final part of his journey was to Egypt. His intention, he wrote, was "to have contact there with Arab culture, which I achieved through plays and by performances of Arab music in the streets and in certain theaters (Academy of Arab music in Cairo)." However, he continues,

> I must confess that by this point I was very tired, nervously and physically, and that it had become very painful to continue to stay in another foreign country without falling into tourism. I decided therefore to end my journey, to spend some time in Paris to get back into composition and afterwards to go to Cologne to review everything again with Stockhausen and my composer friends. It was very important for me to have some time with Stockhausen to look over everything again and to clarify my ideas on the situation.[20]

There is no doubt that Vivier's Asian journey marked him and his music profoundly. Nor is there any doubt that the nearly three months he spent in Bali were the most fruitful and happy part of the journey. Passing through Cologne on his way back to Canada he recorded a two-hour conversation with his friend Kevin Volans that, after the briefest of introductions, is entirely devoted to his memories of, and feelings about, Bali; the other lands he visited, with the exception of Japan, do not even get a mention. Harder, though, is to state the exact nature of the influence of those experiences on his life and music.

His Canadian friends had their own theories. Walter Boudreau, speaking many years later, felt that "Claude reached a certain balance in Bali, away from the Catholic Jesus-Christ-and-the-Devil split in his personality. For Claude, sexual pleasure was still uncomfortably linked to sin, very Catholic, very Jekyll and Hyde—in the east Claude could live out his spirituality in a better way. Claude sexually was like an alcoholic, with these endless cycles of indulgence and avoidance. And he was lucky he was able to travel so easily; no family, no real job, no real apartment."[21] José Evangelista, recalling Vivier's claim that his Balinese experiences had changed him completely, regrets that when he came back to Montreal there was no functioning Balinese gamelan ensemble in the city for him to join. Evangelista founded the gamelan group at the University of Montreal only several years after Vivier's death; one of the distinguished teachers they brought to Montreal, I Nyoman Astita, had known Vivier in Bali.)[22]

The specific influence of Balinese music on certain of Vivier's compositions will be discussed in due course. But we should not forget that the true transformative power of such an experience need not be all that tangible or rational. In one of the notebooks he kept in Asia, after some sketches for the choral work that was intermittently on his mind during his travels (and, in rather different form, would emerge as *Journal*), he suddenly changes his train of thought: "but this is still not the solution—I have to find a solution that is both global and subtle! until now the center of my music has been a melody—<u>a harmony</u>—a series of proportions—this now <u>has to be something different!</u> a subtle body. a system of laws lending my music great plasticity—a movement and a life not so far attained." The two compositions that grew most directly from his experiences both came quickly in the months ahead: *Pulau Dewata*, for variable ensemble, its title meaning "Isle of the Gods," the Indonesian name for Bali; and the piano piece *Shiraz*. He did later write a piece about Japan, but an ancient Japan: *Zipangu*. Other Vivier works whose titles evoke similarly distant places are figments of his imagination. We have no evidence of his having visited Bukhara or Samarkand, which are in Uzbekistan, and, of course, he was nowhere near Paramaribo, capital of Surinam in South America, whose name he may have misspelled in the title of *Paramirabo*.

Something of Vivier's own immediate response to his Asian experience is documented in the conversation he recorded with Kevin Volans in Cologne shortly after his return. Asked by Volans about his motivations for the trip, why he had wanted to go to Bali at all, Vivier replied: "I felt drawn to it; but perhaps life just drew me to Bali.... I wanted to forget completely who I was, to break out from my Judeo-Christian culture. In Bali that really happened." He even enjoyed the taboos, he says, for example, not being allowed to touch a woman; back in Europe he found it at first strange to be kissed by female friends. Probed further, Vivier commented:

> I wanted a kind of freedom from my own history—it's kind of hard to explain—to find back the original of a lot of things, a sort of purity... I don't think [Bali] changed my concept of music, I think it changed my whole personality. I have now a much nicer relationship with my own childhood.... I discovered I just love my own culture, western culture, classical or even jazz—it's much more human than anything I heard in Bali.

Before he set out for Bali, he says, "it was very important for me to be played and to have concerts here and there," but thanks to his journey "I'm very free of that; I don't really care. The only thing I care about is to do *something* musically." A certain type of careerism had been punctured, had been shown to be hollow, by his Balinese experience. In fact, his journey provided a sort of confirmation that it was OK to be himself.

> All my fucking music is always the same thing—I just want to get this purity of expression, where on the one hand you have technique, and on the other hand this total purity and total freedom which go together and which drives your whole personality to a higher level, your own music and your own experience. Because finally my own experience is the experience of other people. My own childhood, or my own "me," belongs to any type of culture; my own fears, fear of the night, or fear of the big beasts. This need, this very need of purity, this need of sun and color and childhood-like things, it's also part of a human being. Before, I was a little afraid of myself; but funnily, I discovered that even in Bali I was so much myself, even if I was speaking Balinese.

It was a kind of reconciliation with himself and with who he was. He had ended his second *Musicanada* piece on Bali with what he called, tongue in cheek, "a pertinent remark," but one that is no less true for having an air of cliché: "I realize, obviously," he wrote, "that this journey finally is only a journey into the depths of myself."[23] From now on he could be more confident about showing the depths of himself, proudly, to the world.

# CHAPTER SEVEN

# " S U B T L E   M U S I C S   /
# F I L L I N G   M Y   S O U L "

## ¹ 9 7 7 ⁻ 7 9

E xactly when Vivier returned to Montreal after his journey to Asia is unclear. There are two conflicting pieces of evidence. One is his let-ter to the Canada Council, already cited, date-stamped March 10, 1977, in which he writes: "I've just arrived in Montreal to realize the second part of my project 'journal d'un voyage en Orient.'" This suggests an arrival date perhaps around the beginning of the month, allowing for a few days to collect his thoughts and to write to them (which he may have felt was an urgent task). The second is the manuscript of a new composition, the organ piece *Les Communiantes*, the date of which poses a conundrum of the sort that biographers love, but is of very little interest to anyone else.

The eleven-page neat copy of *Les Communiantes* is signed "Montréal le 22 janv 77." But measured against all the other documentary sources this date seems odd, indeed improbable. We know Vivier was still in Bali on December 26, 1976, the date of the letter that begins "I will soon have to leave this island"; leaving there a few days later he spent some time in Java, Thailand, then Iran and Egypt, before stopping off for visits in both Paris and Cologne on his way home. The neat copy of the organ piece is unlikely to have been produced during his travels, and could not sim-ply have been dashed off in a day or two immediately upon his return, jet-lagged and exhausted. It must have been the result of many days of work, even at Vivier's relatively swift rate of productivity. The timescale of all these events does not seem to add up. It is not as though the piece had to be written quickly for a particular opportunity—the premiere was not until March 5, 1978, more than a year later, by Christopher Jackson in Montreal's Église de l'Immaculée-Conception. It begins to seem as though the date on the manuscript is incorrect. If so, it would not be the first Vivier manuscript to bear a phantom date.[1] Jackson recalls that Vivier, having been commissioned through the Société des Concerts d'orgue de Montréal series, wanted to do "something Balinese" with the commission; but some parts of his first draft were not playable and a revised version followed. This, Jackson, thinks, might account for the long delay between the ostensible completion date and the premiere.[2] Unless the date as written is simply wrong: should "le 22 janv 77" be "le 22 janv 78?" It is not uncommon to make such slips when writing the date in the early weeks of a new year.

The time Vivier spent in Paris and Cologne early in the late winter or early spring of 1977 was evidently important in helping him to make sense of his Balinese experiences in the context of those two important musical worlds, and also to help him, some time after his student years, to connect those worlds with his new life in Montreal. Of his Paris sojourn we know only that he met briefly with Paul Méfano. We would love to know whether he looked up his friend Gérard Grisey, then at work on his orchestral piece *Modulations*, the fourth piece in the cycle later titled *Les Espaces Acoustiques*, one of the defining statements of the new aesthetic that Hughes Dufourt, a little later, would call *la musique spectrale*.[3] In Cologne Vivier met with various composer friends, spoke with Stockhausen about his travels in Asia, and recorded a long interview with Kevin Volans about his Balinese experiences.

Much had changed in the European new music scene in the short time since Vivier left Germany in the summer of 1974. The musicologist Paul Griffiths has expressed the complexity of the situation in his remark that "just as the single arrow of progress faltered in the 1960s, so [in the mid-1970s] the multifarious subsequent arrows of innovation or reverse began to waver."[4] What we can observe clearly in retrospect, at a time when the number of professional composers working around the world began to increase sharply, is nothing less than the progressive disintegration of the European avant-garde.

In 1977, both in Paris and Cologne, new things were in the air. In Paris, IRCAM, the shiny new music research institute directed by Pierre Boulez and situated next to the brand-new Centre Pompidou, was just about to open its doors, flying the flag for the "official" avant-garde. Simultaneously, young ensembles like L'Itinéraire, founded by Michaël Lévinas, Tristan Murail, Hugues Dufourt, and Roger Tessier, provided an alternative to Boulez's dominance of the city's new music life. In Germany, too, it had been apparent for some years that the established avant-garde was in a rut. We have seen how this had been a complaint at Darmstadt as early as the late sixties, but by now it had become a foreground issue. The backlash against the forty-something generation—not only Boulez (who by this time was composing relatively little new music), but also Stockhausen (who had not been invited to Darmstadt the previous summer, 1976), Ligeti, Nono, and the recent work of Cage—was based on a number of factors. First was the general sense that there was an elitism about the modernist "clique," who were exclusionary and devoted to white, male, bourgeois values. Also, there was a feeling that the interwar generation was not sufficiently concerned with political action; and that their music, by valuing sonic complexity, rational calculation, and performative difficulty, was excluding large numbers of musically curious listeners (and amateur performers) who could not possibly hope to fathom its language.

By the time of Vivier's brief visit to Cologne several new directions were emerging in German music. "When Claude visited us back in Köln he was sort of amused at what we were doing," Kevin Volans recalls.[5] The most prevalent of those beginning to gain attention, though somewhat outside Vivier's own immediate circle of composer friends, was the "New Romantic" tendency (sometimes called the "New Subjectivity"). This was exemplified by the music of Vivier's student colleague Wolfgang Rihm, which combined an Expressionist sensibility close to Mahler and Schoenberg with contemporary techniques (eschewing the most avant-garde), and by that of composers such as Hans-Jürgen von Bose, Detlev Müller-Siemens and Hans-Christian von Dadelsen. Another tendency, more appealing to Vivier, was that named by his friend Walter Zimmermann the "New Simplicity," initially with reference to the "'naïve' pieces of Cage" from around 1950 and Cage's fondness for Satie, music that Zimmermann had proposed as the basis of a festival to be organized that year by WDR.[6] Zimmermann, who was essentially an autodidact compositionally but who had attended lectures by both Stockhausen and Kagel, held an aesthetic position that had strong affinities with American contemporary arts, including the work of Gertrude Stein and John Cage. Richard Toop has argued that the "extreme reduction of means, and cool, unemotional objectivity" in Zimmermann's music "is, at one level, a symbolic purging of European thinking and tradition"—not least, one might add, of the whole German avant-garde as personified by Stockhausen.[7] In 1975

Zimmermann had produced a substantial piano work, *Beginner's Mind*, that scandalized certain areas of the German new music establishment (which, in Kevin Volans's words, accused it of "'musical devolution' with hints of Third-Reich-style anti-intellectualism"[8]) and, in its quiet way, announced the beginning of a new direction in German composition, soon to be enfolded under the name the "New Simplicity." Cologne colleagues like Volans or Clarence Barlow were broadly sympathetic to Zimmermann's position. Barlow had been "out of the whole serial thing" since 1972, as can be heard in early works like *Textmusik* (1971) or . . . *until* . . . (1972), that respond to American minimalism—which Stockhausen, by and large, abhorred—as well as offering the beginnings of a quite individual approach to algorithmic composition. Volans had arrived in Cologne in the summer of 1973 with his mind already full of heterodox ideas. He strongly sympathized with tendencies present in Zimmermann's music and came in time to move away from Stockhausen who, he has said, "gave us all this feeling of serial guilt."[9] At that time, of course, these composers had not the clarity of perspective available to us now: Barlow, returning to Cologne in the spring of 1975 after eighteen months in India, recalls that "when I first saw Walter's music at that time I didn't quite grasp what he was onto," although in time he came to understand it well. In this context, the music that these composers remembered of Vivier himself from his Cologne days—works like *Chants* or *Désintégration*—seemed light-years away from their current concerns, and still under Stockhausen's long shadow. As Barlow puts it, "Claude's was music which frightened me off because of all the vibrato-ing sopranos."[10] But looking at their newest scores early in 1977 Vivier would have noted tendencies in common with his own most recent work (*Learning*, and to some extent *Siddhartha*, neither of which had yet been performed). This perhaps encouraged him in the thought that he and his closest European colleagues were beginning to move in curiously congruent paths.

Following his return to Montreal Vivier found an apartment at 5352 avenue du Parc, a long north–south street in an up-market area of central Montreal near the Parc du Mont Royal, the city's largest green space. Not long thereafter he moved a few doors down the street to an even better apartment, 5304 avenue du Parc #35, in a redbrick complex set off from the street by a small courtyard; this would remain his home for the next four years. Avenue du Parc had been an elegant residential street earlier in the century, but by the late 1970s it had lost some of these qualities and had become a busy commercial thoroughfare. It was also an important Greek area, with many Greek-owned restaurants, bars, and laundries. Vivier soon became a regular at Bar-Salon Skala, a few minutes' walk away on the other side of the street near the intersection with boulevard Saint-Joseph, where he would often go to eat, or to drink beer at the end of the evening.

Soon after his return he attended a concert of the SMCQ. There he encountered the critic Claude Gingras, who reported their conversation in *La Presse* on March 15:

> Encountered at the latest concert of the SMCQ: Claude Vivier. I don't much like his music, I wrote as much, he didn't much like what I wrote, he sent me some letters (which by the way we published), etc. But there's no room to hate each other for this (for so little!). We chatted for a while. Vivier has come back from a stay of six months in Asia: Bali (three months), Japan, Thailand, made possible thanks to a grant from the Canada Council. Above all it was Bali that made an impression on him. Bali, that is to say, above all, music: "The energy, the concentration that people achieve, the speed . . . all that making a totality," says Vivier, who tells of having learned the language and having learned to play the instruments and even of having taken part, as a musician, in the ceremonies. "But I don't want to talk about it, but to work. In Bali, they explain a little how it's done, their music, but they don't talk much about it, like we do here: they play." Presently Vivier is working on a piece for mixed choir and four vocal soloists with accompaniment of percussion, particularly metal; Balinese, Javanese and Thai gongs, which he has brought back with him.

The gongs and other instruments he had shipped back from Indonesia (not as numerous in quantity as Gingras perhaps implies) were important to the new work that had been on his mind during his travels, and that he now set about putting on paper. The working title had been "Journal d'un voyage en Orient," and he had described it to the Canada Council as "a work for choir, 2 pianos and percussion, which will be a vision of the poetic dimension of my journey and a long meditation on contemporary art."[11] In May the work was finished in rough copy, and was titled simply *Journal*. It called for four vocal soloists, choir, and one percussionist. With a performance time of forty-five minutes it was the longest work he had so far composed. He completed a neat copy of the score in November.

The concept of *Journal* seems to have changed fundamentally from Vivier's initial ideas to its finished form, and we are able to trace this change to some extent through the sources that have survived for the work. The idea of a large-scale choral piece that would be a sort of musical travelogue of his Asian adventure had been on his mind months before the journey itself began. The notebooks he kept in Bali are full of verbal sketches for the work, and at one point he tells himself: "Really think in terms of my journey! episodes, a sort of book." His compositional thinking, to judge by the notebooks, was largely concerned with basic principles: he jots down reminders of the necessity to create continuity and discontinuity in the music, and has the idea to juxtapose "active" and "passive" types of music, as well as to contrast solo and group textures, homophony and counterpoint. "Perhaps 2 interleaved plans," he writes: "I. Plan counterpoint in 4 voices / II. Plan of moments." He goes on to write down several types of these Stockhausen-like "moments": "I. concentration on 1 sound—Japan—interval—1 note / II. expressive moment (poetic) . . . Singapore . . . aleatoric writing / III. violent moment . . . masses of sounds. / IV. melody / a very long melody, simple at first sight but complex in its structure and its various aspects." The notebooks also contain a reminder to himself not to forget "the recordings of sirens in Cologne—see on the shoreline if I can find shells."[12]

But in the process of writing the music, the specific connections with his travels (as with the references above to Japan and Singapore) seem to have disappeared, as though pushed out by a guiding spirit, as Vivier describes it in his program note for *Journal*: "While writing the piece, I always felt a presence which wanted me to write this very specific music. Dreams of music came to me so unusual that I had to translate them with my human tools! There is always a discrepancy between pure thought and music. Words came along with the music, in fact, sometimes they added cosmic dimensions, or, better, explained it in a more specific manner."[13] The work finally emerged as a four-part exploration of characteristic themes in the greater journey of life, with sections titled Childhood, Love, Death, After Death. The text, Vivier's own (but including fragments from Lewis Carroll, Novalis, the Requiem Mass and the Bible) makes no reference to Asia.

How should we explain the transformation undergone by *Journal* in its process from conception to realization? Was it that, in retrospect, the Asian journey seemed merely the scaffolding rather than the essence, to be discarded once the real thing came into view? Or is it possible that, having experienced Asia firsthand, its imaginative appeal for him was now lessened? The French writer Gérard de Nerval, in a letter to his friend Théophile Gautier in 1843, clearly expresses the latter dilemma: "You were once reckless enough to have ruined Spain for yourself simply by visiting it. . . . I have already lost—kingdom by kingdom, province by province—the better half of the world; soon I shall no longer know where to find refuge for my dreams. But it is Egypt that I most regret having driven from my imagination, only to provide it with a paltry place in my memories!"[14]

Instead, *Journal*, as it finally emerged, is a birth-to-death sequence of a freely associative kind. The first part, Childhood, opens with a setting of Lewis Carroll's "Jabberwocky" interspersed with moments of cosmic musing ("And you will give life / To these invented gods / These dreamed planets will exist"). This is followed by a quasi-theatrical setting of the old riddle: "What is it that walks at first on four legs, then on two, and finally on three legs?" (Answer: the human being, first crawling, then walking, then walking with a stick.) The section ends again in astral mode: "Our hands will touch the marvellous colours / Our thoughts will blend with the dust of the universe." The second part, Love, opens by calling the names of great lovers—Juliet, Tristan, Isolde, Romeo—and a passage from the First Epistle of John from the New Testament ("Beloved, let us love one another / For love is of God"). The search for love, as Vivier notes, leads us "from the Bible to the brothel," and the text is both witty and, at times, explicitly erotic ("I searched all over the city to find you / And your sex is still throbbing in me"). Perhaps in an autobiographical reference, the pick-up lines briefly shift into German—"Mein freund! Komm doch in die kneipe ein bier trinken" (My friend! Let's go and drink a beer in the pub). But, revealingly, the childhood figures—Pinocchio, Mister Pickwick, Frère Jacques, and the rest—have not gone away, and soon Vivier reaches what is perhaps the central image of the whole section, at the words "Don't leave me in the dark, you know I'm afraid"—words that, at one and the same time, might be spoken by a frightened child to a parent and by a lonely adult cajoling a would-be lover to spend the night with him. This is, without doubt, Vivier speaking of his own fear of the dark, a fear that he retained all his life. The section ends with language of a sort that will later become familiar in the Vivier of *Kopernikus* and *Lonely Child*:

> My friend, my child, my brother
> Finally you have joined me again . . .
> Let's go to see the fairy of marvellous stars
> Let's go to the planet of Cinderellas and Prince Charmings . . .
> Lovers fly away to the sound of the music from the temple of the afterlife
> In Jade, in ruby.

If this second section on Love is a cri de coeur in which Vivier himself takes center stage, with his personal history and his phobias intact, it seems deeply troubling that *Journal* then passes immediately from the turmoil of young love straight to Death, the third section, completely bypassing the middle of life and old age. It is as though there is no time to live—the text exhorts us to drink up ("Trinken bruder! Trinken") so that the "gateway of light," the "bright universe," may open up and accept us. After a setting of a passage from Novalis's *Hymns to the Night*—different from the one Vivier had used two years previously in his *Hymnen an die Nacht*, this time beginning "Nun weiß ich wenn der letzte Morgen sein wird" (I now know when the final morning will dawn)—the voices intone the surname of the poet Vladimir Mayakovsky, the brilliant Russian Futurist who committed suicide at the age of thirty-six. ("In spiritualism, very often, souls trying to make contact with earthlings are those who have committed suicide," writes Vivier in the program note.) This leads to a setting of passages of the Requiem Mass in a mood of great religious solemnity, together with unrepressed cries from the work's accumulated repertory of fears and visions— "Don't leave me alone!" "It's true that, over there, the palaces are made of crystal more precious than the smile of the stars on evenings in June?"—all interspersed with vocal utterances that, the score says, "should sound like crying." The whole section surrenders itself to an orthodox Catholic response to death, with a further setting from the Requiem, "Lux aeterna luceat eis Domine."

In the final section, After Death, we encounter no more religious texts of any kind, only a long text by Vivier himself in his "cosmic" tone, about Light and a celestial existence among "the abstract planets" and "cities of jade and diamond." There are some intriguingly enigmatic moments, for example, at the words:

> Subtle musics
> Filling my soul.
> Suddenly love becomes possible

A moment later, we wonder who the "you" in the phrase is: "Your eyes are no longer eyes but starry openings upon fabulous constellations." Is this Vivier addressing a dead friend? Or words that he imagines being spoken to him?

While the poetic content, imagery, and thematic progression of *Journal* is relatively easy to follow, it is harder, at least on first listening, to make musical sense of this long work. The four parts are relatively distinct, although moments from one bleed through into another. Musically speaking, Vivier tells us that the first section, Childhood, "is constructed around six melodies of evolving complexity, the last being a four-voiced counterpoint."[15] The second section, Love, opens with an endlessly repeated slow tread on two tuned gongs while the choir sustains a Vivier-style tremolo, with hand to mouth, a tenth apart; against this, lovers' names are intoned on pitches that form part of an overtone series on the lower tone, F. Vivier wrote that this section has "a much tighter musical structure evolving through several musical and dramatic units." The third, Death, opens with an "oscillation between two chords"; the section is in "clear cut parts," with half of it "based on a 12-tone chord sometimes transposed half a tone higher." The invocation to Mayakovsky involves a memorable four-note figure that implants itself, ostinato-like, upon the memory; the section ends with "the melody of 'light.'" The final section, "After Death," "thrives in the silence which follows," with the gentle sound of a Balinese gong presaging the closing words.

*Journal* comes to a wonderfully anticlimactic ending in a sudden English-language exchange between the solo tenor and the solo soprano:

Come let's go
ya

But go where? Together into death? But we are already "After Death"; Vivier tells us that these words are "an invitation to more refined and subtle spheres of the universe." We believe him: but is this not also a gesture of Vivier the nascent opera composer, closing the curtain on the charade of art, telling us with a smile that the performance is now over and we can return to our normal lives?

After the enormous effort on *Journal*, Vivier's next piece, *Pulau Dewata*, seems to have been written relatively quickly, in only a few weeks: the manuscript is dated June 19, 1977. If, in *Journal*, the "journey into the depths of myself" remains an inner journey, *Pulau Dewata* is a much more straightforward, open "homage of love" to the Balinese people, "these marvellous people who taught me so much."[16] Here the Balinese connection is too obvious to miss, to the point of being largely undigested. "I wanted to make a simple work," wrote Vivier, "monochrome, a short piece, full of joy . . . with complementary melodies in the Balinese manner."

*Pulau Dewata* is the only work in Vivier's output for which the instrumentation is not specified. The title page informs us that the piece is conceived "for keyboard ensemble or any other ensemble of instruments." In his letter in March to the Canada Council he had written that the second of the works to result from his voyage would be "a work for Javanese and Balinese gongs and other types of metal that I brought back with me

from my journey, here the vision will be fundamentally a religious one";
and although the details are different, *Pulau Dewata* could well be seen
as the realization of this second project. The piece was premiered by the
McGill Percussion Ensemble, to whom it is dedicated, using tuned mallet
percussion; but other versions of the work began to proliferate in Vivier's
lifetime. There is an incomplete early draft of the work for piano and clarinet, although it was never performed in that form; and shortly after the
premiere we encounter new versions for viola, piano, and percussion (by
the Toronto ensemble Array), saxophone quartet (arranged by Walter
Boudreau), and an ensemble of four ondes Martenot.[17] Vivier's friend Jean
Laurendeau, who had the previous year revived *Prolifération*, remembers
a phone call from Vivier excitedly telling him he had just written *Pulau
Dewata* and was sure it would sound good with an ensemble of ondes
Martenot.[18]

"Pulau Dewata" means "island of the gods," signifying both Bali itself
and, by extension, any idyllic place. Several melodic patterns are reminiscent of gamelan pieces, albeit in a fairly general way; and it must be
added that, especially in its percussion version, it is hard not to hear the
piece through the filter of Steve Reich's well-known and highly influential mallet percussion pieces of the 1970s, especially his *Music for Mallet
Instruments, Voices and Organ*, itself inspired by Reich's brief study (in
the United States) of Balinese music. Other near-Balinese characteristics
are the frequent fluctuations of tempo (although Vivier does this by jumps
rather than by the frequent speeding up and slowing down characteristic
of the gamelan), and the occasional close canonic writing in two voices,
similar to the interlocking patterns—*kotekan*—of Balinese music. But of
course the piece would hardly sound Balinese to an Indonesian. "This
piece is a succession of nine melodies deriving from a single one: 1, 2, 3, 4,
5, 6, 7, 8 and 9 sounds," Vivier wrote. "These modes may sometimes recall
Bali because I wanted to write a piece with the spirit of Bali: dance, rhythm
and in particular an explosion of life, simple and obvious. The end of the
piece is the traditional signature of numerous Balinese pieces."[19]

Its pseudo-Indonesian feel aside, the most revolutionary feature of
*Pulau Dewata* in the context of Vivier's own compositional development
is its bold and unashamed return to tonality, or rather to the use of modes
with clearly defined tonal centers. There is a precedent for this in the first
section of *Learning*, which is based on only five notes, C, D♭, E♭, F, and G♭,
with a tonal center of D♭. The first minute of *Pulau Dewata* is a based on a
mode consisting of B♭, C, D, E, F, G♯, and A, with B♭ as clear tonal center;
as the piece proceeds, other pitches enter the fray, but almost always there

is either a clear tonic or an ambiguity between two possible "tonics."[20] This aspect of the work, together with its strongly defined rhythmic character, has made it of great appeal to choreographers both then and subsequently, as well as to some composer colleagues sympathetic to possible exits from Stockhausen-style new music. Clarence Barlow, on hearing the piece in the late 1970s and liking it very much, put it in the same category as recent works by his young Irish contemporary Gerald Barry. Many years later György Ligeti, while feeling that the piece was perhaps not "Vivier at his best," nonetheless sympathized strongly with the fact that Vivier "has invented an orient . . . this is something for which I myself have a great admiration. He made things that are absolutely his own fantasy . . . it's like a non-existent folklore from south-east Asia."[21]

If there is an aspect of *Pulau Dewata* that has failed to learn effectively from the music of Bali, it is perhaps the overall sense of flow through its eleven-minute span. Vivier takes the always dangerous gamble of starting with his most engaging material; the opening section has an irresistible momentum, propelled onward at times by the well-judged use of several beats of rest. But the material that follows—first a passage alternating a ritenuto tempo with a steady one, then a slower passage in unison or two-part homophony—is slightly less characterful. The music resumes at a livelier tempo for a while only to have the energy dissipate once again in a decelerating fifty-five-beat measure (encompassing the composerly conceit of making each of its ten chords one quarter note beat longer than its predecessor, resulting in chords of one beat, two beats, three beats, and so on, with a final sonority of ten beats). Once again the music resumes with lively material, but the stop-start nature of the piece can by this time begin to seem wearisome, and the final section, at a steadier tempo, makes for an inconclusive ending. It is the only example of a Vivier piece that loses energy and momentum as it proceeds; in much of his best music quite the opposite is the case.

Bearing out the truth of his remark to Claude Gingras, "I don't want to talk, but to work," *Pulau Dewata* was immediately followed by Vivier's only other composition to have explicitly Balinese connections, a work for seven dancers who also sing: *Nanti Malam*. It was a collaboration with Le Groupe de la Place Royale, a modern dance company codirected by Jean-Pierre Perreault and the American Peter Boneham, founded in Montreal in 1966, but recently having shifted its base to Ottawa. The piece was partly composed by Vivier and partly devised in collaboration with the dancers, a new working method that he seems to have taken to quite effortlessly. The piece was rehearsed during a summer school under the

University of Ottawa's continuing education scheme, and performances were given on August 4, 5, and 6, 1977, at the Ottawa Teachers College on Elgin Street. The collaboration grew from the fact that Perreault had been to study theater and dance in Asia two years before, and had spent most of his time in Bali. There he—not Vivier—had hatched the title *Nanti Malam*, which means "later, this evening." In the program Vivier is credited as "musical director," and Pauline Vaillancourt, who had premiered *Lettura di Dante* and who had worked with Le Groupe de la Place Royale before, helped "to instruct the dancers in voice techniques." Sometimes the dancers are asked to play the *gangsa*, the Balinese metallophone with strips of metal on a wooden frame struck with a small mallet, the main instrument Vivier himself had played in Bali (in the score he spells it as *ganze*): Perreault had acquired three such instruments during his stay on the island.[22]

*Nanti Malam* is the only mature work Vivier left without a neat score. There are eleven manuscript pages with worked-out material, plus further pages of notes and sketches, mostly with clear rhythmic notation but only a general indication of pitch contour—the piece was, after all, intended for dancers who were not professional singers. It is not specified exactly how this material is to be sequenced, and there seem to be gaps in the continuity, which may well have been filled in by the dance activity. There are alternations between solo and group, and some material that can be treated as pieces of a mobile, the temporal synchronization with other material left to the performers' discretion. A long section calls out names of the stars, a further recurrence of Vivier's astral obsession; the "melody for 7" toward the end presents this obsession at its most hippie-like ("and the stars are flowing around me / they all fill my soul with love eternal"). No audio or video documentation of the performances has survived, which means that any new performance of the work would have to reopen the creative dimension to some extent, using Vivier's existing pages as material for a new structure.

The Ottawa critics embraced the work enthusiastically. The *Citizen* praised the fact that Perreault preferred his dancers not to have to rely on "outside sources like live or even taped music," and noted (in a preview a few days before the premiere) that "much of [Vivier's] work has been concerned with vocal music, and his meticulously pencilled score for *Nanti Malam* is marked with phrases like 'big laugh,' 'nasal mumbling,' and what appear to be strange words but are simply sounds. Perhaps a clue to the work lies in part of a comment which is written at the end of the score: 'I think there are some earthlings among them but I think most come from other realms."'[23] A preview in the French-language *Le Droit*, with a photo of Vivier playing the *gangsa*, noted:

> The musical narrative for *Nanti Malam* is the work of the young Quebec composer Claude Vivier. It's not about illustrating Balinese music, nor of giving the choreographic work an oriental tourist perfume, but of a "testimony to a quality of life" that he breathed in deeply and absorbed. . . . Jean-Pierre Perreault suggested to him a score for dancers, centered around well-defined moments between choreography and musician. The dancers have no particular musical training. Some of them have none at all. But they have the advantage of being available, open-minded, ready to experiment. So Vivier imagined a score with rhythmic models and with almost poetic indications.[24]

When the work traveled to New York's Roundabout Theatre in December the *New York Times* was less convinced, calling it "an experiment of interest," noting, however, that it was "not entirely fortunate" that the performance came hard on the heels of one that month by an actual Balinese troupe. "It is all good and well to come up with do-it-yourself rituals but their appeal pales if they are rituals without content . . . frankly [Vivier's] score is the dominating element in the work and the dancers have been beautifully coached in their vocalizing."[25]

In the summer Vivier had been working on an entirely different composition, which he completed on August 25, and which was quite another sort of response to his Asian travels than were the Balinese-titled pieces. *Shiraz* is a virtuoso work for solo piano, dedicated "to the marvellous pianist Louis-Philippe Pelletier and indirectly to two blind singers who I followed for hours in the marketplace in Shiraz."[26] Vivier's program note further tells us:

> Shiraz—a city in Iran—a pearl of a city, a hard-sculpted diamond—inspired in me a work for piano also sculpted by an idea: the movements of the hands on the piano.
>    The strict four-part writing (two voices per hand) develops in directions that are always homophonic, from which slowly emerges a two-voice counterpoint. A return to these brusque movements and finally a chorale in the form of a question mark.

Louis-Philippe Pelletier had known Vivier since their days together at the Montreal Conservatoire, although they were never close friends. He had played and recorded *Prolifération*, and had the idea to approach Vivier for a new work.

I had asked Vivier to compose a brilliant, virtuosic piano piece featuring double notes, in the style of Schumann's Toccata [in C major, Op. 7,
1832]. He began working on it very shortly thereafter and would often
phone me late at night or early in the morning, while he was composing,
to play for me, at an extremely slow speed, the chord progressions he had
just discovered and which had sent him into raptures. He was anxious to
develop new techniques that would free him from certain habits.[27]

*Shiraz* also provides testimony to the fact that an artist's work rarely develops in a simple, linear fashion—that residues of past manners emerge
even in the midst of the flowering of new ideas. The four-part harmonic
texture, for example, has much in common with Vivier's only other solo
piece for the instrument, *Pianoforte*, written some two and a half years
earlier—and in fact the harmonies themselves have at times a clear family
resemblance to that earlier work, despite the enormous artistic terrain he
had covered in the meantime. But *Shiraz* is also brimful of new ideas, not
least in the extreme muscular virtuosity required in the opening minutes,
something that has no parallel elsewhere in Vivier's output. From its star-
tling opening gesture—fifty-five loud, rapid reiterations of the four-note
chord C–E♭–E–G in the middle of the instrument (a superimposition of
major and minor triads on C)—the music fans out registrally, with the two
hands moving in opposite directions over the keyboard. This creates a vertiginous momentum that gradually yields to a contrapuntal interweaving
of the hands, each in a two-part line. Perhaps it is in this contrapuntal
material, in which the hands partly imitate and partly gainsay each other,
that we encounter the image of the two blind singers in the marketplace,
for *Shiraz* as a whole is one of the least "vocal" and least overtly melodic of
Vivier's works. The "chorale in the form of a question mark" toward the end
of the piece's fourteen minutes stops at an unexpected moment, leaving us
uncertain what has just happened; the avoidance of an "inevitable," tidy
ending is something the piece has in common with an increasing number
of Vivier works, most recently *Siddhartha* and *Pulau Dewata*.

There is no natural successor to *Shiraz* in Vivier's output. For all his
love of the piano—Richard Toop notes that "he was no virtuoso, but he
loved physical contact with the instrument; back in the mid-seventies in
Cologne he would sit for hours singing and playing, sometimes exclaim-
ing (without a trace of hubris) 'It's beautiful, man, isn't it?'"—there is no
further solo piano work in Vivier's catalog, although a new piano work
was one of the pieces he had in mind at the time of his death.[28] In the four
superb chamber works with piano he wrote in the years that followed—
*Paramirabo, Greeting Music, Samarkand*, and *Et je reverrai cette ville*

*étrange*—the instrument is only one component in a rich spectrum of colors. *Shiraz* therefore stands as a sui generis item in its composer's output, somewhat similarly to the places occupied by contemporaneous works like Walter Zimmermann's *Beginner's Mind* or Tristan Murail's *Territoires de l'oubli* in their respective composers' outputs.

The positive experience of *Nanti Malam* led to a second collaboration with Le Groupe de la Place Royale in the autumn. In *Love Songs*, as the new work was called, Vivier's intention was once again to exploit the vocal abilities of dancers using their "natural" voices, rather than to compose for trained singers. Although the first performances were choreographed, Vivier subsequently authorized a concert version of the work intended for the untrained voices of instrumentalists (the piece was done in this way by the Toronto-based ensemble Array in the autumn of 1978, and by various other groups thereafter; in some of the early performances Vivier himself took one of the voice parts). As with *Nanti Malam*, the notation uses a mixture of conventional staff notation and graphic notation where the choice of pitch is left to the individual vocalist, although this time the eighteen-page manuscript is quite complete in itself and clear to follow. The text is a collage of quotations of writings about love by various writers (Shakespeare, Novalis, Hesse), together with fragments of nursery rhymes and passages in an invented language; a few ideas were borrowed from the still unperformed *Journal*. On the title page of the score Vivier wrote that *Love Songs* was "To be staged or not / To be felt not understood / Let tones from the others inspire your own / . . . Never follow the signs but only their spirit. / In this score you do what is appropriate for you to do and leave the rest to the others. / Always be in love." The piece was premiered in Ottawa in November and repeated, with *Nanti Malam*, in New York the following month.[29] Vivier's young friend Rober Racine recalls speaking to one of the dancers in *Love Songs* and asking her how it was working with him. She replied, "It was amazing—but sometimes very exasperating, because Claude ran after us everywhere, in the toilet, in the dressing room, to rehearse—'you have to sing like this—try it, I want to hear how it sounds!'"[30]

Our image of Vivier as he approached his thirtieth birthday in April 1978 is that of a mature composer of vision and drive, with an already impressive catalog of works, who had outgrown the uncertainties of his student years and now spoke and wrote with an ever-increasing sense of artistic confidence and self-belief. Gilles Tremblay came to feel that Vivier was no longer showing him new pieces as a student to a teacher, but one to one, as colleagues. "And he always spoke with marvellous words about his own music."[31] Vivier, Tremblay remarks, was the only freelance composer in Montreal—"but he was a bachelor; still, I think everybody admired him to have the courage to do it." That sense of confidence is publicly apparent in the article "Introspection d'un compositeur," published that year in the short-lived Montreal magazine *Sortir*, edited by Luc Benoit, Paul Chamberland, Georges Khal, and Jean Basile. Although short, this text— already quoted in chapter 1—is the most revealing autobiographical writing of Vivier we possess. Essentially a retrospection of his childhood and adolescence, it also amounts to Vivier's public coming out as a homosexual. It ends with the affirmation: "A single law governs my music: love. And it's also this simple law that should govern our human relationships."[32]

This sense of confidence is also apparent in an interview he recorded with Yves Bouliane in February. He spoke about his ambivalent feelings about postwar serialism and about the need to rethink the concepts of harmony, melody, and counterpoint. He spoke too about the problems of communication, noting something profound about his own music in his remark: "Perhaps solitude is finally the element that I express the most in my music."[33] Going further, the mystical Vivier—the composer of *Musik für das Ende* and *Journal*—speaks to us in this extraordinary comment: "Each person can create their own universe, sonic as well as visual, you know. But at a certain moment, we will no longer have a body. We will be beings . . . pure spirits. That moment will be extraordinary. We will be capable of, of . . . of seeing a music that is much more subtle." And: "My whole existence I accept completely. I also accept that I feel an urgency to write, because it is an urgency. I must write music. I am an *écriveux* [writer] of music."

Part of this increasing sense of maturity showed itself in his wish not merely to fit into the new music world in Montreal but to begin to shape it. On February 17, the Quebec premiere of *Chants* was given at the Nocturnales series at the Faculty of Music of the University of Montreal, with a group of student singers directed by Lorraine Vaillancourt, younger sister of the soprano Pauline Vaillancourt.[34] According to John Rea, who was present, it was the "tremendous vibration," the "magical quality" of that evening at the Nocturnales—the performance beginning at 11:00 p.m.— that led to the idea to perpetuate that feeling somehow. Driving home afterward with José Evangelista, who also had a piece on the programme, Vivier suggested the idea of a new series devoted to contemporary music, one that would be an alternative to the existing institution-based series already happening in the city.[35] Following the first meetings with Vivier, Evangelista, and Lorraine Vaillancourt, Rea got a phone call asking him to join them; the suggestion came from Evangelista, who was a friend ("it was at least partly because I was an Anglo," quips Rea).[36] They began, initially, to plan a repeat of the Nocturnales concert, and then to devise the first season of a series to be called Les Événements du neuf. The name, Evangelista recalls, was suggested by Vaillancourt: it means not merely "new events" but plays on the word "neuf," so the directors would schedule events on the ninth of the month, starting at 9:00 p.m. In the months ahead they would meet from time to time at their various homes, generally at Evangelista's place at Côte-des-Neiges and only occasionally at Vivier's apartment on avenue du Parc (because it was "kind of messy" and Vivier not very domesticated, recalls Evangelista: one time Vivier served them coffee and mistakenly added salt rather than sugar as he was not aware which was which, even in his own kitchen). Vaillancourt recalls that their long meetings would be fueled by chocolate cookies, which Vivier devoured enthusiastically, and by cognac.[37]

The rationale behind Les Événements du neuf, according to Evangelista, was that the SMCQ "was still too straight on one type of music, the international, or more precisely European, avant-garde, and not much else was possible; and we found that was very limiting. We had other ideas. We wanted to be open. We wanted also to try other formats of presentation; that we worked very hard at."[38] Indeed the first communiqué announcing the series proclaimed that the aim was "to present unknown music to the public and to try a new form of concert presentation."[39] Vaillancourt agrees that the series was aimed "more for the community" than for the institutions. All four of them had their own ideas and contacts, so a certain diversity of repertoire choices quickly emerged, with an emphasis on younger composers. Right from the beginning there was the idea that Vaillancourt's students from her Atelier de Musique Contemporaine at the University of Montreal would be a crucial component of the body of performers used. "We had numerous meetings, numerous suppers and soirées with good food and wine," recalls Evangelista; "we were enjoying ourselves." The first concerts were fixed for February, March, and April of the following year, 1979.

The music of the younger generation was also the subject of an article Vivier wrote for *Le Devoir*, which was published on March 18.[40] In it he described the problems still facing Quebec composers, citing examples of Giles Tremblay's long wait for an orchestral commission, the limited review space given to the music of Tremblay, Garant, or himself:

"The composer living today in Quebec is totally isolated from what's go-ing on elsewhere, and this situation . . . is not healthy! . . . That is just to say that contemporary music ought to become a normal thing in musical life and moreover that at the end of the day it should create a real interest for everything that's happening in the field of musical creation!" What the article argues is that young composers should have greater access to, and support from, the prevailing institutions that had relatively recently come into being in Quebec, such as the Société Radio-Canada. There is no sense of Vivier proposing in any way to turn his back on those institutions and start an alternative scene, an aim that would have been madly impractical. The objectives of Les Événements du neuf likewise were supplementary to the status quo, not an attempt somehow to replace it.

Vivier now felt increasingly able to voice his concerns in public, and was the prime mover behind a panel on contemporary music in Quebec held on April 3 at the Conventum. His fellow speakers were Michel Longtin, Walter Boudreau, Michel-Georges Brégent, Lorraine Vaillancourt, Pierre Trochu, José Evangelista, John Rea, and Philippe Ménard. It seems, from a review in Le Devoir, to have been a curious event.[41] Indeed, it was not entirely clear what this band of "young wolves," despite their "superb solidarity," were actually arguing for. Evangelista is quoted as saying that the present young generation of creative musicians in Quebec "is not in conflict with their el-ders . . . it doesn't want to blow up icons, nor to change the world"; much praise is heaped on Garant and Tremblay, perhaps disingenuously ignor-ing many other composers of that older generation, not named, who indeed represented precisely the sort of sterile conservatism these "young wolves" set themselves against. Ultimately, it was the SMCQ that was "politely" at-tacked—it could hardly have been other than polite, with the kindly figure of Maryvonne Kendergi sitting discretely at the back of the hall—for having solidified into an institution with its own sound, its own repertoire, and its own sort of public. Something new was needed, a sort of "quiet revolution" in the new music life of Quebec. But there was no concrete suggestion as to what exactly that "something new" should be. Les Événements du neuf was perhaps as close as Vivier came, at that time, to an answer.

Vivier's professional life had by now stabilized into a steady round of applications for commissions, which he depended on in order to sur-vive. Canadian ensembles could apply through the Canada Council for money to commission a new work, and Vivier was eager to maximize his chances of support by looking to cities outside Montreal for such possibili-ties. (His friend Rober Racine even remembers that at one point, around 1979, Vivier was thinking seriously of moving to Toronto; he had the idea that more money was available for composers there so he would be able to survive better as a composer.)[42] In March the Vancouver-based ensemble Days Months and Years to Come applied to the Canada Council for $3,400 plus $750 copying and reproduction costs for a new work from Vivier.[43] This was a handsome sum, and would make a welcome contribution to the modest income he was used to living on. Just how modest this was is shown by a page surviving among his documents from 1978, which lists the "État des Revenus et Dépenses" for the previous year. It itemizes his "Revenus professionnels" (professional income) as follows:

Radio Canada (Montreal) $650;
Radio-Canada (Montreal) $100;
Festival Singers of Canada $3,500 (the commission for *Journal*);
BMI [Broadcast Music Inc., the performing rights organization], author's rights $429.77.
Total income $4,679.77.

Then come his "Dépenses" (expenses):

Professional association $25;
Technical costs $131.38;
Moving costs $638.18;
Rent (a third of the cost) $615.
Total expenses $1,409.56.

The conclusion: his net income was $3,270.21, about $10,700 (€8,069) in today's currency. And while this was a paltry sum, he seems to have been willing to continue in this way in the years immediately ahead, partly because his recent experience in Ottawa had shown him that any kind of stable teaching job was not something to which he was suited, or really wanted. Moreover, he had developed the bohemian artist's skill of discreetly finding ways to have his somewhat better off friends feed him. John Rea and his then wife Véronique Robert were living on avenue Laurier, a short walk from Vivier's apartment on avenue du Parc. John was teaching at McGill University and was making his own mark as a composer. Although outwardly much less bohemian than Vivier, he greatly admired his friend's "free spirit":

Claude was a person without boundaries ... very creative; you could get a telephone call at any time, a visit at almost any time, you could be caught off guard. Claude had a sort of circuit around his friends in the area around avenue du Parc and he would often unexpectedly arrive just before dinner time. We'd talk about music, he would read, we would read; we were just three young adults shooting the shit. He'd take a little bit of wine, the food was free, and then he'd leave.[44]

Compositionally, the year 1978 is notable for two superb chamber works, as different from each other in technique and emotional range as can be imagined. *Paramirabo*, for flute, violin, cello, and piano, was completed in Montreal in May 1978 on commission from the Canadian ensemble Mozaïk. Its fascination begins with the title: was Vivier thinking of Paramaribo, the capital of Suriname, and simply reversed two of the letters? Such spelling mistakes are not uncommon in his writing, even in French; and, as we have seen, several of his other compositions are named after distant, "exotic" cities.

*Paramirabo*, while a purely abstract work without explicit programmatic content, explores possible relationships between the four players of its ensemble. For much of the time flute, violin, and cello play together in rhythmic unison as a sort of consort, their music set off against the more isolated piano; but all three break away at times for solo passages, as though wanting to express their individuality more openly. A lot of the music explores the world of high-treble harmony, with harmonics on strings, singing into the flute, and, quite prominently, whistling; this latter sonority is used marvelously by Vivier as a way of projecting a range of behaviors ranging from casual insouciance to a sort of teasing, perhaps flirting. After a sustained and harmonically rich coda, *Paramirabo* ends mysteriously with a gasp, almost as though some secret has just been revealed that makes further music making temporarily impossible.

The other work is *Greeting Music*, completed in Montreal on October 15, and scored for piano, flute, oboe, cello, and percussion. While similar in length to *Paramirabo*, the music is utterly different in character and technique. In a program note on the manuscript, Vivier wrote, in English: "'Greeting Music' is in fact a very sad piece. It should be entirely performed with no expression in the face (except the three laughs of the cellist) and the body should just do the movements it needs to perform the piece—the 5 performers should look more like zombies. This piece is somehow related to an hopeless world where nothing is to be done nor felt." The pianist enters the stage first, alone, and during his or her intrada-like solo the other

Jeanne, Claude, and Armand Vivier at home in Pont-Viau, 1957.

First communion, ca. 1957.

With his sister Gisèle, maple syrup time, spring 1958.

Vivier at the Noviciat des Frères Maristes, Saint-Hyacinthe, ca.1966.

A summer outing with family, ca.1967; Gisèle Vivier Labrècque and her husband François, *on either side*; Vivier and his mother Jeanne, *center*.

"A souvenir of his long hair," ca. 1974.

Back in Montreal, 1975. *Musicanada* (1975).

In rehearsal, 1977. Photograph by Laurent Major.

Three of the founders of Les Événements du Neuf, autumn 1978. *Left to right*: Vivier, Lorraine Vaillancourt, José
Evangelista. Photograph by Matilde Asencio. Courtesy of the
photographer.

L'atelier de jeu scénique et l'atelier de musique contemporaine de la Faculté de musique de l'Université de Montréal, en collaboration avec l'École Nationale de Théâtre, présentent:

# l'opéra
# Kopernikus

## de Claude Vivier

| | |
|---|---|
| Direction musicale: | Lorraine Vaillancourt |
| Direction scénique: | Marthe Forget |
| Décor: | Jacinthe Vézina |
| Costumes: | Meredith Caron |

Avec:

Gail Desmarais
David Doane
Michel Ducharme
Jocelyne Fleury-Coutu
Richard Labbé
Christine Lemelin
Shari Saunders
Christian Amesse
Denise Bellemare
Nicolas Desjardins
Denis Ferragne
Jean Gervais
Jasmine Perron
Pierre Tierney

Jeudi et vendredi

## les 8 et 9 mai
## à 20h30 au
## Monument National
1182, St-Laurent
(coin Dorchester)

## Entrée libre

Flyer for the first production of *Kopernikus*, 1980.

Passport photograph, 1979.

Portrait by Alain Renaud, ca. 1979.

Portrait by Jean Billard, 1980. This has become the most frequently reproduced photograph of Vivier, the one that has
fixed his image most firmly in the public consciousness.

Detail from page 2 of the manuscript score of *Lonely Child*, 1980, showing "les couleurs" in the violins. © Boosey & Hawkes, Inc. Reproduced with permission from Boosey & Hawkes Music Publishers Ltd.

With pianist Christina Petrowska Quilico (who premiered *Shiraz*), 1981.

Portrait, 1981.

Vivier in drag, a still from the video film *L'Homme de Pékin*, 1981.

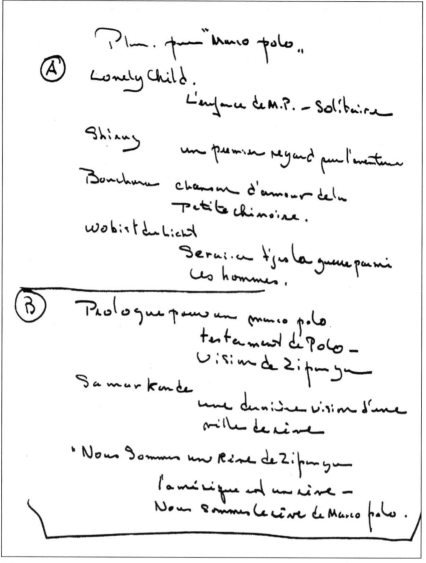

The outline, in Vivier's hand, for the unfinished *opera fleuve* on Marco Polo, 1982.

Walter Boudreau, 1987. Following the death of Serge Garant he became artistic director of the SMCQ, and one of the main champions of Vivier's music in Canada. Courtesy of Walter Boudreau.

Lecture at Centre Culturel Canadien, Paris, November 1982.
Vivier is following the score of one of the recordings played
during the lecture.

players take their places, first the percussionist, then the cellist, then oboe, and finally flute. It is hard to decide whether the mood is formal and solemn or mock-formal and mock-solemn. The pianist's grand octave E♭s are soon joined by a range of consonant intervals in a texture that has shades of *Pulau Dewata*, harmonically and rhythmically, though is a good deal less energetic. With the full ensemble present the music settles for a time into dirge-like material on three pitches, beautifully harmonized, but punctuated absurdly by the pianist playing flexatone. More histrionic gestures are in store: over quasi-Beethovenian reiterations of an A♭–C dyad on the piano, the cello begins to play with exaggerated bow pressure to create a noise texture, and the percussionist produces "screams" on the tam-tam by scraping the metal with the edge of a plastic box. By now the intensity is real; so it is all the more puzzling when, with things beginning to calm down somewhat, the cellist produces a series of laughs. Is the cellist mocking the preceding air of solemnity, or is this an intrusion of barely controlled madness, a sort of cry for help? Subsequently, the ensemble finds a form of unison energy for the only fast passage in the piece, which stops as suddenly as it began. The pianist then plays a mesmeric, repetitive coda as the other players bow and leave the stage; finally the pianist does the same.

*Greeting Music* is hard to "read," either as a musico-theatrical event or autobiographically. The puzzle begins with the title (curiously, as was true also—though for different reasons—with *Paramirabo*); who, or what, is being greeted? (Rober Racine has a memory of Vivier telling him the piece was a tribute to homeless people living on the streets, and was a "greeting" to them.)[45] A note by Vivier on the rough copy of the score says: "Greeting ceremony to be played with lots of concentration"—which hardly elucidates things. The procession onstage and off by the musicians, while reminding us of *Learning*, now seems rather hollow, even futile, with the sense that nothing of what they have to offer will have the power to move or uplift us. But to look for any kind of straightforward "meaning" in this piece, for example, as though it were an expression of personal despair on Vivier's part, is surely misguided. A note scribbled by Vivier in pen on the back of the program for the February 1979 premiere in Vancouver comments that *Greeting Music* was the "strangest piece which ever came to me": sometimes works of art have the power to surprise even their creator, who does not always know exactly what is lurking in the subconscious, waiting to come out.

✶ ✶ ✶

By the time he finished *Greeting Music* another commission application, a much more substantial one, was in the works. This application, dated July 11, 1978, was submitted by the Faculty of Music of the University of Montreal to the Canada Council: it was for an opera, to be completed by April 1979, and to be performed by l'Atelier de Jeu Scénique and l'Atelier de Musique Contemporaine of the University of Montreal directed by Lorraine Vaillancourt. A letter from Vivier dated June 26 confirms his willingness to accept the commission, for both music and libretto. "The work will be ready in spring 1980," he noted, probably meaning the whole production rather than the completion of the score. "My composer's fee"—which was budgeted at $7,000—"should also cover the writing of this libretto."[46] This commission offered him the financial security to devote himself to the work, which occupied him throughout the end of 1978 and the winter and spring of 1979.

Meanwhile he kept busy with other activities. In November he performed with the Toronto-based ensemble Array, as vocalist, in a concert performance of his dance work *Love Songs*. He was convinced the piece could work in an unstaged setting, and Array was a sympathetic vehicle for it—they had successfully performed his *Pulau Dewata* in a version for viola, piano, and percussion earlier that year. The performance was at the Heliconian Club in midtown Toronto, drawing a "good crowd" of fifty people; the reviewer from *Musicworks* noted that the piece "is just long enough that in the wrong hands it could become a disaster, but Array gave it the top flight performance it deserves. The audience loved it and gave the effervescent composer a strong ovation."[47] Back home in December he wrote a program note on Stockhausen's *Mantra* for a forthcoming SMCQ concert, clearly showing that despite the enormous changes in his work in the four and a half years since he finished his studies, his affection for his former teacher remained intact. The year closed for him with three days, December 26–28, at l'Abbaye cistercienne in Oka, his sanctuary away from the world at times of need; he had also been there for a few days at the beginning of July.

In the early weeks of 1979, concurrently with work on his opera, Vivier occupied himself with the new concert series, Les Événements du neuf. A long preview article, "Du 'neuf' en musique," appeared in *La Presse* by Vivier's old adversary Claude Gingras.[48] Gingras quoted Vivier's insistence that this new initiative was in no way a rival to the SMCQ: "in a city of three million, there is only one contemporary music society. There's room for one more—*at least* one more!" (According to official statistics the population of Montreal at that time was only

980,354 with a conurbation of 1,015,420: Vivier's estimate therefore is a bit exaggerated.) Sniffing out history on the verge of repeating itself, Gingras declared that Vivier had turned himself into the same sort of polemicist that Serge Garant had been at the same age; Vivier, he claimed, was the main propagandist (the *"animateur principal"*) in bringing their activities to the attention of the press. José Evangelista, however, disagrees strongly: "Claude was not the sort of charismatic personality who would gather people around him for some common cause, nor did he worry about converting people to his own ideas."[49] Gingras pointed out that of the seventeen works in their first season none (apart from Colin McPhee's *Balinese Ceremonial Music*) was by a Canadian. Vivier replied: "As to the absence of composers from here, it simply happened that way. When we chose our themes, we didn't find anything in our music which corresponded to what we wanted to do." John Rea, looking back, feels that "Gingras's big spread seemed to be his attempt to twist the whole thing, to turn it into a manifesto of sorts, to subvert it, to claim we wanted to show the older generation that what they were doing was not pertinent. This wasn't our intention at all."[50] (The SMCQ at that time was only a decade old; and Gingras was a solid pal of Garant.)

The three concerts of the first season show highly imaginative and original programming. The first, on February 9, was titled "La nouvelle mélodie"; it was dedicated to the Montreal-born cartoonist and silent filmmaker Raoul Barré, one of whose films was shown, and featured Stockhausen's *Tierkreis*, Cardew's *Odes* (from *The Great Learning*), Rzewski's *Struggle Song*, Luis de Pablo's *Very Gentle*, and Berio's *Aria* (from *Opera*). The second concert, on March 9, titled "Musique en bouche," was dedicated to Yves Sauvageau (the dedicatee of Vivier's unperformed *Musik für das Ende*): it featured Kagel's *Die Mutation*, Lois V. Vierk's *Kana*, Peter Eötvos's *Moro Lasso*, Morton Feldman's *Christian Wolff in Cambridge*, La Monte Young's *Composition 1960 no. 7* (the infamous drone piece on the notes B and F♯), and Mesías Maiguashca's *A Mouth Piece*. The third concert, on April 9th, "Les musiques immobiles," was dedicated to Colin McPhee: beginning with his *Balinese Ceremonial Music* for two pianos, it also contained Johannes Fritsch's *Sul G*, Jo Kondo's *Knots*, György Ligeti's *Selbstportrait* (from the *Three Pieces for Two Pianos*), Yuji Takahashi's *Bridges I*, and *Aeolian Harp* by the Polish composer Włodzimierz Kotoński. Each concert was held in a different venue in the city and admission to all the concerts was free. If the influence of Stockhausen is readily apparent on the programming (not only his own *Tierkreis* but works by several of his former associates, Cardew,

Rzewski, Eötvos, Maiguashca, Fritsch), the overall themes are striking: melody ("not a return to melody in the old-fashioned sense of the term," Vivier insisted, "it's *new* melody"); vocal music ("Montreal is full of singers!"); and music with greatly reduced harmonic movement, a characteristic of Balinese music (although it is notable that no early American minimal music was included in this particular program).[51] The series was felt by its four organizers to be a success, although there were issues that remained to be tackled. John Rea remembers that the performances were not always top notch, "because you couldn't persuade the professionals really to get involved in this"; those who were eager to participate were younger people, "sometimes more passionate than competent."[52]

Elsewhere, there were other performances of Vivier's own music. (The three composers among the four directors of Les Événements du neuf— Vivier, Rea, and Evangelista—had resolved not to program their own music in the series, a decision they would, however, later revoke.) *Journal* received its belated premiere performances in Convocation Hall at the University of Toronto on March 30 and 31, 1979, by the Festival Singers of Canada and the percussionist David Kent. The reviews overall were enthusiastic, the *Toronto Star* noting: "A quality of child fantasy permeates the work as Vivier practices the musical equivalent of free association. What he comes up with is a surrealistic collage of images from the attic trunk of memory, rendered in sound. . . . Mysticism and sensuality follow the path of mutual coexistence. Any work so miscellaneously conceived is likely to have its ups and downs and *Journal* is no exception."[53] And on March 16, a new version of *Pulau Dewata* was performed at l'Institut Canadien de Québec, scored for four ondes Martenot, played by l'Ensemble d'Ondes de Montréal led by Jean Laurendeau.

But despite this activity Vivier was not, and never would be, truly content with the status quo of the Montreal scene. In discussing radio broadcasting with a journalist from *La Scène musicale*, he remarked: "the French network of Radio-Canada is not sufficiently integrated in the Montreal musical life, it overuses the LP record. The politics of Radio-Canada are not very lively. They should record more concerts, interview young composers, if not every week then once a month. There is a tendency to interview performers."[54] (It is worth noting that in July the CBC program *Two New Hours*, in a series marking the twentieth anniversary of the Canadian Music Centre, included Vivier among a series of seven features on Canadian composers; the others were Ann Southam, Gilles Tremblay, Walter Buczynski, Hugh Le Caine, Samuel Dolin, and Gabriel Charpentier.) An anecdote recalled by his Ottawa friend Louise

Duchesneau shows the perpetual dissatisfaction that is perhaps an inevitable part of the creative artist:

> I met Claude in the lobby of Place-des-Arts at the Montreal International Competition in 1979. The featured instrument was violin and the imposed piece, *Les Diableries*, was written by François Dompierre. Claude was so upset at the quality of the imposed piece. François Dompierre was, and still is, a very important radio personality and a popular composer in Quebec. The piece he wrote was full of folksy tunes and rhythms. Claude thought the piece was very low level and he was also very hurt that the people responsible for these rather important commissions had not thought of asking him for a piece. He felt he wasn't taken seriously in Canada.[55]

The work he was composing through the end of 1978 and early 1979 was his biggest attempt to date to show Montreal, and the world beyond, just how seriously he should be taken, and what he was now capable of. This was the opera *Kopernikus*, subtitled "Rituel de Mort," cast in two parts playing in total for some seventy minutes. It is scored for seven singers, seven players, and tape. He completed the work, more or less on schedule according to the terms of his commission, on May 14, 1979 ("Deo gratias," says the manuscript). It is dedicated to "my *maître* and friend" Gilles Tremblay. Nearly a whole year would pass before the premiere performances, on May 8 and 9, 1980, at the Théâtre du Monument National on Montreal's boulevard Saint-Laurent, by which time he had moved compositionally beyond even this major work. *Kopernikus* is, however, the most important stepping stone toward the great music of 1980–83, a work of vision and originality that confirmed his place—to the surprise of some of his peers—at the forefront of the Canadian composers of his generation.

# CHAPTER EIGHT

# " A   M Y S T I C A L
E N C H A N T M E N T "

## 1 9 7 8 – 7 9

I n a brief text he prepared for the premiere of *Kopernikus,* Vivier first defended his desire to compose an opera at all, then spoke of the work itself: "Why an opera in 1980? Since its beginnings, opera has always 'represented' archetypes of history, the deep desires of human beings. To 'represent' means to tell a story, characters in their pure state and behavior, therefore a bit excessive. Opera, as a form of expression of the soul and of human history, cannot die. The human being will always need to represent his/her fantasies, dreams, fears and hopes."[1] This last sentence is perhaps as accurate a description of the motivations of this complex work as Vivier would ever give. In the earliest surviving source, a six-page typescript titled "Project for a chamber opera," dated March 13, 1978, we learn that the work was originally to have been another of Vivier's explorations of *Alice's Adventures in Wonderland,* with Alice as the principal character, but "80 years after her experience through the looking glass": the working title was *The Old Alice.*[2] As the work progressed this connection was lessened: the final title is a whimsical spelling of the surname of the Renaissance astronomer Nicolaus Copernicus, and the principal character became Agni, Hindu deity and god of fire, a male god, but represented—as Alice was to have been—by an alto. However, the Alice theme is still present: the work opens with a passage from a letter by Lewis Carroll (the Reverend Charles Dodgson) titled "An Easter Greeting to Every Child Who Loves 'Alice,'" originally appended to a new edition, published in 1890, of his famous book.

Vivier made it quite clear that he identified strongly with the central character of the opera, so much so that we may regard Agni as one of the long list of "Vivier characters" in his work. In a press release, he noted: "Agni is the Hindu god of fire. . . . Fire is my astrological sign. I was born on April 14. I am Aries, the ram. Agni, *c'est moi*. . . . For musical reasons, I represent him by a woman."[3] In contrast, the historical Nicolaus Copernicus barely features in the opera, only appearing at the end to open the gates of "heaven"; Vivier acknowledged that it was the mythic Copernicus that interested him, "the idea of the cosmic searcher, who has begun to look further than the earth," and that he had made no attempt to research the life and thought of the real Copernicus.[4]

Around Agni (created originally by Jocelyne Fleury-Coutu, whose voice Vivier had in mind when composing the role), the other six singers are "mythical beings" who are "in a way her dreams become reality. They accompany her, if you like, towards death, the great passage." Beyond the idea of a journey toward death, there is no real narrative or story being told: the work is "rather a series of scenes. . . . Each scene represents, in a way, 'archetypes.'"[5] Copernicus, the stargazer, is one of these archetypes (he is joined by other astronomers: a whole roll call of them is given in part 2 of the opera). So is Mozart, whom Agni addresses on several occasions. So, more abstractly, are Merlin, King Arthur, the Queen of the Night, and Tristan and Isolde. In an interview given while the work was in rehearsal, the director Marthe Forget explained that all the named characters, figments of Agni's imagination, are finally important only as part of the series of initiations through which Agni must pass on her way to the next world. Vivier agreed, adding that in this regard one could see a clear connection between *Kopernikus* and one of his favorite operas: Mozart's *The Magic Flute*. Later in the same interview Vivier added: "When I wrote my opera, I was influenced above all by Mozart and perhaps to some extent by the cinema of Marguerite Duras." (He protested, however, when Forget jokingly described the piece as "a Stockhausenian *Magic Flute*.")

> In fact the only real connection I recognize is with Mozart's *Magic Flute*. I felt very close to this work when I wrote mine. Of course it's completely different, but the link is considerable between the two. . . . Someone already asked me to define my opera. I replied that it is a *féerie mystique* [a mystical enchantment]. Its two fundamental aspects are dream and spirituality, which are mingled. Besides, I wrote the text and the music at the same time.[6]

Materials in the Vivier Archives make clear that the libretto originally contained a good deal more text than finally ended up in the work, so Vivier's claim that he wrote text and music at the same time should perhaps be understood to mean that the final text was only established in the process of writing the score. Moreover, another significant textual change seems to have occurred during the period of composition: the amount of French text became greatly reduced in favor of an increasing percentage of "langue inventée," lessening the comprehensibility of much of what is sung. A surviving early manuscript libretto dated 1978, originally eleven pages, is entirely in French; but Vivier later added three more pages (dated 1979) in which the "langue inventée" appears only at the end, after Agni has implored the stars to open for her "the gates of paradise."[7] The finished work uses substantial parts of this French text (with occasional phrases in German), but the French is interspersed right from the outset by the invented language. Marthe Forget points out that "this esoteric language is only used by the insiders. When they speak to Agni, who is not yet an insider, the language becomes comprehensible again. But gradually, as she advances in her initiation, she enters more and more into this playing with the 'langue inventée.'"[8] Vivier added: "Often, the 'langue inventée' is mixed with the names of stars, which are innumerable. All this language came from automatic writing. I have always invented my own language." Asked by the interviewer whether the syllables were chosen for their musical value, he replied: "Not necessarily, even though I pay attention to that aspect. It's really from automatic writing."[9]

Acknowledging that he loved many of the operas in the standard repertory—"but I rarely go to see them because I usually don't like the staging" . . . in *Kopernikus*, "as regards staging I didn't want to give precise indications. . . . I made a text explaining each scene, but I leave the choices entirely to the director"—Vivier nonetheless created a work that owes very little to eighteenth- or nineteenth-century operatic convention. One aspect of this is that the instrumentalists (seven or eight, depending on whether one uses a separate percussionist) seem an essential part of the stage action, and indeed have been used in this way in several productions of the opera. The sonorities Vivier chose give the ensemble a Varèse-like abrasiveness: oboe, two clarinets, bass clarinet, trumpet, trombone, and violin, with occasional interjections from the percussion instruments (some of which may be played by the singers). Musically, the work builds on the achievement of a recent work like *Paramirabo* in effortlessly alternating homophonic writing, mostly in four-part harmony, with contrapuntal textures. The instruments themselves sometimes seem symbolic:

the trumpet, Vivier insisted, was "the instrument of death, an important element in the opera." (It is not totally clear why: part 2 opens with a striking and memorable trumpet solo, but dramatically this does not mean that Agni, or anyone else, has died. Perhaps, instead, death is merely calling).[10] A set of tubular bells is used occasionally to mark important moments in the ongoing flow of the music, like bells marking a ritual occasion; and the violin, the only string instrument, is throughout a warmer, more voice-like (and in that sense arguably a more "human") presence than any of the other instruments.

The most striking moments musically are perhaps the final set pieces of each of the two parts. Part 1 ends with an aria, which Vivier calls a Salutation, for coloratura soprano, her melody doubled two octaves higher by glockenspiel, punctuated by tubular bells, and accompanied by drones on trombone, bass clarinet, and low male voices. This beautiful aria is a premonition of the melodic language of later works like *Lonely Child* or *Bouchara*; like them, it ends with an abrupt gesture, the singer giving a loud handclap. Part 2 ends with one of the most haunting passages in Vivier's whole output, a six-measure homophonic chorale ("Prémonition"), repeated four or more times as the singers and musicians process out of the hall. The dissonant tonal harmonies here could not have come from the pen of any other composer, and sum up the chordal explorations he had pursued ever since *Pianoforte*. Once this has faded to near inaudibility with the performers out of the hall, the opera ends, jarringly, with the prerecorded sound of a slamming door.

If *Kopernikus* is ultimately "about" a woman's journey to the next world via a series of initiations, the way in which she and her semi-imaginary companions express themselves on that journey is idiosyncratic, to say the least. Take, for example, the questions Agni poses to Mozart in part 2:

Herr Mozart Herr Mozart monsieur Mozart monsieur Mozart listen to me Is it true that beyond the river the trees talk among themselves that the flowers make music, so marvelous that even the Gods cry is it true monsieur Mozart that the timeless song of the nymphs has seduced the angel of harmony is it true? they told me I could play leap-frog from galaxy to galaxy that my hair will be a path to the hands of the happy planets that the fairy Carabosse has her porphyry castle there I've heard it said that they communicate by music

We may well wonder what sort of character is this, who expresses herself in this childish way—surely not a grown woman, much less a god. Certainly no character in *The Magic Flute* talks anything like this amount of cosmo-babble. But in *Kopernikus* the singers—when they sing in French at all, and not in the invented language—express themselves in these terms almost all the time. The opening of the work, after the Lewis Carroll letter, attempts to seduce Agni (and, by implication, all of us) into the immanence of death, in tones as gentle as those of a mother persuading her child to get ready for bed and to dream sweet dreams:

> [Mezzo:] welcome to the magic land to the land of merlin to the land of wagner hé o the melody of death will invade you very slowly my friend welcome to the land of silence

> [Baritone:] do not worry, death will be gentle like a mother all your friends have all arrived finally you will see the light

Much of the text is taken up with descriptions of the painlessness of death and the beauties of the next world, in terms that are sometimes quasi-re-ligious, sometimes fairy-tale-like ("monks devote themselves to abstract rituals in the secrecy of their opal cloisters"; "the music of lost cathedrals will sound in our ears like rallying cries"; "come to the purifying water of this magic stream which contains the whole universe"). This may well provoke a question: how should we understand the singers' tendency to ex-press themselves throughout in such childish language? Is Vivier perhaps suggesting that childhood is tolerable enough, but that it is better to choose death over the anguish and turmoil of adulthood? Why, finally, has Vivier chosen to devote his largest work to persuading us that death is more beau-tiful than life, indeed altogether preferable to it?

A preview of the work by Claude Gingras appeared in *La Presse* a few days before the premiere. Expecting that Vivier would be unlikely to write opera in the conventional sense, with a story told by means of recitatives and arias, Gingras asked Vivier what the word "opera" meant to him. Vivier replied: "An opera is music put on stage, for one thing. For another, it is an excessive expression of human passions and dreams. In *Kopernikus*, there is a drama, or rather a dramaturgy, but not a dramaturgy born out of a situation of conflict (that is, a relationship between the characters), but rather a dramaturgy that finds its origin in its own way."[11] He added: "We should not try to read any meaning into what happens but try to *feel* what's happening. Not try to *understand*, but to *enjoy* what's happening. It's for that reason that it's written in large part in an invented language." And regarding the choice of seven players and seven singers:

I chose 7 because it's a very beautiful number. Twice 7 makes 14: my birth date. But certainly 4 + 3 makes possible a better balance than two numbers that are the same. The seven instruments allow me to play across the whole musical range. In the high register, I have a violin and also sometimes three clarinets, which also constitute the medium register with the oboe and the trumpet. In the bass I have a trombone. There is also some percussion played by the singers.

Vivier insisted that his *féerie mystique* also had "a sociological dimension": "In a crisis of civilization as profound as the one we are going though now on this planet, the human being perhaps has a need of a return to the fetal state, an intimate one."[12] In an interview with his young friend Rober Racine he first described the structure of the work, then gave a striking prediction for the future:

There are three scenes in the first part, a pause, and three more scenes in the last part. In order: the first is the Salutation to Agni; then the initiation of Agni; then, the big scene of the Meditation; then comes the fourth scene, the Entrance; the penultimate one, which is that of the Stars, then finally the Exit scene. . . . The music is very gentle and slow, like all that of the current period of my work. The opera closes the period of my life I'd call autobiographical.[13]

The reviewers were clearly somewhat perplexed by the work, while recognizing its extraordinary qualities. The title of the review in the *Gazette*, "Overly-long ritual mars *Kopernikus* experience," summed up one point of view.[14] Gilles Potvin in *Le Devoir* wrote:

the composer has limited his resources to fourteen performers, of which seven instrumentalists are placed at the centre of the stage, the characters themselves moving towards the front of the stage and on a tilted semicircular platform. . . . Vivier has written music that is mostly simple and conventional on texts in an invented language, so incomprehensible for the most part. Musically, Vivier has turned his back on pretentious discourse and rhetoric in order to stick to a language that is deliberately austere, even monotonous. . . . Deliberately or unconsciously, he pays homage in turn to Venetian opera and to Monteverdi, to Gregorian chant, to *Pelléas et Mélisande*, to Stravinsky, to the Japanese Noh plays and of course to Stockhausen, whose *Stimmung* can come to the surface at any moment. Despite everything, it is difficult to deny this music a certain coherence, even a poetry which leads sometimes to enchantment.[15]

✳ ✳ ✳

The full year that passed between the completion of *Kopernikus* and its premiere was something of a trial for the always impatient Vivier. But there were other activities to take his mind off things. One, on September 19, 1979, was a further performance of *Chants* at the Théâtre de la Cité Universitaire by the Atelier de musique contemporaine de Montréal directed by Lorraine Vaillancourt, which Vivier felt to be its best to date. Another was the planning of the second season of Les Événements du neuf, which this time offered four events, at 9:00 p.m. on the ninth days of November and December 1979 and January and February 1980. Buoyed up by critic Gilles Potvin's description of their first season as "a successful adventure," the events became even more adventurous in conception. The press release described "four special events, each once again dedicated to a personality from the world of arts and letters": these were the playright and polemicist Claude Gauvreau, the avant-garde composer Pierre Mercure, mezzo-soprano Eva Gauthier, and electronic music pioneer Hugh LeCaine. "The voice again takes a privileged place with 'Poésie sonore.' 'L'arche de Noé' [Noah's ark], a multidisciplinary event, will last a whole night. The atmosphere of the old 'boîte à chansons' will be evoked in 'Café-théâtre' [the evening including Gabriel Charpentier's recent mini-opera *Clara et les Philosophes*]. Finally, the electronic medium dominates 'Au courant de la musique.'" Once again, thanks to subsidy from the University of Montreal, all the concerts were free, and again the venues were all different: the Auditorium of the Musée des beaux-arts de Montréal on rue Sherbrooke, Le théâtre continu on rue Laurier, the Association des vétérans de guerre polonais on rue Prince Arthur, and the Galerie Véhicule Art on rue Sainte-Catherine.

Meanwhile, on October 6, he finished a substantial new work. This was the orchestral piece *Orion*, a commission from the Orchestre Symphonique de Montréal supported financially, with an award of $2,050, by the Canada Council. It was perhaps the most prestigious commission he had yet received, if not the largest in monetary terms; and he was well aware that he would probably wait a long time for another orchestral commission within his native province. With the still unperformed *Siddhartha* on his mind, he may have decided to make this new work, even if intended for a professional performing body, very much less complex. Curiously, toward the end of *Kopernikus* a baritone predicts, to Agni, that in the next world "you will hear the music of Orion and the mystic harmonies of the seven sages": now the prediction was being fulfilled.

Scored for a conventional symphony orchestra, *Orion* plays for about thirteen minutes. From our perspective decades later, the work seems a curious synthesis of materials and gestures recognizable from Vivier's other works (most notably the falling, sometimes teasing interval of the minor third) with very much more conventional moments that unintentionally evoke composers such as Mussorgsky or Janáček.[16] As such, it is unique in his output in giving the impression of wanting to please the large and musically fairly conservative audience for which it was first intended. In reality, the body of Montreal Symphony Orchestra subscribers probably preferred the Sibelius and Mahler that awaited them in the rest of the concert; but the occasion pushed Vivier in a direction that would, as we shall see, have immediate and unexpected consequences for him.

The piece opens with a melody on the trumpet—as in *Kopernikus*, as Vivier remarks in his program note, a symbolic choice ("the instrument of death in the Middle Ages"). The melody, which is constructed in four phrases separated by pauses, then "projects itself upon itself without being able to (or wanting to) break the wall of solitude."[17] In fact, the melody returns, often in fragmentary form, in each of what Vivier regarded as the piece's six sections. Musicologist Jaco Mijnheer sees the piece as progressively destroying the melody:

> The stages of the melody's destruction can be summarized as follows:
> 1. "Harmonization" through the layering of several transpositions, inversions and rhythmic variants of the melody . . . simultaneity of different melodic segments.
> 2. Rhythmic standardization of the segments.
> 3. Gradual transitions between segments.
> In this way, a defining melody consisting of four motifs, each with its own identity, becomes a single stream of pitches without any precise direction.[18]

Vivier himself saw the piece more as "Eternal return, as in history with a capital H, which always impatiently waits for the return of its redeeming saints and its dictators."[19] Whichever interpretation we prefer—progressive destruction or inevitable return—the predominance of the melodic shapes introduced clearly at the outset makes the unfolding of the music relatively easy to follow by ear. Vivier is not shy, also, about using the full orchestral sonorities to color his rich and sensuous harmonies, adding precisely the kind of luxuriant allure to the music that the more angular *Kopernikus* singularly avoided. But the harmonies are of several kinds, that sit in a sometimes uneasy alliance: brassy major triads, such as those at rehearsal number 26, that move from one to the next in a way that all too vividly recalls the music of various well-known early twentieth-century iconoclasts; genuinely exploratory moments, such as rehearsal number 16, where a consort of violins and violas sounding artificial harmonics moves in gentle rhythmic unison with a set of four small nipple gongs played by the percussionist, all set against a low drone; or the passage immediately following this, where the exploration of a harmonic series on a low E♭ takes on a rather New Age lushness (we wonder if Vivier intended the reference to Wagner's Rhine music to be obvious). The piece may be seen unproblematically as a concert overture, or tone poem, evoking the constellation Orion and the awe and wonder of outer space (the working title was *Chant aux Étoiles*). Jaco Mijnheer has, however, suggested a further level of signification:

> In this work, the composer displays in rather clear terms the connection he sees between the cosmos and humanity: on the one hand very intimate and human forms of expression, such as the calls of "hé-o" [into the tamtam] and the wonderfully still percussion interludes, written in a style one could term "meta-Asiatic"; and on the other hand an unbridled orchestra, with very low notes and terrible grinding sounds [the tamtam scraped with a triangle beater], metaphors for unimaginable and inescapable forces.[20]

When the piece was finally premiered by the Orchestre Symphonique de Montréal (OSM), conducted by Charles Dutoit on October 14, 1980 (again, a full year after its completion), the reviewers were a good deal less generous. The reviewer in the *Gazette* seemed disinclined to take it very seriously: "*Orion* . . . makes broad use of orchestral color in a somewhat oriental way—effect depends on repetition rather than on the basic statement. It is difficult to know which aspect of the god Orion, son of P . . . and E . . . , is being demonstrated. Was this Orion killing off all the wild animals on the island of Chios in order to win his bride? The allusion is vague and Vivier's own notes do not help."[21] *Le Devoir* was more censorious:

> In the light of a first listening, this work didn't seem to have the sonorous contrasts which would have been able to impress. Some characteristic things in the trumpet and in the brass keep our attention for a moment, but the large orchestra is treated parsimoniously, the strings being limited to interminable tremoli while we wait for some ideas that finally do not come. Toward the end, however, there is a grand unison theme directly out of Rimsky-Korsakov. Claude Vivier needs to do better in the future.[22]

But it was Claude Gingras in *La Presse* who really brought the knives out: "At the start of the programme: *Orion*, by Claude Vivier, a commission of the OSM. Some ideas here and there, but for the most part a work of incredible banality, already 'old' in sound. I'm sorry to say that I am more and more convinced that Vivier is not a musician."[23]

Walter Boudreau remembers a conversation that suggests that, even at the time he finished the score in the autumn of 1979, Vivier may have realized the essentially conservative nature of *Orion* and was concerned about it. He brought the recently completed score to show to Boudreau, then living in a converted coach house in Outremont. In particular, recalls Boudreau, given the visit to Europe he was now planning, "Claude was really nervous about showing the score to old composer friends there like Gérard Grisey or Tristan Murail, feeling they wouldn't find it avant-garde enough."[24] If Vivier was concerned about falling out of step with developments in western Europe, the month he was about to spend in France, Holland, and Germany was to provide him with an insight that would shape the course his music would take in the years ahead and permanently ensure its relevance in the eyes of his European contemporaries.

CHAPTER NINE

# " O H   B E A U T I F U L
# C H I L D   O F
# T H E   L I G H T "

## 1 9 7 9 – 8 1

O n November 6, 1979, Vivier arrived in France at the beginning of a
month-long stay in Europe. The exact purpose of his visit remains
unknown, though he would surely have been glad to escape the Quebec
winter for a few weeks; and although the visit was not tied to any performances of his music there, it may well have had the aim of promoting
some. After a few days in France, a card postmarked November 15 to his
Montreal friend Thérèse Desjardins announced his arrival in Germany:
"Finally Cologne—and also what you read for me in the cards! The pieces
of mine that are the most appreciated here are those that are the least
appreciated in Montreal! Anyway, some pieces of mine will be played in
Paris and in Cologne."[1] (Regarding what the cards had said, Desjardins
recalls: "We always did card-reading in the family. I did it very often with
Claude. . . . the cards often 'spoke' and Claude's said that the future of his
music was somewhere else than Quebec!!! I used the cards to encourage
him to go and work in Europe. A game, but one that he really liked.")[2] In
Cologne he recorded a radio program about Canadian music. From there
he went to Holland; his passport was stamped in Arnhem on November
18. He gave a seminar at his old stomping ground, the Institute of Sonology
in Utrecht, talking about some recent works, including *Journal*, the most

recent large-scale work of his to have been performed. He was back in Montreal on December 7.

Vivier's trip to Europe that autumn, and particularly the days he spent in Paris, was to transform his musical language. Frustratingly, it is impossible to verify whether he actually met with Grisey or Murail (though it seems from the conversation with Walter Boudreau about *Orion* that he expected to); by 1979 he was relatively out of touch with their recent music, and his renewed encounter with it had the spirit of a new discovery. Whether in conversation, or from the brief flipping through the pages of some of their scores, he came upon the technical idea that, in retrospect, can be seen to be exactly the technique he was looking for, the idea that made possible the composition of the majority of his own works from that point forward.

The technique goes by different names. A literal translation of the French phrase, "l'addition des fréquences" (the addition of frequencies), has never caught on in English. It is sometimes referred to as the "sum and difference" principle of chord generation. François Rose, in a seminal 1996 article on spectral music, calls the technique one of generating "combination tones."[3] Vivier himself referred to the materials so produced, more poetically, as "les couleurs."[4] In the lecture he gave in Paris in November 1982, Vivier acknowledged that the music he was by then composing made use of "a very classical system that Murail uses: a system of *addition des fréquences*."[5] It seems odd that he should describe as "very classical" a system that had been in use for at most a decade. Perhaps he wanted to make the technique seem more of an established practice than it really was. Murail himself modestly remarks: "The idea was in the air anyway. . . . Grisey had used the addition and subtraction of frequencies in a piece like *Partiels*, that was '75, and ring modulation was used by Stockhausen, especially in *Mantra*. There was a group of students of Stockhausen, they called themselves the Öldorf group, they also—and I didn't know this at the time—they were familiar with the ideas of addition and subtraction of frequencies, of harmonic spectra, etc."[6]

The use of combination tones is one of the primary techniques of the French "spectral music" that emerged in the 1970s in the work of Grisey, Murail, and a few others. The term "spectral music" itself began to enter general usage following a 1979 article by Hugues Dufourt; Grisey preferred the term "liminal."[7] And while it would be misleading to categorize Vivier's music—even his later works—as "spectral" in the fullest sense of the term, his music was nonetheless transformed by the use of these techniques from 1980 onward; and he himself was a friend and contemporary of those composers in whose work the spectral aesthetic first came to prominence.

Because the whole spectral approach is so profound, any history of its precursors (who might stretch as far back as Rameau, and include Debussy, Varèse, Scelsi, Messiaen, and many others) becomes immense.[8] Yet whatever its lineage, the new French spectral music was a reaction in part against the prevailing norms of the day: against the serial aesthetic that was still rampant in Paris in the 1970s, and against aleatoric music, improvisation, and collage techniques. Murail has often cited the music of figures like Ligeti and Xenakis as more important in the development of his own thought than the music of Boulez or Barraqué, Cage or Stockhausen (even though the latter's *Stimmung* [1968] may be considered essentially a spectral work).[9] The essence of *la musique spectrale* is its search for compositional models based on sound, rather than on mathematics, or language, or visual imagery. In 1982 Grisey would famously declare: "We are musicians and our model is sound, not literature; sound, not mathematics; sound, not theatre, or the plastic arts, or quantum physics, or geology, astrology or acupuncture!"[10] The permutation of notes was replaced by a scrutiny of the inner life of sounds, which then became models for compositional forms. In the mid-70s Grisey and Murail undertook computer-aided analyses of the waveforms of complex sounds, studies that were sophisticated given the technology of the time but quite primitive in view of the means available today. The natural harmonic series was one such object of study, and an important one; it is the basis of the opening of Grisey's *Périodes* (1974) and his *Partiels* (1975), in which the low E of a trombone creates a spectrum that is simulated by the instrumental ensemble.[11] But the harmonic series was not the only model explored. In spectral music, harmonic spectra have no special priority as musical material over *inharmonic* spectra, which have just as much musical potential: early examples of such "distorted" spectra used as the basis of whole pieces are Grisey's *Jour, contre-jour* (1979) and Murail's *Gondwana* (1980). Models based on formant regions of the spectrum of a sound, rather than the whole spectrum, have also been used as compositional starting points, for example, in Murail's *Désintégrations* (1982). Even smaller units, such as a single interval with its sum and difference tones, can yield material of great richness and complexity, as is the case in the music of Vivier.

Vivier's adoption of a spectral technique such as the use of combination tones is perhaps not surprising given that the ground had already been prepared in his studies with his two main composition teachers, Tremblay and Stockhausen. Tremblay was the most distinguished of Messiaen's

Canadian pupils; he had also learned much from Varèse, who told him "our real master is sound."[12] Thanks to Tremblay Vivier would have absorbed many of Messiaen's ideas, including his "chord of resonance," an eight-pitch aggregate spanning two octaves and comprising harmonics 4–15 of the harmonic spectrum (albeit distorted considerably by the limitations of twelve-note equal temperament). In his treatise *Technique de mon langage musical* (1942), Messiaen also describes his use of "added resonance"—dissonant upper pitches added to a triad in the middle register—and "inferior resonance," dissonant clusters of notes in a low register with triadic configurations above them, citing the complex sounds of percussion instruments such as bells, gongs, and tam-tams as an analogy for this type of harmony. This way of thinking about the nature of sound is highly prophetic of the spectral aesthetic.[13]

Studying with Stockhausen, Vivier became familiar with an even closer precedent to the type of approach he would adopt in his music of the 1980s: the use of ring modulation. More so than *Stimmung*, it is Stockhausen's *Mantra* (1970) for two pianists and live electronics that relates most interestingly to Vivier's later work. Two aspects of *Mantra* are notable in this regard: its use of a single melodic "formula" to determine both large-scale form and small-scale detail; and its use of ring modulation to color the piano timbre. The first of these two features suggests a connection with Vivier's obsession with melody, increasingly the focus of his music from *Learning* of 1976 onward, as we have seen. The other aspect of *Mantra* is of no less consequence: the pianists modify the piano sound by operating a sine tone generator and a ring modulator. This latter device, a common feature on early modular synthesizers, is one that enjoyed a degree of vogue in the late 1960s. A ring modulator takes two signals as input and produces an output containing the sum and difference of their respective frequencies. If, for example, the inputs are two sine waves of 200 Hz and 300 Hz, the output from the ring modulator will be frequencies of 500 Hz (300 Hz + 200 Hz) and 100 Hz (300 Hz – 200 Hz)—the sum and difference tones, respectively. If waveforms richer than sine tones are used as input (in *Mantra*, the sound of the grand pianos) then the output signals from the ring modulator may become very complex; not infrequently the resulting sounds are like bells or various metallic sounds. Ring modulation was seized upon in the early studios as a way of creating inharmonic timbres. As we shall see, the analogous technique used by Vivier generates a sort of harmony that is likewise inharmonic, and not based on the natural harmonic series. Some years later he would remark to Grisey: "I also am writing spectra now. You've influenced me. . . . Only I twist mine a little!"[14]

This, in essence, is the principle used by Vivier in much of his music from 1980 onward to create the complex sonorities that he called, poetically, "les couleurs." His technique does not require the use of electronics at any stage, merely the calculation of the frequency values (in cycles per second) of musical notes. Just as in electronic music, where one pitch is ring-modulated against another, so too do Vivier's calculations involve two pitches. Typically, this is a melody note and the bass note below it: these two pitches are then subjected to an analogy of ring-modulation to produce new sum and difference tones, although in practice Vivier only makes use of sum tones. The dyadic basis of much of Vivier's later music is essential to his use of this technique.

His first work to use this principle is *Lonely Child* for soprano and orchestra, a commission from the Chamber Orchestra of Radio-Canada Vancouver. It uses a text by Vivier himself, partly in French and partly in "langue inventée." He began it after his return from Europe and completed it in Montreal on March 5, 1980. *Lonely Child* is dedicated to Louise Andrée, the Montreal singer and singing teacher, largely as a gesture of gratitude for her help coaching the singers in *Kopernikus*, which was in rehearsal at the time he was finishing the new work. Vivier described the piece as "a long song of solitude."[15]

To show how these new techniques work in practice, let us look at the first voice entry in *Lonely Child*, the first appearance of "les couleurs" in Vivier's output. The orchestral introduction to the piece, the first twenty-three measures, does not use them: the texture is entirely single melodic lines or dyads, always in octaves, punctuated by the occasional chiming of the *rin*, a Japanese percussion instrument that is a crucial ingredient in the overall sonority of the piece. When the soprano enters, with the words "O beautiful child of the light, sleep, sleep, sleep," "les couleurs" appear with her in the first violins, *divisi* in six parts. The first note she sings is an A, against a G in the bass (in the orchestral texture both notes are doubled in octaves). The A of the soprano, 440 Hz, and the G of the second horn and cellos, 196 Hz, when "ring-modulated," produce the combination tone of 636 Hz (440 Hz + 196 Hz, or a + b), a pitch that falls somewhere between the equal-tempered D♯ and E (622 Hz and 659 Hz, respectively); Vivier notates it as an E with a downward-pointing arrow before it, indicating a quartertone lower. (The exact frequency of the quartertone between D♯ and E is 640 Hz, very slightly higher than the pitch in question; but here this slight degree of inaccuracy is not considered to be of much consequence.) The resulting pitch is played by the fifth of the six first violins. Then the process continues: the new pitch, E a quartertone lower, is itself

ring-modulated against the original G: 636 Hz plus 196 Hz gives the combination tone of 832 Hz (a + 2b), almost exactly a tempered G♯ (which is
830.6 Hz); this pitch is taken by player four of the first violins. This new
note is in turn ring-modulated against the G: 832 Hz plus 196 Hz gives
1028 Hz (a + 3b), slightly lower than the tempered C (1047 Hz) although
not by as much as a quartertone (which would be 1017 Hz); Vivier thus
simply writes the note C without any inflection. This C is played by the
third first violin. And so the process continues, with two more, still higher,
combination tones. The total of five combination tones, played together,
make up the "couleur"—the spectral harmony—of the generative interval
G–A.

When the soprano sings her next pitch, a B♭, still against the same G
in the bass, a new set of calculations must begin, yielding a different array of combination tones. The B♭ is 466 Hz, which when ring-modulated
against the G of 192 Hz gives a combination tone of 662 Hz, which falls between E 659 Hz and the quartertone above it (679 Hz); Vivier nonetheless
opts for the quartertone, which he notates as F with a downward-pointing
arrow (in this case artistic taste would seem to have won out over acousti-
cal accuracy, as the combination tone generated is closer to the E). And so
begins the building up of another "color."

This process, with the sheaves of calculations necessary to it, may seem
exhausting, involving massive amounts of precompositional working-out;
but in actual fact the process is somewhat less extensive than we might
imagine, even for this seventeen-minute work. Because of the nature of the
melodic writing in *Lonely Child*, which restricts itself to a relatively modest palette of pitches, a comparatively small number of different melody-
note-and-bass combinations is used. The first extended soprano passage,
which Vivier calls "mélodie 1" (mm. 24–66), uses only fifteen different
such combinations; the second, "mélodie 2" (mm. 78–111) uses thirty-
eight, of which Vivier builds "couleurs" on thirty-six (two combinations
are used only in passing); the third, "mélodie 3" (mm. 113–40), by far the
most elaborate, uses eighty-nine; but "mélodie 4" (mm. 150–80) uses only
eleven.[16]

There is, in this manner of composing, an intriguing paradox: namely,
that so precisely calculated a process of pitch generation (by working out
Hertz values of the first-, second-, third-, and even higher-order combination tones) should yield a considerable amount of approximation when the
results are written down in musical notation. Clearly, the exact Hertz values must be "translated" into values meaningful to performing musicians.
In doing so, Vivier restricts himself to quartertones as a way of augmenting

the limited pitch palette of twelve-tone equal temperament—had he used eighthtones also (as Grisey and Murail had already done in various of their works of the 1970s) the approximations would be less inaccurate but the work would be correspondingly harder to play, the players having to negotiate forty-eight divisions of the octave rather than twenty-four. But in an approach such as Vivier's—and this point has been made by the composer Joshua Fineberg as true of spectral music in general—microtones are simply approximations of a set of frequencies to the nearest available musical pitches. Fineberg claims that "the ear is able to hear past these approximations and hear the underlying frequency structure whenever the approximation is within tolerable limits."[17]

The most striking and, from a compositional point of view, courageous structural feature of *Lonely Child* is its wholesale reliance on an essentially two-part texture of melody and bass, enhanced, "automatically, in a way," by "les couleurs." There is, as Vivier himself was well aware, no real counterpoint to speak of, although even with two voices there is a kind of functional harmony: "For the musical construction," he writes, "I wanted to have total control on the level of expression, control over the musical development of the work I was composing without using chords, harmony or counterpoint. I wanted to achieve a very homophonic music which would transform itself into a single melody, which would be 'intervalized.'"[18] The dyad is a characteristic Vivier sonority; it is to his music what the triad is to tonal music. Earlier works like *Learning* or *Pulau Dewata* had been largely homophonic, their single lines sometimes becoming two-part but rarely contrapuntal. This type of texture reappears in *Greeting Music*, the opening piano solo of which juxtaposes gamelan-style melodic fragments with dyads treated with nineteenth-century-style octave doublings. Dyadic textures also characterize parts of *Kopernikus* and the last section of *Orion*. However, in *Lonely Child* this concentration on melody and bass becomes *the* predominant texture. In the same 1982 lecture mentioned above, Vivier recounts an experience that made him realize the importance of two-part textures: "One day I heard a rehearsal of a chorale by Bach and I only heard two voices; I heard the alto and soprano voices together. It was an extraordinary experience because I heard that the music was still fantastic . . . two sounds superimposed, as an interval, are musically as important as a chord."[19] Vivier's friend Rober Racine remembers asking him on one occasion, "How do you compose?" Vivier "went to the piano, played some chords in a very high register, said 'I compose by colors. Two tones—it's so vast, so infinite, what you can do with two notes.'"[20]

What, then, is this beautiful, innovatory masterpiece ultimately "about?" Almost everyone seems to hear the work as autobiographical, with Vivier himself as the "lonely child" of the title. The text, a curious amalgam of the beautiful and the maudlin, the vivid and the incomprehensible, offers us some possible meanings, but only some. "Oh beautiful child of the light," it begins, "sleep, sleep, sleep on . . . dreams will come / sweet fairies will come to dance with you . . . fairies and elves will celebrate with you / the joyful farandole will intoxicate you." A simple benediction from mother to child? Is Vivier himself, as author of the text, then speaking as his own mother, the mother he never knew, hearing words he so desperately wanted to hear? The second mélodie, with its sudden introduction of invented language ("Ka rè nou ya zo na-ou dè wa ki") pulls us away from the world of possible meanings into linguistic terra incognita. Who is saying these words—is the child now "speaking" to the mother? (We should remember that Vivier did not know his birth mother's own native language, and therefore in which language he should address her.) The text ends in the same benedictory spirit in which it began: "And the hope of time / of time outside time / appears, my child / the stars in the sky shine for you, Tazio, and love you forever." The loved child has now, at the beginning of mélodie 4, acquired a name: Tazio, with its near-resonance with the beautiful youth, Tadzio, of Thomas Mann's *Death in Venice*. This act of naming suggests other possible readings: what had seemed at the outset like the love of a mother for her child can now be understood as love of a sexual, perhaps homoerotic, kind.

The autobiographical, self-revelatory nature of *Lonely Child*, so rich a part of its meaning, has an added poignancy given the fact that Vivier himself never heard the work in concert. Its first performance was for a studio recording by the Canadian radio in Vancouver by the young soprano Marie-Danielle Parent, for whom it was written, and the Chamber Orchestra of Radio Canada, Vancouver conducted by Serge Garant, on January 7, 1981. Vivier himself was not present: recently returned from another trip to Europe, he was unable to attend the session for reasons that are not certain but possibly related simply to a lack of money for a plane ticket. Marie-Danielle Parent has pointed out that although Vivier had a commission fee he did not necessarily have a travel grant to attend the recording: "I remember that Claude had told me he couldn't be there but that he had every confidence in Serge Garant and myself to give a good performance of the work."[21] Although he never heard a live performance of *Lonely Child*, he at least had a copy of the tape made in Vancouver, which he presented several times in lectures and public talks.[22] The first public performance of *Lonely Child* was not until nearly two years later, November 18, 1982, in the Salle Claude Champagne in Montreal, with the same soloist and conductor and the Orchestre des Jeunes du Québec. This, however, was during the period when Vivier was in Paris. The next public performance was given as part of the commemorative concert for Vivier in Montreal on June 2, 1983. By then, the request that ends mélodie 3 of *Lonely Child*—"please give me eternity"—had already been granted.

Vivier had first heard Marie-Danielle Parent singing in a Baroque concert at the University of Montreal in 1978, and immediately fell in love with her voice. She also sang in the performance of *Chants* that Lorraine Vaillancourt was preparing at that time. "It was fantastic to have this guy who likes your voice so much," she says.[23] She decided to repeat *Chants* for her master's examination; Vivier came to the performance with a flower for each of the singers. Parent was at that time preparing for a lot of singing competitions, and included *Hymnen an die Nacht* in her repertory. She found it relatively easy to work on *Lonely Child*, "to enter his special language," partly thanks to this prior experience of his music. Besides, he would often phone her and sing her the music over the phone. She found his "child-like sensibility" easy to relate to. And he would sometimes turn up unannounced to eat with them, adding Parent and her husband Denis Gougeon to the list of suppliers of free meals on his circuit. Even though he was some six years older than her, she felt he began to treat them almost as surrogate parents.

Although he admired the pure, nonvibrato quality of her voice, Vivier, Parent insists, "was open to all interpretations; he told me he'd like to hear *Lonely Child* with Jessye Norman. He was never dogmatic with things like that." In Vancouver she was discussing the score of *Lonely Child* with Serge Garant and remembers Garant saying to her: "You know Claude is so strange—he was always telling me *Lonely Child* is a masterpiece and, you know, I think he's right!" At first she was surprised about the choice of an English title, but came to agree that the English version is stronger than the French; and it was after all a commission for English-speaking Vancouver, as *Greeting Music* had been. She recalls Vivier phoning her about the title, and saying: "*L'enfant seule* is so *moche* [ugly], it's nothing."

Marie-Danielle Parent and Denis Gougeon formed a welcome addition to Vivier's ever-expanding circle of friends in Montreal. His working days were long and intense, so a break from the daily grind of composition always involved sociability of various kinds, and by now he did not lack for it. His daily routine began with a trek outside in search of breakfast. For years his favorite eatery was Dusty's, a few blocks south on avenue du Parc, almost at the corner with avenue du Mont Royal. Then, back home, the day's work would begin, punctuated by phone calls to friends to play and sing what he had written, and to solicit their approval. At night there were bars: Taverne Wilson on avenue Laurier, Bar 5116, the Pit Bar and Bar-Salon Skala on Avenue du Parc itself. The company he was keeping was mixed, but included an ever-increasing number of younger people. John Rea, returning from a sabbatical in Berlin in 1979–80, "met Claude on the street, and went for a drink with him. I met his rather younger friends, to whom he was kind of a hero, and a leader. The only musician I saw him with regularly was Michel-Georges Brégent."[24]

Brégent, who was Vivier's exact contemporary, was a valued drinking buddy as well as a respected colleague. But increasingly, another form of contact was with composers even younger than himself, for whom Vivier was now beginning to seem a force to be reckoned with. Among them was Michel Gonneville, who, although only two years younger, had at least temporarily come to regard Vivier as a sort of mentor. He too had studied with Stockhausen, three years after Vivier, as well as in Belgium with Henri Pousseur. By the late 1970s, Gonneville feels,

> Claude exerted a certain influence around Montreal composers in large part because he was so extroverted and would talk so openly and at any moment about his own musical ideas. Sometimes it could be tiring, about what he was doing, about *pureté*—how many times did he use that word! the purity of childhood, the purity of an interval, the reduction to almost nothing, silence, death, etc. But in talking in this way a lot rubbed off on the other composers around him, who found him an inspiration.

Vivier, he feels, was "the embodiment and even the prophet of a certain postmodern attitude which settled in the later 1980s and '90s."[25] Denis Gougeon, a year younger again than Gonneville, agrees:

> For me and for many other composers, I'm sure, Claude Vivier is the most original voice in the last part of the twentieth century, not only in Canada . . . there was a real kinship that Vivier helped cement, himself, Rea, Evangelista, Brégent, Boudreau; a non-restrictive way of thinking, an eclecticism; respect for the performer; a simplicity; a willingness to experiment with things; a sort of community of thought. Claude would go to all the new music concerts around Montreal, at McGill, at the

University of Montreal, so he was very well informed. He heard my *Voix intimes*, written in New York, for two voices, four clarinets, and percussion, and liked it a lot. He told me: you understand voices.

One of Vivier's legacies, Gougeon feels, is the "new postmodernism in Montreal that Claude's work helped to encourage."[26]

Perhaps the closest of all these friendships by now was with a woman some fifteen years older than Vivier himself, Thérèse Desjardins. Desjardins had bought an apartment on rue Chabot in 1978 after separating from her husband, the politician and author Jacques Hébert, and Vivier spent increasing amounts of time there, becoming a regular fixture at Christmas and at other family celebrations. Walter Boudreau remarks that "the only real family Claude ever had was in those last years with Thérèse and her children," adding: "but it was too late: even that could not compensate for the hurt."[27] Desjardins clearly fulfilled a sort of mother role for him, as well as being interested in, and supportive toward, his music; she was warm-hearted and accepting to all corners of Montreal society, even welcoming into her home the down-and-outs with whom Vivier sometimes associated. She and her daughters passed no judgment on his tendency in the evenings to want to go and "drag in the park," that is, to put on makeup and try to attract men; her daughters would sometimes help him get ready.[28]

Indeed, he was more sexually active now than ever. "Claude would boast about fucking nine guys in a sauna, but you never knew where his deep feelings were," says Boudreau. "He drew a line that none of us managed to cross, and we can only cross it now listening to his music."[29] José Evangelista adds: "I remember that he said things so naturally, not intimate things, but details about his sex life and would shock people at a gathering or a meal, but it was so natural, it was never forced."[30]

In one sense Vivier had less need to be anxious about openly displaying his homosexuality in Montreal than in many other cities. It had not always been so: in 1975 and again the following year, there were large-scale protests after the police raided gay establishments in Quebec and in Ottawa in the buildup to the 1976 Olympics, which were held that summer in Montreal. In 1977, however, the Quebec Charter of Rights and Freedoms was amended to make Quebec the first jurisdiction in the world to prohibit discrimination based on sexual orientation in the public and private sectors. There was a greater feeling of openness toward, and acceptance of, homosexuality than ever before. And while he would now unreservedly display his gay orientation in public, and discuss it in interviews, Vivier would continue on occasion to have sexual contact with women, just as he had done in his student days, without it seeming in any way to threaten his self-identification as a gay man.

For all his need for human company, Vivier was also a voracious reader, reading copious amounts of fiction, works of philosophy, cultural studies, books on cinema, and much else. His shelves were full of books by Marguerite Duras, Hermann Hesse, and Roland Barthes, side by side with classic works of literature, recent studies such as *Bruits* (1977) by Jacques Attali, which he heavily annotated, or *Langage, musique, poésie* (1972) by Nicolas Ruwet, together with much poetry, including many volumes by Quebec writers. His collection also contained much in the area of film studies, including Eric Rohmer's influential little book *L'organisation de l'espace dans le "Faust" de Murnau* (1977). There were many books on Asian subjects, arts and culture: Mircéa Eliade's *Patanjali et le Yoga, Le Sacré et le profane, Le Chamanisme,* and *Forgerons et Alchimistes*; and on Russian culture and history, including Isaiah Berlin's *Russian Thinkers* and Marc Raeff's classic *Origins of the Russian Intelligentsia.* There were also books by Albert Camus, Graham Greene, Samuel Beckett, Marguerite Yourcenar, and other recent fiction. And of course he had many books on music, both technical treatises such as Bartolozzi's *New Sounds for Woodwind* or Schoenberg's *Fundamentals of Musical Composition* and numerous scores, including various pices by Webern and a heavily annotated copy of Bartók's Fourth String Quartet.[31]

The early spring of 1980 was largely taken up with the preparations for the premiere of *Kopernikus* in May, but by the summer he had settled back into composition. He completed a new work, *Zipangu,* for thirteen strings, in Montreal on August 13, a commission from the New Music Concerts series in Toronto. The piece is conceived not for a string orchestra but for thirteen solo players (seven violins, three violas, two cellos, and double bass) with discreet amplification to reinforce the sound. While quite different from *Lonely Child* in terms of mood and overall sonority, the piece is still audibly tingling from his recent exposure to *la musique spectrale.* Tristan Murail, on listening to a recording of the piece that Vivier played for him, found it "very beautiful and strange."[32]

Zipangu, as Vivier explained in the program note, "was the name given to Japan in Marco Polo's time." This is, then, another work inspired by travel to distant lands—and in this case distant not only geographically but in time. But it is also the first reference we find to Vivier's fascination with Marco Polo, the famous Italian medieval traveler, whose writings about his voyages did so much to introduce Europeans to the cultures of central Asia and China. It would be quite a stretch to hear anything pseudo-Japanese, or for that matter pseudo-medieval, in the music, but there is a very audible and immediate link with *Lonely Child*—the phrase near the beginning of that work to the words "les rêves viendront," transposed now above an E fundamental, becomes the main motif of the violin melody that opens *Zipangu*. This phrase, involving only three pitches—the third, the sharpened fourth, and the fifth of the mode—begins, with its recurrence in this piece, to feel something like a Vivier signature: versions of it recur in several later works. It also functions spectrally, by simulating partials ten, eleven, and twelve of a harmonic series above the fundamental. In technical terms there is one main departure from *Lonely Child*, namely, that Vivier does not here use the principle of melody plus bass plus combination tones to construct the texture (although the dense chordal passage beginning at m. 40 comes somewhat close to it in effect); on the other hand, he makes much use of *son "grain,"* a granular sound produced by exaggerated bow pressure, an essential part of the sonic vocabulary of early spectralism (used to marvelous effect in Murail's *Treize couleurs du soleil couchant* of 1978, among other works).[33] Striking, too, are the virtuosic outbursts for a solo violin, near the beginning and end, like a free spirit wishing to detach itself from the swarming mass. In his program note for the premiere Vivier explains the techniques of the piece, here using the word "couleur" differently from its quite specific meaning in *Lonely Child*: "Around a melody, I explore in this work different aspects of 'color.' I tried to 'blur' my harmonic structures by the use of different bowing techniques. In this way I oppose a colored noise obtained by exaggerated bow pressure on the strings with pure harmonics when the players return to normal technique. A melody becomes color (chords), lightens, and returns little by little, as if purified and solitary."[34] There is here a clear urge to explore sound as a medium, in terms that recall some of the discourse around spectral music. With *Lonely Child* and this brilliantly evocative piece, he had found new ways to enrich the technical basis of his music, with the clear possibility of further explorations in these realms. The cul-de-sac of the (then still unperformed) *Orion* was already light years in the past.

In the wake of *Zipangu* Vivier produced another new work, rather rapidly, finishing the score on September 26. The *Cinq chansons pour percussion* were written for David Kent, the Toronto-based percussionist who had played in the premiere of *Journal* the previous year. Recently returned from Indonesia with a collection of percussion instruments, Kent had asked for a solo work that would incorporate them. Vivier was glad to respond, though this is one of the few of his later works to be written without a paid commission. Having by now well and truly assimilated his own Balinese experience, Vivier could not simply step back into the world of *Pulau Dewata*, and the instrumentation he settled upon is a colorful hybrid, involving a Javanese *bonang* or Balinese *trompong* (with sixteen tuned pots in either case), nine Thai nipple gongs (also tuned), two *changs* (Japanese temple bowls) and one low *chang*, and a medium-size Chinese gong.[35] The five parts, which play without a break, each have titles, and Vivier sketched a brief description of their character:

Chanson du matin
a few sounds that reflect each other, on which the mind focuses—that take life in them, upon them—
Chanson à midi
a gentle and tender melody is born—it stops in places to catch its breath
Chanson au soleil
an exuberant hymn to the sun, which continually repeats and never stops
Chanson à la mort
heavy eyes look upon the abyss of a life of meditation
Chanson d'adieu
as in a dream everything is mixed together![36]

In another note he described the musical nature of the piece: "The term 'chansons' is used in the Asian sense and describes five musical statements around a few notes. The piece was worked out in collaboration with its dedicatee, David Kent. . . . The five songs . . . unfold like the cycle of life, changing atmosphere from one to the next. A punctuation by the chang ends each one. The spell of these sonorities comes from the incantatory character of the writing, by repeated formulas, always slightly modified."[37] György Ligeti, in speaking of the Asiatic influence on Vivier's work, remarked that "it's more a question of a conglomeration than an exact influence," and this is absolutely to the point in considering a work like the *Cinq chansons*.[38] It is perhaps impossible not to sound Asiatic, at least to western ears, in a work written for such a collection of instruments. But the rhythmic character of the music is rather different than any specific nonwestern source, so that the overall result does not sound particularly Balinese, or Japanese, or anything else; the marvelous "Chanson à midi," the second piece, has audible connections with the world of *Lonely Child*. The urge to write lyrically for percussion, always Vivier's tendency, here becomes predominant, so that the player has to shape the phrases of the music almost as though they are vocal phrases. The occasional harmonic sonorities that emerge (particularly an interval that in western terms would be called a major tenth, but heard here in various tunings depending on the instruments used) have a wonderful effect, like magic casements through which we glimpse views of a beautiful world just beyond reach. The *Cinq chansons* is also part of the long list of his works that Vivier was never to hear in concert: it was premiered by David Kent in Toronto in June 1982, by which time Vivier had left Canada for the last time. "Perhaps it is one of the many paradoxes in his life," Kent notes, "that a piece he considered to be one of his most personal works was to be shared by everyone except himself."[39]

From another perspective, the *Cinq chansons*, with its immersion in what Ligeti called "a nonexistent folklore of southeast Asia," shows, as do many other works, Vivier completely bypassing what was then (and had been, and would remain) one of the central cultural issues for citizens of his province: the tension between a Quebec that looked back to the old centers of European civilization and one that looked forward to the bright horizons of the New World.[40] It is as though imaginary lands and timeless, ahistorical issues held more attraction for him than real-life ones. (It is interesting in this regard that one of the original suggestions as librettist for the opera he had recently completed was Michel Tremblay, the Montreal playwright and author of *Les Belles-Soeurs*, the play written entirely in *joual* that had enjoyed a *succès de scandale* a decade earlier. But Vivier did not pursue this collaboration, with its potential for a nationalist operatic statement, choosing instead the cultural never-never land of *Kopernikus*.) Perhaps his true feelings on the matter come across in a little text titled "Créativité et cinéma québécois," written this year. "The adjective 'québécois' should certainly not be used to define an *a priori* aesthetic nor a philosophical or political vision," he proclaims, "but for an authentic definition of this kind of cinema": cinema made by someone from Quebec is "cinéma québécois." This, he says, is the important thing to remember in discussions of creativity: "it's actually creativity that redefines, every moment, the word 'québécois.'"[41] Quebec art, or Quebec music, is only defined by what the artist does.

Quebec's relationship with the Old World had always been problematic, not least because of the French tendency to find the Quebecois accent and manners ridiculous. By his own admission Vivier had never felt entirely comfortable in Paris, another visit to which he was now planning; he was conscious of the fact that his native attributes of conviviality, bonhomie, and informality were quite at odds with the stereotypically Parisian traits of snobbishness, hostility to outsiders, and obsession with hierarchy and social status.[42] For the sake of his music, however, the Old World still had much to offer, and he felt it essential to remain visible there. He made another trip to Europe at the end of the year, perhaps with the intention of reaping what he had sown the previous winter. But the only European performances of his music that we can document around this time are two outings of *Pulau Dewata*, one on October 31 directed by Robert HP Platz at Walter Zimmermann's Beginner-Studio in Cologne, and one by the ensemble l'Itinéraire in Paris on November 18, both of which predate his arrival. His passport was stamped in Paris on November 26, 1980, and we have a hotel receipt from Hotel am Neumarkt in Cologne dated December 18: otherwise his exact movements and activities are unknown. In Paris he saw Paul Méfano and played him the tape of *Kopernikus*; Méfano suggested he compose a new string quartet for le Quatuor Français, an idea that Vivier pursued enthusiastically, applying in February to the Canada Council for a commission.

Meanwhile, in Montreal, the third season of Les Événements du neuf had begun. This time the four events were spaced at bimonthly intervals rather than monthly. The first, a performance by The Glass Orchestra—four musicians from Toronto improvising on glass objects—was held in a studio at the University of Quebec, on the night of November 8–9, beginning, uncharacteristically, at 11:00 p.m. The second, "À la recherche du tango perdu," with tangos by Satie, Stravinsky, Lehár, Krenek, and Weill, then real Argentinian tangos by Piazzolla, Paulos, and Villodo, followed on January 9, 1981, two days after the premiere in Vancouver of *Lonely Child*. (It would be upsetting to think that Vivier gave up plans to hear the Vancouver performance because of his loyalty to the activities of Les Événements du neuf.) The third, "Carnets de voyage," followed on March 9, and was exclusively devoted to works by the organizers themselves, Evangelista, Rea, and Vivier (*Chants*). Finally, "La nouvelle mélodie II" in May brought music from Cologne, with Stockhausen's *Indianerlieder* and pieces from Walter Zimmermann's cycle *Lokale Musik*.

Despite the prodigious amount of new music he was now producing, Vivier was now more active than ever in the Montreal music world. He made frequent trips to the Radio-Canada studios to record his contributions to Musique de Canadiens, a series hosted by musicologist Louise Bail Milot, with broadcasts in February and March devoted to the Toronto scene. (The previous autumn he had taken part in a broadcast titled "Musique et jeux scéniques" to promote the forthcoming concerts of Les Événements du neuf.) The Musique de Canadiens series would give him a platform to talk about almost anything he wanted, and he was also paid, albeit modestly, for his contributions. In the middle of February he was at the Department of Music at Carleton University in Ottawa as one of the invited guests at their festival of Canadian music. There, on the afternoon of Monday 16, he lectured on his opera *Kopernikus* and presented a recording. A review that appeared in *Le Droit* the following day reports in remarkable detail the introspective nature of his talk:

> The final work of his "autobiographical" period, a ritual outlet which will liberate him—perhaps—from the young boy in him, who, singing the Midnight Mass, contracted the virus for a certain kind of music. . . . "Kopernikus" ends in symbols, contrary in approach to the upsurge of a whole series of works including "Love Songs" and "Journal." The process was hastened along, in a way, by a long stay in Asia where the loss of identity highlighted his true identity, and in another way by a reaction against the musical objectivity that sculpted his musical education at the feet of Darmstadt, of Stockhausen and acoustical criteria. . . . More traditional than some of his previous works, will "Kopernikus" be the final proof or the beginnings of a new Vivier? His next opera "Marco Polo" will tell us.[43]

CHAPTER TEN

# " THE PASSIONATE LOVE FOR MUSIC THAT SOMETIMES STOPS ME FROM COMPOSING "

## 1981–82

The *Le Droit* review of Vivier's Carleton University talk in February 1981 provides the earliest mention we have of the new opera he was now planning. If the musical portrait he had produced some months before of Marco Polo's Zipangu was the first musical manifestation of this, he was at work now on an even more ambitious part of the edifice: the *Prologue pour un Marco Polo*, a twenty-five-minute cantata for five singing voices, speaking voice, six clarinets, two percussion, thirteen strings, and tape, which he completed in Montreal on March 1, 1981. The work was commissioned by Radio-Canada as an entry for the 1981 Paul Gilson Prize of the Communauté des radios publiques de langue française. For this reason the premiere performance, conducted by Lorraine Vaillancourt, was for a radio recording, as had been the case with *Lonely Child*. He dedicated the score to Thérèse Desjardins.

Vivier departs in this work from his usual practice of writing both words and music himself. He told an interviewer later in the year: "I gave myself the goal of working at least once in my life with a writer to make an acceptable text."[1] The *Prologue* was a collaboration with Quebec poet Paul Chamberland, who had come to attention in the mid-1960s for his strongly nationalistic collections *Terre Québec* and *L'Afficheur hurle*, as well as for his cofounding of Quebec's political and cultural magazine *Parti Pris*, a radical publication that, during the five years of its existence, advocated an independent, socialist Quebec that would reject the implications and the rhetoric of "French Canada." In Vivier's *Prologue*, however, the theme of Quebec nationalism is not in evidence, unless somehow one is to take Marco Polo and his voyages symbolically. Vivier wrote that the piece was "A melancholy look at the drama of Marco Polo—and above all a meditation on a state of being—that of the misunderstood searcher."[2] (Is an obscure kinship perhaps being hinted at between Polo and Jacques Cartier, the French explorer who first described and mapped the shores of the Saint Lawrence River, claiming Canada for the French? In any case, there is nothing in the work itself, either text or music, to support this hypothesis.)

Years later Chamberland told the musicologist Paul Griffiths that he had enjoyed the collaboration with Vivier on the *Prologue*.

> The figure of Marco Polo he already had in his head, and so for me it was—well, "easy" would not be the word, because I had to work, but it was a question of being on that level. And that excited me. From the beginning I listened attentively to what Claude said, and to the rhythm of how he spoke, which was very rapidly, staccato. . . . When I got home I wrote down things, sometimes phrases, and let that work, one might say. Then I would go to his place—which was in indescribable disorder, scores everywhere. He played what he had written at the piano, and I came with my words, and a kind of circuit was formed. He was a seer, a *listener*. There was one writer we had in common, as a reference: Aurobindo. What fascinated me was that he already was in that visionary world . . . nobody is entirely self-sufficient, but he had an autonomy in his thinking. He had a passion to make something *be*. He felt himself inspired, at the service of something. Yet at the same time he wasn't egocentric. There was a complete absence of vanity in him. . . . There coexisted in him an abandoned child and a kind of being like an angel, who had completely a sense of his gravity.[3]

As Vivier explained in his program note, the *Prologue pour un Marco Polo* uses not only Chamberland's words but "three levels of language": "literary French, a language that speaks more about Polo than allows him to speak, and also a language that, thanks to the music, guides us to another, invented language, which is that of the general incomprehension that poor Marco hit up against."[4] By the first of these, "literary French," Vivier is surely referring to Chamberland's text; regarding the last he provides a justification, if such be needed, for the use once again of the invented language. (One wonders if he had been criticized, or teased, for the use of the *langue inventée* in earlier works and felt the need to defend himself.) The second phrase, "a language that speaks more about Polo than allows him to speak," would seem to refer to one of the oddest aspects of the work: its penultimate section originally included the playback of a short taped conversation between Vivier and Chamberland about the mythology of Marco Polo, so that—in a strikingly postmodern way—the two creators would be heard talking about the subject of their creation during its actual performance. Although integrated into the 1982 Radio-Canada recording of the work, the original tape was then apparently erased by the engineers who did not seem to realize the need to preserve it. The conversation, at least in its original form, can therefore no longer be a part of any live performances of the work.[5]

The form of the *Prologue pour un Marco Polo* is unique in Vivier's output, consisting as it does of eight discrete sections that follow each other without pause. Their succession is highly convincing: each has its own mood and its own particular configuration of the available sound sources, and the whole work builds and releases intensity in a way that never loses the listener's interest. (Ligeti judged the work to be one of Vivier's most perfect, with "an absolutely remarkable large-scale architecture."[6]) As with Nicolaus Copernicus, Vivier admitted that the historical Marco Polo was of considerably less interest to him than the symbolic one: to him, Polo was a dreamer, a misunderstood explorer, "someone who tried to say something and didn't succeed," the whole figure "quite desperate." (Vivier never explained why he insisted that Polo was misunderstood or, for that matter, why this extremely rich and successful man—if we leave aside his time in prison—was so "desperate.") So, in Vivier's *Prologue*, Polo encounters a Sage "who understands Polo but also makes fun of him"; we feel the sadness, from Polo's perspective, of Zipangu, "a land glimpsed but not reached." Polo has a "solo de la solitude," his consolation being music, which "blurs everything and becomes the state of grace for lonely visionaries." Then comes a vision of death, juxtaposed with a vision of the immortality of Marco Polo as symbol; and finally Polo's testament, sung by a female voice, "a long solo climbing ever higher, the voice of God becoming almost the voice of madness." The work is thus a free fantasy on themes of isolation, misunderstanding, mockery, lack of recognition, and ultimately the hope of immortality. Surely we cannot overlook the autobiographical element even in this apparently historical conception.

In the premiere of the work, the intense, compelling soprano solo that forms its last part (to the words "Errant o chercheur méconnu") was sung by Pauline Vaillancourt, the singer who had premiered *Lettura di Dante* some eight years previously. "For me this was his best work," she says. "Again very difficult writing for the voice, but effective." She loved the suspended feeling of the long soprano line at the end, with its feeling of "going beyond ourselves, more than normal." She had heard but not particularly liked *Kopernikus*, finding it "a bit confused, too many words. I think Vivier came back to the purity in *Marco Polo* that *Lettura di Dante* had, that I miss in the works in between."[7] There are definite shades of *Kopernikus* in the sound world of this new piece, with its inner ensemble of clarinets, and in its harmonies; but the rich, spectrally derived textures of *Lonely Child* and *Zipangu* make their mark here too, and the combination-tones principle is once again used in parts of the score. Vivier in the *Prologue* shows himself to be master of his sound world: elements familiar from earlier works, such as the use of Asian percussion (*rins* and Balinese gong) are here perfectly integrated with the string-and-wind chordal textures and the singing, shouting, and teasing voices, in a world where what Paul Griffiths has described as the self-indulgent "infantilism" of parts of *Journal* or *Kopernikus* is wholly absent.[8]

Merely ten days after finishing the score of the *Prologue pour un Marco Polo*, Vivier put the final signature on the fifty-three manuscript pages of another major work, substantial, ambitious, and entirely different from its predecessor: *Wo Bist du Licht!* for mezzo-soprano, strings, percussion, and tape. It seems impossible to believe that this music, with its extensive use of the combination-tones principle and therefore a huge amount of precompositional calculation, could have been entirely composed in the period between March 1 and 11. There must surely have been some degree of overlap in the composition of the two works. Vivier described *Wo Bist du Licht!* as a "meditation on human suffering." The original working title, "L'enfant aux étoiles," was jettisoned in favor of the more urgent title, a phrase from Friedrich Hölderlin's poem *Der blinde Sänger*. *Wo bist du Licht!* is unusual in Vivier's output in being his only work (arguably, since the student piece *Musique pour une liberté à bâtir* in 1968–69) that shows a concern with recent political events, specifically North American ones. A sketch among his papers describes an idea for a radiophonic work to be called *Discours politique*, which has features in common with *Wo bist du Licht!* but without the singer. It was planned as a "history of the twentieth century from 1945 (the atomic bomb) and the first steps of man on the moon / the end of the Vietnam war."[9] But the work that emerged is more nuanced and ambiguous in its standpoint than this early sketch suggests.

Even in a work of twenty minutes' duration Vivier sets only certain lines of Hölderlin's thirteen-stanza poem, in German, interspersing them with multiple repetitions of the title phrase and a long passage in the *langue inventée*. A further dimension is provided by the tape, which contains four pieces of spoken material. The first is part of Martin Luther King's famous 1963 speech "I Have a Dream," followed by a recording in situ of the assassination of Robert Kennedy, the two forming material that Vivier described as "emotional text, with a very great significance for America." Later comes a recording with Vivier himself reading parts of the Hölderlin *Der blinde Sänger*; and, right at the end of the work, a recording that the score describes simply as "femme vietnamienne" but that consists of two radio announcers, in French, in an "almost neutral tone," describing torture, their words thereby having "an enormous emotional impact." But it is the Hölderlin poem, Vivier tells us, that "contains within it the secret of my work": "An old blind man recalls his past, marvelous visual images; greenery, the wings of clouds, etc. The present is evoked by auditory images: thunder, earthquakes. He looks for light, for freedom, perhaps for death."[10] Two blind singers in a marketplace in Iran, we recall, had been the inspiration for *Shiraz* some four years earlier; but this blind singer is a rather different character, an end-of-life image of a lonely individual recalling the beauties of the past.

We may wonder what connection Vivier felt between Hölderlin's old man (here, like Agni, represented by a woman) and the collection of taped material he assembled for *Wo bist du Licht!* A starting point was perhaps the idea of freedom. Just as the blind singer, as Vivier interprets him, is searching for freedom, so too the Martin Luther King tape with its endlessly repeated "Let freedom ring" bears the same message ("Let freedom ring from the mighty mountains of New York! Let freedom ring from the heightening Alleghenies of Pennsylvania! Let freedom ring from the snowcapped Rockies of Colorado! Let freedom ring from the curvaceous slopes of California!").[11] Vivier's musical ear was doubtless responsible for his choosing the more incantatory latter part of King's speech, with its rhythmic reiterations, rather than the more discursive and argued opening sections. But the fact that the last moments of this tape overlap with the 1968 recording of Robert Kennedy's assassination seems to give a rather different message. Is Vivier acknowledging that the dreams of the 1960s, for freedom and everything else, have turned sour? The subsequent recording of descriptions of torture in the Vietnam war would seem to emphasize this. It is another incursion in Vivier's work of themes of violence and human brutality. The blind singer, dreaming of past beauties and "perhaps [of] death," can be seen as implicitly acknowledging that all hopes of paradise in this world are in vain.

Musically, *Wo bist du Licht!* is a tour de force for the solo mezzo-soprano (sung in the first performances by Joscelyne Fleury-Coutu, his Agni in *Kopernikus*); once she begins, some three and a half minutes into the piece, she stops only rarely until the very end. Technically speaking, as Vivier's program note tells us, "we hear a slow development . . . a spectral music merging with the contours of a sine wave." The work begins with the electrifying sound of the strings loudly playing a dyad G–B in octaves with excessive bow pressure, a noisy, quasi-electronic sound, with occasional punctuations by bangs on a bass drum and Balinese gong. Here, Vivier's spectral vocabulary is used to generate a mood of terror, which abates slowly, only to return. Once the singer enters, however, this opening music does not recur. The singer's melody and its bass line are used to generate combination tones, exactly the technique used in *Lonely Child*, though here with even larger chords made possible by the bigger string group. This creates a massive and densely microtonal texture. Later the constituent tones of these chords are grouped into repeating mobiles, creating a vertiginous swirl under the voice and the banging and chiming of the percussion. When the singer shifts into the *langue inventée*, the string texture is progressively taken over with whirling triplet figures in the strings, with a percussionist doubling the vocal line rhythmically on a set of brake drums that give a harsh and only approximately pitched shadow to the melody. The result, to the listener, is music of an incredible intensity that in this respect goes beyond parts of the *Prologue pour un Marco Polo*. Vivier's wish to grab the listener, to pin the audience to their seats, has never felt more urgent.

The violence that is a striking part of both the music and what might be called the documentary content of *Wo bist du Licht!* is not without a sort of parallel in an aspect of Vivier's personal life: his increasing interest in, and attraction to, the sadomasochistic practices that were an aspect of the gay scene in Montreal as elsewhere.

In discussing this aspect of Vivier's life we have little solid information to go on, as his gay friends are not at all forthcoming on the subject (which may of course suggest that there is actually relatively little to be forthcoming about). His friend Lambert Ferrand remarks that, like many gay men of his acquaintance, Vivier was attracted to the stereotype of the "tough guy," the leather-clad, muscular, biker type.[12] Sophie Hébert, the youngest daughter of Thérèse Desjardins, who was about sixteen when she got to know Vivier, says: "Claude knew I had a lot of weird people in my life, and he was interested in that. I was involved in the Hell's Angels since I was very young, and Claude wanted to know all about that. He was fascinated with the look, and the scary part. He wanted to go to the extreme."[13]

Vivier seems to have wanted to share this fascination even with friends who were not at all part of that world. His young friend Rober Racine— musician, visual artist, and writer, and the dedicatee of *Wo bist du Licht!*— recalls an occasion in the late spring of 1982 when Vivier finally had a recording of the work and wanted to play it for him. He invited some other friends, "some guys whom I didn't know and felt a bit uncomfortable with," says Racine. "It was a beautiful sunny day. I said to Claude how powerful I found [the piece]. I wanted to stay more with Claude and talk, stay with this music and him": but Vivier was going on to a party with his other friends and Racine did not want to join them. "Violence is fascinating," he comments, "erotic also. You can go each time one step further."[14]

Some years later a journalist interviewed Racine about his memories of this aspect of Vivier's life: "One evening, [Vivier] brought his friend Rober Racine to the boulevard Saint-Laurent, to a tavern where transvestites, beggars and other homeless people gathered. At the back of the room there was a guy who looked so scary that he seemed to have come straight out of Dante's Hell. That guy, he told Racine, was with him in the orphanage. 'My music is here,' he added, gesturing around the room full of lost souls."[15]

As to Vivier's actual involvement in sadomasochistic practices, however, we have very little information, and even some recollections by friends that suggest a different overall picture. Sophie Hébert recalls Vivier's participation in a performance by her friend Daniel Guimond in 1981:

> We had a studio, first called Scrap Gallery, and then Galerie Limite— Claude was there all the time—on St Catherine and St Laurent, next to the prostitute part, all painted in black. We had people come from Europe, an exchange thing. And we did a sort of happening, called *Mon Corps*, where my boyfriend—actually he wasn't my boyfriend at the time—where he was whipped. Claude whipped him, in German, and he's screaming in German, and he's counting, he's at eight, and he turned to me, and he said, should I go on? Or should I stop? Because he didn't want to hurt him.[16]

Vivier's thoughts on sexuality and art formed a large part of an interview he gave that spring to Daniel Carrière, which appeared in the magazine *Le Berdache* in its July–August 1981 issue. The author begins by describing the new apartment to which Vivier had moved that March, his
first move in four years. No. 7 Chemin de la Côte-Sainte-Catherine was
only some fifteen minutes walk away from his place on avenue du Parc, in
the direction of the Parc du Mont Royal; he lived in apartment #1102 in a
huge, seventeen-floor 1960s building known as the Tour Suisse.[17] This gave
him an astonishing view and did not represent a real change of neighborhood: all his friends and his old haunts were just as handy as before. "His
place is in an astonishing disorder 'which is sometimes the beautiful effect
of art' (anonymous), a small grey apartment on the eleventh floor of an
impersonal high-rise. The piano takes up all the space. It's a nervous man
who receives me, always running after an event that excites him, passionate about the cinema, a friend of all creation but extremely critical, a great
gossip with a crazy laugh." Carrière comments that "for the first time, to
my knowledge, someone defends the thesis of a 'gay' music. Composed
by a gay man, available to the majority for the raising of a gay consciousness." But Vivier's own words are perhaps not quite so straightforward.
He is describing the lack of dramatic action in *Kopernikus*, for which he
says several people criticized him: "As the basis of *Kopernikus* I wanted
absolutely no conflict. In this sense, it's from *Kopernikus* onwards that I
began to discover a type of sensibility I wanted to express that was very
very individual." He quotes a phrase of Annie Leclerc, "the universal has
brought us the face of the particular," and continues:

> Male discourse, the way it is presented to us in western civilisation, is a
> discourse that obliges us to be strong, great, dominating, which obliges
> music to be goal-oriented, which obliges opera to have conflicts, to put
> the universal on stage. It is this that, on the level of sensibility, is called
> into question. Right now what we see is an enormous crisis of civilization,
> an extremely profound one, and which can be expressed in terms that
> feminists like Annie Leclerc have revealed in a very brilliant way. Ever
> since the Greeks we are obliged to live with a macho complex in works of
> art. . . . When I talk about a gay discourse in that sense, a gay discourse, as
> much as a feminist discourse, is a way of putting people on an equal foot-
> ing without discrimination. For me a gay discourse completely throws
> into question any particular sensibility, whether homosexual or hetero-
> sexual. This puts the debate on a higher level. It's no longer important
> if my sexuality expresses itself in a homosexual way, it must be possible
> to surpass that in order to discover things, for example: I no longer pity

the fact that I'm a queer, in transcending that I discover things that the heterosexual, whose sexuality is never called into question, doesn't have the chance to encounter. It's this that makes some heterosexuals today question their sexuality, and in this sense there is a gay movement that affects heterosexuals as well as homosexuals.

A footnote on this subject is provided by a conversation Vivier had around this time with Rober Racine. "I once said to Claude," Racine recalls, "that I'd like to write a book about him and his music. Vivier's first response was 'You have to say I love women!' One time when I called him on his birthday he seemed a bit spaced out and said he was in the seventh heaven, having spent the previous night with a woman."[18]

Vivier's move to his new apartment on the Chemin de la Côte-Sainte-Catherine coincided with a piece of momentous news: *La Presse* on March 31 announced that he had been named Composer of the Year 1981. The Composer of the Year was an award created by the Canadian Music Council, and given to composers across the whole of Canada (the previous three incumbents were R. Murray Schafer, Gilles Tremblay, and Harry Freedman). Vivier was, by some years, the youngest composer ever to be given the award, and it seems to have been partly in recognition of the achievement of *Kopernikus*, premiered the previous year. A good deal of publicity followed. Perhaps the most interesting of these reported conversations was with the young composer Sylvaine Martin, who published a feature on him in *La Scène musicale*. She quotes Vivier as saying:

> I think that my musical language, and my attitude to contemporary music, shocks people who are interested in the future of contemporary music here as elsewhere. . . . I believe that *Kopernikus*, and *Orion*, are works that are disturbing. . . . I wrote them in reaction against a certain kind of contemporary music that wants composing today to be the equivalent of inventing structures. It's madness, the delirium of a structuralism that wants to be the only generator of real works of art and which forbids any inspiration provoked by what I call musical emotion.

The talk then turned to more composerly matters:

> In my case a melody is often the origin of a whole work. I compose this melody, then I sing it in my head the whole day long, until it develops

by itself and takes on its own shape. It may sometimes suggest the large-scale form of the piece as well as the organization of its smaller parts. . . . I need to feel "close" to my musical material, to live it.[19]

When the news of his award was made public he was on his way to Toronto for the premiere of *Zipangu*. Still needing to make economies wherever he could, he stayed at the YMCA Metropolitan Toronto, on College Street in downtown, paying only fifteen dollars for a room (and one dollar for membership). The program, a New Music Concerts event on Saturday April 4, began with Scelsi's spellbinding *Canti del Capricorni* sung by the composer's preferred interpreter, Michiko Hirayama; the second half began with a new concerto for harp and strings by Marjan Mozetich, followed by the first public performance—four years after its completion—of *Shiraz*, given by the young pianist Christina Petrowska, now the wife of his old friend Michel-Georges Brégent. The reviewer from the *Toronto Star* complained that in the Mozetich the thirteen-piece string ensemble "looked bored and sounded sloppy. . . . The strings were more attentive for Montrealer Claude Vivier's *Zipangu*." But she sounds mystified by the piece itself, simply quoting from Vivier's program note: "[the] piece attempted "to 'blur' the harmonies through different bowing techniques and exploited a range of colors, mostly dark."[20] Vivier returned by train to Montreal the following day.

The Composer of the Year award was conferred by Governor General Ed Schreyer in a ceremony at Rideau Hall, in Ottawa, on April 12. Also receiving awards were the ensemble Canadian Brass, the conductor Mario Bernardi, and the pianist Glenn Gould. The event was followed that night back in Montreal by a gathering of no less significance from Vivier's own perspective: a party at the home of his friend Lambert Ferrand in which *Shiraz* was performed again, this time by its dedicatee Louis-Philippe Pelletier, and at which the guests of honor were none other than the writer Marguerite Duras and her boyfriend Yann Andréa. The sixty-seven-year-old Duras, alcoholic and irascible, had for years been one of the artists Vivier most admired, as much for her films as for the novels on which her reputation mostly rested. That day she had given an interview, later included in the collection *Marguerite Duras à Montréal*, and she seemed to be enjoying her time in the New World, behaving flirtatiously at the party.[21] In Duras he had an example of an artist who had made a mark in two media simultaneously: given Vivier's own burgeoning interest in the cinema, it is tantalizing to wonder whether she might not have become a role model for him in the years ahead.

Véronique Robert has suggested that Duras's influence may be perceptible in a little text titled "Imagine" that Vivier wrote around this time, a curious dialogue between himself and an anonymous interlocutor, probably intended (because of the incorporation of passages of music, from *Chants* and *Lettura di Dante*) for radio broadcast. The "subject"—if the term can be applied to so freely imaginative a text—is the relationship between music and time, a subject that seems to have been increasingly on Vivier's mind at this period. The "Vivier character" (we assume he imagined himself reading one of the voices) begins by trying to imagine a music entirely made of memories, a kind of eternal music that exists outside time. Then, his imagination turns to "this music of silence which exists deep inside me" and, immediately thereafter, to the purity of his childhood conception of music, the music heard in the *messe de minuit*, the music he has always associated with a vision of God (reflected in "Ho visto Dio" at the end of *Lettura di Dante*). However, the vision does not have to be of God: it could also be "a café in Paris on the street, beauty, a pure beauty no sooner seen than it disappears." At the end comes perhaps the most revealing passage of all: "But, you know, it's difficult to imagine music. . . . Always these memories, these musics that superimpose themselves on our thoughts. And there is love . . . the passionate love for music that sometimes stops me from composing. It takes hold of me like a lover who never wants to leave me, whom I can't stare freely at, whom I couldn't paint even on the oldest canvas." The enigmatic conclusion is that one could die for love as one could die for music, but that one could also make operas, "like *Kopernikus*." As long as one is able to create, the implication seems to be, there is no need to die.[22]

Whether or not there is any connection with these last-expressed thoughts—the exact date of "Imagine" being unknown—the first work he composed in his new apartment on the Chemin de la Côte-Sainte-Catherine is testament to a new development in his life: by the spring of 1981, he had a boyfriend. The work in question is *Bouchara*, subtitled "chanson d'amour," for soprano solo, wind quintet, percussion, string quintet, and tape. Although intended as part of the Marco Polo opera, it also had a more personal significance: the manuscript bears the dedication "à Dino Olivieri."[23]

It is Vivier's astonishing achievement in the first half of 1981 to have followed two outstanding compositions with a third, as different as can be imagined from either of them. *Bouchara*, at twelve minutes, is more modest in scale than the *Prologue pour un Marco Polo* or *Wo bist du Licht!* but its perfectly judged mood of melancholy and passionate longing adds new emotions to his music while building upon the technical achievements of the preceding works. The piece's introduction, taking fully two minutes, is arguably his most note-perfect use of a dyadic texture of melody and bass line. The voice is doubled an octave lower by horn, and joined by clarinet and cello; any further instrument would seem superfluous, so ideally has Vivier sculpted the dimensions of his sound world. When the full ensemble enters with sonorous chords of combination tones (exactly the same principle as "les couleurs" of *Lonely Child*, although here employing winds as well as strings), we have the feeling of an enormous increase of scale, as though stepping back to admire a vista that until then had been largely curtained off. Throughout, the voice remains the center focus, and we are placed directly into the singer's world, in all its fervent intensity. Only the final sonority—the recorded sound of a foghorn and the gentle lapping of waves—offers us a perspective outside the frame, perhaps suggesting that love, no matter how powerful, must undergo separation, a journey to an unknown end. *Bouchara* is one of only a few works to be entirely written in the *langue inventée*; in the text it is only the two syllables of "Dino" that provide anything recognizable.

Vivier's relationship with Dino Olivieri, lasting at most a year, was perhaps the most prolonged and relatively stable of his life. Dino was a few years younger, and was part of the younger crowd with whom Vivier was spending increasing amounts of his time. But the relationship was far from straightforward. Sophie Hébert, who was part of their circle and had come to regard Vivier "like a brother," describes Dino as "a lost kid," and recalls: "Claude's relation with Dino was very tough for him, because as far as I know he wasn't always happy in that relationship. He was surprised by his own reaction to Dino. Dino was weak in a certain way, he needed Claude, and I think Claude loved the fact that someone needed him so much, more than anything else. Claude was in a way too concerned; it was more like a father and son relationship at times." Dino, like most others in their circle, was an occasional drug user, and Vivier asked Sophie "a lot about drugs, what various drugs did to you, their effects. He wanted to know because of the effects on Dino. He was surrounded by people on drugs." She has no recollections of Vivier himself being an active part of any drugs scene:

> Claude didn't smoke pot because he'd tried it and he said it made him weird, paranoid. I don't remember Claude on drugs. I don't even remember Claude drinking a lot. Occasionally at the end of the night he would come back to the bar where I worked and he would be drunk. And we used to not let him come in the bar. Sometimes I would go with him across the street and say, now you go home. Because when he was drunk

he was a bit too much. Screaming too loud, sitting, hugging, and all that, but in a way that was a bit too much. We had to sort of put a brake on. But this would be about 3 o'clock. When he was drunk he was the same guy but louder and more emotional.[24]

After the extreme concentration on the voice in his previous three compositions, Vivier spent the late summer working on his first instrumental chamber work since *Greeting Music* more than three years earlier. *Samarkand*, for piano and wind quintet, a Canada Council commission for Louis-Philippe Pelletier and the Quintette à vent du Québec, was completed on September 17. (The manuscript is rather cryptically titled: "SAMARKAND [and the dance of time was stopped by sad news . . .].") He had had renewed contact with Pelletier in connection with the Quebec premiere of *Shiraz*, which took place at the Festival d'Orford in July, and was reminded of the demands he could make from the pianist in this new work. *Samarkand* is one of the most brilliantly sonorous of Vivier's chamber works, demanding enormous energy and stamina from all six musicians. Musically, it explores two novel and performatively challenging domains: the world of spectral harmony, calling for microtonal inflections from the wind players that produce chords corresponding to the intervals of the harmonic series (rather than the combination tones of his recent music); and second, more so than anywhere else in Vivier's output, a range of pulsing, proportional rhythms (5 in the time of 4, 6 in the time of 5, even 9 in the time of 8, etc.) in the ensemble. This makes for a continuously changing rhythmic momentum, which abates only briefly around the midpoint of the work's thirteen minutes, and then resumes.

The opening of the work, led by the piano, is melodic in orientation, with the musicians playing in rhythmic unison much of the time. The individual lines incorporate various embellishments, sometimes melodic, sometimes irregular trills or the pulsing of a single note or chord. Before long, the music settles into a long passage based almost entirely on pulsation, filled with dynamic ebb and flow, like waves on a beach. This section is based on large chords, with the microtonal wind parts adding a spectral "halo" around the equal-tempered harmony of the piano; occasionally little scalic figures emerge and disappear amid the pulsing. After an emphatic E-flat spectral chord, the rhythmic unison begins to drift apart with the emergence of the carefully calculated proportional rhythms, the piano part at times giving the illusion that it is dragging behind the slightly faster-moving wind quintet. This gradually winds down to much slower, sustained music. As activity resumes, the horn begins to inject a sequence of arpeggio-like phrases, ascending the natural harmonic series on various fundamentals. This gesture—by now a commonplace of Vivier's language—has a clearly symbolic meaning: an image of purity, here in the midst of turbulent surroundings. Its effect, as these figures continue through the last section of *Samarkand*, is first to counterpoint, and eventually to calm, the reenergized music surging around it, prefiguring the work's uneasy close on a spectral harmony over an E-flat fundamental.

With *Samarkand* complete, another commission was waiting, this time a new piece for Toronto's Array for a concert in February. Vivier's collaboration with Array had become as satisfying as that with any of the ensembles in Canada. At home in Montreal his main champion was now Lorraine Vaillancourt, who had conducted the premieres of two of his most recent major works, and would soon conduct a third; in a sense she had taken over the role played in his life by Serge Garant and the SMCQ during his first years back in Quebec after his studies in Europe. Array, a small ensemble, was flexible in instrumentation. They had already performed *Love Songs*, *Pulau Dewata*, and *Paramirabo*, so the idea of a new work specially for them was only natural.

However, the work Vivier produced that October—*Et je reverrai cette ville étrange*, for piano, viola, cello, double bass, trumpet, and percussion—is unique in his output for not really being new but a recasting of parts of the earlier, unperformed *Learning*, from 1976. Whereas this might conceivably have resulted from panic, from lack of time to devise a new work by a deadline, this explanation seems unconvincing: first, because Vivier had previously produced plenty of pieces in short amounts of time; and second, with more than three and a half months between completion of the score and the premiere, time pressure would not seem to be an obvious factor. We may wonder, then, about other explanations: was he suffering a creative block? Or were there perhaps external pressures in his life sapping his ability to concentrate on creative work?

By the autumn of 1981, there were nearly a dozen works in Vivier's catalog, out of a total of about forty-five, that had not yet had public performances. This seems a rather high percentage. But if we discount early student works (pre-*Chants*), the several small-scale Tremplin-commissioned pieces that had not yet been done in concert, and recent works whose premiere had simply not yet happened, that leaves only two: the orchestral work *Siddhartha* and the chamber work *Learning*. In the case of *Learning*, it may be that he had simply given up hope of this difficult piece being performed anytime in the near future, and found the music too good to allow it to languish in the bottom drawer. If so, no special explanation for the concept of *Et je reverrai cette ville étrange* is necessary; music history is full of similar examples of composers recycling earlier works.

And that is precisely what Vivier has done here. The piece is cast in six parts, with the last a reprise of the first, each part being one of the "mélodies" from *Learning*. Some of the music has been remeasured to make it more easily readable, and Vivier specifies how the melodies should be distributed among the ensemble (mostly a matter of choice of octave register); otherwise, he has resisted the temptation to change or revise any of the material, for example by using some of the spectral techniques of his most recent works. The piece therefore is not truly representative of the 1981 Vivier, but a curious flashback to an earlier stage of his creative development. Overall, the new piece plays for fifteen minutes, less than half the length of *Learning*; many of the melodies that he has not chosen to reuse are those that are most idiomatic to the original scoring for violins.

For all that, *Et je reverrai cette ville étrange* has a special flavor and a coherence that raises it far above the level of a simple makeweight in Vivier's output. The sheer sonority of the work is beguiling and original, with the trumpet set alongside a trio of low strings (viola, cello, double bass) and an attractive mini-gamelan of piano (doubling celesta) and percussion (tuned and untuned). The determined concentration on unaccompanied melody has an element of courage, as though Vivier is showing us just how little artifice he needs in order to make music. However, the critics and some of his friends were not so convinced. The premiere, in Toronto's Trinity United Church on February 12, 1982, drew a negative review in the *Sunday Star*: "Claude Vivier's *Et je reverrai cette ville étrange* reasserts the importance of one of the least exploited elements in contemporary composition, good old-fashioned melody. Indeed, the piece is very nearly pure melody, the players—trumpet, viola, cello, bass, piano, celesta and Indonesian nipple gongs—spending most of their time in unison, with lingering gong strokes interrupting their linear progress. The music seems to aspire to hypnosis and in its place achieves dullness by virtue of holding to the same dynamic level and purposely restricting its expressive means. Less isn't always more."[25] Thérèse Desjardins, hearing a tape of the performance back in Montreal, told him in no uncertain terms that this was not the sort of music he should be producing and that he needed to get out of Montreal to revitalize his creative energies.[26]

✶ ✶ ✶

Desjardins's reaction to *Et je reverrai cette ville étrange*, while apparently extreme, was perhaps fueled by the unprecedented situation in which Vivier found himself by the winter months of 1982: he was suffering from a prolonged creative dry spell, the most extreme of his whole adult life. Between early September 1981, when he completed *Samarkand*, and his departure for Paris the following June, he produced almost no new music at all (if we discount *Et je reverrai cette ville étrange*). Nor do we have any knowledge of abandoned or unfinished music in progress through all those months. The only exception is a tiny choral piece, *A Little Joke*, dated December 2 and dedicated to Sylvaine Martin. But this is no more than a *feuillet d'album* that could have been produced in one sitting, not the product of substantial compositional effort.

It is of course quite possible that he was suffering from a form of creative burnout. The twenty-one months from the time of beginning work on *Lonely Child* to the completion of *Samarkand* had seen the composition of seven outstanding works, most of them large-scale, playing for more than two hours in total. It is hardly surprising that some sort of a break would have been welcome. But his Montreal lifestyle, with its ever-expanding range of social activities and friendships, may have played its part. Sophie Hébert is convinced that his relationship with Dino Olivieri had simply become too demanding: "Claude couldn't write at one point. He was very concerned about Dino. He said I *think* I love Dino. I'm not sure he didn't leave Montreal for all of that. I think it helped him to make that decision. The relationship was no longer anything positive in his life. And, you know, they had strange parties in the apartment on Saint-Catherine. Something was preparing itself somehow in the scheme of things."[27]

The end of 1981 was marked by the writing of words, rather than of notes. On December 24, he finished a little text titled "Pour Gödel," which was published in the new year in a new journal titled *Trafics*. Ostensibly inspired by a reading of Douglas R. Hofstadter's book *Gödel, Escher, Bach*, which John Rea had recommended to him, and Thérèse Desjardins had given him as a present, the article describes itself as "an article about time," and begins with the declaration: "Time is the most important parameter in music, without it music would not exist." He describes time as the main subject in his two most recent compositions (without naming them), citing the enormous decelerando in what must surely be *Samarkand*, and the "forgetting any division of time," leaving only "empty spaces of time surrounded by melody," in what must be *Et je reverrai cette ville étrange.* Observing the human fixation upon "directional linearity," the discussion itself then takes a decidedly nonlinear turn:

> The plane geometry of human space allows me to think of sound as the point of non-contact between melancholy and hope (the past and the future).
>
> Melancholy is all that is no longer, but which still exists in the form of a memory, of traces left in the heart of a woman and a man, which allows the being to understand, because melancholy allows us to look at the past with a tenderness that objectivizes events and brings them back to a single point: memory. Melancholy, among human beings, is often confused with sadness. Sadness is an image of the past that lives on and would like to become eternal in the mirror of the future.
>
> Hope is an imaginary space where everything is possible, where dreams exist. Often, alas, this dream is conceived and organized not by creative forces but by political forces. That is what I call a politicized imagination. The point of non-contact is called despair.
>
> Earthly terminology having alas already classified the three results of despair as submission, suicide, and the imaginative (creation), I propose the fourth solution: revolution.
>
> And I imagine that the point of contact, which would reestablish the continuum of space–time, could be called melancholy hope, referred to by some as love and by others as death.[28]

It is astonishing how easily Vivier shifts gears from what was shaping up to be a discussion of the role of time in music to these extremely personal reflections, almost as though he were desperate to have his position understood in all its illogicality. The three results of despair, he says, are submission, suicide, and the creative imagination: the fourth is revolution. Surely the personal voice behind this strange utterance is clear. Having evidently himself chosen to follow the creative imagination as an alternative to suicide or submission—and the text "Imagine," discussed earlier, had stated a similar position—now he is contemplating a new path: revolution. What can he mean?

One possible interpretation, the reality of which was not yet certain at the time he wrote these words, is that he is talking about revolution in the form of physical escape: not only from Montreal, or from Canada, but from the very life he was by then leading. In October he applied to the Canada Council for their Arts Grant "A," for the year June 1982 to May 1983, asking for a total of $19,000 plus $1,000 for travel ("Montréal–Paris–Cologne"). He wrote:

During this year, I have the firm intention of composing an opera—for which the libretto will be a montage of philosophical and political texts. An *opéra en fresque*. Seven singers, a chamber orchestra and tape. I need to work freely for a year on a work that doesn't depend on a commission—concentrating entirely on my own compositional needs. In addition, I have to go for a month to Paris and Cologne partly to preserve my musical contacts (very important for a composer today) and to continue to have myself performed there.[29]

From this statement two things remain tantalizingly unclear: first, the relationship of this planned *opéra en fresque* to the Marco Polo opera he had begun, whether they are the same thing or whether this was a new project; and second, whether he was already planning to spend the whole year away from Montreal (the application does not really imply this, merely that he wants to make another European trip with the aim of promoting his music there). Of course, it may be that he was simply being cautious—in the first case, because the Canada Council had already supported the Marco Polo opera in the form of commissions for several of its component pieces; and in the second because, having just been named Composer of the Year, to propose to disappear from the country that had so recently honored him in this way may have seemed rather ungrateful. But by the time of the Canada Council's press release the following May announcing that he was one of the four successful grantees that year in Music, his plans to leave Montreal were firm.

The last substantial creative product from Vivier's final months in Montreal is his first venture in a new medium: film. He had dedicated *Samarkand* to Daniel Dion, a young Montreal artist and filmmaker who, with his friend Philippe Poloni—the dedicatee of *Zipangu*—had recently graduated from art school and had begun to work with video, then a very new medium. (At that time, they sometimes functioned under what they admit was the rather grandiose name Dion/Poloni International.) Vivier would come to their openings and look at and discuss their work with them. They had a friendly, often intense, exchange on all matters artistic—on one birthday they gave Vivier a copy of Pier Paolo Pasolini's *Les Dernières Paroles d'un Impie*, a collection of his interviews with Jean Duflot. Poloni has inscribed the book "parce que Claude a de belles oreilles" (because Claude has beautiful ears).[30]

Vivier now came to them with a proposal to work together. The idea to make a film can hardly have come as a surprise, given the depth of his interest in the cinema (John Rea describes him as a "film buff"). He had produced an outline of sorts, an experimental kind of autobiography, an exploration of themes in his own life.[31] And while the filmmakers followed the outline in general terms (Vivier is credited as having devised the "scenario") there was a good deal of improvisation during the actual filming; Dion and Poloni believed very much in the inspiration of the moment. *L'Homme de Pékin*, as the video was finally named, plays for some eighteen minutes.[32] It most certainly avoids the linearity Vivier had questioned in "Pour Gödel": the brief scenes seem quite separate from one another (sometimes literally so, through the use of a totally red screen for short periods of time, and later a blue screen), and they occasionally recur, either whole or in part, further obliterating any sense of progression. Certainly nothing resembling a narrative emerges. What stays in the memory are the vividness of many of the images themselves and the enduring sense of Vivier here displaying sides of himself not accessible elsewhere.

The autobiographical aspect works on several levels at once, most immediately by involving crucial people from his own life, specifically his parents and his boyfriend. Several of the early scenes involve Vivier sitting on the floor in an empty gymnasium (at the University of Montreal) having makeup applied to his face by a woman, who seems dissatisfied with her work, while a young man—played by Dino Olivieri—hovers close by. Then we see Vivier himself applying body paint to the young man's naked back. Later, the young man recurs robed in white, priest-like or angel-like, processing around Vivier lying supine on the ground, with operatic music (from Gluck's *Alceste*) sounding ceremonially on the soundtrack; we are not sure if "Vivier" is sick and ailing or actually dead. Toward the end of the film we see the real Vivier on a visit to his parents, sitting on a couch looking with them at childhood photographs, as if to say: this is where it all began; this is why I ended up like this. A further autobiographical aspect is the use on the soundtrack of fragments from two of his own works, from either end of his career so far: the tape piece *Homage: Musique pour un vieux Corse triste* and his opera *Kopernikus*.[33]

There is perhaps a more hidden autobiographical significance to the film's several scenes of Vivier in the nude. "He was very influenced by those naked statues from Thailand and places like that," says Daniel Dion, "by the aesthetic of those statues. And Vivier had absolutely no shame whatsoever about nudity, or about sexuality—he had no inhibition about kissing a man in front of everybody. He was totally uninhibited in telling you about his sexual encounters. For him, nudity was a natural thing; and in the film, this element of nudity was a very strong signature somehow. He was totally free, could do anything he wanted with his body." These nude scenes, which variously show Vivier masturbating, chasing a clothed friend around a swimming pool (that of the Tour Suisse, the apartment complex where he now lived), or imitating dance positions reminiscent of Asian dance forms, perhaps Balinese or Indian, had, Dion insists, "a serious purpose behind it; it's not just shocking." Vivier was "a very provocative man, you know, he was playing with many frontiers, with music, with life and death, with combining all kinds of music. . . . I think in this movie you see a part of him that's oniric, whether it's a dream or its real: where is truth and where is fiction?"[34]

The filmmakers were themselves often surprised by Vivier's improvisatory imagination. "The scene with the chairs, for example," says Dion, "when he's running after me with the chair: that's another element of improvisation. I think he was supposed to walk through the chairs like he was walking in an empty church, and then suddenly something happened and he started running after me." The noise of the wooden fold-up chairs crashing into one another as Vivier runs around the swimming pool banging into them makes an impression of unrestrained chaos, like a party gone wild. Similar in effect is the scene of Vivier jumping into the pool fully clothed, and the later scene of three naked male bodies swimming in the water. This may simply be youthful, unrestrained exuberance: but Philippe Poloni feels there was something else to it, something darker. "It was a very strange energy for me and for Daniel because we were not used to this kind of energy. In everyday life Claude was constantly at the edge, like someone walking on a tightrope all the time . . . the equilibrium was not right."[35]

Poloni says that for him the most stunning image in L'Homme de Pékin is the last shot of Vivier singing, where only his head is seen. They had decided to crop the image so his head appears at the bottom of the screen, in the center. Dion says: "when we first saw the cropped image we had to laugh. But after many years we realized it was a very significant and unfortunately very heavy picture. For me this picture is announcing his death somehow." Poloni agrees: "I think Claude was possessed by this kind of death-energy."

Vivier's role in L'Homme de Pékin—as both scriptwriter and protagonist—was creatively fulfilling on many levels, and the film should be seen as part of his oeuvre as much as that of the filmmakers themselves. He would surely have made more films had he lived. And we wonder how his filmic imagination would have informed the design and staging of the operas he was now planning.

The fourth season of Les Événements du neuf, 1981–82, was the last in which Vivier would play an active role. In fact, the series was experiencing difficulties, with a press release announcing that the group was reducing its activities: "The lack of subsidy has obliged them to cancel the first half of the season." But they managed to put on, in collaboration with Cinéma Parallèle, a minifestival titled "Trois jours de musique vocale," promising "a varied panorama of vocal musics, traditional as well as contemporary." *La Presse* published a review of the May 7 concert, with Claude Gingras grudgingly complimentary to Vivier's ten-year-old *Chants*.[36] (The series was to survive for several more seasons.) Later that month Vivier took part in the colloquium "Who's afraid of contemporary music?" organized by the Canadian League of Composers in Montreal. He was his usual outspoken and provocative self, arguing as always for greater support for the living composer. At the same time, he had no desire to burn any bridges in the Montreal scene, even though he was now preparing to leave the city for an extended period.

Before he left he did the rounds of many of his composer friends. Gilles Tremblay recalls that "we had much still to talk about. We planned to discuss 'l'esprit de finesse'; he wanted to know what I meant by finesse. I was thinking of Pascal, 'l'esprit de finesse,' or 'l'esprit du géometrie.'"[37] But the philosophical discussion was not to be. Louis-Philippe Pelletier recalls a more practical discussion:

> During the summer of 1982, shortly before his ill-fated trip to Paris, I had invited Vivier for dinner and, just as we were about to sit down at table, we decided to go over *Shiraz* together. Since he was not satisfied with the work's proportions, he decided to cross out measures 166 to 187. I believe he considered this section redundant so I have never played it again. I had also commented that the very conventional A7 chord in the measure preceding the return to the first tempo fell rather flat. He immediately picked up his pencil and reharmonized the chord as G♯, C♯, G, A, and D♯ in the extreme high register. Unfortunately, these changes did not appear in the Salabert edition published after Vivier's death."[38]

By now he had tapes of the studio recordings of both the *Prologue pour un Marco Polo* and *Wo bist du Licht!* so was able to play them to

friends. The ever-practical Walter Boudreau was bothered by a few aspects of these pieces: "I felt the beginning of *Wo bist du Licht!* should be
rebarred. And some things were crazy—like the voice with brake drums;
it's very hard for the singer. And there were balance problems in general.
I felt Claude's weaknesses were mostly technical. He never sat behind a
music stand, he had a lack of practical knowledge, so you'd lose time in
rehearsals." But he could never "give shit" to his friend about this, "because you haven't got what you haven't got. And this side of things might
have improved had Claude lived."[39] John Rea admits to "many diverse
feelings" on hearing these late pieces, "maybe even jealousy." Of what?
"Of Vivier's ability to be consequential with respect to himself; you know
what kinds of steps you can take and you take them." He wondered how
a singer should deliver those melodies "with those nonsense words that
are stuck in the throat, founded in pain. Do you give it the beautiful
treatment? Music is beautifying." These late works, Rea says, are a kind
of autobiographical mirror—he cites Freud on narcissism, "malignant
self-love," being disappointed by the image in the mirror. "I felt some of
these pieces are maybe overly precious: a dial is being turned up." Asked
if he felt the late pieces came over in any way as a cry for attention, a cry
for help, he replies: "this was a part of him I didn't want to know about
then. Maybe because I was unsure of myself."[40]

We do not know, finally, why Vivier chose to spend the year 1982–83 in
Paris in particular. Perhaps it was simply that returning to Germany would
have felt too much like déjà vu, a repeat of his student years. And perhaps,
although still very much a Germanophile at heart, he felt a greater urge
than ever before to try France, to fight some new battles.

    In itself, Vivier's decision to go to Europe for an extended period needs
little explanation. Boudreau remarks simply: "for Claude, the performance
possibilities here were in immanent danger of drying up. Everyone in
Canada who would commission him had already done so; he was starting
to go round in circles. A composer's life could be much more interesting in
Europe. So many more venues, easy travel, cities more closely knit."[41] He
fully expected Vivier would come back to Montreal a year later with an opera, and then, after a while, go off again. Rea agrees: Vivier had "exhausted
the possibilities in Quebec rather quickly, the commissions were drying
up. There was no place left to go."[42] Added to this was his complicated
emotional situation and his wish to start a new chapter in that phase of his

life. But there is also the tantalizing idea expressed in "Pour Gödel": that if, conventionally, the three results of despair are submission, suicide, and the creative imagination, the fourth possibility is revolution.

Before departure he left many of his possessions with Thérèse Desjardins, who had offered to store them while he was away. On the day of his departure in June, she drove him to the airport. Michel-Georges Brégent came with them to see him off. Desjardins today insists on her very strong intuition, then, that it was the last time they would see Vivier alive.[43]

# CHAPTER ELEVEN

# "IT'S ONLY IN THINKING ABOUT MUSIC, AND ABOUT SOUND, THAT I CAN BE HAPPY"

## 1982–83

In all probability Vivier arrived in Mitterrand's France in a mood of optimism and even relief following the recent fruitless months in Montreal. A letter to the Canada Council a few weeks later thanks them for their grant "which saved me from a deep compositional crisis."[1] It was the third time he had left his native city for an extended period, but unlike previous times he was not traveling to terra incognita: by now he knew Paris fairly well. The most immediate problem, finding a place to live, he solved quickly. A card postmarked June 21, 1982, to Thérèse Desjardins says he has found a furnished apartment, three rooms, with phone, at 22 rue du Général-Guilhem, in the eleventh arrondissement between the avenue de la République and the boulevard Voltaire, for 2,000 francs per month (equivalent to roughly €630 today). "For the first time in my life I feel *good* in Paris!"

The nine months that Vivier spent in Paris are documented, in what for his biographer is luxurious detail, in a collection of correspondence with

Desjardins. (Her letters to him, in contrast, seem not to have survived.) There are fourteen letters and two postcards, the earliest postmarked June 21, 1982, and the last dated February 12, 1983. This has the virtue of being the most substantial collection of letters we possess from Vivier to any one single correspondent, and is a testament to the role Desjardins now played in his life, as friend and confidante. The correspondence also allows us to follow his state of mind during these months, a period of time when his life, externally, was fairly uneventful.

A letter postmarked July 2 declares that he is already installed in the rue du Général-Guilhem and composing. He repeats what he had already told her last time, that this was "one of the rare times I've felt very good in Paris"; and thereafter he moves on to more reflective matters about music. "What is very strange musically is that the only music that can really inspire me now is my own music—and I think that's perfectly normal." He complains that "it's hard here to get to know people," also about how expensive Paris is; on the other hand, "I've found what I wanted: *solitude* and the space to think. . . . Soon my piano will arrive, because for composing I really need my instrument."[2]

But the solitude did not last long, as he could not resist the temptation of a week's visit to Darmstadt, his first in eight years. If the status of the Ferienkurse as a stronghold of modernism had not really changed, the dramatis personae were now different. The Stockhausen era was a thing of the past: the new guiding spirit and leading intellectual presence was the English composer Brian Ferneyhough, who was soon to assume the role of overall coordinator of the composition courses. "Throughout this period," notes the composer Christopher Fox, "Ferneyhough dominated the Ferienkurse: not as Stockhausen had dominated earlier, by running series of lectures, analysis and composition seminars, and open rehearsals so extensive they consumed participants' attention, but by the exhilarating rigor of the discourse which he extrapolated from his composing."[3] Moreover, 1982 was the year of the visit by L'Itinéraire, the ensemble spearheaded by Grisey, Murail, and others, bringing the cultural and aesthetic clash between the French new music and the German into sharp focus. "L'Itinéraire in Darmstadt, it's like Tintin in America!" wrote Grisey. "Amused by the serial heroics of which Brian Ferneyhough seemed at the time the ultimate representative, the brave little French set out not on a pilgrimage, but to conquer the Mecca of serialism."[4] Vivier himself showed little sign of wanting to become embroiled in a cultural battle between two musical cultures he valued so highly, telling Desjardins that during his week there he had "seen some friends, talked a bit, felt rather bored there but prepared a lecture I have to give in Germany and in Paris."[5] And he managed to network efficiently, arranging for several performances of his works in the new year in Paris and in Germany, the most pressing of which was a commission for a new work for l'Itinéraire.

Back in Paris his life remained quiet. "Paris in the summer is very calm," he wrote to Desjardins in the middle of July—"you should write to me from time to time, because the summer in Paris is a bit lonely, and I still don't dare to leave for fear of losing my familiarity with this city, it needs to tame me." However, there were things that livened it up. "I had my first romantic encounter in Paris. . . . I'm glad that at least the ice is broken in that department." Other than that, his main entertainment was the cinema. "I've seen lots of films, including *Passion* [by Jean-Luc Godard] (fantastic, sensual), *Céline et Julie vont en Bateau* [by Jacques Rivette] (marvelous) and many others!" And he had been composing: "it's strange but I'm not in any hurry, a sort of calm has come over me—a feeling of security but not idleness." The piece in question he describes as "a piece about counterpoint—I need to do that before taking the leap into my opera." It seems that initially the connection between the music he had now started to compose and the new opera was not clear, largely because of his indecisiveness about aspects of the latter. "I really want to do an opera but it's strange; although I want to do the opera I haven't succeeded in finding a subject, I can see instead a dramatic work without a subject in which the drama would be music itself!"[6]

The new music he was beginning that July was originally to have a "rather classic orchestration": string quintet, piccolo, flute, oboe, clarinet and bass clarinet, horn, electric organ and percussion, "but no voice—strange." With the substitution of a second clarinet in place of the oboe, and the addition of voice, this is exactly the instrumentation of the *Trois airs pour un opéra imaginaire*, which it would eventually become. He told Desjardins that his Cologne friend Peter Eotvös, now the principal conductor of the Ensemble Intercontemporain based at IRCAM, "gave me a strange piece of criticism: I have a very good sense of the big public—but I mustn't be afraid of that, I should just write operas and three years from now I'll be very well known as a composer."[7]

The Montreal musical world occasionally intruded into his Parisian isolation, and in August he wrote, at the request of Michel-Georges Brégent, a short text honoring Gilles Tremblay on his fiftieth birthday, which was published in the magazine *Sonances* in October. In a different vein, the philosophical speculations about the nature of music that had found form during his last year in Montreal (in texts such as "Pour Gödel") continued to fascinate him, and on August 19, he set down some thoughts under the title "Que propose la musique?" Here again the ostensible subject is the various ways in which music works with time. "The interval between the past moment and the future moment, if it exists, would be the eternal, and it's the eternal that makes music vibrate," he wrote. "The impossibility of living fully in this interval, which would throw human beings into a sort of black hole of consciousness, created music; the desperate desire of the woman and the man who live this astonishing contradiction in their skins created these vibrations of eternity, these tunnels toward non-time placed in historical time, these magical writings marking the complex canvas of time of the human being, these signs hiding our despair." Here he is arguing quite explicitly for a mystical view of music's power, in an optimistic tone that emphasizes his own strong attachment to his chosen art form. "It is in this refined atmosphere and on multiple levels that music occupies this space forbidden by analytical speculations, the interval between acceptance and negation, between love and death, a place so present in the human spirit that the Greeks called it Acheron. A hopeless Acheron, eternally breaking the continuum of space–time and calling music what others call desire."[8] Acheron, of course, is one of the rivers of the ancient Greek underworld across which the ferryman Charon would transport the dead: here Vivier seems to equate the river with the place "between love and death," a place outside the space–time continuum in which music becomes confounded with desire. As a flight of the imagination, this one is certainly unusual. And while there is no mistaking the belief that emerges in music as a transformative power in our lives, a place of hope, the curious ending seems to suggest that music—like the river Acheron—is also a conduit to the next world.

The calm of the Parisian summer was violently punctured on August 9 with a bombing and shooting attack on a Jewish-owned restaurant, Chez Jo Goldenberg, on the rue des Rosiers in the Marais district. Six people were killed and more than twenty injured. "Two days earlier I was walking there calmly," Vivier reported to Desjardins the following day. "In some Jewish or Arab cafés you feel an enormous tension—people fight easily and get angry as well—all very aggressive—but it seems that these deep emotions, as animal as they are, will need to explode totally one day, and certainly not in love." He was very sensitive to the racial tensions in Paris, something that was largely foreign to his Montreal experience. "I've never before experienced racism and its animality so deeply in my skin." And he speculated on the causes: "In Paris . . . you see the deep scars of the west and the Jewish people at the center of this whirlwind of suffering and fear—we are all Jews and Arabs, I mean we all carry within us seeds that tend toward self-destruction, the *Christian* west is caught between a past (the Jewish faith) and a future, more or less (the faith of Mohammed) and this with no relation to the theological content of these two belief systems." His conclusion was a pessimistic one: "My dear Thérèse, the world is rushing to its end, very dangerously."[9]

Despite his sensitivity to these tensions, Vivier was not temperamentally the type to adopt the role of passive bystander. We recall that among his fantasies about his origins was his half-belief that he was Jewish, albeit on the basis of absolutely no evidence. Desjardins's son Bruno Hébert recalls an evening with Vivier at his mother's place in Montreal when they played ouija, and the "oracle" calling out (in answer to Vivier's question "who am I?") the name "Jew." Hébert says that even though they were obviously just fooling around, it seemed to encourage Vivier in the belief that he was indeed Jewish, so much so that he was capable of walking into an Arab bar in Paris and declaring he was Jewish.[10] If true, this act was surely not meant as provocation but rather the opposite, a declaration of identity in order to provoke tolerance—extending the hand of friendship even at risk, as it were, of having it bitten off. But we may read it also as a sign of Vivier's way of not hiding away from potential violence but of trying to pacify it by direct confrontation.

Otherwise, he was now firmly in working mode. "As I told you on the phone," he wrote to Desjardins, "I'm not going to leave Paris, I'm staying home (I even made my first spaghetti sauce), I listen to the radio a lot (right now to marvelous Iranian vocal music), I compose, go to the cinema, to gay bars, and sleep." By the time of this letter, August 10, he was hard at work on what he was then calling his *Cinq airs pour un opéra imaginaire*, and had made a neat copy of the first four minutes of music. He feels that "it will be rather sad music. It will also probably be one of my most beautiful and deepest works. I've been thinking a lot about music, and life, but particularly about music because it's only in thinking about music, and about sound, that I can be happy. . . . This piece I'm doing is an important bridge to cross before beginning the opera, technical work, obviously, a rediscovery (A) of counterpoint (B) of more dramatic musical time, closer to speech, with *atomic* elements of different kinds." In a postscript he notes: "I'm working very hard, and I'm very afraid musically, although I think that my 5 airs will be very beautiful."[11]

The relationship of the *Trois airs pour un opéra imaginaire*, the final score of which was completed at the beginning of November, to the new opera project remains unclear, and possibly was unclear to Vivier himself.

The clearest statement of his intentions comes in a letter to the Canada Council in mid-August, telling them that he was working hard at the opera, "of which the first part or introduction is literally an air. . . . This air will be the introduction to the opera—technically I need to begin the opera with the effect of a real musical 'Blow up.' This 'air' will by the way be done Paris after Christmas by the ensemble l'Itinéraire—a good way of selling the rest of the project which will clearly be more ambitious and large-scale."[12] This is clear enough: but whether or not that intention remained, as his thoughts on the opera took slightly more definite form in the months ahead, is uncertain and, as we shall see, the surviving outline in Vivier's hand of the new operatic project has no obvious place where the "Airs" might appear, certainly not at the beginning.

What is sure is that the *Trois airs pour un opéra imaginaire* stands as a richly rewarding independent work, one of Vivier's finest scores, and a definite departure in a new direction from the music he had composed in Montreal. In his own terms, its main innovation is the rediscovery of counterpoint, a musical technique that he had wilfully and bravely eschewed in most of the music since *Lonely Child*. The dyadic textures of many of those works had been a more satisfactory basis on which to build his chords of combination tones, the technique he had explored extensively and with great imagination in 1980–81. Perhaps he felt he had gone as far as he could, at least temporarily, in that direction, and that textural principles he had consciously bypassed in the process would now refresh his compositional imagination. Such is abundantly the case in the *Trois Airs*.

The piece is "about 13 minutes—but a very dense thirteen minutes."[13] The program note he wrote in early January for the forthcoming premiere describes the music in almost entirely technical terms; and while this was not uncharacteristic of some of his recent program notes (such as that for *Wo bist du Licht!*) we may wonder whether he was trying to adhere to the Parisian fashion for intellectual descriptions of new music ("a public, oh! so far from its heart and so close to its intellect"):[14]

This work is literally what the title suggests. The main elements of my piece are: a spectrum with regular pulsation moving towards an irregular and individual pulsing; from this pulsing arises a series of short, brilliant lines rocketing towards the highest register. The rhythm thus produced flattens out more and more to become pure duration. Everything becomes homophonic only to break up once again, becoming contrapuntal and stabilising in an orchestration that becomes ever thinner and moves more and more towards the high register. Finally there is an abrupt return to homophony, moving towards a sound / noise from the whole ensemble, which shatters brutally on a pure interval in order to allow a return to spectral writing.[15]

Once again the vocal part uses the "langue inventée" exclusively, as had *Bouchara*, emphasizing the tendency Vivier himself had noted toward a concentration on pure music even in this would-be operatic context ("a dramatic work without a subject where the drama will be music itself"). The three sections make an effective contrast in terms of mood, the first flowing and restless, the second becoming playful in its use of extended techniques for the singer, though achieving at the end a beautiful serenity; whereas the last, the shortest of the three, is relentlessly intense, with the voice climbing to its highest register, the singer's line punctuated by disconsolate whacks on the bass drum. At least vocally, the music is certainly "operatic"—even, as Vivier acknowledged, impassioned in the manner of Italian bel canto—while the instrumental writing shows a high degree of virtuosity and an apparently effortless command of his timbral and harmonic resources.[16]

During the long days of composition in the summer he took a companion: a dog, Dewa. It can hardly be coincidental that the dog's name matches the first syllables of the *Trois airs pour un opéra imaginaire*, "dè wa," which he had composed by then: a case of life seeming to follow art. "She is very nice," he told Desjardins, "and completely Parisian, in other words a bit of a thug and a snob!" Whether the dog was intended merely for company or for some sort of protection he does not say, though the same letter goes on to talk about the visible police presence in Paris—"plain-clothes policemen keep watch with enormous weapon and metal detectors! The Canadian embassy has had threats." He had dined with François Cloutier of the Maison du Québec, to discuss a plan of giving talks on Canadian music, including one on his own work at the Centre Culturel Canadien. "I read *L'Eté 80* by Duras, extraordinary," the letter continues, "and now I'm reading Hermann Broch's *Les Somnambules*. . . . Despite the little contact I have with the French milieu I keep on, and am maintaining quite a feverish intellectual activity! perhaps it's to do with this slow life I'm leading at the moment, where I'm allowing my thoughts to take me over."[17]

Also in Paris that autumn was Pauline Vaillancourt, whom he was delighted to see, but who was not at all pleased when he told her he wanted to work with another singer on the forthcoming premiere of the *Trois airs*. "I invited her to dinner to try to calm her down, but no luck, alas!"[18] With the exalted, intense moods of the *Trois airs* in mind it is interesting to discover from his correspondence that one of the composers he was spending time listening to that autumn was Mahler—a letter in mid-September announces he is about to go to a concert with Mahler's Seventh Symphony conducted by Hans Zender. "Mahler is perhaps the musician with whom I have the most in common, an exaggerated sensibility, Schmalz and at the same time a deep desire for purity, but an almost libidinal purity—a harmony of Judeo-Christian opposites, in balance—and moreover a horror of origins, in fact all the inherent complexes of a Jew and a Christian."[19] In contrast, a gala concert he attended marking John Cage's seventieth birthday was much less to his liking, and he found the mostly recent music presented "pretty shitty" (though he made an exception for Cage's ballet *The Seasons* of 1947).[20]

Professionally speaking, things were moving a little faster by the autumn, with his Parisian circle beginning to expand. He had met with representatives of the music publishers Ricordi who were interested in publishing his music, and new commissions were coming his way, including a piano piece for Stuttgart—"I'm going to do an étude on the passage from the spectral world to the harmonic world, in fact using the harmonic and spectral material from the end of my 'air for an imaginary opera.'"[21] By now he was planning to stay three years in Europe to build up solid contacts. But this did not imply distancing himself from Canada: he was trying to get himself an invitation to teach at the Banff Centre the coming summer, and he had been talking to the musicologist Harry Halbreich about a joint lecture tour on music in Quebec.[22]

The horror of world events intruded once again in the middle of September, and a long letter to Desjardins recounts his upset at the massacre of hundreds of Palestinian and Lebanese Shiite Muslim civilians in Palestinian refugee camps in Beirut by a Lebanese Christian Phalangist militia. He marched in a demonstration against the slaughter, and recounts how, in tears, he went into a bar and found a Palestinian man also grieving; Vivier bought him a beer and the two sat, without speaking, united in their distress. "I could only cry, only shudder, before a horror like that, and I can only shiver when they still look for 'the' guilty ones (like in cheap crime novels) as I strongly believe that we're all guilty and that wars should become rugby matches and that 'power' can go to hell!"[23]

The opera project that had been his main reason for coming to Paris had still not really gotten properly started by the autumn (on October 8 he wrote, "I still have a serious libretto problem"). But at least he was by now more and more convinced that he had found a good subject—or, perhaps more accurately, a good backstory—on which to base the work. Before he left Montreal his friend Véronique Robert had told him of an astonishing new theory that had recently come to light concerning the death of Tchaikovsky, one of his favorite composers. The generally held version of events was that the great composer had contracted cholera (at the age of fifty-three) by drinking a glass of contaminated water during the epidemic that was then raging in Russia, only a few days after the premiere of his Sixth Symphony. But even at the time there were those who questioned this explanation, and an alternative had already begun to circulate, though was never officially accepted: that Tchaikovsky had committed suicide.

The new theory—the one that seized Vivier's imagination—was first aired publicly by the Russian musicologist Alexandra Orlova after her emigration to the west in 1979.[24] This theory held that the composer's death was indeed from suicide, but not because of despondency, such as depression over the end of his marriage, but for a more shocking reason: the suicide was "ordered" by a court of honor consisting of several of the composer's Petersburg schoolfriends because of the rumors spreading about his homosexual infatuation with his young nephew, Vladimir Davydov. (In a slightly different version of this story, Tchaikovsky's death was ordered by Czar Alexander III himself, who had been informed of another of the composer's homosexual affairs.) Even today the matter has not been conclusively settled, and perhaps never will be. "Vivier was shocked by these allegations," writes Véronique Robert, "and immediately dreamed of making them the basis of an opera."[25] And in this case, unlike his lack of interest in the real Copernicus or Marco Polo, he did some reading on the historical Tchaikovsky—specifically, the book *Tchaïkovski* by Michel Rostislav Hofmann published by Éditions du Seuil in 1959, highlighting all the quotations from Tchaikovsky's letters, as though the composer's own words had special significance for him.[26]

In a letter in October Vivier gives the first clear, if still sketchy, outline of his thoughts about how this story might be handled. His idea was to use the structure of the Requiem Mass as the framework of the piece, "and on the basis of the Latin text work by association or opposition of ideas." Somewhat as in *Kopernikus*, the characters were to be partly symbolic and partly representatives of real people: Tchaikovsky himself was also Saint Sebastian, the early Christian martyr; Tchaikovsky's patron Nadezhda von Meck, a sorceress; Czar Alexander III, an emperor/alchemist; Tchaikovsky's mother, the Virgin Mary; and Tchaikovsky's lover, Joan of Arc. He imagined "choral music which is a Requiem and on the stage sung or spoken scenes that internalize, or extrapolate from, etc., the seven parts of the Requiem Mass." And he had begun tentatively to imagine the beginning: "I dreamed the dramatic form of the first scene of Tchaikovsky—a large male choir, very deep voices—minor third (C♯–E), calls and shouts—superimposed on this, the speech of the czar—First words: the darkness of history. In the end I'll have a lot of French texts—I'm placing this opera in the line of Dante, Mozart, and Bataille."[27] Actual musical ideas seemed to depend upon the establishment of a satisfactory dramatic conception and structure. In mid-October he was able to report that "musically the Requiem scene is taking shape as well as the last scene"; but if he made any musical notations for the opera they have not survived. His thoughts turned to using a Mozart-sized orchestra and only twelve singers in total. The search for a libretto remained elusive, and at one point he contemplated using "classic texts (Romeo—Macbeth, etc.)," as well as texts from the Requiem (some "backwards"), and from Goethe and Novalis. Judging from his correspondence, the idea at this point seemed to be to make a textual collage, rather in the manner of *Journal*. And he wanted to integrate film into the staging. "So Tch would become a film opera!"[28]

The last stage of work on the Tchaikovsky opera that we are able to document consists of a nine-page manuscript scenario in Vivier's hand, undated, but probably written late in 1982. There are no musical notations, but a clear dramatic outline, every bit as detailed as the one he had produced some years earlier for *Kopernikus* (though, as in that case, this verbal scenario would surely have been modified had he lived to work on the music). The excepts below show the seven sections of the work, each corresponding to part of the Requiem structure, and what he calls the "argument" for each scene:

Requiem + Kyrie
Argument: your death will be a lie / you will be judged by your peers / Sodomite, you will become a true aristocrat of our Holy Russia.
Absolvé Domine
Argument: Tch [illegible] voluntarily commits suicide following the trial; he was in fact a "petit bourgeois" who wanted to rise to the high circles of the Russian bourgeoisie.
Dies Irae
Argument: Tchaikovsky's trial / Tchaikovsky is guilty of not belonging to the pure and noble race. / Tchaikovsky accepts death in order to reintegrate the pure and noble race.
Domine Jesu Christe

Argument: unconsciously, women have directed Tch.'s life—his mother
gave him his pathological sensibility and a love for music—Joan of Arc
exemplified the myth of the pure, virginal woman, and Mme von Meck
gave him the illusion of pure love but with a hidden jealously tending
toward destruction.
Lux aeterna—Agnus Dei
Argument: In committing suicide Tch. embraces the law of power—we
are attending a suicide marriage—and the poison that cancels out the
poison of sin is concocted by the three symbolic women in Tch.'s life.
Libera me
Argument: the love that Tch. feels for his Lover is the love he feels for
a martyr; he takes on the role of the martyr in assuming responsibility
for his own death—his mother has brought him in contact with his own
mirror.
In paradisum
Argument: Tchaikovsky again reaches the heights of power, a power that
will be destroyed in '14–'18 and its sequels Hiroshima and Vietnam.

He had enthused Harry Halbreich about the project, and they exchanged
some ideas about a possible production; Halbreich's wife Elisabeth also
became interested in the idea, sending Vivier pages of notes on the evolving conception, and there was even talk of her becoming his librettist. But
from the end of 1982 onward the idea receives almost no further discussion in Vivier's correspondence.

In November he gave two lectures on his work, the first on November 1,
at Feedback Studios in Cologne at the invitation of his friend Johannes
Fritsch. (Fritsch subsequently used a recording of Vivier's lecture in his
composition *Testament Vivier* [1983] for wind quintet, piano, and tape).
From there he went to Stuttgart and gave a presentation to some composers in the city—"tough," he told Desjardins.[29] Then on the evening of
November 23, he presented a lecture at the Centre Culturel Canadien in
Paris, with the title "Spectral color as developed in three works: in search
of the new melody." This was a discussion of his recent compositional practice, during which he presented three recent works on tape: *Lonely Child*,
*Wo Bist du Licht!*, and *Prologue pour un Marco Polo*. A tape recording survives, showing this talk to be the most detailed of all his public discussions of his own music. Among the ideas he mentions, rather in passing,
is the fact that in his music to that point he had made a purely intuitive

relationship between the invented language syllables and "les spectres," but that he had been thinking of a more rigorous relationship that could be developed in the future. And in the question session at the end the subject of his Marco Polo opera came up: Vivier remarked that he'd like the mise-en-scène to be not at all connected with a story, expressing his admiration for the work of Robert Wilson and other directors "where the music has become the opera."[30]

The photographs of Vivier's lecture at the Centre Culturel Canadien show him wearing a black leather jacket that he had borrowed for the occasion from his Montreal friend Philippe Poloni, who was spending some months in Paris. Daniel Dion, their other collaborator on *L'Homme de Pékin*, was in the city more briefly, and the three spent time together. Poloni recalls that he and Vivier had found a tiny restaurant near Notre Dame where they would go once a week for steak frites and cheap red wine. They would attend openings, enjoy occasional dinners with friends, and show their faces at parties at the Canadian Cultural Centre.[31] Yet for all that, and especially with the Christmas season approaching—a time of year that always reminded him of the orphan he was—Vivier's mood took an unexpected turn as the new year approached. A long letter to Thérèse Desjardins, dated January 3, 1983, pours out his emotions about an unexpected feeling that had overtaken him, which he clearly identifies by its name: homesickness.

The simple fact is that now, after six months away, Vivier was desperately missing Montreal and his large circle of friends there. He was shocked by the feeling, partly because he had felt at something of a dead end in his last months before departure, and partly because he saw himself as "a creator who wants to be universal, without boundaries": but what he missed most was Montreal's "human warmth, which seems impossible for me to find in Paris." The letter goes on to explain, totally rationally, what he is missing most:

> All the wonderful friendships I experienced there I don't find in Paris! No-one to phone when I'm composing, no-one to confide in, no-one I can talk to about my existential anguish. In fact a great loneliness—at my age (nearly 35!) . . . I also find it very hard in Paris to be a composer who is certainly respected but without the deep love I felt in Montreal . . . now I truly understand the pain of exiles and the uprooted, and perhaps for the first time in my life I accept something that I've always systematically refused—I'm a Montrealer, my roots are there and not in a vague, imaginary country like that of my [birth] parents. . . . To put it another way, I need the kind of affection that Paris can't give me and I

have to give priority to affection over a European pseudo-career which will happen anyway.[32]

His conclusion: that what he was now craving was stability above all, a life in which he would be based in Montreal but would travel to Europe once or twice a year in the effort to promote his music. He even thought he would return to Canada in April or May once the concert season ended in Paris, "because I won't have anything more to do here."

While he expresses his hope that the letter will not seem too disconcerting, and reassures Desjardins that she must not worry about him, nothing that he writes suggests any feelings of despair or panic. It is, on the contrary, a very level-headed assessment of his present situation and mood, with clear thoughts about the future and about his changing needs as a maturing artist. It comes as a surprise, then, to find in the penultimate paragraph a passing mention of the new work he has begun to compose on commission from the Groupe Vocal de France, with a German title so raw and shocking that it must have stunned Desjardins as it has stunned others subsequently: *Glaubst du an die Unsterblichkeit der Seele* (Do you believe in the immortality of the soul).

When he wrote to Desjardins again, on January 7, he reported having finished the first six minutes of this new work, with its unconventional scoring for twelve voices, three synthesizers, percussion, and electronics. (Curiously, there is no mention of any connection with his two operatic projects, so we must assume that this was intended as a stand-alone work.) He copied out for her benefit a text he had written for what he called the "immobile" part of the work (which he was conceiving overall as having two "poles," mobility and immobility). If she had been worried about his emotional state following the previous letter, this text—the first he had written in French since parts of *Lonely Child*—would scarcely have set her mind at rest:

> I was cold, it was winter
> in fact I thought I was cold—
> perhaps I was cold.
> God, however, told me I would be cold.
> Perhaps I was dead.
> It was not so much being dead
> I was frightened of as dying.
> Suddenly I felt cold
> very cold—or I was already cold.
> it was night and I was afraid.

✶ ✶ ✶

In view of the loneliness that pours out in his letters to Thérèse Desjardins in the early days of the year, the rest of January 1983 was to bring a welcome surprise: he was falling in love. He met a young American writer named Christopher Coe, who was spending some time in Paris. Coe was at that point not at all known: his two novels, *I Look Divine* and *Such Times*, were only published some years later. The second of them, *Such Times* (1993), is a fictionalized memoir that partly describes in detail the author's relationship with a composer named "Claude." And while there seems little doubt that the fictionalized character is modeled closely on Vivier, it also departs in certain very definite ways from the truth: we must therefore attach great caution in reading Coe's book for biographical accuracy.

In *Such Times*, for example, the protagonist-author, Timothy, meets "Claude" supposedly in 1987, four years later than in reality; and on one occasion they attend a concert to hear a piece for oboe and piano by "Claude" (there is no such work in Vivier's catalog). The lack of obvious verisimilitude carries on into the surprising visual resemblance the protagonist sees between "Claude" and one of his favorite paintings: "Claude is the man I knew in Paris who reminded me of *Portrait of a Man*, the Hans Memling painting that hangs in the Frick Collection. Claude, as I have said, was a mistake I made. Claude was my lunacy."[33]

From a biographical perspective, one important aspect of Coe's book that is anachronistic is its forthright discussions of AIDS and its consequences. Although the disease was already present among high-risk groups in the United States in the 1970s, it was not named (by the US Centers for Disease Control and Prevention) until July 1982. The first cases of it had only been reported some months previously. But the disease was still very little understood, and its recognition as a virus followed only in 1984, with the name HIV (for human immunodeficiency virus) being adopted in 1986 (in French it is known as SIDA, for *Syndrome d'Immuno-Déficience Acquise*).[34] The references to AIDS in Coe's book would not have been possible in early 1983, and could only have been made in retrospect. More important, we do not know if Vivier himself was aware of the disease, either by name or simply as a new sort of illness that was spreading widely in the gay community: his letters make no mention of it.

In *Such Times*, the protagonist, Timothy, is alone in Paris, looking for an unprotected sexual encounter with a gay man, apparently to make it uncertain that he will ever be able to blame his contracting AIDS on his long-term boyfriend, Jasper (who, in the novel, subsequently announces his infection and dies from it). "What I'd wanted was *one* other possible exposure . . . so that if in five years, or ten, I found myself infected, I would not be able to point to Jasper." He finds "Claude" upstairs in a bar just north of the Louvre in a "joy room," with Eartha Kitt projected on large video screens and her songs booming loudly over large speakers. Three men are linked together in a "chain fuck." "The man in the middle, who was slamming and being slammed, reached out to me." It is "Claude": "I chose Claude because he was the man in the middle." They walk together to the rue Tiquetonne, where they first make love; Timothy likes the lingering smell of French cigarettes on the clothes of "Claude." Thereafter, they go back to the apartment of "Claude," where there is a mattress on the floor and, through a doorless passage, a living room "with clothing for all seasons strewn about." There is a piano—and here again the correspondence with reality breaks down—a cello in one corner, and a saxophone.

None of Vivier's small circle of Paris friends ever met Christopher Coe. Philippe Poloni, for example, says he never met him but heard quite a bit about him: "they were going out a lot, it was very intense. Claude sort of mellowed down with him, he wasn't going to bars so much. They'd go to a restaurant and have dinner. I think Claude was very happy with this man. But I remember Claude finding out that Christopher had a boyfriend in New York. Christopher was stunned that Claude had no inheritance, neither money, property, nor effects. Claude was shocked by this, we had a long conversation about it. I began to think Christopher was perhaps a cruel person."[35]

The affair may well not have lasted more than a couple of weeks. Coe returned to New York at a certain point, and the two never saw each other again. (In *Such Times*, Timothy does not tell his boyfriend Jasper about the rue Tiquetonne "or the five times after it," which further suggests, if the detail can be believed, that his encounter with "Claude" was a fairly brief one.) And in a letter to Desjardins on January 24, Vivier comments casually that "my lovesickness is over, it was marvelous, now I'm returning quietly to composing"; but, a few pages later, "Christopher just called me, I think he's madly in love with me—it's so strange—he told me he was crying on the plane—it's a strange feeling to be loved with so much passion! Who knows, maybe I'll go to New York to live with him!"

Meanwhile he was making progress with *Glaubst du an die Unsterblichkeit der Seele,* despite a curious hesitancy that had recently overtaken him. "It's strange but I have a blind fear of composing, of making mistakes. I've finished (?) about eight minutes of my piece but I don't dare to write the last three as I'm so afraid of mistakes! Anyway I'll get over it, I'm sure . . . Finally the problem with the piece I'm working on now is that I want to write for large orchestra!"[36]

In fact, the striking sound world of the new piece was quite unlike any he had devised to that time, the sounds of the three synthesizers (a PPG, a "string synth," and a Korg Polysix) lending the texture a somewhat cold, impersonal aura, the impression intensified by the use of a vocoder to process the sounds of some of the voices. This opening part—the first three minutes—is surely the "immobile" music to which Vivier refers: a tenor at one point comments, "it's so strange, this music that doesn't move." Yet for all that, it is music of nervous tension and incident: loud spoken outbursts in the invented language by the first tenor are doubled or answered by Thai gongs, their approximately pitched dialogue an effective contrast against the immobile chords in voices and synthesizers. After his confession that "I never knew how to love," the tenor is cajoled by an alto into singing her a love song. So begins the second section, in which the tenor's high, sustained melody holds its own with difficulty against the vocalizing of the first soprano, in a rising and falling wave of intensity that threatens to drown him out.

All this, brilliantly imagined and vivid though it is, cannot prepare us for the chilling section to follow. Here a narrator, speaking through a vocoder, recites a text that must rank as one of the most unforgettable in late twentieth-century music. His words are accompanied by swelling chords, many of them overtone sonorities ("chords of resonance," in Messiaen's terminology) in the synthesizers and voices, while a solo soprano sings the text quoted above ("I was cold, it was winter . . ."):

It was a Monday or a Tuesday, I don't remember anymore.
but that's not important, what's important is
what's important is the event that would take place that day
that would take place that day
it was grey, I recall, so I decided to take the métro.
I even had to buy tickets, having none on me.
I walked along the platform a little
and I lit a cigarette to kill my boredom
I knew the train was coming from the metallic rumbling. the long blue
    vehicle came to a stop. so I headed for one of the doors, lifted the
    latch and went into the carriage, the front one I think. the space was
    practically empty,
only opposite the bench I was sitting on a slightly wrinkled old woman
    smiled as she read her newspaper.
a priest was reading his breviary. the woman had a kindly look,

> sitting as she was to one side so as not to disturb anyone.
> sitting on my bench I had the impression that something would happen
> to me that day, something essential to my life.
> it was then that my eyes, looking round randomly,
> fell upon a young man with a strange, upsetting magnetism.
> I could not help staring at him.
> I could not take my eyes off the young man.
> it seemed like he'd been in front of me for all eternity.
> then he spoke to me, he said: "quite boring this metro, huh?" I didn't
> know how to answer and said,
> rather embarrassed to have been caught staring: "yes, quite." then com-
> pletely naturally the young man came to sit beside me and said:
> "my name is Harry." I replied that my name was Claude.
> then with no other form of introduction he took from his dark black
> jacket, probably bought in Paris, a dagger, and struck it straight into
> my heart.

Given the events that would soon befall him, this text—with the most true-to-life of all the "Vivier characters" in his output, the only one to actually share his name—seems possessed by an uncanny prescience. Even by the most level-headed of his friends it has been widely interpreted as Vivier predicting immanent danger, even his own death. (We should remember, though, that "Claude" in *Glaubst du an die Unsterblichkeit der Seele* survives the attack and lives to tell the tale).

The coincidence—or, perhaps, the eerie sense of life following art—begins to become even more incredible given a horrible event that occurred just after he wrote the text. In the letter of January 24 to Thérèse Desjardins, already quoted above, Vivier—as was his habit by that time—copied out the draft of this text simply to keep her appraised of the development of his new work, commenting quite matter-of-factly: "I hope you like it, it's my best piece of prose." Late the very next day, January 25, he brought home a man he had met in a bar, hoping to share a night of intimacy. Instead the man grew violent, stabbed Vivier in the neck with a pair of scissors, and made off with his money. Clarence Barlow, who was visiting from Cologne, recalls the incident.

> I took the last metro to Claude's place. When I got in he wasn't there. So I just lay down on this camp cot that he'd got there and tried to sleep. That was about 12:30 or 1 o'clock or something. Then I heard Claude coming in but I could hear that he was with somebody: I heard two male voices. And I thought, "Oh God, is this going to go on all night?" There was just a thin door between me and them. I thought I'd never get to sleep. I think

I remember seeing the face of this chap through the crack in the door; I must have left that door open. The light was on in the passage. I think I saw a clean-shaven, smooth-looking young chap, slightly swarthy complexion. I remember them talking in hushed voices in the other room—I couldn't understand a word. Suddenly I heard rapid footsteps down the stairs. I thought he'd forgotten his cigarettes or something, he's gone to get some. But then Claude put the light off in the passage and everything got quiet. I decided to go off to sleep, and I managed to. And the next day when I woke up he showed me that he'd been slashed with a pair of scissors—superficially, he wasn't bleeding or anything—and the guy had used the same pair of scissors to cut his phone line. He didn't know how to fix the phone. So I cut the wires and folded them together so the phone would work again and that's how he was able to call people and tell them what had happened. He also told me that the man had seen me lying on my bed, and he'd wanted to rob me as well. And Claude made up a little story, said "Oh, you can forget him, he borrowed 30 francs from me this morning, he's got no money at all." And so I was left alone.[37]

In fact Vivier had rushed round to Philippe Poloni's place. "Philippe has been marvelous with me—I cried in his arms—he was incredibly tender with me—we talked a little, he looked after me and he also took care of this wound in my being which touched my soul to its depths," he told Thérèse Desjardins.[38] Shocked though he was, Poloni also tried to impart a few home truths to his injured friend: "He was like a little kid, completely unaware that people could do that. I told him, are you so naive? You know that kind of thing happens in bars. Especially in the gay bars, people go there, pretending they're gay, and when they're back in your house they're only looking for money or drugs or whatever."[39]

The incident clearly shocked Vivier deeply, not least because all his years of casual encounters in bars had never before resulted in anything like this. He seemed not to understand that Paris was more dangerous than Montreal in this respect. "Now I understand the horror of rape," he wrote to Desjardins, "and the difficulty of talking publicly about it." With his telephone working again he managed to get through to her for a long talk, which comforted him, but in a letter on January 26, he described to her his dark feelings in the aftermath of the attack:

I'm suffering, Thérèse, my soul is really suffering, my body has been penetrated by scissors and a part of me that I thought was secret has been torn, has been revealed, and I saw something that I took for nothingness but which was not nothingness. I'm afraid, Thérèse, and I think it's myself that I'm afraid of. I'm afraid of this infinite emptiness which I'm

not afraid of. Death has been totally demystified. . . . Altogether I think
I'm frightened of dying and that's what I've been so violently confronted
with. . . .

But I'll say it again, Thérèse, I'm afraid, afraid of myself, I'm afraid
of failing in my task—I'm so stupid, so weak, so incapable of living my
creative solitude fully and that is what I have to force myself to do. I
don't think that in the years ahead I'll compose as much as previously,
I have to refine everything, find the voice of the lonely child who wants
to embrace the world with his naive love—the voice that we all hear and
want to inhabit forever.[40]

It is a disturbing letter, although still remarkably self-possessed, quite
without hysteria. Barlow persuaded him that he needed to get out of Paris
for a few days to recover, so Vivier agreed to drive back to Cologne with
him and his wife Clair. Barlow remembers it as a strange trip: "Claude
was shattered, but trying to put on a brave face," and Barlow and his wife
were experiencing strains in their relationship. Barlow and Vivier light-
ened the atmosphere by singing Catholic hymns, respectively in English
and French simultaneously. When they reached Cologne, Vivier asked
to be set down at a gay bar, King Georg, on Ebertplatz. Barlow recalls: "I
remember saying, 'but Claude, you said to us in the car you'd never go to
a gay bar again in your life!' He said, 'Yes, I meant in Paris.'"[41] He stayed
with the young Quebec composer Denys Bouliane, who was then living
in Cologne.[42]

What might be called the psychic aftermath of the attack placed a
heavy burden on Vivier, but its real effect on him is impossible to trace
clearly. There are no more letters to Thérèse Desjardins (only one postcard
a couple of weeks later from Nice), so we have only the recollections of
friends who saw him thereafter, recollections that are perhaps inevitably
tinted by the tragic event that was to occur in early March. The fact that
his correspondence with Desjardins stops at this point does not in itself
necessarily signify anything disturbing, as professionally, the month of
February was a very busy one for him, with performances, travel, and new
projects all clamoring for attention.

By now, discussions were proceeding with both Ricordi and Salabert
regarding publishing his music. He was keen to find a publisher if only to
reduce the amount of time he had to spend making cassettes and standing at photocopiers in order to have copies of his pieces to send to interested parties. A European publisher was an obvious choice because no
publisher in Quebec had the same potential to disseminate his music:
the Canadian Music Centre, which had handled his works to that point,

was geared more toward promotion than actual publication (although in 1980 they had produced a handsome engraved version of his *Lettura di Dante*). Both publishers were impressed by the number of performances he was now getting, and Ricordi had expressed interest in publishing all the works of the Marco Polo opera.[43] *Samarkand* and *Bouchara* were performed in Nice on February 13 (Vivier himself conducted *Samarkand*), and *Bouchara* was given again the following day at the Centre Pompidou in Paris, its official premiere, with the singer Evelyne Razimowsky and the ensemble 2E2M directed by Paul Méfano. A postcard to Desjardins from Nice reports how pleased he is that the musicians like his music, and adds: "I feel very happy . . . I think they like me a lot here. I think I have an insatiable need to be loved! . . . *Bouchara* is marvelous and sad."[44] Back in Paris he wrote to the German conductor Michael Zilm with a long list of corrections and errata on the score of *Bouchara* for its forthcoming Stuttgart performance.

The last surviving business letter we have from Vivier was written in Paris on February 23, to the conductor Philippe Dourguin in Montreal. It concerns three large-scale projects he had in mind, for which he was hoping to secure the financial backing to make productions possible. The first is the long-projected "opéra fleuve" on Marco Polo. This would consist, he told Dourguin, of "scenes, like scenes in a film." In this last outline, the work was to consist of seven parts:

1st part

| | |
|---|---|
| Lonely Child— | (chamber orchestra + voice) |
| | Marco's childhood—loneliness. |
| Shiraz— | (piano solo) |
| | a first glimpse of adventure |
| Bouchara— | (2 quintets, perc etc soprano) |
| | love song of the little Chinese woman. |
| Wo bist du Licht— | (string orchestra (20) perc—mezzo) |
| | will there always be war among men? |

2nd part

| | |
|---|---|
| Prologue pour un Marco Polo— | (6 clar, 13 strings, 2 perc, 5 voices) |
| | the testament of Polo—vision of Zipangu |
| Samarkande— | (wind quintet and pno) |
| | a last vision of the city of Dreams |
| "Nous sommes un rêve de Zipangu"— | (orchestra choir 3 soloists sop mezzo tenor) |
| | America is born of a dream—we are the dream of Marco Polo! |

This would be, he told Dourguin, "a sort of premiere." Another suggestion, less ambitious than this two-hour, evening long work, would be for him to compose a new work "directly related to Jacques Cartier," some thirty minutes long, for soloist, choir, and orchestra. For this he would need a commission. Then finally, there was "the opera I've barely begun to work on," which he was now calling *Tchaikowsky, un réquiem Russe*. Of the three suggestions, the one he himself was most keen to promote was the Tchaikovsky opera, which he was now planning to begin composing in June with a view to a premiere in 1985.[45] Dourguin replied encouragingly on March 10, proposing to meet in Paris in the second half of April to work further: but Vivier never saw his reply.

On March 2, *Bouchara* was performed, by the soprano Ingrid Ade, at the Keplersaal Planetarium in Stuttgart as part of a Canada Day. The program, conducted by Michael Zilm, was of chamber works by Canadian and Stuttgart composers, including pieces by Vivier's friends John Rea and Robert Aitken. It was the last concert Vivier attended.

# CHAPTER TWELVE

# " I N   Q U E B E C   P E O P L E
# D I E   E A S I L Y "

## 1 9 8 3 —

T he tragic news first became public in Quebec in a notice in the *Journal de Montréal* on Sunday, March 13, 1983. Under the title "Claude Vivier Strangled," the paper reported:

> The composer of music Claude Vivier, 35 years old [correctly, 34], originally from Montreal, was discovered strangled, yesterday afternoon in his Paris apartment where he had been living for less than a year. . . .
> Alerted by friends who had not heard from the victim for several days, the police gained entry to the apartment after breaking through the door. They discovered the dead body of the composer in his room, strangled under a mattress. The apartment had been ransacked.[1]

An obituary, by Claude Gingras, followed in *La Presse* the next day: "I didn't much like his music. However it was with infinite sadness that I took out his dossier to add the last information concerning him. CLAUDE VIVIER (1948–). Now it should read: CLAUDE VIVIER (1948–1983). It's never nice to add, in this way, the date of death to someone's name."[2] A more extended and thoughtful obituary followed in *Le Droit* a few days later. "The inner journey can lead to precipices," wrote the journalist J. J. Van Vlasselaer. "This XXIst century Romantic, like all true Romantics, took risks in order to find himself. So the absurd hands of a vicious strangler have stifled one of the musical glories of our country."[3]

To his friends, almost as upsetting as the news of his murder was the thought that Vivier's body had lain undiscovered in his apartment for more than four days before the Paris police had forced entry. As the full picture slowly began to emerge, the real tragedy of his death became all the more apparent. And while the events of the night of March 7–8, 1983, are straightforward to describe, aspects of their interpretation have unleashed a controversy that has raged ever since, and will perhaps never be satisfactorily resolved.

On the night of Monday, March 7, Vivier was drinking in a bar—which has never been reliably identified—in the Belleville neighborhood, not far from his apartment on rue du Général-Guilhem. He found himself attracted to a young man there and invited him home for the night. Here, immediately, questions arise that cannot be answered: was this the first time Vivier had picked up a would-be lover in Paris since the savage attack at the end of January? And should we understand this as an irresponsible act of ignoring the implicit dangers, or as a more positive wish to regain faith and confidence in this sort of casual encounter?

Once back in Vivier's apartment, the young man turned aggressor. One of the earliest published accounts of the events, by Harry Halbreich, claims that Vivier was "stabbed twenty-four times, strangled, his mouth stuffed with paper to stifle his cries."[4] But the identity of the murderer—or murderers, as for some time the French police entertained the idea that more than one man had committed the crime—was utterly unknown, and his (or their) motives unclear.

An alarm bell already rang the following day, Tuesday, March 8, as Vivier was due to give the first of the joint talks he had organized with Halbreich on the subject of music in Quebec: lectures had been planned for Paris, Milan, London, and Düsseldorf. Halbreich wrote:

> On the day of the first planned lecture, I turned up for the appointment we had fixed for that afternoon to rehearse a bit but there was no sign of Claude. I became worried very quickly, because by nature he was absolutely punctual and precise about work-related matters. I called his place all afternoon but there was no reply, and in the evening, when I gave the talk, alone, alas, I knew something serious had happened. I had to leave for Brussels, and I asked my sister to inform the police. That Saturday my sister telephoned me, in tears, and told me that they had found him.[5]

Speculations began almost immediately about what had actually happened in Vivier's apartment on the night of the murder. "French police have run out of leads after clearing the four early suspects in the killing," reported the *Globe and Mail.*

> Vivier, who was living in a low-income quarter of Paris, was found stran-gled and stuffed under a mattress. He had been the victim of a sex-related assault in January, which originally led to speculation that the murder also was a *crime passionnel.* But according to Thérèse Desjardins, one of three Montreal people mandated by the Vivier family to handle the com-poser's scores and personal effects, this theory has been discounted, and police are now investigating the discovery of a large deposit in Vivier's bank account. "Claude did not live with much money," Mrs Desjardins said, "so this was not normal." Mrs Desjardins also reported that Vivier had expressed fear for his life to a Paris music publisher the day be-fore his death. There was, however, no evidence of forced entry into his apartment.[6]

The bank credit mentioned, deposited on January 12, was for 27,050 francs—about €7,800 in today's currency. Who exactly made the deposit remains unknown.

Vivier's body was transported to the Institut Médico-Légal in the elev-enth arrondissement in preparation for cremation, which took place on March 23 at the Crématorium de la Ville de Paris in the Cimetière de l'Est on boulevard Ménilmontant. From there authorization was granted for transportation back to Montreal for burial. A small ceremony was held in his memory. Louise Duchesneau recalls:

> When we went to Claude's funeral in Paris (with Denys Bouliane and his then wife) we met up with Gérard Grisey and Tristan Murail who had known Claude in Paris. Gérard said that there were three things which were equally important to Claude: movies, music and gay bars. At the funeral, the cloth that covered the casket fell at some point to reveal a simple wooden box (Claude was cremated right after the funeral). Tristan Murail also spoke and played some Balinese music as this was one of Claude's favorites.[7]

An inventory was made of the possessions in his Paris apartment, which included a dozen tapes, a number of copies of scores of his works, a few books, manuscript paper, various items of clothing, notepads, a leather belt, a yellow leather tie, two pairs of glasses, a "wooden statuette of a wild boar," and a "plaster statuette of a cherub."[8]

Back in Montreal a ceremony was held in his memory on April 14—which would have been his thirty-fifth birthday—at the Église

Saint-Albert-le-Grand. The music performed included the psalm setting from *Ojikawa*, one of the earliest works in his catalog. His ashes were placed in the Salon Funéraire Dallaire, on boulevard Saint-Martin in Laval. The "Autorisation testamentaire" drawn up on March 13 on behalf of Vivier's parents, Armand and Jeanne Vivier, had authorized Thérèse Desjardins "to undertake all the legal measures concerning ways of returning the ashes as well as the belongings of Claude Vivier to Canadian soil": the testament had been signed by Jeanne Vivier, Armand Vivier, Marcel Vivier, Gisèle Vivier Labrecque, and her husband François, and Vivier's friend Jean Billard. From this point onward, Desjardins became the custodian of all his effects. An official memorial concert followed on June 2 in the Salle Claude Champagne, including *Pianoforte, Shiraz, Pièce pour flûte et piano, Prolifération*, the saxophone quartet version of *Pulau Dewata, Love Songs*, and *Lonely Child*.

The terrible truth about the identity of Vivier's murderer followed some months later, and by the end of October the news was widely covered in papers and magazines in Paris, Montreal, and elsewhere. He was a young homeless French criminal, then twenty years old, named Pascal Dolzan.

✶ ✶ ✶

Dolzan was apprehended in the last week of October in a bar on Paris's Place de Clichy. He was taken to police headquarters on the Quai des Orfèvres, where he immediately confessed—not just to Vivier's murder but also to that of two other men a month previously. A pattern immediately became apparent: all three of his victims were homosexuals. A reporter for *Le Parisien* noted: "Of average height, rather ordinary looking, he calmly tells of his murders without emotion, in the tone of a normal conversation." His first two victims were discovered together, murdered in their apartment on rue Véron on February 15. Vivier's murder was thus some three weeks later, during which time Dolzan had been in hiding from the police. "Immediately," the report continues, "the police tended toward the theory of a 'truqueur' [a trickster], specialized in the racket of this kind of victim."[9] A "truqueur," in this context, is a criminal who pretends to accept the advances of homosexuals in order only to have an opportunity to rob them and even, as in these cases, to harm or kill them. In August, Dolzan had also attacked and robbed, but not killed, a tourist near the Centre Pompidou. "In the evenings when I've drunk and smoked a bit I lose track of what I'm doing," Dolzan told the police.[10] And now a strong, if additional, motive for Vivier's murder became clear: "Claude Vivier, a homosexual, had met the young vagabond in a cafe in Belleville and had invited him home to finish the evening. Pascal Dolzan admitted that he had killed the composer by stabbing him with a knife in order to steal his wallet containing several thousand francs."[11] A final detail is suggested in one published source, but not confirmed in any other: that in Vivier's case Dolzan had accepted a "sadomasochistic assignment negotiated for 400 F by the victim in a bar in Belleville. . . . 'For Dolzan,' the police explained, 'his crime was simply a sadomasochistic ritual that ended up badly. . . . A simple accident, according to them, in a necessarily dangerous profession.'"[12]

Three years later, Dolzan was sentenced to life imprisonment. The report in *La Presse* gave a fuller account of the murder than had appeared previously:

> Twenty years old at the time, the young man subjected the Quebec composer to multiple violences, particularly in strangling him with a dog collar. Then the murderer regained his composure. Subsequently he rummaged around in the kitchen and filled the toilet bowl with dog food, pushed down by a bottle recalling the knife he had just used to stab the victim many times.
>
> The young homosexual [*sic*] pleaded irresponsibility. By way of extenuating circumstances, the defense emphasized that his childhood in public care was responsible for his psychological problems. The psychiatrist experts did not agree.[13]

News of Vivier's murder, and the progressive discovery of what had happened that night on the rue du Général-Guilhem, sent shock waves through the Montreal new music world. "I was very surprised at what happened," says Gilles Tremblay, "completely surprised":

> I think nobody could have made a prophecy of any kind. He was living very intensively, like a person who has to do as many things as possible as soon as possible. Once he told me, "Oh Gilles, you are going to live very long!" But he was living dangerously. You know, when he died we were very sad. But in a certain way I was furious. I was furious against him. You know, you don't have the right, when you have such talent, to be so stupid! In the last months I did not know what was going on in his mind. I learned from other people that he would go into a café in Paris full of

Arab people, and say, I am a Jew. Just to see the faces of the people. A sort
of provocation. In certain places you cannot make jokes. People think
that he really wanted to die, that he was looking for that. I could not sign
to this idea. Because he liked life. He had no tendency for suicide at all.
But at the same time, *Do you believe in the immortality of the soul*; why
this title? It's a mystery.[14]

Others are not so convinced that Vivier's death was a pure accident.
Harry Halbreich commented: "In the month preceding his death, he had
been attacked. . . . we begged him to move, but he ignored these warn-
ings, driven by who knows what horrible fascination with the darkness
that he was so afraid of."[15] Walter Boudreau says he always felt Vivier
was not destined to live a long life, "because I think most of the time
life was unbearable for Claude. So it's not fun—being here and only suffering."[16] Might it be, in short, that there was something willed about
Vivier's death, that he himself courted death, even finally provoked it?
That his death could, as Thérèse Desjardins has sometimes suggested, be
considered a sort of suicide?[17]

"His death appalls by its inevitability," wrote Paul Griffiths.[18] Those who
adhere to this view tend to point to Vivier's work as a form of evidence.
And it is undeniably true that few contemporary artists, especially composers, have been quite so obsessed with death, all the way from *Musik für das
Ende* in 1971 to *Glaubst du an die Unsterblichkeit der Seele* in 1983, sixteen
pages of which were found on his desk after his death.[19] *Chants, Lettura di
Dante, Journal, Kopernikus, Lonely Child*, and *Wo bist du Licht!* are explicitly
about death, in whole or in part. Yet for all that, at least as many works are
not about death: not just the purely instrumental ones, but those that treat
of other themes such as love, or travel. And for all the death-haunted artists in Vivier's century who killed themselves—Paul Celan, for example, or
Sylvia Plath—there are surely as many who did not, all the way from Samuel
Beckett to Marilyn Manson. "For me, the man and his work are very different," says Lorraine Vaillancourt. "His work is pure, and he was absolutely
the inverse. He was burning the candle at both ends."[20]

Another cross-section of his friends are equally convinced that Vivier's
death was in no sense a suicide. José Evangelista saw him in Paris about a
month before his death, when the two had dinner with Tristan Murail. He
found Vivier full of excitement about forthcoming projects, and declaring
how he thought his music had been too simple and that he wanted from
now on to compose more complex music.[21] Michel Gonneville agrees: "although Claude was obsessed by death he wasn't a suicidal type."[22] And
Bruno Hébert remarks simply: "One thing you got to remember about

Claude: really, he wasn't that fucked up."[23] Denys Bouliane expresses an important distinction, feeling that Vivier, in these last weeks, was "playing with fire; music was becoming a stage, and at a certain point he couldn't differentiate so clearly between his life and his art." However, in the last months, Bouliane met him a few times and "he was not in disarray"; although complaining about not having enough performances, he was "not depressed."[24] John Rea sees the widely held notion that Vivier was "playing with fire" differently: "'flirting with danger' is what we say, we on the other side; from Claude's point of view, he wasn't 'flirting with danger' at all."[25]

Might it not be, however, that these viewpoints do not actually contradict each other? That whereas in general Vivier was an artist filled with ideas, living at top speed in order to realize them, something in Paris— maybe even in the very last weeks in Paris—had pushed him over the edge, into a sort of darkness that until now he had only observed from the precipice? Pauline Vaillancourt spoke to him shortly before his death, talking about the Marco Polo opera among other things. "My feeling was he lived in situations of danger. A lot. I remember some calls in panic." Panic about what? "He told me he was afraid. I met him a few days before his death and he was really anxious. . . . He knew something would happen, he knew it was his last opera, he knew."[26] Daniel Dion recalls:

> [In Paris] we'd see Claude regularly, every couple of days and in the last few weeks Philippe [Poloni] spent a lot of time seeing him and also sharing some of the anguish or fantasy that Claude was going through. I'm no psychologist: I think somewhere it has a bit to do with the childhood, the lonely child, *Do you believe in the immortality of the soul* and all these works. I think there's a relationship to death, or a flirting with death, that's very present. Both extremes—the exuberance of Claude and his openness to everybody and anything, and the other side of the coin was that really strong worry or fear of living and dying, so they came to together. I guess it's typical of genius sometimes that these extremes come in one package.[27]

Poloni himself remarks that Vivier's death was not a surprise to him:

> I had a feeling it was coming, because he was always looking for new experiences, he was always going to these strange bars, encountering those boys who were just looking for money. Claude was a perpetual lonely person, in Paris no more so than anyplace. He would go at nights to gay bars like Le Central, in Le Marais. After the first attack he came to my place and started crying. He was going toward love, and wanting attention, and in reaction he received violence. He had two lives: during

the day working, eight hours a day; during the night, exploding; nights would often go late towards the morning, drinking. I think if Claude didn't die like that he would have died of AIDS. I think his path was going that way.[28]

Was there, as some of his friends vaguely remember, a real "menace" that was threatening him during the last weeks in Paris? Gilles Tremblay re-members Nellie Boufathal of the publisher Salabert telling him that Vivier "told her he had some *menace*, he had the insight that something could be wrong, so she told him, 'don't go back to your apartment, go anywhere else.' So she knew this situation. It is clear that none of his Montreal friends knew what was going on. Sometimes somebody needs help."[29] It is true that the journey back to the rue du Général-Guilhem at night—and at the time of his death it was dark by 6:00 p.m.—was not an altogether pleasant one. The orangey glow of the streetlamps may have seemed rather sinister; we recall his teacher Urbain Beauvais's remark that "Claude was excessively sensitive." However, the recollection by various people of Vivier saying that there was a "menace" needs to be treated with caution as this is a type of remark that can acquire exaggerated significance in the light of what hap-pened to him subsequently. He may have been talking about nothing more than the rough atmosphere in the bars he frequented, or some other situa-tion different from his customary life in Montreal. Or he may not.

How one regards Vivier's death—as inevitable, as a type of suicide, or as a meaningless accident—is, in the end, an individual matter, a distillation from opinions, theories, and possible readings of motivations and tenden-cies. It is, finally, an area where no real "explanation" is possible. In what follows I should like to offer a purely personal understanding of that death, based on my reading of all the available sources and the sense I have devel-oped—as someone who never met the composer—after years of working on his biography.

It is my opinion that Vivier was the victim of what today would be called a "hate crime," a crime in which the perpetrator intentionally tar-gets the victim because of the victim's perceived membership of a certain group, defined in this particular case by sexual orientation. While the term itself is relatively recent, incidences of hate crimes are older than recorded history. In other words, if the question one poses is "why was Vivier mur-dered?" the answer—as simple as it is horrible and unacceptable—is, in my opinion, because he was a homosexual. This explanation is, of course, consistent with Pascal Dolzan's targeting of his two previous victims: in this light, Vivier was a wholly unwilling victim who did not in any way actively seek his own death.[30]

I take this view not least because of the absence of any solid, incontrovertible evidence that Vivier, even in these last weeks, showed clear suicidal tendencies—in my reading of the documentary sources there simply is no such evidence. As we have seen, he was as full of new projects for the future as ever, and his career was going from strength to strength. This of course does not in itself imply that, inwardly, another range of darker emotions was not stirring. And it is undeniably the case that the January attack had been intensely traumatic for him. But it would then seem strange that these darker emotions did not manifest themselves externally—there is no cry for help, no first failed attempt, no suicide note. A love of and a craving for intense experience, certainly, but that was nothing new; an abandon to new situations and adventures, yes, to a limited extent. We must remember that he invited both the January attacker and Dolzan to his own apartment, rather than going with them to theirs. This does not seem the action of a man who has given up on life.

In the immediate aftermath of his death, the *Trois airs pour un opéra imaginaire* received its premiere on March 24, at the Centre Pompidou by l'Itineraire directed by Yves Prin with the soprano Brenda Hubbard. It was a memorable, if for many listeners intensely sad, occasion. Among those in the audience was Olivier Messiaen. Gérard Grisey commented:

> The exaggerated lyricism of Claude Vivier, which has no equal in its emotional and affective weight other than the prosody of Janácek, was however in many ways the absolute opposite of the preoccupations of the musicians of l'Itinéraire. Their point of intersection was the teaching of Gilles Tremblay, himself a pupil of Messiaen, with its great attention given to melody, to harmonic richness, and to homophony. With the perspective of a few years, I find that this marvelous musician possessed to a very high degree a freshness, a sense of melody, authentic emotion, and an economy of means which we in turn could have enriched if he had lived in Paris for a longer time.[31]

Posthumous recognition of Vivier's achievement was not slow in coming. As early as 1985, the Almeida Festival in London mounted a retrospective of his works curated by Pierre Audi (to mixed critical response). Five years after his death no less a figure than György Ligeti declared that Vivier was "the most important and original composer of his generation."[32] Ligeti spoke to Peter Hanser-Strecker of Schott in Germany about publishing Vivier's scores; and although this did not happen, it was Ligeti, with help from Thérèse Desjardins, who recommended the music to the Dutch conductor Reinbert de Leeuw, who, since the mid-1990s, has been the most tireless European champion of Vivier's music. De Leeuw recorded and toured a concert of Vivier's last works, the pieces on which his reputation rests; and, with the director Pierre Audi, mounted productions of the opera *Kopernikus* and the first production of the unfinished "opéra fleuve" *Marco Polo* (which, because their version was somewhat different from what we know of Vivier's intentions, they named *Rêves d'un Marco Polo*). This operatic double bill played at the Holland Festival in 2000 and again in 2004. With the announcement in 2005 of publication by Boosey and Hawkes in New York of Vivier's entire oeuvre, the future of the music now seems secure.

"It seems to me that in Quebec people die easily," wrote Vivier in 1978:

and it's in a wholly Quebec "sensibility" (an adolescent one) that we must look for the solution. An extreme sensibility which, alas, because of a pseudo-male environment, can often only suffer. So many are dead, and I myself do not want to die of this strange malady, which is perhaps why I have written this introspective text in the context of a book on the oppression of a sensibility and the free expression of love. . . . A single law governs my music: love. And it's also this simple law that should govern our human relations.[33]

Through music, and the search for love, he had found a reason to live, and those reasons remained true to the end. "Lives that are cut short are a real problem in the history of the arts," remarks John Rea, "because ultimately such lives were never really tested."[34] Indeed: all that remains now is the work, an exuberant font of richness, invention, and beauty that continues to uplift and to inspire.

# APPENDIX ONE

## Chronology of Compositions

T his descriptive chronology of Vivier's works is based on a study of all the known manuscripts of the composer, together with information gleaned from his correspondence, interviews, and various other documentary materials. It builds upon the information given in Jaco Mijnheer and Thérèse Desjardins, "La chronologie des oeuvres de Claude Vivier: historisation de la déshistoire." The description "not performed in Vivier's lifetime" in the list below means there is no known documentation of a public performance; it is possible that at least some of these works may have been rehearsed, perhaps in Vivier's presence. The standard order of instrumentation is used here: flute.oboe.clarinet.bassoon—horn.trumpet. trombone.tuba—perc—other—violin1.violin2.viola.cello.doublebass. All Vivier's works are now published by Boosey & Hawkes.

### 1968: *Quatuor à cordes #1*

Two movements only are extant: first movement 15 pp., second movement 12 pp. (originally marked at top "3° mouvement," but crossed out and "2° pièce" written above). It is not clear whether the second of the surviving movements is actually complete. The manuscript is undated. Premiered August 10, 1968, under the name *Quatuor en deux mouvements*, at a concert titled "Musique d'Aujourd'hui" at Festival Orford 68 at Magog, Quebec. The performers were participants in the Centre JMC Orford: Hansheinz Schneeberger and Anka Moravek, violins; Norbert Blume, viola; Eric Wilson, cello; conductor Marius Constant. First professional performance: June 2005, Zephyr Kwartet, Holland Festival, Amsterdam, the Netherlands.

## 1968: *Ojikawa*, for soprano, clarinet, and percussion (four timpani and vibraphone)

Two manuscript scores are extant: the first incomplete, 7 pp.; the second complete, 8 pp., the definitive version. Neither manuscript is dated. Text by Vivier. Premiered March 1969, at the fifth Symposium of Student Composers, McGill University, Montreal.

## 1968–69: *Musique pour une liberté à bâtir*, for women's voices and orchestra

The manuscript is in several parts: a first part of 23 pp., then a short aleatoric second part of 2 pp. (at the start of which Vivier has written "the 3 events of this part are to be played in any order, following each other without pause"); then a long section, 24 pp., with the title "Musique pour une liberté à bâtir II." (This "part II" is possibly a later replacement for the originally aleatoric part 2.) The manuscript is undated. Not performed in Vivier's lifetime.

## 1969: *Prolifération*, for piano, percussion, and ondes Martenot

The original manuscript from 1969 is apparently no longer extant; only the score of the 1976 revision is known. A page headed "Solo de piano pour Prolifération" has the date March 10, 1975; this seems to have been a first step in the revision of the piece. The manuscript of the revised version consists of a title page plus 14 pp., and is signed "Montréal le 24 avril 76." Originally written for the ondist Jean Laurendeau, and his trio partners Gabriel Dionne, percussion, and Louise Forand, piano. Premiered April 1970, at the New England Conservatory of Music, Boston, in a concert as part of a symposium of works by young composers. European premiere March 31, 1972, at the ninth Festival d'Art Contemporain in the Théâtre du Casino municipal, Royan, France.

## 1970–71: *Hiérophanie*, for soprano and ensemble (2.0.1.0, 1.3.2.0, 2 perc)

Two manuscript versions are extant: the first signed "Heidelberg, août 1970," 89 pp., with the remark "this is not the definitive version; it's a first version!" added later at the end; and a second version, much neater, 56 pp., signed "Montréal le 8/1/71." Not performed in Vivier's lifetime.

World premiere September 18, 2010, by Sarah Wegener, soprano, with MusikFabrik conducted by Emilio Pomarico, Cologne, Germany.

### 1971: *Musik für das Ende*, for twenty voices (in three groups, 2S, A, T, B; 2S, A, T, B; 4S, 3A, 2T, B), the singers also playing percussion

The manuscript consists of five introductory pages, a to e; then 7 pp. of the score itself, signed "Köln juli 71 Amen!" plus an annexe of 2 pp. "Peter Eötvos und Joachim Krist gewidmet und die Leute [*sic*] die heute sterben werden gewidmet." Not performed in Vivier's lifetime. Premiered January 20, 2012, Parochialkirche, Berlin, Germany, RIAS Kammerchor conducted by Hans-Christoph Rademann.

### 1971–72: *Deva et Asura*, for ensemble (2.2.2.2, 2.3.2.0, strings–1.1.1.1.1)

The manuscript consists of a title page plus 31 pp., signed "Utrecht le 8 janvier 1972." Not performed in Vivier's lifetime. World premiere October 8, 2008, by ensemble unitedberlin conducted by Andrea Pestalozza, Berlin, Germany.

### 1972: *Variation I,* for tape

The four-track stereo master, made at the Institute of Sonology, has the date February 22, 1972. 10'27". "Réalisé par Claude Vivier et Luctor Ponse."

### 1972: [untitled], for tape

Composed in collaboration with Peter Hamlin at the Institute of Sonology for a multimedia event on the theme of chance at the University of Utrecht. The label on the original tape has the date March 10, 1972. The box says: "Peter Hamlin Hall-music (right track) / Claude Vivier Stair-music (left track) / Random Music (Stadium Generale: Toeval [chance]), 1972, c.35mn." Vivier himself described this work as an "environment for an exhibition" (Canada Council grant application, 1972).

### 1972: *Hommage: Musique pour un vieux Corse triste,* for tape

The stereo master, made at the Institute of Sonology, has the date May 8, 1972. 27'30". "Réalisé par Claude Vivier et Luctor Ponse."

**1972:** *Désintégration,* **for two pianos (with optional tape); second version for two pianos and six strings (4.2.0.0) (with optional tape), 1974**

Manuscript of first version consists of 38 pp., signed "Paris le 26 août 1972 / Deo gratias." Revised version for two pianos, four violins, and two violas; manuscript cover page, layout page, plus 97 pp., signed "1974 3 April Köln." First version (with added strings) premiered March 1973 at Champigny, France, by Ensemble 2E2M directed by Paul Méfano. Revised version performed at the Hochschule, Cologne, in late July 1974, and again at Darmstadt on August 2, 1974, by Herbert Henck and Christoph Delz, with Saschko Gawriloff and pupils (Kalevi Aho, Vjera Katalinic, Andreas Pflüger, Jacqueline Ross, and Claes Pearce).

**1972–73:** *Chants,* **for 2 sopranos, 2 mezzo-sopranos, and 3 contraltos ("pour 3 voix de femmes principales et 4 voix secondaires de femmes")**

Manuscript title page and 68 pp., signed at the bottom of the first page "© Claude Vivier, 1972" and at the end "Deo gratias." Commissioned (retrospectively, in 1975) by the Secrétariat d'État à la Culture de France. Premiered March 1974 in Cologne: Gale Olivier, Beate Göttke, Gisela Prinz, Eileen Firmstone, Evelyn Freund, Ulla Zacharias, Annie Ditmayer, voices, conducted by Vivier. Quebec premiere: February 17, 1978, Atelier de Musique Contemporaine directed by Lorraine Vaillancourt, at Nocturnales, Faculty of Music, University of Montreal.

**1973:** *O! Kosmos,* **for SATB chorus**

Two manuscript scores, one 3 pp. dated "Köln 13/2/73," another 4 pp., less neat, no date. Text by Vivier. Canadian premiere May 1976 by the Festival Singers of Canada conducted by Elmer Iseler, Toronto.

**1973:** *Jesus erbarme dich,* **for SATB chorus**

Two manuscript scores, both 2 pp., with "© Claude Vivier, 1973" written at the bottom of the first page. Canadian premiere May 1976 by the Festival Singers of Canada conducted by Elmer Iseler, Toronto. Performed by the Festival Singers in November 1977 in Europe (London, Cambridge, Paris, and Bonn).

## 1974: *Lettura di Dante*, for soprano and ensemble (0.1.1.1, 0.1.1.0, percussion [cymbales antiques, claves, bongo, nipple gong, tam-tam], strings—0.1.0.0)

Manuscript title page plus 55 pp., signed "Koeln den 16/7/74. Deo Gratias." Dedicated to Peter Eötvos. Premiered September 26, 1974, Salle Claude-Champagne, University of Montreal: Pauline Vaillancourt, SMCQ conducted by Serge Garant. Repeated September 27, 1974, at Centre National des Arts, Ottawa.

## 1975: *Pièce pour flûte et piano*

Manuscript, 5 pp., dated "Montréal le 16/2/75." Premiered June 22, 1975, Tremplin International Competition (performers unknown).

## 1975: *Pièce pour violon et piano*

Manuscript, 5 pp., dated "9/3/75" [March 9, 1975]. Premiered June 22, 1975, Tremplin International Competition, by Gwen Hoebig, violin; pianist unknown.

## 1975: *Pièce pour violoncelle et piano*

Manuscript, 5 pp. Written for the Tremplin International Competition, but not performed there. No known performance in Vivier's lifetime.

## 1975: *Hymnen an die Nacht*, for soprano and piano

Words by Novalis (from *Hymns to the Night*) and the composer. Manuscript, 4 pp., no date. Premiered June 22, 1975, Tremplin International Competition (four performances, by different sopranos).

## 1975: *Pianoforte*, for piano

Manuscript, 5 pp., no date. Premiered June 22, 1975, Tremplin International Competition (six performances, by different pianists, including the competition winner, Louis Lortie).

### 1975: *Pour guitare*, for guitar

Manuscript, 3 pp. (Originally "Pièce pour Guitare et Piano.") Premiered May 1, 1976, by Michael Laucke, La Maison des Arts, La Sauvegarde. Written for the Tremplin International Competition but not performed there; retrospectively dedicated to Michael Laucke.

### 1975: *Improvisation pour basson et piano*

Manuscript, 5 pp. Not performed in Vivier's lifetime.

### 1975: *Liebesgedichte*, for SATB soloists, 0.2.1.1, 2.2.0.0. ("Trois quatuors: voix, bois et cuivres")

Manuscript, first copy, 110 pp., dated "deo gratias Montréal le 17/4/48" [*sic*; correctly, April 17, 1975]; a second manuscript, 112 pp., is dated "Montréal le 5 mai [1975]." Texts: fragments in Latin from Virgil's Eclogues (Bucolics), a passage in French from Psalm 131, and passages in Vivier's "invented language." "L'oeuvre est affectueusement dédiée à Maryvonne Kendergi." Premiered October 2, 1975, by the SMCQ conducted by Serge Garant (vocalists unknown), Salle Pollack, McGill University, Montreal.

### 1975: *Pour violon et clarinette*

Manuscript, 3 pp., signed "Halifax le 5/8/75." Premiered by Luis Grinhauz and Jean Laurendeau, at the Musée d'art contemporain à la Cité du Havre, Montreal.

### 1976: *Siddhartha*, for large orchestra (in eight instrumental groups: 3.4.4.3, 4.3.3.1, 8 percussionists, piano, strings)

Manuscript signed "ottawa le 28 Février" [1976]. Dedicated to Michel-Georges Brégent. Not performed in Vivier's lifetime. Premiered March 14, 1987, Montreal, by the Orchestre Métropolitain de Montréal conducted by Walter Boudreau.

## 1976: Revision of *Prolifération* (1969)

Title page plus 14 pp., signed "Montréal le 24 avril 76." This revision was probably connected to the performance at the Centre Culturel Canadien in Paris in October that year.

## 1976: *Learning,* for four violins and percussion (claves and Balinese gong) and tape

Manuscript, 21 pp., signed "le 11/8/76." The manuscript bears the subtitle "Ceremony of the Beginning." "Dédié à Martin Foster." Not performed in Vivier's lifetime. World premiere June 2005 by Zephyr +, Holland Festival, Amsterdam, the Netherlands.

## 1976: *Woyzeck,* for tape

Incidental music for a marionnette theater production at the Centre National des Arts, Ottawa, directed by Felix Mirbt. Premiered October 4, 1976, Ottawa.

## 1977: *Les Communiantes,* for organ

Manuscript: title page plus 11 pp., signed "Montréal le 22 janv 77." "Dediée à Luc Courchesne. D'après un tableau de Louise Thibeault." Premiered March 5, 1978, at Église de l'Immaculée-Conception, Montreal, by Christopher Jackson.

## 1977: *Journal,* for four solo voices, SATB chorus, and percussion (one player)

Manuscript, pp. 1–47 in a copyist's hand, pp. 48–93 in Vivier's hand; a later score, 70 pp., in Vivier's hand. Dated on title page "May 1977" (the same page for both versions) and at the end of the second score "Montréal le 15 nov. 1977." "Dedicated to Elmer Iseler." Commissioned by the Festival Singers of Canada through a grant of the Arts Council of Canada. Premiered March 30 and 31, 1979, Convocation Hall, Toronto; soloists Billie Bridgman, soprano, Sandra Graham, mezzo, Robert Missen, tenor, Giulio Kukuruga, bass; and David Kent, percussion; Festival Singers of Canada conducted by John Barnum.

## 1977: *Pulau Dewata,* for variable ensemble ("for ensemble of keyboards or any other combination of instruments")

Manuscript: title page plus 7 pp., signed "Montréal le 19/6/77." "L'oeuvre est amicalement dédiée au Groupe de Percussions de McGill." Premiered January 28, 1978, by the Groupe de Percussions de McGill. First performance of version for viola, piano, and percussion: January 28, 1978, Arraymusic concert at The Art Works, Toronto. Premiere of version for quartet of ondes Martenot: March 16, 1979, l'Ensemble d'Ondes de Montréal, l'Institut Canadien de Québec. Premiere of version for saxophone quartet, arr. Walter Boudreau: March 2, 1980, Le Quatuor de saxophones Pierre Bourque, Les Concerts Couperin, Petit Séminaire de Québec.

## 1977: *Nanti Malam,* for seven voices

Manuscript: 11 pp. plus various further pages of notes and sketches, some numbered, some with letters, but no final neat score. Premiere performances August 4, 5, and 6, 1977, by Le Groupe de la Place Royale at the Ottawa Teachers College, Elgin Street, Ottawa: choreography by Jean-Pierre Perreault. Performed in New York, Roundabout Theater, December 14, 1977.

## 1977: *Shiraz,* for piano

Manuscript, 12 pp., dated "Montréal le 25/8/77." Dedicated "to the marvelous pianist Louis-Philippe Pelletier and indirectly to two blind singers whom I followed for hours in the marketplace in Shiraz." Premiered April 4, 1981, New Music Concerts, Toronto, by Christina Petrowska-Brégent. Quebec premiere by Louis-Philippe Pelletier, July 28, 1981, Salle Gilles Lefebvre, Festival d'Orford.

## 1977: *Love Songs,* for seven voices

Manuscript: title page plus 15 pp. plus added 3 pp. ("love song melody I," "melody of the end," "melody II"). Premiered November 1977, in Ottawa, by Le Groupe de la Place Royale, choreography by Peter Boneham. Performed in New York, Roundabout Theater, December 15, 1977. Premiere of concert version by Array, Toronto, November 18, 1978.

## 1978: *Paramirabo*, for flute, violin, cello, and piano

Manuscript: title page plus 31 pp., "Montréal le 13 mai 78." Commissioned by ensemble Mozaïk with funding by the Canada Council. Performed by Mozaïk (Katherine Cash, violin, Kristina Melnyk, cello, André-Gilles Duchemin, flute, and Mario Duchemin, piano), date unknown. Performed by Array, Toronto, February 28, 1980.

## 1978: *Greeting Music*, for piano, flute, oboe, cello, percussion (tam-tam, plastic box, vibraphone, marimba, tubular bells, flexitone, rattle, bass drum)

Manuscript: title page, 2 pp. notes, plus 14 pp. score, "Montréal le 15 octobre 1978." "For 'Days Months and Years to Come.'" Premiered February 25, 1979, by Days Months and Years to Come, Vancouver.

## 1978–79: *Kopernikus [Opéra—Rituel de Mort]*, opera in two acts, for seven singers, seven (or eight) players—0.1.2.bcl.0, 0.1.1.0, perc (played by singers), strings—1.0.0.0.0, and tape

Manuscript signed "Montréal le 14 mai 79 / Deo gratias." Text by Vivier. "Dédié à mon maître et ami Gilles Tremblay." Premiered Thursday May 8, and Friday May 9, 1980, Théâtre du Monument National, Montreal; l'Atelier de jeu scénique de la Faculté de Musique de l'Université de Montréal; Pierre Godin, director; Marthe Forget, mise-en-scène; Jacinthe Vézina, décors; Meredith Caron, costumes. Conducted by Lorraine Vaillancourt.

## 1979: *Orion*, for large orchestra (3.2.cor anglais.2.E♭ clar.3; 4.2.2.1; harp; three percussion [tubular bells, vib, mar, crotales, bass drum, four rin, nipple gong, four small nipple gongs, three tam-tams, Chinese gong, two metal plates, woodblock], strings)

Manuscript: title page plus 40 pp., "Montréal le 6 octobre 1979." Commissioned by the OSM with funds by the Arts Council of Canada. "Dédié à Louise Laplante." Premiere performances October 14 and 16, 1980, by l'Orchestre symphonique de Montréal conducted by Charles Dutoit, Salle Wilfrid Pelletier, Montreal.

## 1980: *Lonely Child*, for soprano and chamber orchestra (1.picc.2.2.2, 2.0.0.0, perc, strings [6.5.4.3.2])

Manuscript: two title pages plus 30 pp., "Montréal le 5 mars 1980." Text by Vivier. Commissioned by l'Orchestre de chambre de Radio Canada, Vancouver. "L'oeuvre est dédiée à Louise Andrée." Premiere (radio recording) January 7, 1981, by Marie-Danielle Parent, Chamber Orchestra of Radio Canada, Vancouver conducted by Serge Garant, Vancouver. Concert premiere, November 18, 1982, in the Salle Claude Champagne, Montreal, Marie-Danielle Parent, l'Orchestre des Jeunes du Québec conducted by Serge Garant.

## 1980: *Zipangu*, for thirteen strings (7.0.3.2.1)

Manuscript signed "Montréal le 13 aout 1980." "Dédié à Philippe Poloni." Premiered April 4, 1981, New Music Concerts, Toronto, conducted by Robert Aitken. Performers: Ann Armstrong, Moshe Hammer, Nancy Mathis, Josie Pelog, Joe Pepper, Pauline Salesse, and Karen Zafer, violins; Leslie Malowany, Douglas McNabney, and Douglas Perry, violas; John Helmers and Peter Schenkman, cellos; Joel Quarrington, double bass.

## 1980: *Cinq Chansons pour Percussion*, for solo percussionist playing Asian instruments

Manuscript: two title pages plus 10 pp., "Montréal le 26 sept 1980." In five parts: Chanson du matin; Chanson à midi; Chanson au soleil; Chanson à la mort; Chanson d'adieu. "Dédié à David Kent." Premiered June 1982 by David Kent, Toronto.

## 1981: *Prologue pour un Marco Polo*, for five singing voices, speaking voice, four clarinets, two bass clarinets, two percussion, thirteen strings (4.3.3.2.1), and tape

Manuscript: two title pages plus 55 pp., dated "Montréal le 1 mars 1981." Texts by Paul Chamberland and Claude Vivier. "Commande de Radio Canada pour le prix Paul Gilson." "Pour Thérèse Desjardins." Premiere: studio recording by Radio-Canada, 1982. Pauline Vaillancourt, Marie Laferrière, David Doane, Michel Ducharme, and Yves Saint-Amant, voices; Jacques Lavallée, narrator; CBC Montreal instrumental ensemble conducted by Lorraine Vaillancourt.

## 1981: *Wo Bist du Licht!* for mezzo-soprano, twenty strings (6.5.4.3.2), percussion, and tape

Manuscript: title pages plus 53 pp., "Montréal le 11 mars 1981." Text by Hölderlin. Dedicated to Rober Racine. Premiere: studio recording by Radio-Canada, 1982. Jocelyne Fleury-Coutu, mezzo, with a string orchestra conducted by Lorraine Vaillancourt. Concert premiere: April 26, 1984, Salle Pollack, Montreal; Jocelyne Fleury-Coutu, mezzo-soprano, ensemble conducted by Serge Garant.

## 1981: *Bouchara [chanson d'amour]*, for soprano solo, 1.1.1.1, 1.0.0.0, percussion (Chinese gong, Balinese gong, tam-tam, bass drum, tubular bells, superball), string quintet (1.1.1.1.1), tape

Manuscript: title page plus 10 pp., no date [spring or early summer 1981]. Text by Vivier. "Dédié à Dino Olivieri." Premiered February 14, 1983, Evelyne Razimowsky, soprano, 2E2M conducted by Paul Méfano, Centre Georges Pompidou, Paris. Performed March 2, 1983, Keplersaal Planetarium, Stuttgart, Ingrid Ade, soprano, Studio-Ensemble Stuttgart conducted by Michael Zilm.

## 1981: *Samarkand*, for piano and wind quintet

Manuscript, 14 pp., "Montréal le 17 sept 1981." (Manuscript says: "SAMARKAND [et la danse du temps fut arrêté par une triste nouvelle . . .]"). "Pour Daniel Dion." Commissioned by the Quintette à vent du Québec and Louis-Philippe Pelletier. Premiered February 13, 1983, in Nice, conducted by Vivier.

## 1981: *Et je reverrai cette ville étrange*, for piano, viola, cello, double bass, trumpet, and percussion (celesta, vibraphone, trompong, chang, Balinese gong, tam-tam)

Manuscript: title page plus 4 pp. "Montréal le 26 oct. 1981." "Dédié à Claude Chamberlan." "For Array with support from the Ontario Arts Council." Premiered February 12, 1982, by Arraymusic, Trinity United Church, Toronto. Performers: Mike Malone, trumpet; Douglas Perry, viola; John Helmers, cello; Roberto Occhipinti, bass; Henry Kucharzyk, piano; Beverley Johnston, celesta; David Kent, percussion.

## 1981: *A Little Joke,* for SATB voices

Manuscript: title page plus 3 pp., "Montréal le 2 décembre 1981." Text by Vivier. "Pour Silvaine" [Sylvaine Martin]. Not performed in Vivier's lifetime.

## 1981–82: *L'homme de Pékin,* video

Film by Daniel Dion and Philippe Poloni; scenario by Claude Vivier.

## 1982: *Trois airs pour un opéra imaginaire,* for soprano and ensemble (1.picc.0.2.bcl.0, 1.0.0.0, percussion, strings [1.1.1.1.1])

Manuscript: 28 pp., "Paris le 3 novembre 1982." Text by Vivier. "Oeuvre dédiée à l'itinéraire." Premiered March 24, 1983, at the Centre Georges Pompidou, Paris; Brenda Hubbard, soprano, with l'Itineraire directed by Yves Prin. Not performed in Vivier's lifetime.

## 1982–83: *Glaubst du an die Unsterblichkeit der Seele,* for voices, narrator, 3 synthesizers, 2 percussion, electronics

Manuscript 16 pp. (unfinished?). Text by Vivier. Commissioned by the Groupe Vocal de France. Premiered April 20, 1990, in Montreal, Ensemble vocal Tudor de Montréal, Ensemble SMCQ conducted by Walter Boudreau. Not performed in Vivier's lifetime.

# APPENDIX TWO

## Selected Discography

This list of recordings of Vivier's works, ordered alphabetically by title, gives information on those recordings that are, or have been, available commercially on compact disc and on DVD. It builds upon the information presented in Johanne Rivest, "Claude Vivier: les oeuvres d'une discographie imposante," in *Circuit* 2 nos. 1–2 (1991): 137–61.

### *Bouchara*

Performed (1995) by Susan Narucki and the Asko and Schoenberg Ensembles conducted by Reinbert de Leeuw on *Claude Vivier*, Phillips 454 231-2, 1996. Performed by Marie-Danielle Parent and L'Ensemble de la SMCQ conducted by Walter Boudreau on *Claude Vivier*, ATMA Classique ACD2 2252, 2001. Performed (2004) by Susan Narucki and the Asko and Schoenberg Ensembles conducted by Reinbert de Leeuw on *Rêves d'un Marco Polo*, Opus Arte OA 0943 D (2-DVD), 2006.

### *Chants*

Performed by the Atelier de musique contemporaine de la Faculté de Musique, Université de Montréal conducted by Lorraine Vaillancourt, on *Claude Vivier—Anthology of Canadian Music*, Radio Canada International ACM 36 CD 1-4, 1990. (Originally released on LP CCL-33-131, 1981.) Performed by Les Jeunes Solistes conducted by Rachid Safir on *Claude Vivier: Chants . . . .*, Soupir S 206, 2003.

## Cinq Chansons pour Percussion

Performed by David Kent on *Claude Vivier: Zipangu*, Les Éditions Doberman-Yppan DO 99, 1988; also included on *Claude Vivier— Anthology of Canadian Music*, Radio Canada International ACM 36 CD 1–4, 1990. Performed by Arnold Marinissen on *Traces of Cultures*, BVHaast 0303, 2003. Performed by Christian Dierstein on *Claude Vivier*, Kairos 0012472KAI, 2006.

## Désintégration

Performed by Kristi Becker and Ursula Kneihs on *Claude Vivier: Complete Piano Works*, Pianovox PIA 529-2, 2000.

## Et je reverrai cette ville étrange

Performed by Arraymusic on *Strange City/Ville Étrange*. Artifact Music ART 002, 1988.

## Glaubst du an die Unsterblichkeit der Seele

Performed by Susan Narucki and Johan Leysen with the Holland Festival Singers and the Asko and Schoenberg Ensembles conducted by Reinbert de Leeuw on *Fifty Years Holland Festival*, Globe 6903, 1997. Performed by Susan Narucki, Claron McFadden, Tomoko Makuuchi, Lani Poulson, José Scholte, Helena Rasker, Terence Mierau, John van Halteren, Charles Hens, Richard Lloyd Morgan, James Ottaway, Harry van der Kamp, Johan Leysen, and members of the Asko and Schoenberg Ensembles conducted by Reinbert de Leeuw on *Rêves d'un Marco Polo*, Opus Arte OA 0943 D (2-DVD), 2006.

## Greeting Music

Performed by L'Ensemble de la SMCQ conducted by Walter Boudreau on *Claude Vivier*, ATMA Classique ACD2 2252, 2001.

## Hymnen an die Nacht

Performed by Pauline Vaillancourt and Jean-Eudes Vaillancourt on *Claude Vivier—Anthology of Canadian Music*, Radio Canada International ACM 36 CD 1–4, 1990. (Originally released on LP RCI 631, 1987.)

## *Jesus erbarme dich*

Performed by the Tudor Singers of Montreal conducted by Patrick Wedd on *Choral Works of Quebec*, CBC Records MVCD 1039, 1991. Performed by Les Jeunes Solistes conducted by Rachid Safir on *Claude Vivier: Chants* . . . ., Soupir S 206, 2003.

## *Journal*

Performed by Les Jeunes Solistes conducted by Rachid Safir on *Claude Vivier: Chants* . . . ., Soupir S 206, 2003.

## *Kopernikus*

Performed by Yolande Parent, David Doane, Pauline Vaillancourt, Michel Ducharme, Marie-Danielle Parent, Yves Saint-Amant, Jocelyne Fleury, and ensemble conducted by Lorraine Vaillancourt, on CBC Centrediscs CMC-CD3890. Performed by Claron McFadden, Tomoko Makuuchi, Marion van den Akker, Lani Poulson, Karl Daymond, Richard Lloyd Morgan, Harry van der Kamp, Johan Leysen, and members of the Asko and Schoenberg Ensembles conducted by Reinbert de Leeuw on *Rêves d'un Marco Polo*, Opus Arte OA 0943 D (2-DVD), 2006.

## *Les Communiantes*

Performed by Pierre Bousseau on *Pierre Bousseau au grand orgue de la cathédrale Notre-Dame du Havre*, Adda 581240, 1991.

## *Lettura di Dante*

Performed by Pauline Vaillancourt and the Ensemble of the SMCQ conducted by Serge Garant on *Claude Vivier—Anthology of Canadian Music*, Radio Canada International ACM 36 CD 1–4, 1990. (Originally released on LP RCI 411, 1975.)

## *Lonely Child*

Performed by Marie-Danielle Parent and the Orchestre Métropolitain conducted by Serge Garant on *Claude Vivier—Anthology of Canadian Music*, Radio Canada International ACM 36 CD 1–4, 1990; also included on *Montréal Postmoderne*, Centrediscs CMC-CD 5194, 1994. (Originally

released on LP CMC 1384, 1984.) Performed (1995) by Susan Narucki
and the Asko and Schoenberg Ensembles conducted by Reinbert de
Leeuw on *Claude Vivier*, Phillips 454 231-2, 1996. Performed (2004) by
Susan Narucki and the Asko and Schoenberg Ensembles conducted by
Reinbert de Leeuw on *Rêves d'un Marco Polo*, Opus Arte OA 0943 D (2-
DVD), 2006.

## Love Songs

Performed by Les Jeunes Solistes conducted by Rachid Safir on *Claude
Vivier: Chants . . . .*, Soupir S 206, 2003.

## Orion

Performed by the Orchestre Métropolitain conducted by Walter Boudreau
on *Orchestre Métropolitain*, CBC Records SMCD 5106, 1991. Performed
by the WDR Sinfonieorchester Köln conducted by Peter Rundel on *Claude
Vivier*, Kairos 0012472KAI, 2006.

## Paramirabo

Performed by Lise Daoust, Denise Lupien, Claude Lamothe, and Louis-
Philippe Pelletier on *Claude Vivier: Zipangu*, Les Éditions Doberman-
Yppan DO 99, 1988; also included on *Claude Vivier—Anthology of
Canadian Music*, Radio Canada International ACM 36 CD 1–4, 1990.

## Pianoforte

Performed by Louis-Philippe Pelletier on *Claude Vivier—Anthology of
Canadian Music*, Radio Canada International ACM 36 CD 1–4, 1990.
(Originally released on LP RCI 625, 1987.) Performed by Kristi Becker on
*Claude Vivier: Complete Piano Works*, Pianovox PIA 529-2, 2000.

## Pièce pour flûte et piano

Performed by Lise Daoust and Louis-Philippe Pelletier on *Claude Vivier:
Zipangu*, Les Éditions Doberman-Yppan DO 99, 1988; also included on
*Claude Vivier—Anthology of Canadian Music*, Radio Canada International
ACM 36 CD 1–4, 1990. (Originally released on LP RCI 535, 1982.)

## Pièce pour violon et clarinette

Performed by Swantje Tessmann and Sebastian Borsch on *Keyworks*, Karnatic Lab Records KLR 022, 2009. Performed by Luis Grinhauz and Michaël Dumouchel on the LP *Montréal Postmoderne*, CMC 2085, 1986.

## Pièce pour violon et piano

Performed by Denise Lupien and Louis-Philippe Pelletier on *Claude Vivier: Zipangu*, Les Éditions Doberman-Yppan DO 99, 1988.

## Pièce pour violoncelle et piano

Performed by Claude Lamothe and Louis-Philippe Pelletier on *Claude Vivier: Zipangu*, Les Éditions Doberman-Yppan DO 99, 1988; also included on *Claude Vivier—Anthology of Canadian Music*, Radio Canada International ACM 36 CD 1–4, 1990.

## Prolifération

Performed by Jean Laurendeau, Louis-Philippe Pelletier, and Serge Laflamme on *Claude Vivier—Anthology of Canadian Music*, Radio Canada International ACM 36 CD 1–4, 1990. (Originally released on LP RCI 358, 1973.)

## Prologue pour un Marco Polo

Performed by Pauline Vaillancourt, Marie Laferrière, David Doane, Michel Ducharme, Yves Saint-Amant, Jacques Lavallée, and the Ensemble instrumental de Radio-Canada, Montreal, conducted by Lorraine Vaillancourt on *Claude Vivier—Anthology of Canadian Music*, Radio Canada International ACM 36 CD 1–4, 1990. (Originally released on LP RCI 626, 1987.) Performed (1995) by Susan Narucki, Alison Wells, Helena Rasker, Peter Hall, James Ottaway, Harry van der Kamp, and Johan Leysen, and the Asko and Schoenberg Ensembles conducted by Reinbert de Leeuw on *Claude Vivier*, Phillips 454 231-2, 1996. Performed (2004) by Susan Narucki, Claron McFadden, Helena Rasker, Terence Mierau, James Ottaway, Harry van der Kamp, Johan Leysen, and the Asko and Schoenberg Ensembles conducted by Reinbert de Leeuw on *Rêves d'un Marco Polo*, Opus Arte OA 0943 D (2-DVD), 2006.

## Pulau Dewata

Version for percussion ensemble: performed by the McGill Percussion
Ensemble conducted by Pierre Béluse on *Claude Vivier—Anthology of
Canadian Music*, Radio Canada International ACM 36 CD 1–4, 1990.
(Originally released on LP RCI 478, 1978.) Arr. John Rea for ensemble:
performed by the Nouvel Ensemble Moderne conducted by Lorraine
Vaillancourt on *Bali in Montreal*, UMMUS UMM 104, 1992. Version
for quartet of ondes Martenot: performed by the Ensemble d'Ondes de
Montréal on *Ensemble d'Ondes de Montréal*. (Two other versions of *Pulau
Dewata* have only ever been available on LP: the version by Arraymusic for
viola, percussion, and piano on *Claude Vivier* LP CMC 1384, 1984; and the
version for saxophone quartet performed by the Quatuor de saxophones
de Montréal on *Vue sur les jardins interdits*, LP SNE 515, 1985.)

## Shiraz

Performed by Louis-Phillippe Pelletier (1983) on *Claude Vivier—Anthology
of Canadian Music*, Radio Canada International ACM 36 CD 1–4, 1990;
also included on *Montréal Postmoderne*, Centrediscs CMC-CD 5194, 1994.
(Originally released on LP CMC 1384, 1984.) Performed by Kristi Becker
on *Claude Vivier: Complete Piano Works*, Pianovox PIA 529-2, 2000.
Performed by Louis-Phillippe Pelletier (1999) on *Shiraz: oeuvres de Vivier
et Brégent*, Disques Pelléas, CD-0111, 2002. Performed by Marc Couroux
on *Rêves d'un Marco Polo*, Opus Arte OA 0943 D (2-DVD), 2006.

## Siddhartha

Performed by the Orchestre Métropolitain conducted by Walter
Boudreau on *Orchestre Métropolitain*, Centrediscs CMC-CD 3188, 1988;
also included on *Claude Vivier—Anthology of Canadian Music*, Radio
Canada International ACM 36 CD 1–4, 1990. Performed by the WDR
Sinfonieorchester Köln conducted by Peter Rundel on *Claude Vivier*,
Kairos 0012472KAI, 2006.

## Trois Airs pour un Opéra Imaginaire

Performed by Ingrid Schmithüsen and L'Ensemble de la SMCQ conducted
by Walter Boudreau on *Claude Vivier*, ATMA Classique ACD2 2252, 2001.

## *Wo bist du Licht!*

Performed by Marie-Annick Béliveau and L'Ensemble de la SMCQ conducted by Walter Boudreau on *Claude Vivier*, ATMA Classique ACD2 2252, 2001. Performed by Kathryn Harries and the Asko and Schoenberg Ensembles conducted by Reinbert de Leeuw on *Rêves d'un Marco Polo*, Opus Arte OA 0943 D (2-DVD), 2006.

## *Zipangu*

Performed by I Musici de Montréal conducted by Yuli Turovsky on *Claude Vivier: Zipangu*, Les Éditions Doberman-Yppan DO 99, 1988; also included on *Claude Vivier—Anthology of Canadian Music*, Radio Canada International ACM 36 CD 1–4, 1990. Performed (1995) by the Asko and Schoenberg Ensembles conducted by Reinbert de Leeuw on *Claude Vivier*, Phillips 454 231-2, 1996. Performed (2004) by the Asko and Schoenberg Ensembles conducted by Reinbert de Leeuw on *Rêves d'un Marco Polo*, Opus Arte OA 0943 D (2-DVD), 2006.

# NOTES

The following abbreviations are used throughout the notes and bibliography:

ACV   Archives Claude Vivier, University of Montreal.
AFV   Archives, Fondation Vivier, Montreal.
ÉCV   Robert, Véronique, ed. "Les écrits de Claude Vivier." *Circuit: Revue Nord-Américaine de Musique du Xxe siècle* 2, nos. 1–2 (1991): 39–135.

## Preface

1. The documentary was later reissued in DVD format as part of Claude Vivier, *Rêves d'un Marco Polo*, Opus Arte OA 0943 D (2006).
2. Brégent, Michel-Georges. Unpublished liner notes intended for a CBC LP of Vivier's music (1984), AFV.

## Chapter One

1. Crawford and Legget, "Ground Temperature Investigations in Canada," 2.
2. The statistics, notoriously unreliable as regards the matter of illegitimate births, are those of the Bureau fédéral de la statistique, Ottawa, as summarized in Malouin, *L'Univers des Enfants en Difficulté au Québec*, 119.
3. "La crèche Saint-Michel": Gisèle Vivier Labrècque, quoted in Bourassa, "Vivier courait les églises de Pont-Viau," 22.
4. Gisèle Vivier Labrècque, handwritten note on letter of February 28, 1951, from Paul Contant, director of La Société d'adoption et de protection de l'enfance, Montreal, to M. et Mme. Armand Vivier, AFV.
5. Malouin, *L'Univers des Enfants en Difficulté au Québec*, 95.

6. Lévesque, *La Norme et les Déviantes*, 105.

7. Lévesque, *La Norme et les Déviantes*.

8. Vivier, "Notes on *Journal*" (original in English), ÉCV, 79–81.

9. Lazar and Douglas, *Guide to Ethnic Montreal*, 145.

10. Philippe Poloni, interview with the author, Montreal, November 14, 2002 (conducted in English).

11. Vivier, "Introspection d'un compositeur," ÉCV, 92–93.

12. Thérèse Desjardins, interview with the author. My interviews with Mme Desjardins began in Cologne in February 2002 and were continued on numerous occasions and in various locations subsequently (conducted in French and English).

13. Vivier, program note for *Chants*, ÉCV, 55.

14. Michel-Georges Brégent, unpublished liner notes intended for CBC LP of Vivier's music (1984), AFV.

15. Gisèle Vivier Labrècque to Thérèse Desjardins, personal communication.

16. Chantale Quesney, e-mail to the author, July 30, 2004. Original in French.

17. See Roy, *Mémoire d'asile*.

18. Gisèle Vivier Labrècque, interview with the author, Montreal, November 11, 2002 (conducted in French and English).

19. Ibid.

20. At the bottom of this letter Gisèle Vivier has written: "Baptism St Enfant Jésus du Milen / Confirmation at Pont Viau, Laval Qué / Birth certificate kept in les Écoles de Pont Viau / date of birth 14 April 1948 / adopted in 1951 / rue St Denis ancien palais de cours Juvenile adoption legale." AFV.

21. Gisèle Vivier Labrècque, interview with the author.

22. Ibid.

23. Linteau et al., *Histoire du Québec Contemporain*, 212.

24. Gisèle Vivier Labrècque, interview with the author.

25. Gisèle Vivier Labrècque to Thérèse Desjardins, personal communication.

26. Gisèle Vivier Labrècque, interview with the author.

27. Ibid. Vivier as an adult had a fear of sleeping in the dark, and would generally sleep with a light on; this fear would seem to have its origins in his childhood.

28. Thérèse Desjardins, interview with the author.

29. Gisèle Vivier Labrècque, interview with the author.

30. Ibid.

31. Bruno Hébert, interview with the author, Contrecoeur, July 6, 2002 (conducted in English).

32. Thérèse Desjardins, interview with the author.

33. Gisèle Vivier Labrècque, interview with the author.

34. Gisèle Vivier Labrècque quoted in Bourassa, "Vivier courait les églises de Pont-Viau," 22.

35. Gisèle Vivier Labrècque, interview with the author.

36. Vivier, letter to Thérèse Desjardins, January 3, 1983, AFV.

37. Jeanne Vivier, interview with the author, Montreal, November 11, 2002 (conducted in French).

38. Bertrand Lamoureux, e-mail to the author, December 4, 2002. Original in French.

39. Frère Jean Loiselle, interview with the author, Saint-Jean-sur-Richelieu, Quebec, November 8, 2002 (conducted in French).

40. Bertrand Lamoureux, e-mail to the author, September 13, 2003. Original in French.

41. Frère Jean Loiselle, interview with the author.

42. Vivier, "Musique," ÉCV, 39–40.

43. Robert, ÉCV, 41n1.

44. Vivier, "Serge Bélisle," ÉCV, 42–43.

45. Jeanne Vivier, interview with the author.

46. Frère Jean Loiselle, interview with the author.

47. Vivier, "Introspection d'un compositeur," ÉCV, 92.

48. Vivier, lecture at the Centre Culturel Canadien, Paris, November 23, 1982: recording in AFV.

49. Vivier interviewed by Claude Cubaynes, 1981: recording in AFV.

50. Philippe Poloni, interview with the author.

51. Frère Urbain Beauvais, interview with the author, Saint-Jean-sur-Richelieu, Quebec, November 8, 2002 (conducted in French).

52. Denis Gougeon, in the radio feature, "Claude Vivier ou la Montée au ciel de l'Homme qui riait toujours," by Catherine de la Clergerie and Marie-Hélène Bernard, France Culture (1991).

53. Gilles Beauregard, interview with the author, Montreal, November 11, 2002 (conducted in French).

54. Ibid.

55. Bertrand Lamoureux, e-mail to the author, December 4, 2002.

56. Gilles Beauregard, interview with the author.

57. Vivier interviewed by Claude Cubaynes, 1981: recording in AFV.

58. Robert, ÉCV, 46.

59. Vivier, "Noël," ÉCV, 43–45.

60. Gilles Beauregard, interview with the author.

61. Frère Urbain Beauvais, interview with the author.

62. Gilles Beauregard, interview with the author.

63. Bertrand Lamoureux, personal communication. Original in French.

64. Robert, ÉCV, 43.

65. Thérèse Desjardins, interview with the author; Clarence Barlow, interview with the author, Amsterdam, August 11, 2002 (conducted in English).

66. Bertrand Lamoureux, e-mail to the author, September 13, 2003.

67. Vivier, "Introspection d'un compositeur," ÉCV, 92.

68. Gilles Beauregard, interview with the author.

69. Frère Urbain Beauvais, interview with the author.

70. Bertrand Lamoureux, e-mail to the author, September 13, 2003.
71. Cited by Véronique Robert, ÉCV, 43.
72. Jeanne Vivier, interview with the author.
73. Ibid.
74. An anonymous neighbour of the Vivier family in Pont-Viau, quoted in Bourassa, "Vivier courait les églises de Pont-Viau," 22.
75. Bertrand Lamoureux, e-mail to the author, December 4, 2002.
76. Gisèle Vivier Labrècque, quoted in Bourassa, "Vivier courait les églises de Pont-Viau," 22.
77. The manuscripts remained for many years in the possession of the Montreal organist Yvon Godbout, who found them among some old papers and placed copies in the Fondation Vivier in 1999.

## Chapter Two

1. "Horrible building": Walter Boudreau, interview with the author, Montreal, November 14, 2002 (conducted in English); "poor soundproofing": Jean Laurendeau, interview with the author, Montreal, November 14, 2002 (conducted in French).
2. A brief history of the Conservatoire de Musique can be found on their website: http://www.conservatoire.gouv.qc.ca/le-conservatoire/a-propos-du-conservatoire/historique-359/ (accessed October 16, 2013); see also *Les Origines du Conservatoire de Musique du Québec*, the catalog of an exhibition held in the Edifice Ernest-Cormier, Montreal, October 1–14, 1987 (Archives nationales du Québec, 1987).
3. Daudelin, "Entrevue avec Gilles Tremblay."
4. Grescoe, *Sacré Blues*, 270.
5. Borduas, *Refus global*. The translation given here is slightly modified from the version found in *The Canadian Encyclopedia*, online at http://www.thecanadianencyclopedia.com/articles/refus-global-manifesto (accessed October 3, 2012).
6. Grescoe, *Sacré Blues*, 34.
7. Linteau et al., *Histoire du Québec Contemporain*, 421.
8. Dickinson and Young, *Short History of Quebec*, 305.
9. Grescoe, *Sacré Blues*, 270.
10. Trudeau quoted in Moore, "New Look North of the Border," 88.
11. John Rea, interview with the author, Montreal, November 10, 2002 (conducted in English).
12. Vincent, *La vie musicale au Québec*, 99.
13. Marie-Thérèse Lefebvre, "Les débuts du modernisme musical à Montréal," in Ridout and Kenins, *Célébration*, 73–79.

14. Michel-Georges Brégent, unpublished liner note intended for CBC LP of Vivier's music, 1984, AFV. Gilles Tremblay also remembered this piece (interview with the author) and thought Vivier had later destroyed it.

15. Gilles Tremblay, interview with the author, Montreal, November 5, 2002 (conducted in French and English).

16. Gilles Tremblay in "Claude Vivier," radio documentary by Maryse Reicher, released as part of *Anthology of Canadian Music: Claude Vivier*, Radio Canada International, ACM 36, 1990.

17. "Gilles Tremblay: un portrait."

18. Gilles Tremblay interviewed by Jean Deschamps on the Canadian television program "Rencontres," January 13, 1974: transcript in Canadian Music Centre, Montreal.

19. John Rea, interview with the author.

20. Walter Boudreau, interview with the author.

21. Gilles Tremblay, interview with the author.

22. Ibid.

23. Michel Gonneville, interview with the author, Montreal, September 17, 2003 (conducted in French).

24. Toop, *György Ligeti*, 74.

25. Robert Leroux, e-mail to the author, September 22, 2003. Original in French.

26. Bertrand Lamoureux, e-mail to the author, December 4, 2002. Original in French.

27. Michel-Georges Brégent, "Témoignage," in the program book for the Concert Commémoratif in memory of Vivier, Salle Claude Champagne, Montreal, June 2, 1983.

28. Walter Boudreau, interview with the author.

29. Ibid.

30. Ibid.

31. Harry Somers, "Preamble" to the score of Somers, *Voiceplay* (Toronto: Canadian Music Centre, 1971).

32. John Rea, e-mail to the author, November 15, 2002.

33. Vivier's quartet was therefore played by an ad hoc group of students, not by the professional Quatuor à cordes Orford, which had formed at the Centre d'art d'Orford three summers earlier with completely different personnel.

34. In the first movement, measure 27, for example, Constant has written 3½/8 rather than Vivier's 7/16, clearly with the intention of maintaining the eighth-note pulse common to the surrounding measures.

35. Constant's inscriptions on the manuscript of the *Quatuor* posed a challenge in the critical edition of the work I prepared in 2004–7 for publication by Boosey and Hawkes; my decision finally was to remove all of Constant's additions from the text itself and to relegate them to the critical notes that follow the score.

36. Gilles Tremblay, interview with the author.

37. Curiously, the text of the psalm as used by Vivier in *Ojikawa* is different than that found in the French-language Bible most widely used in Quebec at the time, the "Bible Crampon" (the translation by Augustin Crampon, canon of the Cathedral of Amiens, first published posthumously in 1904).

38. Robert, ÉCV, 48n1.

39. "I remember *Ojikawa* well": Gilles Tremblay, interview with the author.

40. Jean Laurendeau, interview with the author.

41. Laurendeau, "Témoignage," in the program book for the Concert Commémoratif in memory of Vivier, Montreal, June 2, 1983.

42. Jean Laurendeau, interview with the author.

43. R.N., "Les Élèves Canadiens Plus Intéressés Par La Musique Nouvelle."

44. Jean Laurendeau, interview with the author.

45. Potvin, "Présence du Québec à Royan." Laurendeau has no recollection of Vivier being present when they played *Prolifération* in Royan in March 1972; Jean Laurendeau, interview with the author.

46. *Prolifération* was performed on October 25, 1976, at the Centre Culturel Canadien in Paris and was billed as the French premiere, which was not in fact the case, though it was the French premiere of the revised version. The concert, "Musique pour Ondes Martenot," also included a piece by Vivier's friend Tristan Murail, who performed as one of the two ondes players in his own *Mach 2.5* (1971).

47. Jean Laurendeau, interview with the author.

48. Robert Leroux, e-mail to the author, September 22, 2003.

49. Gilles Tremblay, interview with the author.

50. Martin Foster, e-mail to the author, October 6, 2011.

51. Dickinson and Young, *Short History of Quebec*, 321. Ironically, Quebec separatists unintentionally helped Trudeau to victory: at the 1968 Saint-Jean-Baptiste Day parade, held in Montreal on the eve of the June election, rioting separatists threw rocks and bottles at the grandstand where Trudeau was seated. Rejecting advice from his aides that he take cover, Trudeau remained seated, facing the rioters, showing no sign of fear. The incident was covered widely in the media and gave a further boost to his already considerable public image.

52. Gilles Tremblay, interview with the author.

53. From the beginning to two measures after figure 9; from two measures after figure 9 to figure 16; from 16 to 23; from 23 to 29; from 29 to 42; and from 42 to the end. Vivier, "Arcana: Edgar Varèse" (April 1970), unpublished analysis, Centre de Documentation, Conservatoire de Musique, Montreal.

54. See Bernard, *Music of Edgard Varèse*.

55. Laurendeau, "Témoignage," in the program book for the Concert Commémoratif in memory of Vivier, Montreal, June 2, 1983.

56. Bertrand Lamoureux, e-mail to the author, December 4, 2002.

57. The property in Oka was sold in 2007 and the monks, now greatly reduced in number, moved north to the newly built L'abbaye Val Notre-Dame in Saint-Jean-de-Matha.

58. Père André Picard, letter to Thérèse Desjardins, August 10, 1993, AFV. The letter records that Vivier's stays in 1970 were February 10–14 and June 4–9.

59. Toop, *György Ligeti*, 41–42.

60. *Darmstädter Beiträge zur Neuen Musik* 13 (Mainz: B. Schott's Söhne, 1973), 87–128. In German, the titles of Stockhausen's lectures were "Mikro- und Makro-Kontinuum"; "Metacollage und Integration"; "Expansion der Temposkala"; "Rückkopplung"; "Spektralharmonik / Expansion der Dynamik"; and "Raummusik."

61. Clarence Barlow, interview with the author, Amsterdam, August 11, 2002 (conducted in English).

62. Long thought to be of unknown origin, scholars now believe the hymn can be attributed to Athenaeus, son of Athenaeus: see Pöhlmann and West, *Documents of Ancient Greek Music.*

63. The Salve Regina is also used toward the end of Francis Poulenc's opera *Dialogues des carmélites* (1956), but this may well be coincidence rather than an instance of Vivier borrowing the idea from Poulenc.

64. Eliade uses the term "hierophany" as early as his *Le Mythe de l'éternel retour* (1949). Vivier owned copies of Eliade's *Patanjali et le Yoga* and *Forgerons et alchimistes*, and had almost certainly read other works.

65. Eliade, *Myth and Reality*, 6.

66. A copy of Vivier's application to the Canada Council in October 1970 is among the papers of AFV.

67. "Yves Sauvageau," Centre des Auteurs Dramatiques, accessed October 23, 2013, http://www.cead.qc.ca/_cead_repertoire/id_auteur/238.

68. Vivier, "Introspection d'un compositeur," ÉCV, 93. Vivier bought a copy of Sauvageau's posthumous collection *Les Mûres de Pierre* shortly after its publication in Ottawa in 1977.

69. Vivier, "L'acte musical," reprinted in Duguay, *Musiques du Kébèk*, 291–94, and in ÉCV, 49–51.

70. The translation given here is from Artaud, translated by Mary Caroline Richards, 13.

71. Vivier, "Notes du soir," ÉCV, 51–53.

72. "Écouter avec sa troisième oreille," accessed August 17, 2010, http://compositeur.raoulduguay.net.

73. Duguay, "Témoignage," in the program book for the Concert Commémoratif in memory of Vivier, Montreal, June 2, 1983.

74. The photograph is reproduced in "Stockhausen au Québec," a special issue of *Circuit: Musiques Contemporaines* 19, no. 2 (2009): 10.

75. Vivier, registration form for the Institute of Sonology, Utrecht, June 20, 1971: photocopy in AFV.

76. André Roy, interview with the author, Montreal, November 12, 2002 (conducted in French and English).

77. Vivier, registration form for the Institute of Sonology, Utrecht, June 20, 1971: photocopy in AFV. In English.

# Chapter Three

1. Vivier, registration form for the Institute of Sonology, Utrecht, June 20, 1971: photocopy in AFV.

2. Clarence Barlow, interview with the author, Amsterdam, August 11, 2002 (conducted in English).

3. Thériault, "Et j'entendis une voix réciter Dante."

4. Vivier, introductory text to the score of *Musik für das Ende*, in ÉCV, 53.

5. Vivier, *Musik für das Ende*, p. 6 of the manuscript.

6. Vivier to Pierre Rochon, undated letter [between June and September 1971], ACV.

7. Pugin, "Through the Spectrum," 15.

8. Vivier to Pierre Rochon, undated letter [between June and September 1971], ACV.

9. Clarence Barlow, interview with the author.

10. Ibid.

11. Gottfried Michael Koenig, interview with the author, Buren, the Netherlands, August 19, 2002 (conducted in English).

12. Stan Tempelaars, interview with the author, Nieuwegein, the Netherlands, August 15, 2002 (conducted in English).

13. Vivier to Pierre Rochon, undated letter [ca. February–April 1972], ACV.

14. "List of New Compositions Realized in the Institute of Sonology 1971/72," 187–89.

15. Gottfried Michael Koenig, interview with the author.

16. Ibid.

17. Peter S. Hamlin, e-mail to the author, December 7, 2010.

18. Annemarie Ponse Smalt, interview with the author, Nieuwersluis, the Netherlands, August 15, 2002 (conducted in English).

19. Frits Weiland, interview with the author, Groningen, August 17, 2002 (conducted in English).

20. Knut Sönstevold, e-mail to the author, February 4, 2003.

21. Barry Truax, e-mail to the author, December 7, 2010.

22. Machleen Batelaan, interview with the author, Amsterdam, August 19, 2002 (conducted in English).

23. Ibid.

24. Vivier to Pierre Rochon, undated letter [ca. February–April 1972], ACV.

25. Photocopy in AFV.

26. Vivier to Pierre Rochon, undated letter [ca. February–April 1972], ACV.

27. Ibid.

28. Peter S. Hamlin, e-mail to the author, December 7, 2010.

29. Vivier, grant application to the Canada Council, October 12, 1972: photocopy in AFV.

30. Peter Hamlin, e-mail to the author, December 7, 2010.

31. Thériault, "Et j'entendis une voix réciter Dante."

32. Vivier to Pierre Rochon, undated letter [ca. February–April 1972], ACV.

33. Louis Andriessen, interview with the author, IMS/IAML conference, University of Amsterdam, July 7, 2009.

34. The composer James Dashow recalls Ligeti's frequent stuttering (" . . . uh uh uh uh . . . oh oh oh ah ah ah ah") while trying to remember which language he was speaking at any given time. "The technicians at Darmstadt who recorded the lectures for posterity made a tape collage out of his stutters, cutting out everything but the ah ah ah ah OH OH OH uh uh uh uh etc., which made the rounds of the students in the last days. Ligeti was enraged." James Dashow, e-mail to the author, March 24, 2004.

35. Clarence Barlow, interview with the author.

36. "Very impressed": Walter Boudreau, interview with the author. Boudreau himself was less convinced by Radulescu's work.

37. James Dashow, e-mail to the author, March 24, 2004.

38. Walter Boudreau interview with the author. Vivier had heard *Stimmung* previously (at the latest by September 1971), as he compares Stockhausen's *Sternklang* unfavorably to *Stimmung* in the letter to his friend Pierre Rochon cited above.

39. James Dashow, e-mail to the author, March 24, 2004.

40. See Iddon, *Dissolution of the Avant-garde*, chapter 4. Criticisms of the aesthetic rigidity of Darmstadt had been expressed at least a decade earlier. See Attinello, Fox, and Iddon, *Other Darmstadts*.

41. Toop, *György Ligeti*, 142.

42. James Dashow, e-mail to the author, March 24, 2004.

43. Walter Boudreau, interview with the author.

44. Toop, liner notes to *Vivier: Complete Piano Works*, Pianovox PIA 529-2 (2000).

45. Vivier, program note for the first recording of *Chants*, reprinted in ÉCV, 56.

# Chapter Four

1. Vivier, "Mantra de Stockhausen," ÉCV, 94.

2. Gilles Tremblay, interview with the author, Montreal, November 5, 2002 (conducted in French and English).

3. Kevin Volans, interview with the author, Knockmaroon, Ireland, August 27, 2006 (conducted in English).

4. Richard Toop, e-mail to the author, August 15, 2002.

5. Clarence Barlow, interview with the author, Amsterdam, August 11, 2002 (conducted in English).

6. Tremblay cited in Griffiths, "Vivier," in Griffiths, *Substance of Things Heard*, 186.

7. Kurtz, *Stockhausen*, 194.

8. "A wonderful month of May 1974/ dear Vivier/ with warmest wishes/ Stockhausen." (The reference in the first line is to the opening song of Schumann's *Dichterliebe*, setting a poem by Heine.) Stockhausen gave Vivier a copy of his booklet *Vier Kriterien der Elektronischen Musik* published by Droste Verlag Düsseldorf, inscribing his wishes for a good new year 1974.

9. Several such film extracts are currently available on YouTube: see, for example, "Stockhausen on 'Sounds,' 1972," posted on YouTube by "Zero Budget Film School," August 6, 2007, http://youtube.com/watch?v=pIPVc2Jvd0w&feature=related.

10. Clarence Barlow, interview with the author.

11. Stockhausen in Cott, *Stockhausen*, 26.

12. Vivier interviewed by Claude Cubaynes, Radio-Canada, November 1981: recording in AFV.

13. Gilles Tremblay, interview with the author.

14. Thérèse Desjardins, interview with the author.

15. Parts of this sketchbook were published in the folder "Kompositions-Kurs über SIRIUS" distributed at the Stockhausen Courses in Kürten in 2000. Stockhausen adds: "I came upon the information about Sirius, the central sun, in Lorber's *Kosmos in geistiger Schau*." Jakob Lorber (1800–1864) was a Christian mystic and visionary (and a one-time violin pupil of Paganini) who, around the age of forty, claimed to hear an inner voice that he believed to be the voice of Jesus Christ. He produced an enormous body of writing, much of which was supposedly dictated to him by his inner voice.

16. Richard Toop, e-mail to the author, August 17, 2002.

17. Walter Zimmermann, personal communication, October 2008.

18. Vivier, application form to the Canada Council, dated October 12, 1972: photocopy in AFV.

19. Vivier, program note for the first recording of *Chants*, reprinted in ÉCV, 55.

20. Mennesson, "The Word Has Its Own Scent, Its Colour, Its Soul."

21. Kevin Volans, interview with the author.

22. Clarence Barlow, interview with the author.

23. Vivier, undated letter written from Neuhöfferstrasse 32 in Cologne (therefore, sometime in 1973–74) to François Bertrand of Radio-Canada: photocopy in AFV. The other two works were *Prolifération* and *Chants*. The proposed broadcast was to be the third of three: the first was to have been devoted to the music of Stockhausen and the second to Kagel and the Feedback group (Johannes Fritsch, Rolf Gehlhaar, and David Johnson). The project did not materialize.

24. Vivier, undated letter to Serge Garant [February 1973 or slightly earlier; the address is Vogelsängerweg 26]: copy in AFV.

25. Vivier, letter to Yves [?], undated [early 1973]: copy in AFV.

26. Regarding *Chants*, Vivier wrote "I believe I'll have it finished by June 1st and maybe earlier," undated letter to Serge Garant [ca. February 1973]: copy in AFV.

27. Nathalie Méfano to Thérèse Desjardins, June 17, 1988: AFV. Original in French.

28. Méfano, in De la Clergerie, "Claude Vivier ou la Montée au ciel."

29. Toop, liner notes to *Vivier: Complete Piano Works*.

30. Vivier, application to the Canada Council for a "Bourse de Perfectionnement pour Artiste" for 1974–75, dated "15/10/1974" [correctly, October 15, 1973], and date-stamped October 23, 1973: photocopy in AFV.

31. Vivier to Pierre Rochon, undated letter [March or April 1973]: ACV.

32. Letter to Vivier from Hugette Hébert, secretary of the SMCQ, May 17, 1973; Vivier to Jacques Hovsépian, received July 3, 1973: copies in AFV.

33. Toop, "Shadows of Ideas."

34. Walter Zimmermann to the author, personal communication.

35. Clarence Barlow, interview with the author.

36. Ibid.

37. Vivier to Pierre Rochon, undated letter [March or April 1973]: ACV.

38. John McAlpine, personal communication, May 25, 2011.

39. Kevin Volans, interview with the author.

40. Richard Toop, e-mail to the author, August 15, 2002.

41. Vivier to Serge Garant, June 17, 1973: copy in AFV.

42. Vivier, postcard to Walter Zimmermann, postmarked July 18, 1973: photocopy courtesy of Walter Zimmermann.

43. Vivier to Pierre Rochon, August 9, 1973: ACV.

44. Richard Toop, e-mail to the author, August 17, 2002. The possible relationship of Stockhausen's use of ring modulation in *Mantra* to the development of spectral techniques in Vivier's music around 1980 is discussed in my article, "On Claude Vivier's *Lonely Child*."

45. Richard Toop, e-mail to the author, August 15, 2002.

46. Toop, "Shadows of Ideas."

47. Richard Toop, e-mail to the author, August 15, 2002.

48. Vivier to Pierre Rochon, May 8, 1973: ACV.

49. Richard Toop, e-mail to the author, August 15, 2002.

50. Vivier to the Canada Council, date-stamped November 23, 1973: photocopy in AFV. In this letter he mentions that one of his intentions is to "finish a piece for orchestra": we know nothing further about this piece.

51. Vivier to Serge Garant, June 17, 1973: reproduced in Lefebvre, *Serge Garant*, 64.

52. Lefebvre, *Serge Garant*, 64.

53. Vivier to Serge Garant, March 8, 1974: reproduced in Lefebvre, *Serge Garant*, 66.

54. Thériault, "Et j'entendis une voix réciter Dante."

55. Gojowy, "Summe eine Melodie, die gut is."

56. Vivier to Serge Garant, undated [ca. April 1974]: reproduced in Lefebvre, *Serge Garant*, 68.

57. Ibid.

58. Vivier to Maryvonne Kendergi, undated [May 1974]: photocopy in AFV.

59. "Neither of which": Iddon, *Dissolution of the Avant-garde*; "melodic qualities," José Evangelista, interview with the author, Montreal, November 6, 2002 (conducted in English).

60. Bruck, "Rasch gealtert."

61. v.L., "Die Tänzerin und der Kontrabass." Curiously, in a letter of Vivier dated August 30, 1976, to the Canadian Music Centre authorizing them to reproduce his works "for the purpose of performance, analysis and deposit in the Centre's music library," he makes an exception not only for early, unperformed works such as *Hiérophanie, Musik für das Ende*, and *Deva et Asura*, but also for *Désintégration*: had the bad reviews shaken his confidence in the work? In an interview with Kevin Volans in 1977, he states that the work had been "a disaster" in Darmstadt but quite successful in Cologne.

62. Misch and Bandur, *Karlheinz Stockhausen*, 518.

63. "The minutes . . .": Iddon, *Dissolution of the Avant-garde*, 60; "[f]or all that . . .": Misch and Bandur, *Karlheinz Stockhausen*, 518.

64. Misch and Bandur, *Karlheinz Stockhausen*, 557.

65. English translation in Iddon, *Dissolution of the Avant-garde*.

66. Griffiths, *Encyclopaedia of Twentieth-Century Music*, 58.

67. Iddon, *Dissolution of the Avant-garde*, 62.

68. Martin Iddon, e-mail to the author, July 10, 2003.

69. Vivier, report to the Canada Council, undated [ca. March 1977]: copy in AFV.

70. Gingras, "De Stockhausen à Claude Vivier."

71. Walter Boudreau, interview with the author, Montreal, November 14, 2002 (conducted in English).

72. von der Weid, "Drowned in His Dying Song."

73. Richard Toop, e-mail to the author, August 15, 2002.

74. Griffiths, *Substance of Things Heard*, 188.

75. Lesage, "Claude Vivier, *Siddhartha*, Karlheinz Stockhausen."

76. Volans quoted in Gilmore, "Wild Air," 24.

77. Cott, *Stockhausen*, 32–33.

78. Richard Toop, e-mail to the author, August 15, 2002.

# Chapter Five

1. Pauline Vaillancourt, interview with the author, Montreal, September 24, 2003 (conducted in French).
2. Thériault, "Et j'entendis une voix réciter Dante."
3. Gingras, "De Stockhausen à Claude Vivier."
4. Vivier, "Lettura di Dante," ÉCV, 60.
5. Thériault, "Et j'entendis une voix réciter Dante."
6. Tilley, "Eternal Recurrence."
7. Vivier, "Lettura di Dante," ÉCV, 60–61.
8. Potvin, "Ouverture de la saison à la SMCQ."
9. McLean, "SMCQ Opens New Season with Return of Garant."
10. Gingras, "Varèse et les autres."
11. Vivier's letter is reprinted in ÉCV, 64–65. Some eighteen months later, a letter of Vivier passionately protesting Gingras's review of Boudreau's *Variations I* at an SMCQ concert was published in *La Presse*, March 29, 1976, under the title of "Boudreau ne méritait pas ça!" It is reprinted in ÉCV, 66–68.
12. Gilles Tremblay, interview with the author, Montreal, November 5, 2002 (conducted in French and English).
13. Walter Boudreau, interview with the author, Montreal, November 14, 2002 (conducted in English).
14. *Lettura di Dante* was the first of Vivier's works to be released commercially on disc, appearing on a Radio-Canada LP (RCI 411, 1975) in a recording by the performers who had premiered it. It was coupled with Robert Aitken's *Shadows—Part II "Latita"* (1973).
15. Rochon, "Vivier veut exprimer l'élément canadien par la musique," 6, 19.
16. Thériault, "Et j'entendis une voix réciter Dante."
17. Vivier, "Lettura di Dante," ÉCV, 60.
18. Rochon, "Vivier veut exprimer l'élément canadien par la musique."
19. Tannenbaum, "The Brief and Turbulent Life of Claude Vivier."
20. Rochon, "Vivier veut exprimer l'élément canadien par la musique."
21. *La Scène musicale* of September–October 1975 announced that the Arts Council of Canada had given $2,000 for the commission of eight pieces for the competition; this is not quite the same as the six months' payment of $400 mentioned in Vivier's letter of December 4, 1974.
22. Information from the "Request for Part-time Teaching" form submitted by Vivier to the University of Ottawa, September 18, 1975: photocopy in AFV.
23. Rochon, "Vivier veut exprimer l'élément canadien par la musique."
24. Samson, "Le pianiste Louis Lortie." Gwen Hoebig recalls: "As far as I remember there was great disappointment at that time as Vivier did not attend the competition" (e-mail to the author, April 27, 2011).

25. I am indebted to Michael Laucke for providing me with a scan of his annotated copy of *Pour Guitare*, with an inscription by Vivier that reads: "Affectionately for Michael Laucke, a friend of music / and may the musical harmony in your heart always express itself through your guitar."

26. Not all performers of the piece have been able to achieve the extreme dynamic independence of the hands called for by this passage: a particularly successful example is the recording by Kristi Becker on her CD *Vivier: Complete Piano Works* (2000).

27. This combination of instruments was something Vivier intended to explore further. Writing to the Canada Council in early March 1977, following his return to Montreal from Asia, he describes three projected works that he hopes will result from his experiences. The first is what became *Journal*; the second sounds close to *Pulau Dewata*; and the third, which never materialized, was "a series of pieces for clarinet and violin which will be a technical vision of my journey." Copy in AFV.

28. Jean Maheu, director of the Secretariat d'État à la Culture in Paris, letters to Vivier (care of Paul Méfano, Ensemble 2E2M in Champigny), August 27, 1975; September 11, 1975. Photocopies in AFV.

29. "Not liked": Carolyn Jones, "An Interview with Claude Vivier" (1981), in Belkin, Gagné, and Lefebvre, *Regards sur la Musique Actuelle au Quebec*. "A catastrophe": Walter Boudreau, interview with the author.

30. A photocopy of the contract, signed by Vivier on September 18, 1975, is in AFV.

31. Vivier showed the manuscript of the work to Gilles Tremblay, who wrote him (on April 28, 1975) two pages of comments, some of which draw attention to details in the score that might not work in performance, and others of which note, admiringly, some effective moments in the score. A photocopy of Tremblay's letter is in AFV.

32. Maryvonne Kendergi, "Témoignage" in the booklet for the "Concert Commémoratif" in Vivier's memory, Montreal, June 2, 1983.

33. Vivier, "Liebesgedichte," ÉCV, 65.

34. Ibid., 65–66.

35. It may be reading too much into Vivier's words to hear a faint echo here of Stockhausen's description of his *Telemusik* (1966): "TELEMUSIK is not a collage anymore. Rather, through the process of intermodulation, old objects trouvés and new sounds, which I produced in the electronic studio, are combined into a higher unity: a univers-ality of past, present and future, of distant places and spaces: TELE-MUSIK." Stockhausen, sleevenotes to the LP of *Telemusik* (Deutsche Grammophone Gesellschaft, 137012).

36. Lonchampt, "La musique au Canada."

37. Potvin, "La semaine de musique: un concert harmonieux."

38. Vivier to Harry Halbreich, March 10, 1976: photocopy in AFV.

39. These reviews were reported in *La Scène musicale* on June 5, 1976, and August 7, 1976, respectively.

40. Vivier to Walter Zimmermann, undated [ca. March 1976]. Copy courtesy of Walter Zimmermann.

41. Louise Duchesneau, e-mail to the author, September 2, 2011.

42. Gilles Tremblay, interview with the author.

43. Desjardins, in De la Clergerie, "Claude Vivier ou la Montée au ciel."

44. Van Vlasselaer, "Quand Claude Vivier s'appèle 'Nyonan Kenyung.'"

45. Ligeti, "Sur la musique de Claude Vivier," 13.

46. Lesage, "Claude Vivier, *Siddhartha*, Karlheinz Stockhausen," 110. Stockhausen's famous description of tempo relations was first set out in his article "Wie die Zeit vergeht," first published in *Die Reihe* 3 (1957), and reprinted in Stockhausen, *Texte 1*, 99–139.

47. Lesage, "Claude Vivier, *Siddhartha*, Karlheinz Stockhausen," 111.

48. Some of these markings may be by Foster, who recalls: "I have a very dim recollection of Claude's asking me to look over something he wrote sometime after I returned to Montreal from New York in 1980, but what that may have been I really can't recall. In the early 80s a lot of composers were interested in having me perform their works. It could have been around that time that Claude showed me *Learning*." Meeting Vivier again, Foster noticed a difference from their years together as students in Tremblay's class: "From 1970 to 1976 I was a student at the Juilliard School. I had dinner with Claude a couple of times when he came to New York, and I was struck by how much he had changed. Québec independence [which had been important to Vivier back then] was now utterly irrelevant. His composition style had evolved considerably, largely due to the time he had spent outside Quebec." Martin Foster, e-mail to the author, October 6, 2011.

49. The *Woyzeck* production would also tour France and Belgium in late January and early February 1978, with performances in Bourges, Grasse, Nevers, Creusot, Dijon, Cergy-Pontoise, Orléans, Amiens, Brussels, and Liège.

50. *Canadian Theatre Encyclopedia*, s.v. "Mirbt, Felix," last updated April 24, 2009, http://www.canadiantheatre.com/dict.pl?term=Mirbt%2C%20Felix.

51. Felix Mirbt to Thérèse Desjardins, personal communication. Kevin Austin's "A History of the McGill Electronic Music Studio," December 1990, posted on the website of the Canadian Music Centre mentions Vivier as having worked in their studios, but does not specify what he worked on (updated by Alcides Lanza, 2001, http://www.musiccentre.ca/node/65774).

# Chapter Six

1. Carolyn Jones, "An Interview with Claude Vivier" (1981), in Belkin, Gagné, and Lefebvre, *Regards sur la Musique Actuelle au Quebec*.

2. "The relation of the sacred and art": Gilles Tremblay, interview with the author.

3. Rogers, "Travelogue pour un Marco Polo," 29.

4. Vivier interviewed by Kevin Volans, Cologne, 1977; copy courtesy of Kevin Volans.

5. The seven-page manuscript is reprinted, in incomplete form, as "Japon," ÉCV, 68–69.

6. At one point in his description Vivier writes: "the sound of the *claves* announces the beginning and end of the piece. A musician dressed all in black punctuates the action with two pieces of wood struck against a wooden plate." This use of the claves is very close to what happens in Vivier's own *Learning*, completed (but not performed) before his journey to Asia. Might it be that the role of the percussionist in *Learning* was only added after the fact, after his Japanese experience? The role of the percussionist is described only in the five pages of typed verbal notes that preface the score; the music manuscript pages, which bear the August 1976 date, do not include a percussion part (which admittedly does not really need to be notated at all).

7. Vivier, "Trois lettres de Bali," ÉCV, 70.

8. Vivier, interview with Claude Cubaynes, November 1981. Among the books in Vivier's library was *Island of Bali* by the Mexican painter and anthropologist Miguel Covarrubias, a classic originally published in 1937, and a new third edition of which had appeared in 1976. He also admired Colin McPhee's *Music in Bali*, which he described to Kevin Volans (without remembering the author's name) as a "very good book." Vivier interviewed by Kevin Volans; recording courtesy of Kevin Volans.

9. Vivier interviewed by Kevin Volans, Cologne, 1977.

10. The source of this quotation has not been identified.

11. Reprinted in ÉCV, 72–73.

12. Vivier interviewed by Kevin Volans.

13. Gilles Tremblay, interview with the author, Montreal, November 5, 2002 (conducted in French and English).

14. Steve Reich, for example, writing of his studies in Ghana in 1970, commented, "I was overwhelmed by their music, like being in front of a tidal wave, and there I was, just me, with several thousand years of a whole continent's music washing over me. I found myself wondering where, as a composer, my studies were taking me." Reich, *Writings About Music*, 57.

15. Vivier, "Trois lettres de Bali," ÉCV, 73.

16. Ibid., 74.

17. Under the title "Heureux qui comme Ulysse," this was reprinted in full in ÉCV, 74–79. In a letter to the Canada Council date-stamped March 10, 1977, he mentions: "I'm working at the moment on an article on the music of Thailand and also on my experiences in Egypt"; sadly, neither of these articles seems to have materialized: AFV.

18. A photocopy of this CV, dating from 1980, is in AFV.

19. Vivier, undated letter to Canada Council [February or early March 1977]: photocopy in AFV.

20. Vivier, undated letter to Canada Council [February or early March 1977]: photocopy in AFV.

21. Walter Boudreau, interview with the author, Montreal, November 14, 2002 (conducted in English).

22. José Evangelista, interview with the author, Montreal, November 6, 2002 (conducted in English).

23. Vivier, "Trois lettres de Bali," ÉCV, 79.

# Chapter Seven

1. The original manuscript of *Liebesgedichte* (before the neat copy of the score completed a few weeks later) bears the inscription "deo gratias Montréal le 17/4/48" [correctly, April 17, 1975]—"4/48," of course, being his birth month and year, a date he was used to filling in on application forms and elsewhere.

2. Christopher Jackson, interview with the author, Montreal, October 2, 2003 (conducted in English). Vivier had known Jackson since their student days at the Montreal Conservatoire.

3. Dufourt, "Musique spectrale." Grisey wrote of this: "Various nomenclature was advanced: liminal, differenial, spectral. For better or worse, the term spectral was retained by the musical milieu following an article by Hugues Dufourt." Grisey, *Écrits*, 197.

4. Griffiths, *Modern Music and After*, 255.

5. Kevin Volans, interview with the author, Knockmaroon, Ireland, August 27, 2006 (conducted in English).

6. Walter Zimmermann, e-mail to the author, April 22, 2011.

7. Toop, "Walter Zimmermann," in Morton and Collins, *Contemporary Composers*.

8. Volans, program note in the score for Volans, *Nine Beginnings* for two pianos (1976–79) (London: Chester Music).

9. Volans quoted in Gilmore, "Wild Air," 24.

10. Clarence Barlow, interview with the author, Amsterdam, August 11, 2002 (conducted in English). An interesting perspective on the aesthetic coherence in the work of some of the young Cologne-based composers at this time is given in Fox, "Where the River Bends."

11. Vivier, undated letter to Canada Council [February or early March 1977]: photocopy in AFV.

12. Vivier, from notebooks kept during travels in Bali, 1976: ACV.

13. Vivier, "Notes on *Journal*" (original in English), ÉCV, 79.

14. Nerval, "To My Friend Théophile Gautier," in Nerval, *Selected Writings*, 194–95.

15. Vivier, "Notes on *Journal*" (original in English), ÉCV, 79–81.

16. Vivier, "Pulau Dewata," ÉCV, 89.

17. Of the Array performance at The Art Works in Toronto on January 28, 1978, Ronald Hambleton in the *Toronto Star* wrote: "Also surprising was Claude Vivier's *Pulau Dewata* (1977) for keyboard, viola and xylophone. Based on Balinese idioms, it was both simple and subtle, and of all the works that night, was most warmly received by the audience."

18. Jean Laurendeau, interview with the author, Montreal, November 14, 2002 (conducted in French).

19. Vivier, "Pulau Dewata," ÉCV, 89.

20. Walter Boudreau suggests that the choice of intervals in *Pulau Dewata* had to do with the tuning of the upright piano Vivier had at that time. Walter Boudreau, interview with the author.

21. Ligeti, "Sur la musique de Claude Vivier," 13.

22. Southworth, "Dancers Find Their Voices."

23. Ashley, "Dance for the Senses, but not the Intellect."

24. Van Vlasselaer, "Quand Claude Vivier s'appèle 'Nyonan Kenyung.'"

25. Kisselgoff, "Dance: The Debut of Montreal Group."

26. Vivier, program note for *Shiraz*, reprinted in ÉCV, 89.

27. Pelletier, liner notes for *Shiraz: oeuvres de Vivier et Brégent*. Disques Pelléas CD-0111 (2002).

28. Toop, CD liner notes to *Vivier: Complete Piano Works*, Pianovox PIA 529-2 (2000).

29. The Vivier pieces were reviewed enthusiastically by the New York critics: see Dunning, "Dance: Montrealers Try All Arts"; and Jowitt, "Dance."

30. Rober Racine, interview with the author, Montreal, October 16, 2003 (conducted in English).

31. Gilles Tremblay, interview with the author, Montreal, November 5, 2002 (conducted in French and English).

32. Vivier, "Introspection d'un compositeur," ÉCV, 93.

33. Vivier interviewed by Yves Bouliane, February 15, 1978: transcript in ACV.

34. *Chants* was performed again on March 22 and 23, 1978, at Conventum on rue Sanguinet, a short-lived venue in an area of topless cabarets. A review by Françoy Roberge, "Evangelista et Vivier au Conventum," appeared in *Le Devoir* on March 29, 1978: "[*Chants*] bears witness to an enormous musical culture, it is balanced and with a very nuanced harmony that sometimes recalls Messiaen. . . . A work of high spiritual quality, *Chants* uses the power of language and the force of elocution, but, despite the affirmation of the author who claims 'the musical structure depends as much on the text as the music,' it's the music that dominates primarily . . . if Vivier himself talks about 'Romanticism' with regard to

*Chants*, the work does not at all come across in the colours of Romantic passion. Ultimately, we think more of Gregorian chant or of post-impressionist vocal music than of Romanticism."

35. José Evangelista, interview with the author, Montreal, November 6, 2002 (conducted in English).

36. John Rea, interview with the author, Montreal, November 10, 2002 (conducted in English).

37. Lorraine Vaillancourt, interview with the author, Montreal, November 15, 2002 (conducted in English and French).

38. José Evangelista, interview with the author.

39. Quoted in the ninth anniversary brochure of Les Evénements du Neuf, 1986–87: copy in AFV.

40. Reprinted in ÉCV, 90–91.

41. Roberge, "La jeune musique en quête d'épanouissement."

42. Rober Racine, interview with the author. Racine adds that Vivier was very conscious of the standard of living in different countries, the political climate, the value of currency; in that sense he was "absolutely not a tourist."

43. Days Months and Years to Come was founded in 1974 by conductor Alex Pauk; in 1982 the ensemble changed its name to Magnetic Band.

44. John Rea, interview with the author.

45. Rober Racine, interview with the author.

46. Vivier to the Conseil des Arts, Montreal, June 26, 1978: photocopy in AFV. Vivier's "État des Revenus et Dépenses" for 1979, however, lists a "bourse de travail" for $6,000; perhaps the sum he received was slightly less than originally requested.

47. Horwood, "Array Concerts October 21 & November 18 1978."

48. Gingras, "Du 'neuf' en musique."

49. José Evangelista, interview with the author.

50. John Rea, interview with the author.

51. Vivier cited in Gingras, "Du 'neuf' en musique."

52. John Rea, interview with the author.

53. William Littler, "Singers Banish Cobwebs."

54. Proulx, "Moyens d'Élaborer la Programmation."

55. Louise Duchesneau, e-mail to the author, September 3, 2011.

# Chapter Eight

1. Vivier, "Kopernikus: Opéra—Rituel de Mort," ÉCV, 95.

2. Vivier, "Project for a chamber opera" (1978), unpublished typescript, AFV.

3. Vivier quoted in Gingras, "Le dernier Vivier: un opera."

4. Vivier quoted in Moisan, "*Kopernikus* ou l'histoire d'une oeuvre lyrique Québécoise," an interview with Vivier, director Marthe Forget, and conductor Lorraine Vaillancourt.

5. Ibid.

6. Ibid.

7. Vivier, "Livret de Kopernikus" (1978–79), fourteen-page unpublished typescript, AFV.

8. Moisan, "*Kopernikus* ou l'histoire d'une oeuvre lyrique québécoise."

9. Ibid.

10. Vivier in Moisan, "*Kopernikus* ou l'histoire d'une oeuvre lyrique québécoise."

11. Vivier in Gingras, "Le dernier Vivier: un opera."

12. Ibid.

13. R.R., "Le mysticisme onirique."

14. Bailey, "Overly-long Ritual Mars *Kopernikus* Experience."

15. Potvin, "Kopernikus: un coup d'audace de Claude Vivier."

16. Vivier's friend Rober Racine recalls that when Vivier got the OSM commission for *Orion* he wanted to study some standard orchestral works but did not have a record player himself, and very few scores. Racine invited him over so they could listen at his place: he recalls on one occasion César Franck's symphony on the turntable, and Vivier on the floor following the score. Rober Racine, interview with the author, Montreal, October 16, 2003 (conducted in English).

17. Vivier, "Orion," ÉCV, 121.

18. Mijnheer, liner notes to the recording of *Orion* by the WDR Sinfonieorchester Köln conducted by Peter Rundel, Kairos 0012472KAI (2006).

19. Vivier, "Orion," ÉCV, 123.

20. Mijnheer, liner notes to the Kairos recording of *Orion*.

21. McLean, "Violinist Gidon Kremer Shows He Is Extraordinary."

22. "Reviews," *Le Devoir*, October 25, 1980.

23. Gingras, "Dutoit: un Mahler nouveau."

24. Walter Boudreau, interview with the author, Montreal, November 14, 2002 (conducted in English). Although he was hurt at the time by the reviews, several years later Vivier played a recording of the work for his musicologist friend Harry Halbreich, who liked it: "I'm therefore reconciled with *Orion*!" Vivier to Thérèse Desjardins, January 24, 1983: AFV.

# Chapter Nine

1. Vivier to Thérèse Desjardins, postmarked November 15, 1979: AFV.

2. Thérèse Desjardins, e-mail to the author, October 2, 2012.

3. Rose, "Introduction to the Pitch Organization of French Spectral Music"; esp. 20–29.

4. Vivier, "Lonely Child," ÉCV, 108.

5. Vivier, lecture at the Centre Culturel Canadien in Paris, November 23, 1982, "La couleur spectrale développé dans trois oeuvres: à la recherche d'une nouvelle mélodie": recording in AFV.

6. Tristan Murail, interview with the author, telephone, October 21, 2003 (conducted in English).

7. Grisey, "Lettre à Hugues Dufourt," originally written July 5, 1980, and re-printed in Grisey, *Écrits*, 281.

8. The best to have appeared so far in English is Anderson, "A Provisional History of Spectral Music."

9. As we have seen, Vivier had heard *Stimmung* at the latest by September 1971. And yet it had no immediate consequences for his musical thinking. For years his language (that of *Lettura di Dante* or *Liebesgedichte*) seemed rooted in an earlier phase of Stockhausen's work.

10. Grisey, *Écrits*, 53.

11. Here we are talking not of actual resonance (of the type Grisey would explore in his *Prologue* [1976] for solo viola and optional resonators) but of simu-lated resonance; a complex sound—in this case, a low trombone note—is treated as though broken down into its component partials and reconstituted by the en-semble. This technique has become known as "instrumental synthesis."

12. Gilles Tremblay, interview with the author, Montreal, November 5, 2002 (conducted in French and English).

13. Messiaen, *Technique de mon Langage Musical*; see chapter 14.

14. Grisey, "Autoportrait avec l'Itinéraire" (1991), in Grisey, *Écrits*, 199.

15. Vivier, "Lonely Child," ÉCV, 108. According to his "income report 1980," the commission he received was $3,200: AFV.

16. Vivier's calculations of the combination tones used in *Lonely Child*, as seen in his sketches, contain a good many errors. These would seem to be the result of doing the calculations by hand, rather than with a calculator or computer, prob-ably at Vivier's characteristic high speed. The errors remained for the most part undetected by him and were incorporated into the score. In studying the work, I found what seem to me more than ten inexplicable pitch choices out of the sev-enty-five combination tones in "mélodie 1" alone, the only plausible explanation for which is mathematical error. And yet, possible though it would be, it somehow seems utterly repugnant to imagine a "corrected" version of the score. See my ar-ticle, "On Claude Vivier's *Lonely Child*."

17. Fineberg, "Guide to the Basic Concepts and Techniques of Spectral Music," 84.

18. Vivier, "Lonely Child," ÉCV, 108.

19. Vivier, lecture at the Centre Culturel Canadien, Paris, November 23, 1982. In the same lecture he commented: "my music before *Lonely Child* used a harmonic language that always had a certain historical connection to a particular past." José Evangelista remembers being "very struck by the melodic invention" in *Lonely Child*, making a connection with Stockhausen's *Indianerlieder*, and talking with

Vivier about the lack of counterpoint, joking that he should write some real counterpoint like their more conservative senior colleague Jean Papineau-Couture. José Evangelista, interview with the author.

20. Rober Racine, interview with the author, Montreal, October 16, 2003 (conducted in English).

21. Marie-Danielle Parent, e-mail to the author, September 18, 2004. Original in French.

22. "Claude must have heard this version," notes Marie-Danielle Parent, "because he gave me some excellent comments" (e-mail to the author, September 18, 2004). The recording by Parent and the Orchestre métropolitain de Montréal conducted by Serge Garant, presently available on the CD *Montréal Postmoderne*, is not the Vancouver performance but a later one, recorded in the Salle Claude Champagne in Montreal some months after Vivier's death.

23. Marie-Danielle Parent and Denis Gougeon, interview with the author, Montreal, November 17, 2002 (conducted in English and French).

24. John Rea, interview with the author, Montreal, November 10, 2002 (conducted in English).

25. Michel Gonneville, interview with the author, Montreal, September 17, 2003 (conducted in French).

26. Marie-Danielle Parent and Denis Gougeon, interview with the author.

27. Walter Boudreau, interview with the author, Montreal, November 14, 2002 (conducted in English).

28. Thérèse Desjardins, interview with the author.

29. Walter Boudreau, interview with the author.

30. Evangelista, in De la Clergerie, "Claude Vivier ou la Montée au ciel."

31. In chapter 4, "Connecting Motive-Forms," of Schoenberg's book, Vivier has highlighted the paragraph that reads: "A well-balanced melody progresses in waves, i.e. each elevation is countered by a depression. It approaches a high point or climax through a series of intermediate lesser points, interrupted by recessions. Upward movements are balanced by downward movements; large intervals are compensated for by conjunct movement in the opposite direction. A good melody generally remains within a reasonable compass, not straying too far from a central range." Schoenberg, *Fundamentals of Musical Composition*, 16.

32. Tristan Murail, interview with the author.

33. Murail remarks that he himself admired the use of the technique in George Crumb's *Black Angels* (1970): Tristan Murail, interview with the author.

34. Vivier, "Zipangu," ÉCV, 109.

35. The instrumentation of this piece has made performances of it a rarity, and right from the outset Vivier realized that substitutions might have to be made. David Kent remembers: "My gongs for which he wrote the piece are in fact a mixture of Thai, Balinese and Javanese gongs." David Kent, e-mail to the author, April 4, 2011.

36. Vivier, "Cinq Chansons pour Percussion," ÉCV, 109–10. The individual movement titles he gives in this program note are slightly different from those in the score; it is those latter that are given here.

37. Vivier, manuscript program note for *Cinq Chansons pour Percussion*: copy in AFV.

38. Ligeti, "Sur la musique de Claude Vivier," 12.

39. Kent, liner note to *Cinq Chansons*, included in the booklet of *Claude Vivier—Anthology of Canadian Music*, Radio Canada International ACM 36 CD 1–4, 1990.

40. Ligeti in De la Clergerie, "Claude Vivier ou la Montée au ciel."

41. Vivier, "Créativité et cinéma québécois," ÉCV, 118.

42. As late as June 1982 he would write: "For the first time in my life I feel *good* in Paris!" Vivier to Thérèse Desjardins, postmarked June 21, 1982: AFV.

43. Van Vlasselaer, "Claude Vivier et 'Kopernikus.'"

## Chapter Ten

1. Carrière, "Claude Vivier."

2. Vivier, "Prologue pour un Marco Polo," ÉCV, 111.

3. Chamberland quoted in Griffiths, *Substance of Things Heard*, 193.

4. Vivier, "Prologue pour un Marco Polo," ÉCV, 111.

5. A transcription of the conversation can be found in ÉCV, 112. With to-day's digital technology it would be possible, in theory, to disentangle the voices of Vivier and Chamberland from the surrounding music; but so far no one has attempted this time-consuming task.

6. Ligeti, "Sur la musique de Claude Vivier," 12.

7. Pauline Vaillancourt, interview with the author, Montreal, September 24, 2003 (conducted in French).

8. Griffiths, *Substance of Things Heard*, 190.

9. Vivier, (verbal) sketches for a projected radiophonic work titled *Discours politique*, three pages, unpublished manuscript, AFV.

10. Vivier, "Wo Bist du Licht!" ÉCV, 119–20.

11. The full text of King's speech is available, among other places, at http://www.usconstitution.net/dream.html (accessed September 29, 2012).

12. Lambert Ferrand, interview with the author, Montreal, September 19, 2003.

13. Sophie Hébert, interview with the author, Contrecoeur, September 20, 2003 (conducted in English).

14. Rober Racine, interview with the author, Montreal, October 16, 2003 (conducted in English).

15. De Billy, "La deuxième vie de Claude Vivier," 86–89.

16. Sophie Hébert, interview with the author. See also "Daniel Guimond," *Frontalepoésie*, accessed September 30, 2012, http://guimond.wordpress. com/a-u-t-e-u-r-s/.

17. His Bank of Montreal statement dated March 31, 1981, is, for the first time, addressed to Vivier at 7, Côte-Ste-Catherine # 1102, Montréal, Qué, H2V 1Z9: AFV.

18. Rober Racine, interview with the author.

19. Martin, "Claude Vivier nommé compositeur de l'année."

20. Jones, "New Concerto Ushers in Spring."

21. Duras, *Marguerite Duras à Montréal.*

22. Vivier, "Imagine," ÉCV, 123–25.

23. In the interview with Daniel Carrière in *Le Berdache* (July–August 1981), Vivier remarks: "I've done the prologue, a piece for strings and the love song," thereby allowing us to situate the composition of the undated *Bouchara* to before the summer of 1981; strangely, this list does not include either *Lonely Child* or *Shiraz*, both subsequently considered part of the scheme. He goes on: "I'm composing it a bit like a soap-opera, that is to say that it's part of a large cycle that I really want to produce, I'm trying to have the possibility of doing it in Banff."

24. Sophie Hébert, interview with the author.

25. Littler, "Reviews."

26. Thérèse Desjardins, interview with the author.

27. Sophie Hébert, interview with the author.

28. Vivier, "Pour Gödel," ÉCV, 125–26.

29. Vivier, application form to the Canada Council, undated [October 1981]: photocopy in AFV.

30. Vivier's copy is now in AFV.

31. No such written script has survived among the papers of the Fondation Vivier. Daniel Dion recalls that "it wasn't really a scenario, just a rough synopsis of ideas. There was no real formal scenario" (Daniel Dion, interview with the author, Montreal, November 13, 2002 [conducted in English]). Among the papers of the Vivier Archives is a one-page outline, titled "Wittgenstein," which reads like a very sketchy outline of a film divided into twenty-one numbered scenes; among them are descriptions of scenes or activities that ended up in the finished *L'homme de Pékin* ("le maquillage," Alceste de Gluck," "les photos," "danse nu," "dino claude—l'ange," etc.).

32. About the title, Dion comments: "At the time we were really into branding, it seems like it's something today companies do, but at that time our label was Dion/Poloni. We used to joke and say, oh, my horoscope sign is Ferrari, and my ascendant is Gucci … it was all about that. We were just playing. *L'Homme de Pékin* has a historical, anthropological aspect, the Peking man, who was he exactly? So it fitted with Claude who was into a lot of archaeology, Samarkand, the middle east, Asia. I think he liked it immediately." Daniel Dion, interview with the author.

33. Rober Racine, who had a functioning reel-to-reel tape recorder, recalls Vivier bringing round the tape of *Hommage* during this time. Vivier wanted to hear it in the dark with the lights off. Racine recalls it as a "sound fog." Rober Racine, interview with the author.

34. Daniel Dion, interview with the author.

35. Philippe Poloni, interview with the author, Montreal, November 14, 2002 (conducted in English).

36. Gingras, "De 'longues' heures de 'musiques vocales.'"

37. Gilles Tremblay, interview with the author, Montreal, November 5, 2002 (conducted in French and English).

38. Pelletier, liner notes for *Shiraz: oeuvres de Vivier et Brégent*. Disques Pelléas CD-0111 (2002).

39. Walter Boudreau, interview with the author, Montreal, November 14, 2002 (conducted in English).

40. John Rea, interview with the author, Montreal, November 10, 2002 (conducted in English). Cf. also Rea, "Reflets dans l'eau . . . bénite."

41. Walter Boudreau, interview with the author.

42. John Rea, interview with the author.

43. Thérèse Desjardins, interview with the author.

# Chapter Eleven

1. Vivier to the Canada Council, August 22, 1982: copy in AFV.

2. Vivier to Thérèse Desjardins, postmarked July 2, 1982: AFV.

3. Fox, "British Music at Darmstadt 1982–92," 22.

4. Grisey, "Autoportrait avec l'Itinéraire," in Grisey, *Écrits*, 197.

5. Vivier to Thérèse Desjardins, July 21, 1982: AFV.

6. Ibid.

7. Ibid.

8. Vivier, "Que propose la musique?" ÉCV, 130.

9. Vivier to Thérèse Desjardins, August 10, 1982: AFV.

10. Bruno Hébert, interview with the author, Contrecoeur, July 6, 2002 (conducted in English).

11. Vivier to Thérèse Desjardins, August 10, 1982: AFV.

12. Vivier to the Canada Council, August 22, 1982: copy in AFV.

13. Vivier to Thérèse Desjardins, October 8, 1982: AFV.

14. Vivier to Thérèse Desjardins, January 7, 1983: AFV.

15. The text given here is from a manuscript in Vivier's hand in AFV, and is slightly different from the version given in ÉCV, 131.

16. Vivier to Thérèse Desjardins, September 27, 1982: AFV.

17. Vivier to Thérèse Desjardins, August 20, 1982: AFV.

18. Vivier to Thérèse Desjardins, September 17, 1982: AFV.

19. Ibid.

20. Vivier to Thérèse Desjardins, September 27, 1982: AFV.

21. Vivier to Thérèse Desjardins, September 20, 1982: AFV.

22. Vivier to Thérèse Desjardins, September 27, 1982: AFV.

23. Vivier to Thérèse Desjardins, September 20, 1982: AFV.

24. The definitive account of Orlova's theory is her 1990 book *Tchaikovsky: A Self Portrait*, published long after Vivier's death; but accounts of her theories had appeared in numerous secondary sources since 1979.

25. Robert, ÉCV 131–33n1.

26. Vivier's copy is now in AFV.

27. Vivier to Thérèse Desjardins, October 8, 1982: AFV.

28. Vivier to Thérèse Desjardins, October 16, 1982: AFV.

29. Vivier to Thérèse Desjardins, November 8, 1982: AFV.

30. Vivier, lecture at the Centre Culturel Canadien in Paris, November 23, 1982: recording in AFV.

31. Philippe Poloni, interview with the author, Montreal, November 14, 2002 (conducted in English).

32. Vivier to Thérèse Desjardins, January 3, 1983: AFV.

33. Coe, *Such Times*, 112.

34. Grmek, *History of AIDS*, 4.

35. Phillipe Poloni, interview with the author.

36. Vivier to Thérèse Desjardins, January 24, 1983: AFV.

37. Clarence Barlow, interview with the author, Amsterdam, August 11, 2002 (conducted in English).

38. Vivier to Thérèse Desjardins, January 26, 1983: AFV.

39. Phillipe Poloni, interview with the author.

40. Vivier to Thérèse Desjardins, January 26, 1983: AFV.

41. Clarence Barlow, interview with the author.

42. Vivier had been on a jury the previous year that had awarded Bouliane a CBC prize for his chamber work *Jeu de société*.

43. Vivier to Philippe Dourguin, February 23, 1983: photocopy in AFV.

44. Vivier to Thérèse Desjardins, February 12, 1983: AFV.

45. Vivier to Philippe Dourguin, February 23, 1983: photocopy in AFV.

# Chapter Twelve

1. "Claude Vivier étranglé."

2. Gingras, "Adieu, Claude Vivier!"

3. Van Vlasselaer, "La mort d'un compositeur."

4. Halbreich, "Vivier Tragique."

5. Halbreich, "Mon ami Claude Vivier." This article is based on an interview with Halbreich in Brussels on March 17, 1983, by Denys Bouliane.

6. Kaptainis, "Vivier's Music 'Will Last.'"

7. Louise Duchesneau, e-mail to the author, September 3, 2011.

8. List attached to a letter from the Department of External Affairs, Ottawa, August 2, 1983, to Thérèse Desjardins: AFV.

9. "Trois fois meurtrier à vingt ans."

10. "Le meurtrier présumé de trois homosexuels arrêté," in an unidentified newspaper [October 1983]: photocopy in AFV.

11. "Pascal, 20 ans, avoue le meurtre de trois homosexuels," 11. Dolzan was known to frequent a bar named Le Transfert on rue de la Sourdière: see "C'était il y a trente ans . . . Les Années Gai Pied," *Yagg*, accessed October 21, 2012, http://thd75010.yagg.com/2012/02/26/1984/. In a 1986 article, Peter Tannenbaum suggests Vivier met Dolzan in the "Galaxy Bar on the rue des Manteaux Blancs" [correctly, rue des Blancs-Manteaux]; but no source for this is given, and the article is full of small mistakes, planting doubts about the reliability of the author's information. Tannenbaum, "The Brief and Turbulent Life of Claude Vivier."

12. N.B., "La 'java' meurtière de Pascal Dolzan," in an unidentified newspaper [October 1983]: photocopy in AFV. In 1983, 400 French francs ws roughly equivalent to €100 in today's currency.

13. Viau, "La prison à vie pour le meurtrier de C. Vivier."

14. Gilles Tremblay, interview with the author, Montreal, November 5, 2002 (conducted in French and English).

15. Halbreich, "Vivier Tragique."

16. Walter Boudreau, interview with the author, Montreal, November 14, 2002 (conducted in English).

17. Thérèse Desjardins, interview with the author.

18. Griffiths, *Substance of Things Heard*, 197.

19. The tantalizing question remains in regard to whether *Glaubst du . . .* should be considered an unfinished work. On one hand, there is no date on the last page of the manuscript, a highly unusual occurrence in Vivier's scores (although it is also true of *Bouchara*); on the other hand, it is hard to imagine quite what could have come after the chilling ending.

20. Pauline Vaillancourt, interview with the author, Montreal, September 24, 2003 (conducted in French).

21. José Evangelista, interview with the author, Montreal, November 6, 2002 (conducted in English).

22. Michel Gonneville, interview with the author, Montreal, September 17, 2003 (conducted in French).

23. Bruno Hébert, interview with the author, Contrecoeur, July 6, 2002 (conducted in English).

24. Denys Bouliane, interview with the author, Montreal, October 13, 2003 (conducted in English).

25. John Rea, interview with the author, Montreal, November 10, 2002 (conducted in English).

26. Pauline Vaillancourt, interview with the author.

27. Daniel Dion, interview with the author, Montreal, November 13, 2002 (conducted in English).

28. Philippe Poloni, interview with the author, Montreal, November 14, 2002 (conducted in English).

29. Gilles Tremblay, interview with the author.

30. When I presented this view in my keynote lecture at the Journée d'étude Claude Vivier, held at the University of Montreal in April 2008, it met with a good deal of resistance from many Vivier aficionados and even some of his friends, whose collective attitude seemed to be, as one person put it, "there's more to it than that." However, the composer Denis Gougeon, who was present, told me that exactly the same view as mine had been expressed to him shortly after Vivier's death by Tristan Murail.

31. Grisey, *Écrits*, 199.

32. "J'estime qu'il est le compositeur le plus important et original de sa gé-nération": György Ligeti, letter to Thérèse Desjardins, May 28, 1988: AFV.

33. Vivier, "Introspection d'un compositeur," ÉCV, 93.

34. John Rea, interview with the author.

# BIBLIOGRAPHY

A ll previously unpublished writings by Claude Vivier in this book are used by permission of the Fondation Vivier. All the texts are in French unless otherwise noted, and the translations here are my own. The great majority of Vivier's manuscripts, or photocopies thereof, are located in two sources: the Archives of the Fondation Vivier, Montreal, and the Claude Vivier Archives, University of Montreal. Published writings by Vivier, unless otherwise stated, are here quoted from the texts as given in Véronique Robert, ed., "Les écrits de Claude Vivier" (see below).

Anderson, Julian. "A Provisional History of Spectral Music." *Contemporary Music Review* 19, no. 2 (2000): 7–22.

Artaud, Antonin. *The Theatre and its Double*. Translated by Mary Caroline Richards. New York: Grove Press, 1958.

Ashley, Audrey M. "Dance for the Senses, but not the Intellect." *Citizen* (Ottawa), July 30, 1977.

Attinello, Paul, Christopher Fox, and Martin Iddon, eds. *Other Darmstadts*. *Contemporary Music Review* 26, no. 1 (2007): whole issue.

Bail, Louise. "Introduction à *Kopernikus:* Pistes de réflexion autour du sacré." *Circuit: Musiques Contemporaines* 18, no. 3 (2008): 9–26.

Bailey, Bruce. "Overly-Long Ritual Mars *Kopernikus* Experience." *Gazette*, May 12, 1980.

Belkin, Alan, Mireille Gagné, and Marie-Thérèse Lefebvre, eds. "Regards sur la Musique Actuelle au Quebec: entrevues avec des compositeurs québecois." Typescript copy in CMC, Montreal.

Bernard, Jonathan. *The Music of Edgard Varèse*. New Haven: Yale University Press, 1987.

Borduas, Paul-Émile. *Refus global*. In *The Canadian Encyclopedia*. Historica Dominion Institute, 2012. http://www.thecanadianencyclopedia.com/articles /refus-global-manifesto. Accessed October 3, 2012.

Bourassa, Jocelyn. "Vivier courait les églises de Pont-Viau pour jouer de l'orgue." *L'Hebdo de Laval* (Quebec), March 15, 1996.

Bruck, Werner. "Rasch gealtert: Konzert mit Werken zeitgenössischer Komponisten in der Aula der Musikhochschule." *Kölner Stadt-Anzeiger*, July 31, 1974.

Carrière, Daniel. "Claude Vivier." *Le Berdache*, July–August 1981.

"Claude Vivier étranglé." *Journal de Montréal*, March 13, 1983.

Coe, Christopher. *Such Times*. New York: Harcourt Brace Jovanovich, 1993.

Cott, Jonathan. *Stockhausen: Conversations with the Composer*. London: Robson Books, 1974.

Crawford, C. .B., and R. .F. Legget. "Ground Temperature Investigations in Canada." *Engineering Journal* 40, no. 3 (1957): 2–6.

Daudelin, Robert. "Entrevue avec Gilles Tremblay." *Journal des Jeunesses Musicales du Canada* (January 1962): n.p.

De Billy, Hélène. "La deuxième vie de Claude Vivier." *L'actualité* (Montreal), April 15, 2001.

de la Clergerie, Catherine, and Marie-Hélène Bernard. "Claude Vivier ou la montée au ciel de l'homme qui riait toujours." Radio documentary, France Culture (1991). AFV.

Dickinson, John, and Brian Young. *A Short History of Quebec*. Montreal: McGill-Queen's University Press, 2003.

Dufourt, Hughes. "Musique spectrale." Paris: Société Nationale de Radiodiffusion, Radio-France (March 1979): n.p. Reprinted in *Conséquences* nos. 7–8 (1986): 111–15.

Duguay, Raôul, ed. *Musiques du Kébèk*. Montréal: Éditions du Jour, 1971.

Dunning, Jennifer. "Dance: Montrealers Try All Arts." *New York Times*, December 17, 1977.

Duras, Marguerite. *Marguerite Duras à Montréal*. Edited by Suzanne Lamy and André Roy. Montreal: Spirale, 1981.

Eliade, Mircea. *Le Mythe de l'éternel retour*. Paris: Gallimard, 1949.

———. *Forgerons et alchimistes*. Paris: Flammarion, 1956.

———. *Myth and Reality*. New York: Harper and Row, 1963.

———. *Patanjali et le Yoga*. Paris: Éditions du Seuil, 1972.

Fineberg, Joshua. "Guide to the Basic Concepts and Techniques of Spectral Music." *Contemporary Music Review* 19, no. 2 (2000): 81–113.

Fox, Christopher. "British Music at Darmstadt 1982–92." *Tempo*, no. 186 (1993): 21–25.

———. "Where the River Bends: The Cologne School in Retrospect." *Musical Times* 148, no. 1901 (2007): 27–42.

"Gilles Tremblay: un portrait." *Musicanada* 24 (November 1969).

Gilmore, Bob. "Claude Vivier and Karlheinz Stockhausen: Moments from a Double Portrait." *Circuit: musiques contemporaines* 19, no. 2 (2009): 35–49.

———. "On Claude Vivier's *Lonely Child*." *Tempo*, no. 61 (2007): 2–17.

———. "Wild Air: The Music of Kevin Volans." *Journal of Music in Ireland* 6, no. 6 (2006): 22–29.

Gingras, Claude. "Adieu, Claude Vivier!" *La Presse*, March 14, 1983.

———. "De 'longues' heures de 'musiques vocales.'" *La Presse*, May 10, 1982.

———. "De Stockhausen à Claude Vivier." *La Presse*, September 24, 1974.

———. "Du 'neuf' en musique." *La Presse*, February 3, 1979.

———. "Dutoit: un Mahler nouveau." *La Presse*, October 15, 1980.

———. "Le dernier Vivier: un opera." *La Presse*, May 3, 1980.

———. "Varèse et les autres." *La Presse*, September 27, 1974.

Gojowy, Detlef. "Summe eine Melodie, die gut is: Stockhausens Werkstatt in Köln / Seine Schüler stellen sich vor." *Frankfurter Allgemeine Zeitung*, March 11, 1974.

Grescoe, Taras. *Sacré Blues: An Unsentimental Journey Through Quebec.* Toronto: Macfarlane Walter and Ross, 2000.

Griffiths, Paul. *Encyclopaedia of Twentieth-Century Music.* London: Thames and Hudson, 1986.

———. *Modern Music and After.* 3rd ed. Oxford: Oxford University Press, 2010.

———. *The Substance of Things Heard: Writings About Music.* Rochester, NY: University of Rochester Press, 2005.

Grisey, Gérard. *Écrits: ou l'invention de la musique spectrale.* Edited by Guy Lelong and Anne-Marie Réby. Paris: Éditions MF, 2008.

Grmek, Mirko D. *History of AIDS.* Translated by Russell C. Maulitz and Jacalyn Dufflin. Princeton: Princeton University Press, 1990.

Halbreich, Harry. "Mon ami Claude Vivier." *Sonances*, July 1983.

———. "Vivier Tragique." *La Croix*, April 12, 1983.

Horwood, Michael S. "Array Concerts October 21 & November 18 1978." *Musicworks* 6 (Winter 1979): 15.

Iddon, Martin. "The Dissolution of the Avant-Garde, Darmstadt 1968–1984." PhD diss., University of Cambridge, 2004.

Jones, Gaynor. "New Concerto Ushers in Spring." *Toronto Star*, April 6, 1981.

Jowitt, Deborah. "Dance." *Village Voice*, January 2, 1978.

Kaptainis, Arthur. "Vivier's Music 'Will Last.'" *Globe and Mail*, July 2, 1983.

Kisselgoff, Anna. "Dance: The Debut of Montreal Group." *New York Times*, December 15, 1977.

Kurtz, Michael. *Stockhausen: A Biography.* London: Faber and Faber, 1992.

Lazar, Barry, and Tamsin Douglas. *The Guide to Ethnic Montreal.* Montreal: Véhicule Press, 1992.

Lefebvre, Marie-Thérèse. *Serge Garant et la Révolution Musicale au Québec.* Montreal: Éditions Louise Courteau, 1986.

"Le meurtrier présumé de trois homosexuels arrêté." Unidentified newspaper, October 1983 (copy in AFV).

Lesage, Jean. "Claude Vivier, *Siddhartha*, Karlheinz Stockhausen: La nouvelle simplicité et le *râga.*"*Circuit: Musiques Contemporaines* 18, no. 3 (2008): 107–20.

Lévesque, Andrée. *Making and Breaking the Rules: Women in Québec, 1919–1939.* Translated by Yvonne M. Klein. Toronto: McClelland and Stewart, 1994. Originally published as *La Norme et les Déviantes* (1989).

Levesque, Patrick. "L'élaboration du materiau musical dans les dernières oeuvres vocals de Claude Vivier." *Circuit: Musiques Contemporaines* 18, no. 3 (2008): 89–106.

Ligeti, György. "Sur la musique de Claude Vivier: propos recueillis par Louise Duchesneau." *Circuit: Revue Nord-Américaine de Musique du Xxe siècle* 2, nos. 1–2 (1991): 7–15.

Linteau, Paul-André, René Durocher, Jean-Claude Robert, and François Ricard. *Histoire du Québec Contemporain.* Vol. 2. Montreal: Boréal, 1989.

"List of New Compositions Realized in the Institute of Sonology 1971/72." *Interface: Journal of New Music Research* 1, no. 2 (1972): 187–89.

Littler, William. "Reviews." *Sunday Star*, February 14, 1982.

———. "Singers Banish Cobwebs." *Toronto Star*, March 31, 1979.

Lonchampt, Jacques. "La musique au Canada: un dynamisme sans complexes." *Le Monde*, October 6, 1975.

Maconie, Robin, ed. *Stockhausen on Music.* London: Marion Boyars, 1989.

Malouin, Marie-Paule, ed. *L'Univers des Enfants en Difficulté au Québec Entre 1940 et 1960.* Quebec: Éditions Bellarmin, 1996.

Martin, Sylvaine, "Claude Vivier nommé compositeur de l'année." *La Scène musicale*, July–August 1981.

McLean, Eric. "SMCQ Opens New Season with Return of Garant." *Montreal Star*, September 27, 1974.

———. "Violinist Gidon Kremer Shows He Is Extraordinary." *Gazette*, October 18, 1980.

Mennesson, Christine. "The Word Has Its Own Scent, Its Colour, Its Soul." Liner notes to the CD *Vivier: Chants . . .* Paris: Soupir, 2003.

Messiaen, Olivier. *Technique de mon Langage Musical.* Paris: Alphonse Leduc, 1944.

Mijnheer, Jaco, and Thérèse Desjardins. "La chronologie des oeuvres de Claude Vivier: historisation de la déshistoire." *Circuit: Revue Nord-Américaine de Musique du Xxe siècle* 2, nos. 1–2 (1991): 17–29.

Misch, Imke, and Markus Bandur. *Karlheinz Stockhausen bei den Internationalen Ferienkursen für Neue Musik in Darmstadt 1951–1996: Dokumente und Briefe.* Kürten: Stockhausen-Verlag, 2001.

Moisan, Daniel. "*Kopernikus* ou l'histoire d'une oeuvre lyrique québécoise." *Aria* 2, no. 1 (Spring 1980): n.p.

Moore, Gilbert D. "New Look North of the Border." *Life*, April 19, 1968, 88–90.

Morton, Brian, and Pamela Collins, eds. *Contemporary Composers.* London: St James Press, 1992.

N.B. "La 'java' meurtière de Pascal Dolzan." Unidentified newspaper, October 1983 (copy in AFV).

Nerval, Gérard de. *Selected Writings*. Translated by Richard Sieburth. London: Penguin Books, 1999.

Orlova, Alexandra. *Tchaikovsky: A Self Portrait*. London: Oxford University Press, 1990).

"Pascal, 20 ans, avoue le meurtre de trois homosexuels." *Libération*, October 29–30, 1983.

Pöhlmann, Egert, and Martin L. West, eds. *Documents of Ancient Greek Music: The Extant Melodies and Fragments*. Oxford: Clarendon Press, 2001.

Potvin, Gilles. "Kopernikus: un coup d'audace de Claude Vivier." *Le Devoir*, May 12, 1980.

———. "La semaine de musique: un concert harmonieux." *Le Devoir*, October 10, 1975.

———. "Ouverture de la saison à la SMCQ." *Le Devoir*, September 28, 1974.

———. "Présence du Québec à Royan." *Le Devoir*, April 15, 1972.

Proulx, Michelle. "Moyens d'Élaborer la Programmation." *La Scène musicale*, May–June 1979.

Pugin, Tristram. "Through the Spectrum: The New Intimacy in French Music (I)." *Tempo* 212 (2000): 12–20.

Rea, John. "Reflets dans l'eau . . . bénite. Douze images impures: la vie et la musique de Claude Vivier." *Circuit: Revue Nord-Américaine de Musique du Xxe siècle* 1, no. 2 (1991): 71–79.

Reich, Steve. *Writings About Music*. London: Universal Edition, 1974.

Rhéaume, Martine. "Évolution d'un style musical—comment Vivier passe-t-il d'une oeuvre à l'autre?" *Circuit: Musiques Contemporaines* 18, no. 3 (2008): 73–88.

Ridout, Godfrey, and Talivaldis Kenins, eds. *Célébration*. Toronto: Canadian Music Centre, 1984.

Rivest, Johanne. "Claude Vivier: les oeuvres d'une discographie imposante." *Circuit: Revue Nord-Américaine de Musique du Xxe siècle* 2, nos. 1–2 (1991): 137–61.

R.N. "Les Élèves Canadiens Plus Intéressés Par La Musique Nouvelle." *La Scène musicale*, June 5, 1970.

Roberge, Françoy. "Evangelista et Vivier au Conventum." *Le Devoir*, March 29, 1978.

———. "La jeune musique en quête d'épanouissement." *Le Devoir*, April 6, 1978.

Robert, Véronique. "Prologue pour les écrits d'un compositeur." *Circuit: Revue Nord-Américaine de Musique du Xxe siècle* 2, nos. 1–2 (1991): 31–37.

———, ed. "Les écrits de Claude Vivier." *Circuit: Revue Nord-Américaine de Musique du Xxe siècle* 2, nos. 1–2 (1991): 39–135.

Rochon, Pierre. "Vivier veut exprimer l'élément canadien par la musique." *La Scène musicale*, May–June 1975.

Rogers, Stephen. "Travelogue pour un Marco Polo [My Travels with Claude?]: A Journey Through the Composer's Life and Work in 10 Days." *Circuit: Revue Nord-Américaine de Musique du Xxe siècle* 18, no. 3 (2008): 27–51.

Rose, François. "Introduction to the Pitch Organization of French Spectral Music." *Perspectives of New Music* 34, no. 2 (Summer 1996): 6–39.

Roy, Bruno. *Mémoire d'asile: la tragédie des enfants de Duplessis.* Montreal: Éditions du Boréal, 1994.

R. R. [Rober Racine]. "Le mysticisme onirique: le théâtre contemporain devient près de l'opéra." *Virus* (May 1980).

Samson, Marc. "Le pianiste Louis Lortie grand vainqueur des Concours de musique du Canada." *Le Soleil*, June 25, 1975.

Sauvageau, Yves. *Les mûres de Pierre.* Montreal: Librairie Déom, 1977.

Schoenberg, Arnold. *Fundamentals of Musical Composition.* Edited by Gerald Strang and Leonard Stein. London: Faber, 1967.

Southworth, Jean. "Dancers Find Their Voices." *Ottawa Journal*, August 4, 1977.

Stockhausen, Karlheinz. *Texte 1.* Cologne: Verlag M. DuMont Schauberg, 1963.

Tannenbaum, Peter. "The Brief and Turbulent Life of Claude Vivier." *Music Magazine*, May–June 1986.

Thériault, Jacques. "Et j'entendis une voix réciter Dante . . . .: Claude Vivier à la SMCQ." *Le Devoir*, September 20, 1974.

Tilley, Janette. "Eternal Recurrence: Aspects of Melody in the Orchestral Music of Claude Vivier." *Discourses in Music* 2, no. 1 (Fall 2000), http://library.music.utoronto.ca/discourses-in-music/v2n1a3.html.

Toop, Richard. *György Ligeti.* London: Phaidon Press, 1999.

Toop, Richard. "Shadows of Ideas: On Walter Zimmermann's Work." Lecture given at Weingartener Tage für Neue Musik, November 15, 2002. http://home.snafu.de/walterz/toopwz.html. Accessed April 17, 2010.

"Trois fois meurtrier à vingt ans." *Le Parisien*, October 28, 1983.

Van Vlasselaer, J. J. "Claude Vivier et 'Kopernikus.'" *Le Droit*, February 17, 1981.

———. "La mort d'un compositeur." *Le Droit*, March 19, 1983.

———. "Quand Claude Vivier s'appelle 'Nyonan Kenyung.'" *Le Droit*, August 4, 1977.

Viau, René. "La prison à vie pour le meurtrier de C. Vivier." *La Presse*, November 26, 1986.

Vincent, Odette. *La vie musicale au Québec: Art lyrique, musique classique et contemporaine.* Quebec: Les Editions de l'IQRC, 2000.

v.L. "Die Tänzerin und der Kontrabass." *Darmstadter Tagblatt*, August 5, 1974.

von der Weid, Jean-Noël. "Drowned in His Dying Song." Liner notes for Vivier, *hants . . .* Paris: Soupir, 2003.

# INDEX

# Eastman Studies in Music

Ralph P. Locke, Senior Editor
Eastman School of Music

Additional Titles of Interest

*Elliott Carter:*
*Collected Essays and Lectures, 1937–1995*
Edited by Jonathan W. Bernard

*Elliott Carter's "What Next?":*
*Communication, Cooperation, and Separation*
Guy Capuzzo

*From Boulanger to Stockhausen:*
*Interviews and a Memoir*
Bálint András Varga

*György Kurtág:*
*Three Interviews and Ligeti Homages*
Bálint András Varga

*Leon Kirchner*
*Composer, Performer, and Teacher*
Robert Riggs

*The Pleasure of Modernist Music:*
*Listening, Meaning, Intention, Ideology*
Edited by Arved Ashby

*The Sea on Fire: Jean Barraqué*
Paul Griffiths

*Three Questions for Sixty-Five Composers*
Bálint András Varga

*The Twelve-Tone Music of Luigi Dallapiccola*
Brian Alegant

*The Whistling Blackbird:*
*Essays and Talks on New Music*
Robert Morris

A complete list of titles in the Eastman Studies in Music series
may be found on our website, www.urpress.com.

Claude Vivier's haunting and expressive music has captivated audiences around the world. But the French-Canadian composer is remembered also because of the dramatic circumstances of his death: he was found murdered in his Paris apartment at the age of thirty-four. With unrestricted access to Vivier's archives and through interviews with Vivier's family, teachers, friends, and colleagues, musicologist and biographer Bob Gilmore tells here the full story of Vivier's fascinating life, from his abandonment as a child in a Montreal orphanage to his posthumous acclaim as one of the leading composers of his generation.

Expelled from a religious school at seventeen for "lack of maturity," Vivier gave up his ambition to join the priesthood to study composition. Between 1976 and 1983 Vivier wrote the works on which his reputation rests, including *Lonely Child*, *Bouchara*, and the operas *Kopernikus* and *Marco Polo*. He was also an outspoken presence in the Montreal arts world and gay scene. Vivier left Quebec for Paris in 1982 to work on a new opera, the composition of which was interrupted by his murder. On his desk was the manuscript of his last work, uncannily entitled "Do You Believe in the Immortality of the Soul." Vivier's is a tragic but life-affirming story, intimately connected to his passionate music.

Bob Gilmore is a musicologist and performer and teaches at Brunel University in London. He is the author of *Harry Partch: A Biography*.

"Claude Vivier lived a life we had thought extinct: that of the doomed creative genius, casting off masterpieces from an unstoppable ride into the abyss. Bob Gilmore brings immediacy, sensitivity and care to telling the story of Vivier's life, while also guiding us through and into some of the most breathtaking music of the late twentieth century. This is a necessary book, and an exciting one."

—Paul Griffiths, author of *The Sea on Fire: Jean Barraqué*

"Vivier's 'marvelous dream universe' is researched and presented by Gilmore with a wealth of colorful detail and respect, allowing the reader an insightful vision into the world of this extraordinary composer."

—Barbara Hannigan, soprano